Art Galaxie

Masters

OF CONTEMPORARY FINE ART

VOLUME II

Art Galaxie
www.artgalaxie.com

Published by Art Galaxie Ltd
Av. do Atlântico nº 16 - 14º Piso,
Escritório 8 - 1990-019 Lisbon
publishing@artgalaxie.com

Founder and Curator
Pedro Boaventura
Design
Art Galaxie Design
Sylvia Gomes
Front Cover
"Kopera P15", painting
by Tomasz Alen Kopera

ISBN 978 989 20 7103 9

INTRODUCTION

Some things that I do love in the creative process and which is found within artists, is the germination, the life that they have, the energy that they emanate, their development and evolution. Their amazing proliferation and the ability which they present in terms of propagation and contagion. As opposed to destructive energy, creative energy is able to shake the atoms, flare up the spirits and produce endorphins.

A fascinating artistic movement ruled by originality, freshness and even by emotion, changes our reality and existence into a more beautiful and transcending thing, an experience that becomes more precious and cheerful. An explosion of light, shape and colour which sprouts of the intricate texture of its creator's mind, based on his intellect, ideas, envisions, dreams, life and sometimes even in his most hidden, recondite and intimate self.

Through his own imagination, the messages reach the broadest audience with a new interpretation of the world. The reinvented and rewritten world, posing a sensorial and cognitive challenge. An admirable new landscape which induces a reinforced pleasure, both at an intellectual and idleness level. And it is with this pictorial poetry that major secrets are revealed to us, knowledge and techniques that uncover a great mastery. It's a good thing to have the opportunity to step inside the artists' world and mind, and to be able to stroll through them.

One of the intents of producing this book is so we can share this magic with you. It's with great pleasure that we invite and promote these artists, an excellent collection of contemporary artists whose art speaks for itself. Painting, Sculpture, Drawing and Digital Art are the main categories that one can find in this edition. Throughout this book, you will have the chance to go around the globe and you can also take an exceptional path through the world of arts. You'll be able to find a rich expressiveness and a range of styles, techniques and motifs. An inspiring journey that is going to provide you with a fresh view on the Contemporary Art movement and trends. An experience that will urge you to go even further, in terms of knowledge and creativity.

If you want to get to know more about these and some of our other artists, in addition to this book, you can access their artwork on our Art Portal (now totally renewed). Adding to these annual editions of Masters of Contemporary Fine Arts, we're also putting together several editions dedicated to each category. I invite you to learn more about our collection of Masters. Masters of Painting, which is currently in its production stage, will be published in a couple of months. Soon after, Masters of Sculpture, Masters of Drawing and Masters of Digital Art will follow, thus contributing to a more in-depth outlook on every one of these mediums.

Art Galaxie is an artistic project and is in constant motion. It is comprised by artists and over its three years of life has always been an organization fed by energy, enthusiasm and love for art. Profit was never its goal, but rather being genuinely helpful when it comes to spreading art and promoting the artists, actions particularly important in times of recession, in which art and culture investments fall very short of what is desirable.

I hope you enjoy this book as much as we have in creating it.

Pedro Boaventura
Founder and Curator of Art Galaxie

INDEX

INDEX

INDEX

ALEJANDRO ROSEMBERG

PAINTING - ARGENTINA

www.a-rosemberg.com

Alejandro was born in Córdoba, Argentina in 1981. He attended The National University of Cordoba, where he obtained a degree in Fine Arts, at the same time forming himself with master Claudio Bogino in the classical method of painting based on the tradition of the great Italian masters. He furthered his education on colour under Graydon Parrish, at the Grand Central Academy of New York.

Many think that his artworks look like photographs and categorize them as being Hyperrealistic, but Hyperrealism is not a technique, rather an artistic movement which tries to reproduce reality with photographic objectivity and quality.

On the contrary, his intention when he paints is not photographic but pictorial, using technique as an instrument to express a particular vision of the world. In that sense, he chooses realism because of its accessible language which, like a bridge, facilitates the connection between the painting and its spectators: it allows them an approach to art without requiring any previous knowledge.

Alejandro feels that painting is a way thinking, and that the images are texts. Through his works he reflects upon the world in which he lives and on the space that art occupies in it, working particularly on two concepts: beauty in an ample sense and craft as its support; values that have been devalued throughout the last century and yet so necessary to the development of human beings and art.

Right: Camille I, 2013, oil on canvas, 50 x 37cm

Victoria I, 2007, oil on canvas, 70 x 50cm

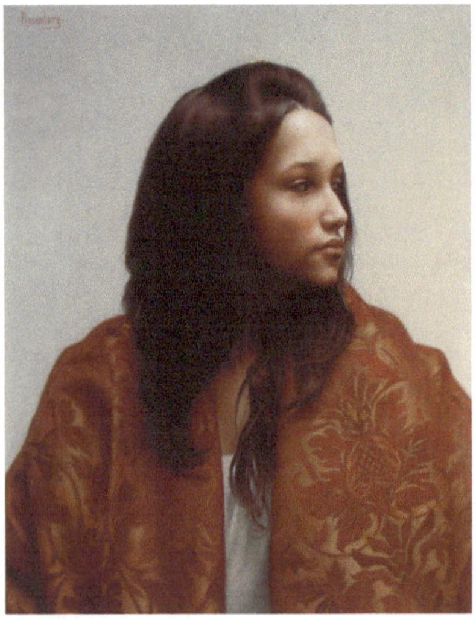

Muse Series - painting no. 1, 2010, oil on canvas, 80 x 60cm

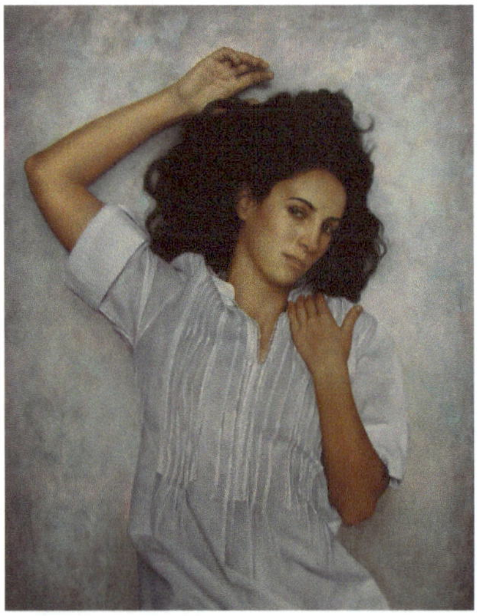

Camille 3, 2013, oil on canvas, 50 x 37cm

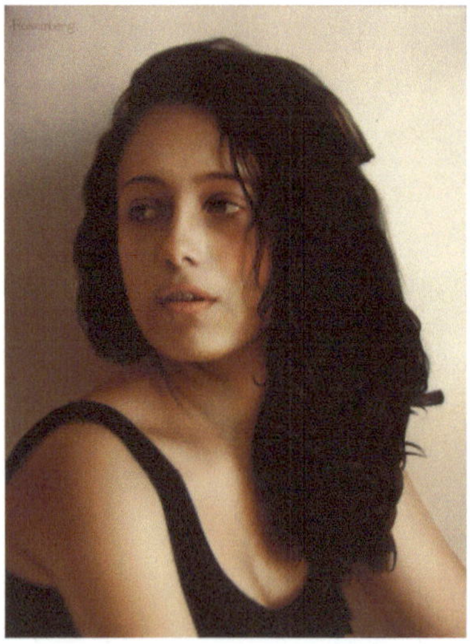

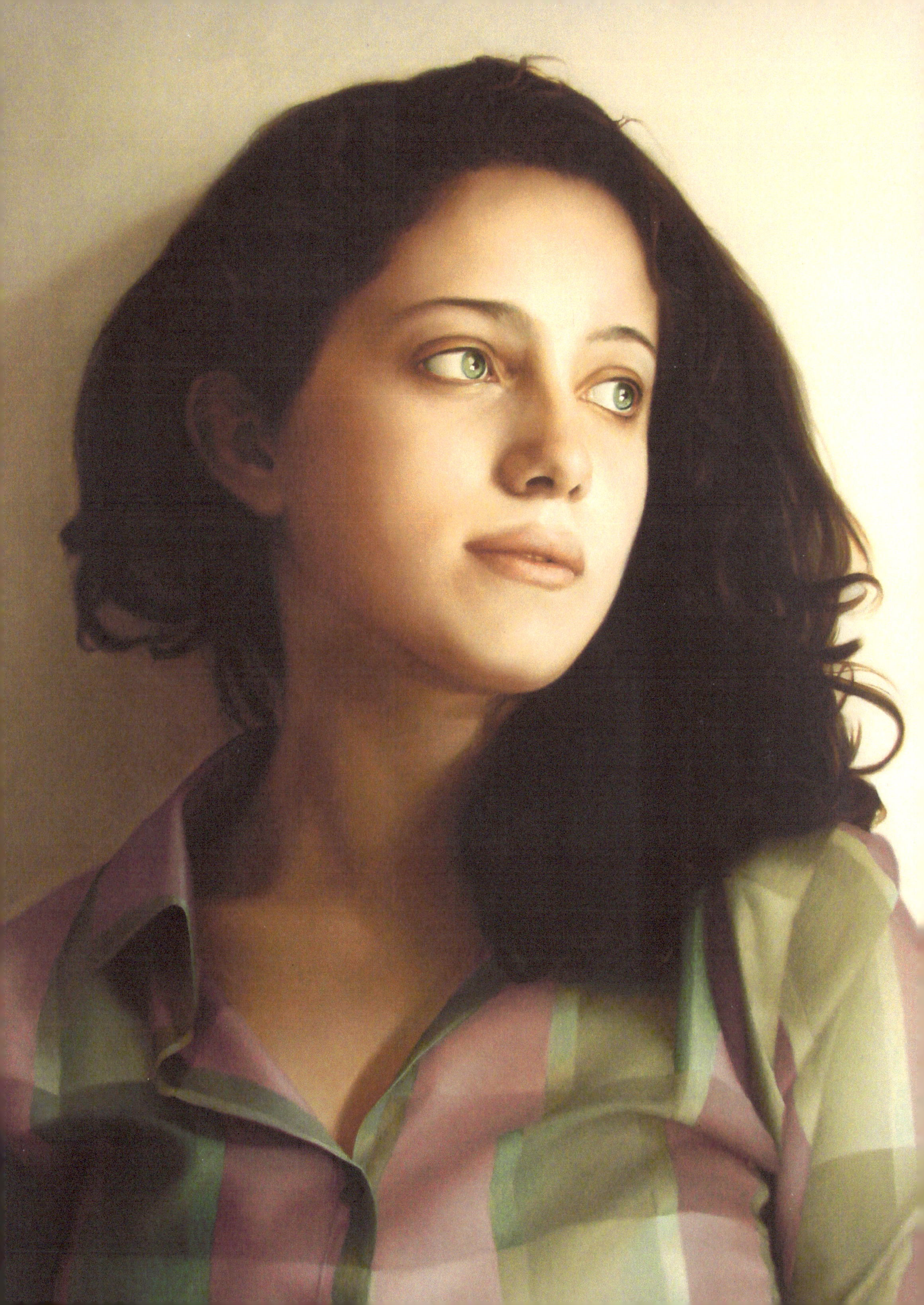

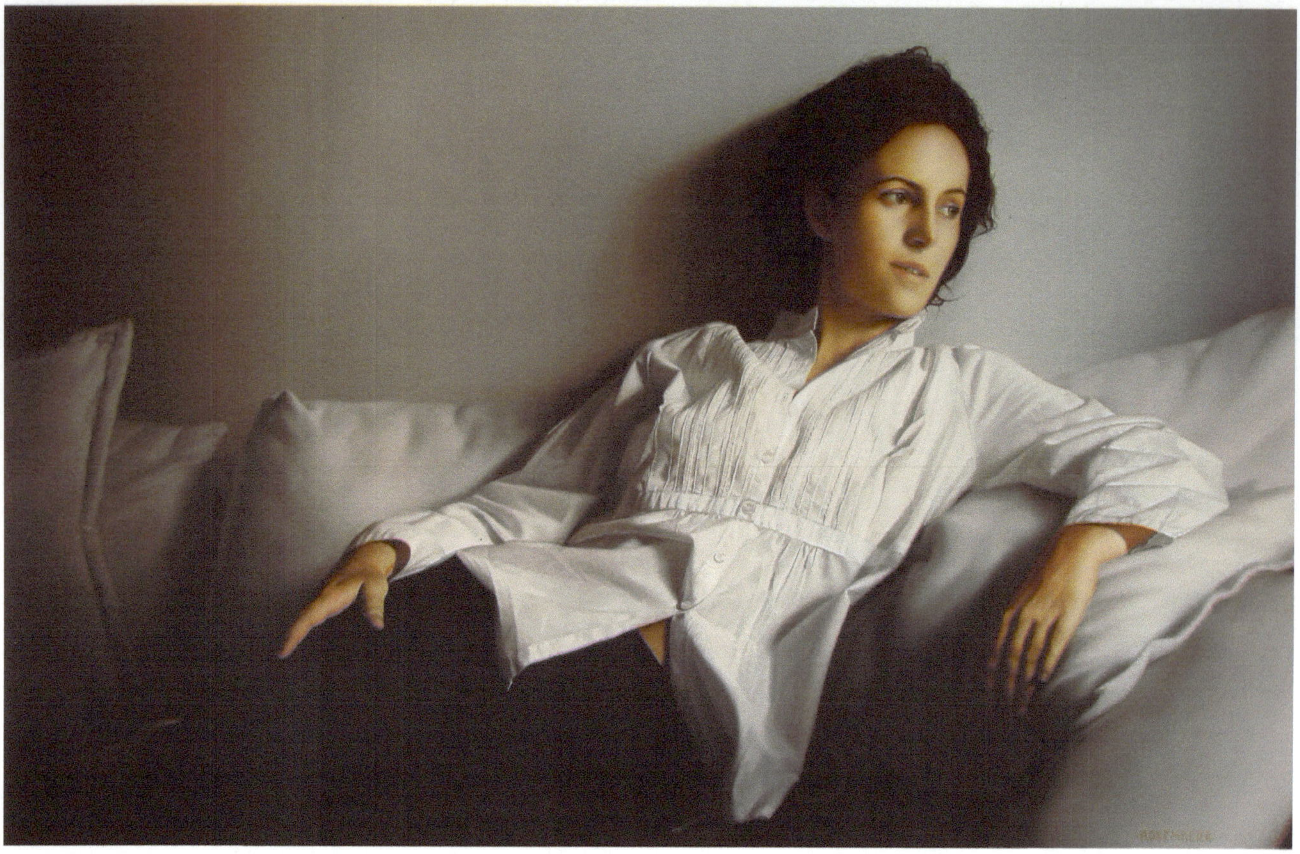

Juliana Series - Painting no. 2, 2011, oil on canvas, 80 x 120cm

Sunday Morning Series - Painting no. 2, 2012, oil on canvas, 50 x 90cm

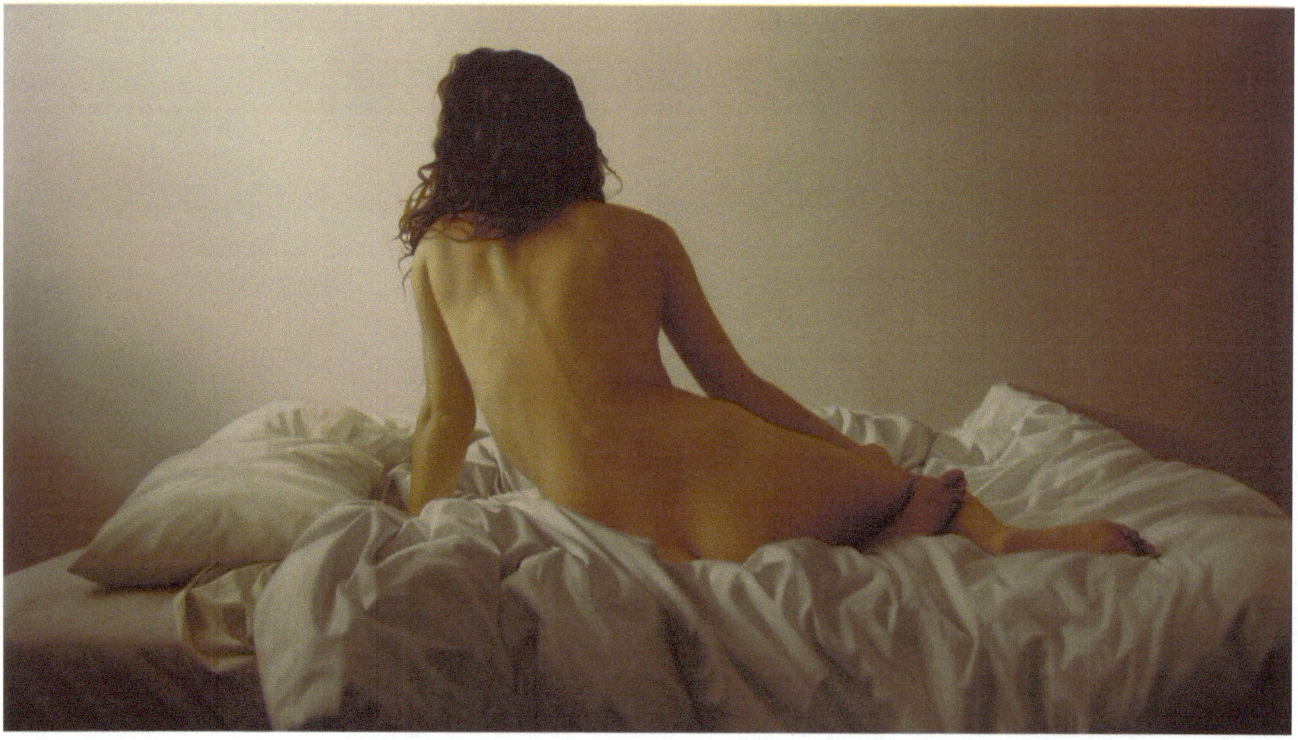

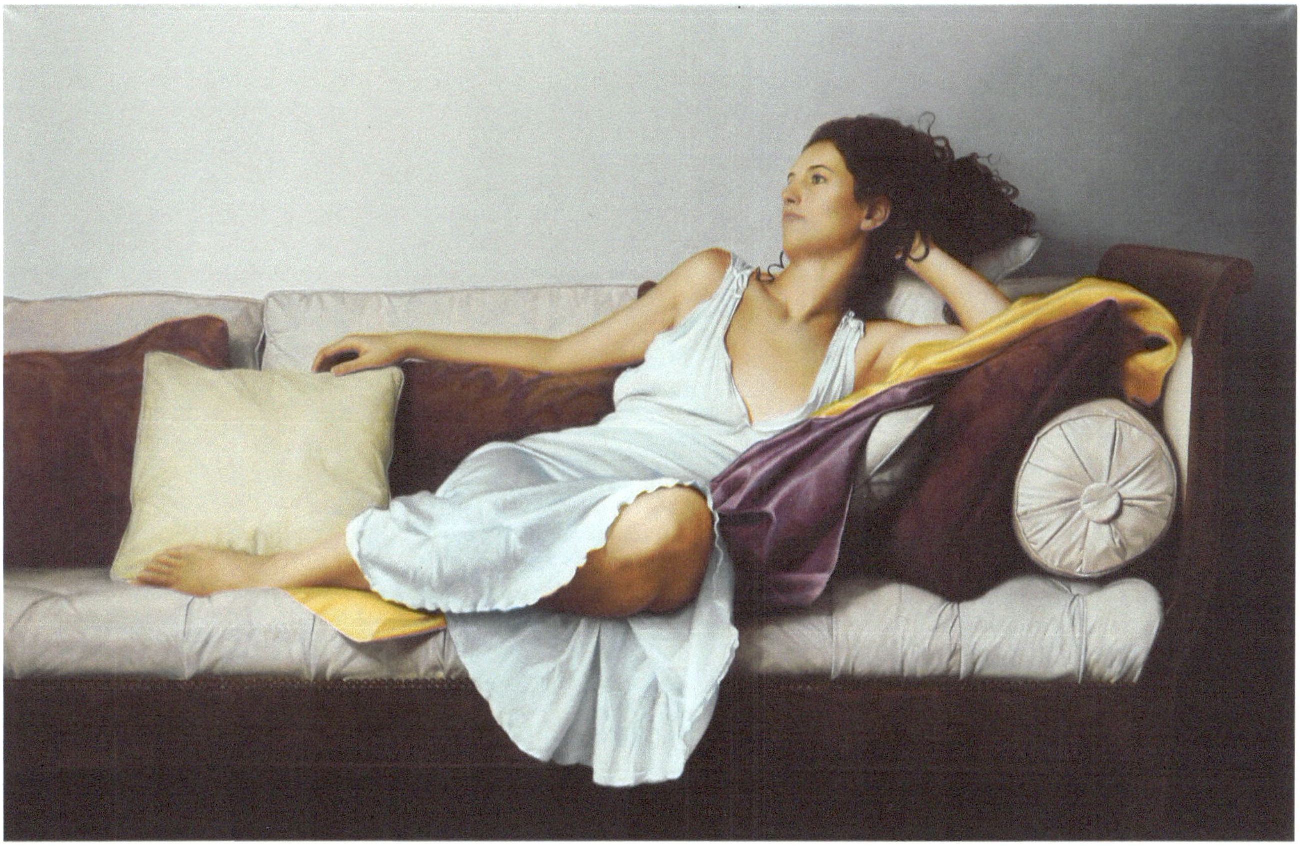

Juliana Series - Painting no. 3, 2011, oil on canvas, 50 x 80cm

Spring Series - Painting no. 1, 2015, oil on canvas, 60 x 110cm

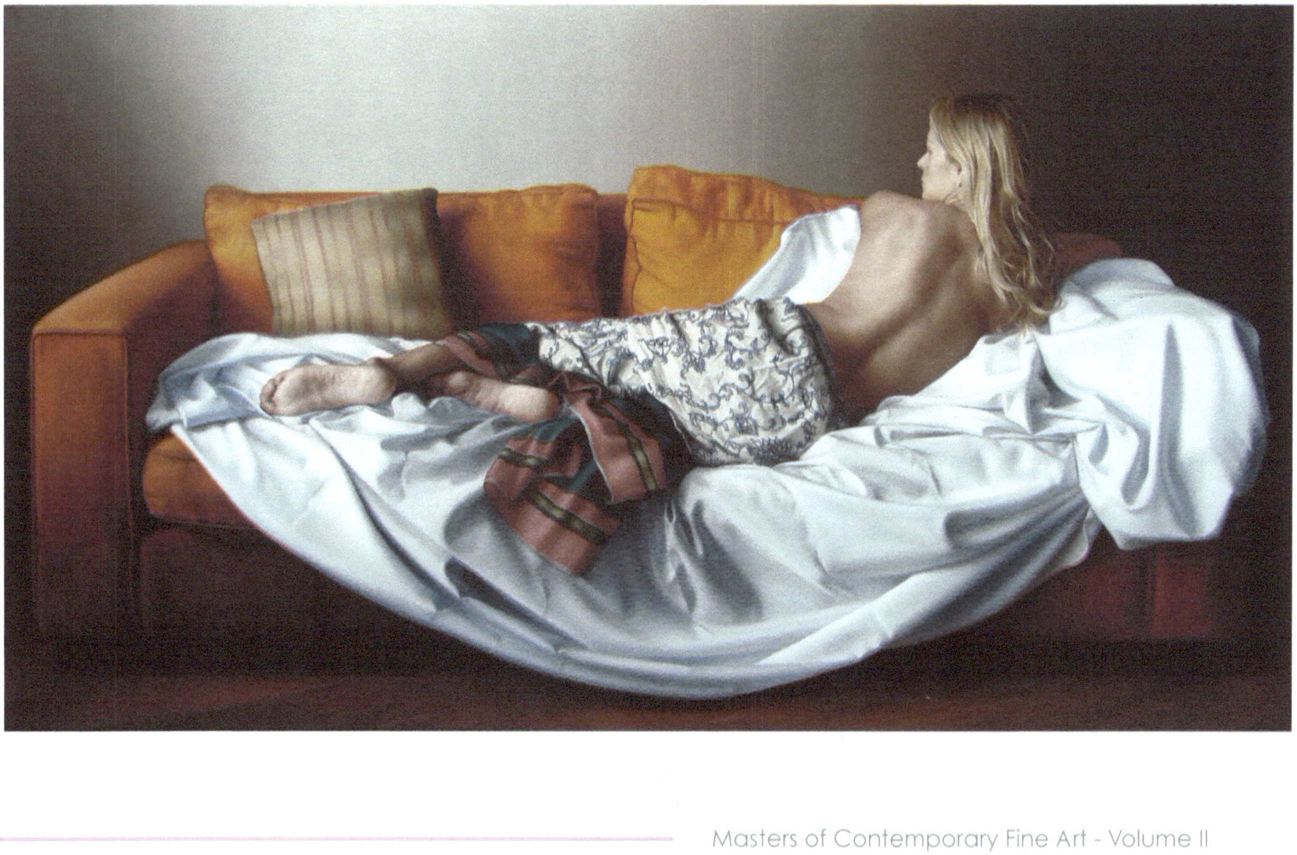

CARLO MIRABASSO

PAINTING - ITALY

www.carlomirabasso.it

Carlo Mirabasso is an Italian painter who was born in Tivoli, Rome.

After attending the First Art High School in Rome during the 70s, he spent the 80s and 90s honing his skills while he supported himself on a career in advertising, design, and illustration. Eventually, that path led him to realize the fullness of his dream, and he became a professional artist in the early 90s.

Around that time, he shifted his focus to metaphysical compositions, developing his own style based on wood panels, and in 1996, he chose to begin painting full time. His work has since been put on display throughout the world, in cities such as Rome, Florence, Milan, London, Auckland, Providence, and Taipei.

In Carlo's work, there is a certain inscrutable quality that can be taken as a unique perspective of reality. Carlo takes images, places, and events and runs them through his own metaphysical lens, producing what is for the viewer a sensory experience unlike any other. Influences on his paintings are many and derive especially from daily life or memories from the past.

Although his work can at time be jarring, he tries to incorporate an over-arching sense of serenity into each piece as well, finding peace among the chaos that is modern life. Unbound by the narrative of his work, he intentionally leaves much of his painting open to interpretation.

La Buona Occasione, oil on canvas, 70 x 70cm

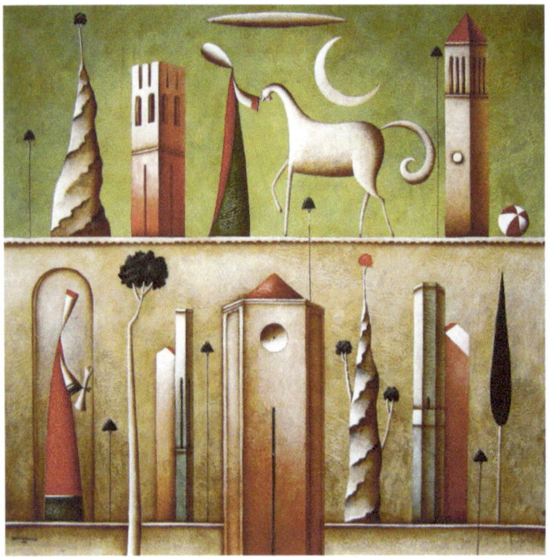

Passeggiando Nel Borgo, oil on canvas, 70 x 100cm

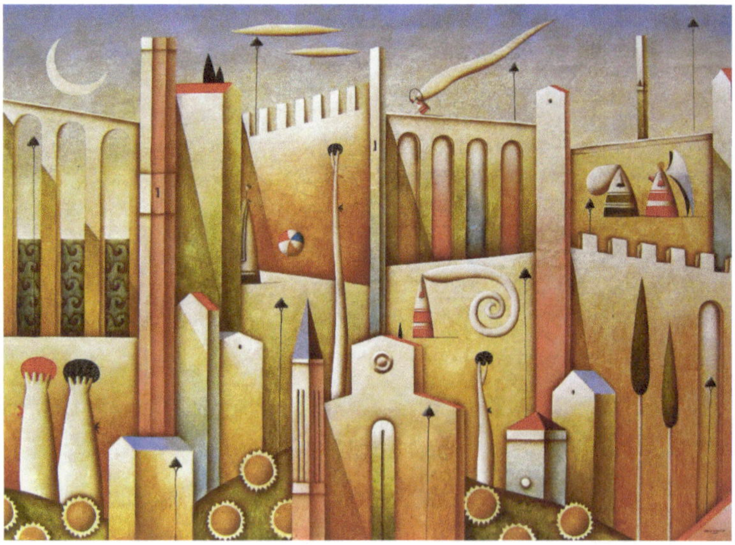

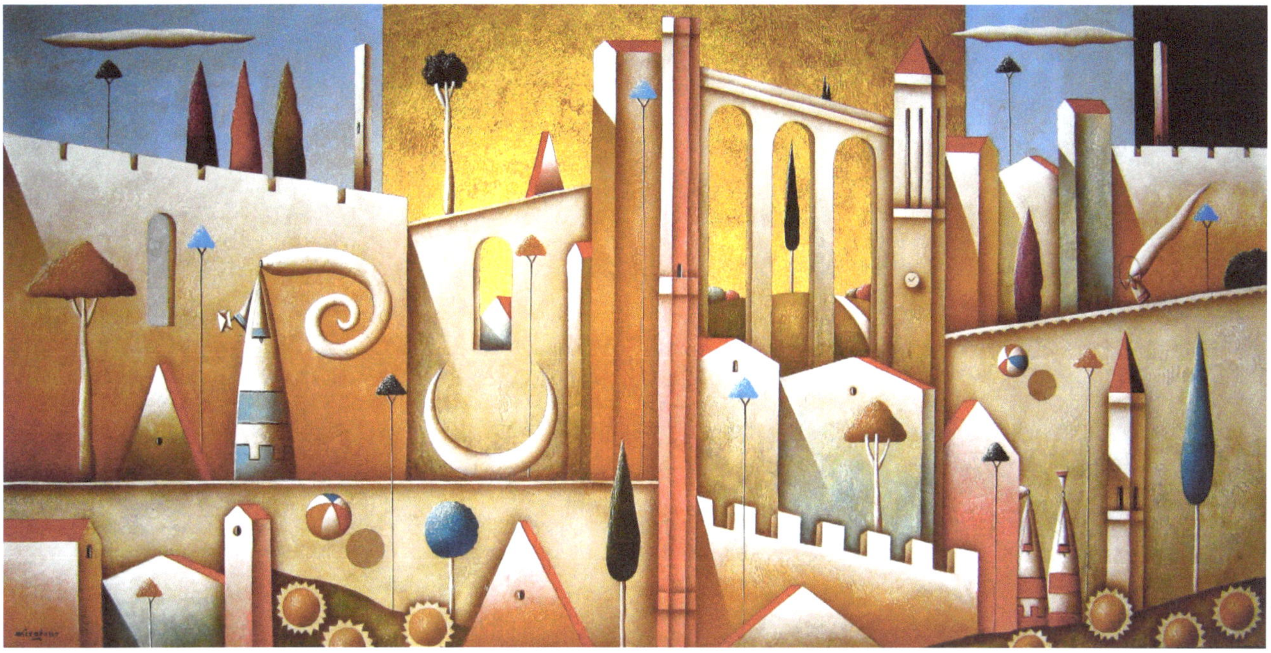

Il Primo Appuntamento, oil on canvas, 50 x 100cm

La Gioia Ritrovata, oil on canvas, 50 x 100cm

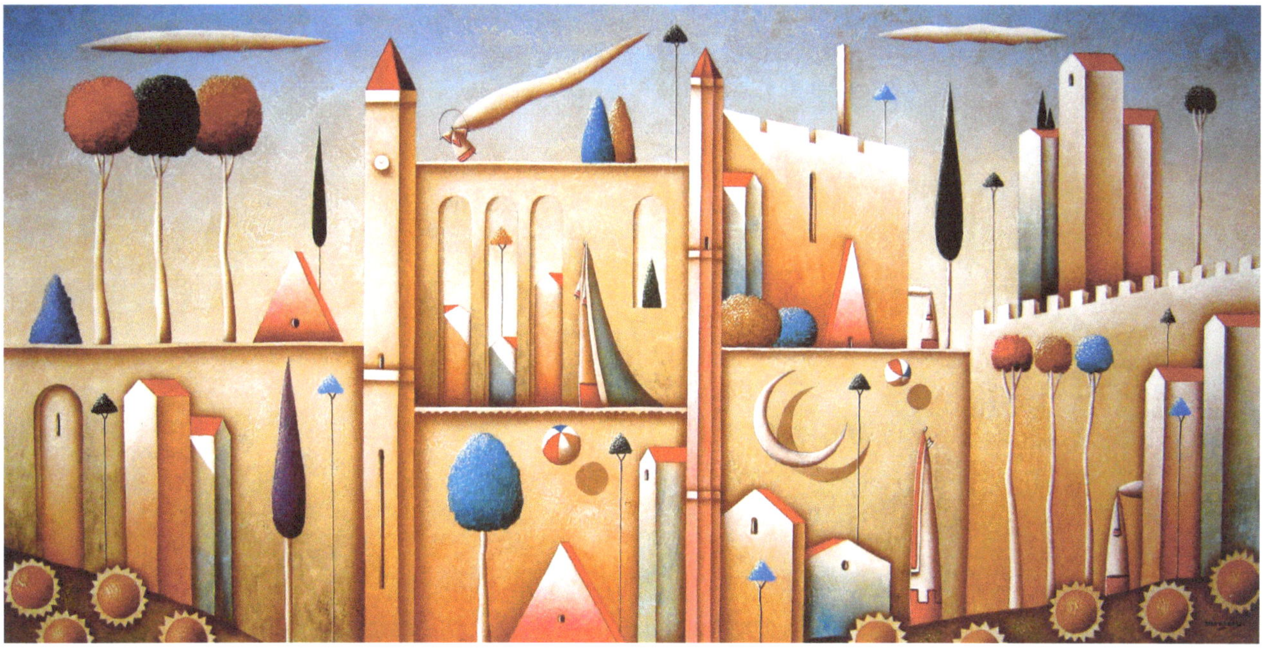

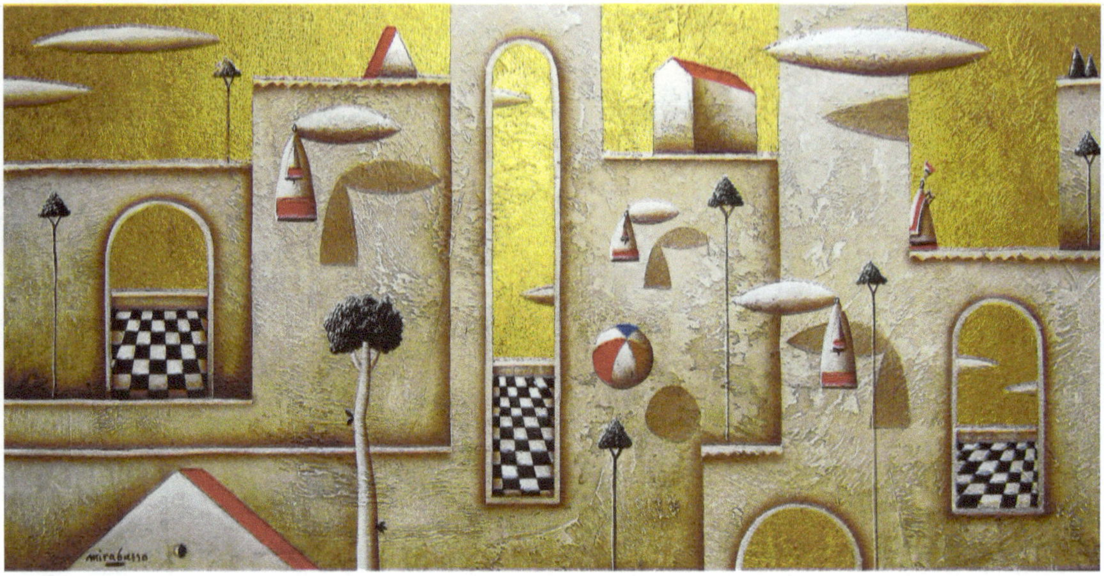

Apparizioni Simultanee, oil on canvas, 20 x 40cm

La Saggia Decisione, oil on canvas, 70 x 70cm

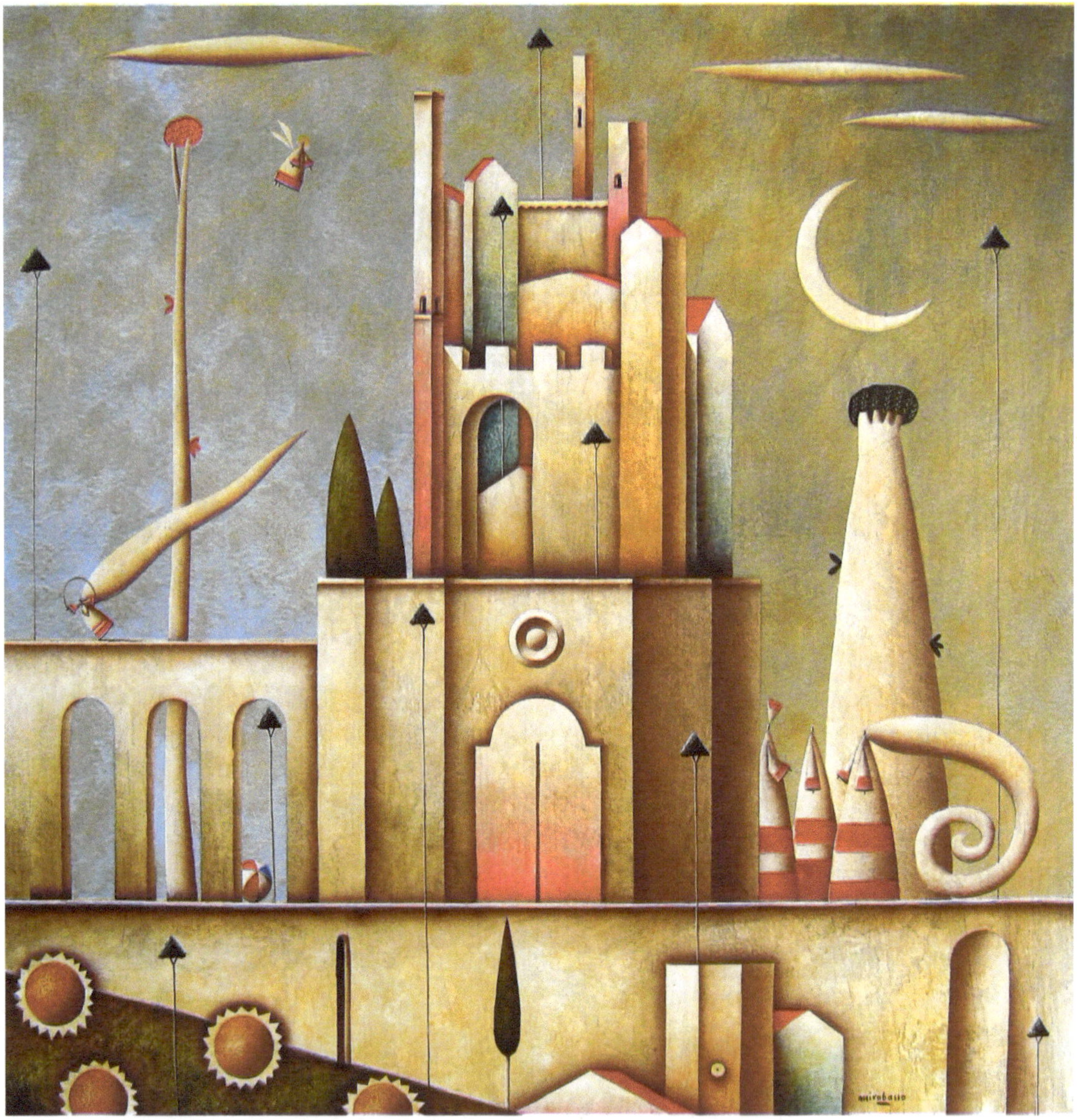

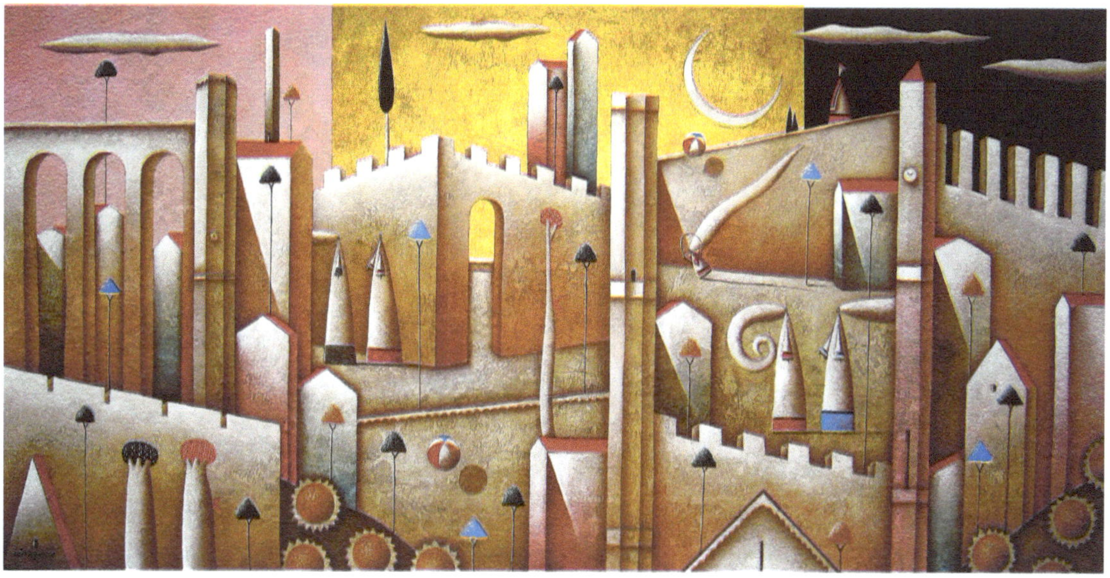

La Lieta Notizia, oil on canvas, 50 x 100cm

Tre Appuntamenti, oil on canvas, 50 x 50cm

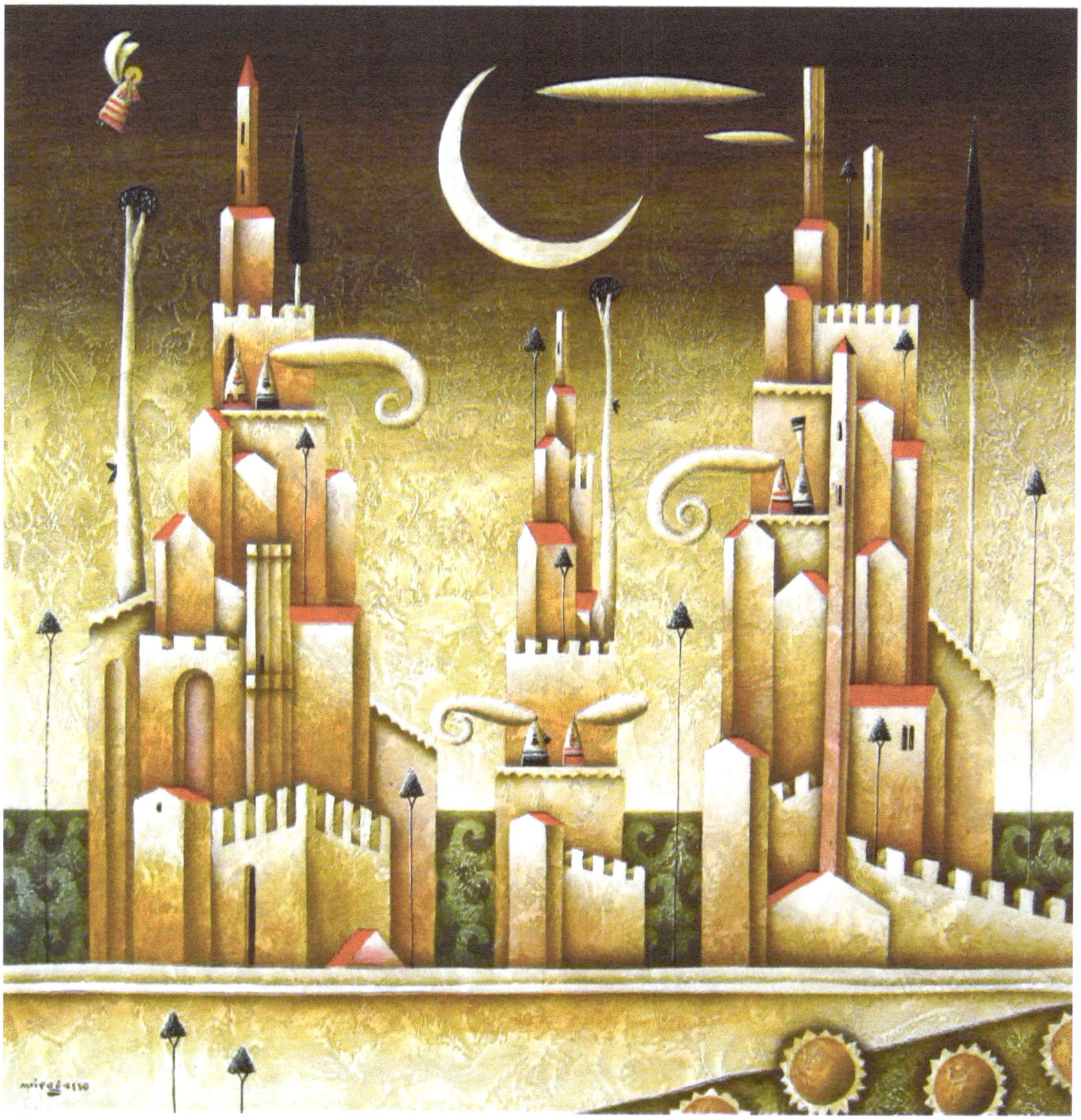

CESAR SANTOS

PAINTING - CUBA

www.santocesar.com

Cesar Santos is a painter who has studied at Miami Dade College, the New World School of Arts, and the Angel Academy of Art in Florence, the last of which he graduated after spending time under the tutelage of Michael John Angel, who himself was a student of the artist Pietro Annigoni.

Since his entry into the art world, Cesar has become known for the striking expertise of his techniques, which illustrates a particular harmony between the natural and the conceptual. He consistently produces works that are provocative without being reaction-seeking, a natural extension of his unassuming-yet-dramatic personality.

Cesar has completed a number of solo shows to date, most notably "Syncretism" at Eleanor Ettinger Chelsea Gallery in New York, "Beyond Realism" at Oxenberg Fine Arts in Miami, and "New Impressions" at the Greenhouse Gallery in San Antonio. He has quickly become recognized as a leader of his generation, placing first at a competition run by the Metropolitan Museum of Art and awarded the 2013 Miami Dade College Hall of Fame Award in Visual Arts.

A world traveler, he has spent time in the United States, Europe, Latin America, and Asia, practicing his art wherever he goes and building upon a repertoire that resembles more and more the definition of global.

Right: Self Portrait with Palette, oil on canvas, 130 x 107cm

The Three Graces, oil on linen, 142 x 188cm

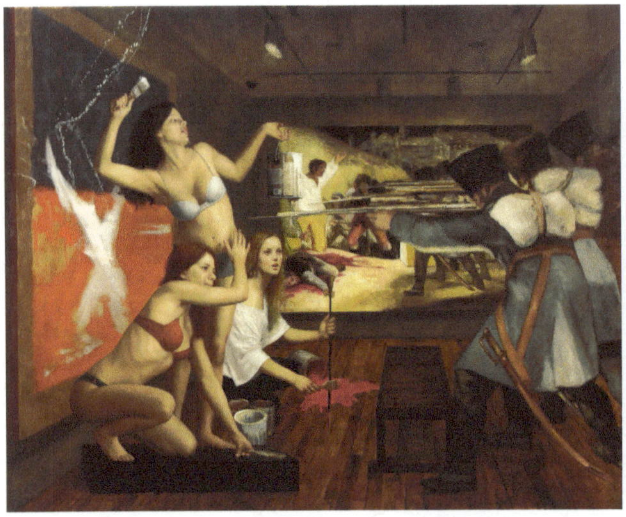

Matisse's Niece, oil on linen, 99 x 69cm

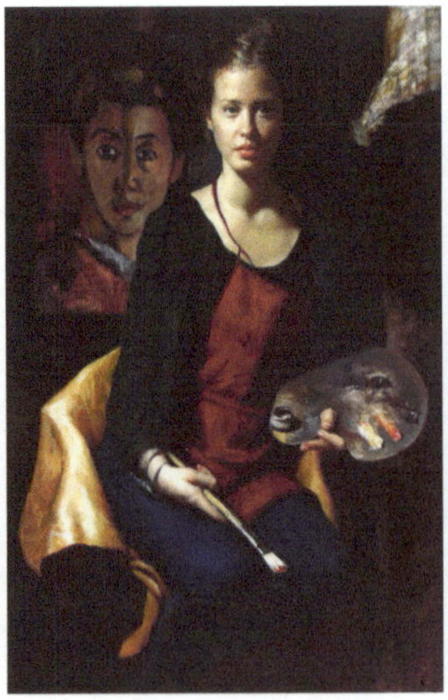

Matisse in Vermeer's Corner, oil on linen, 119 x 76cm

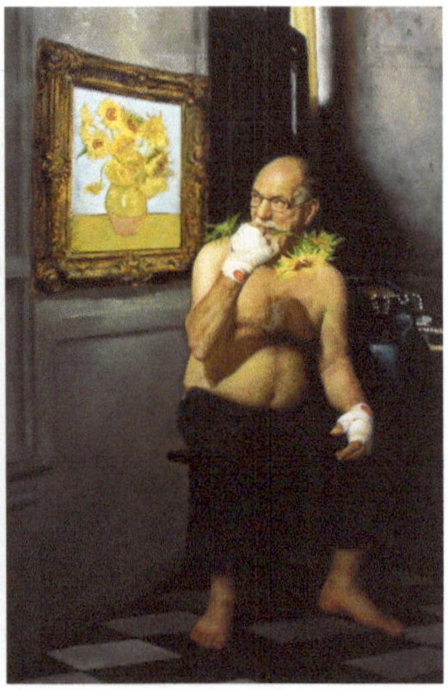

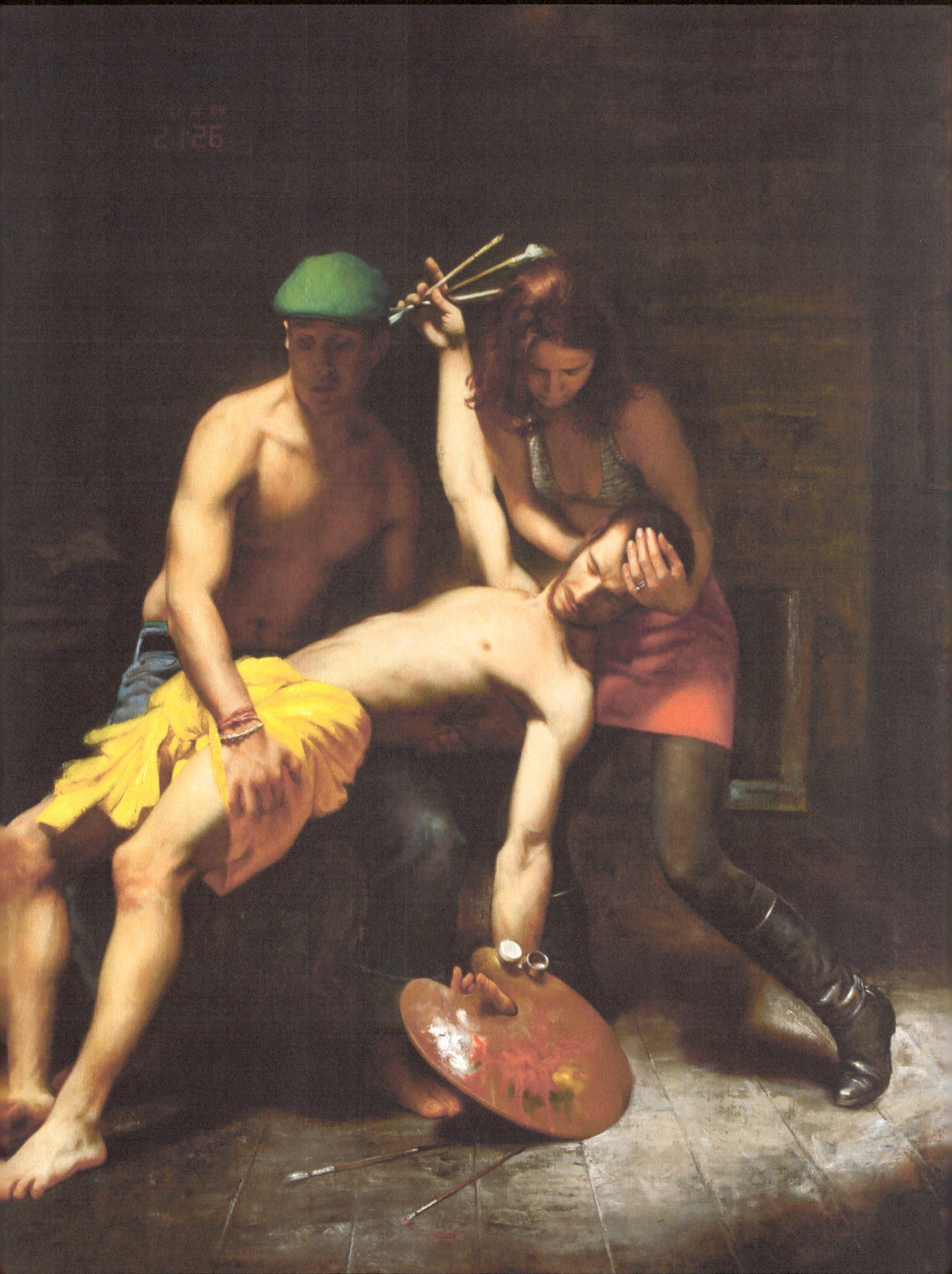

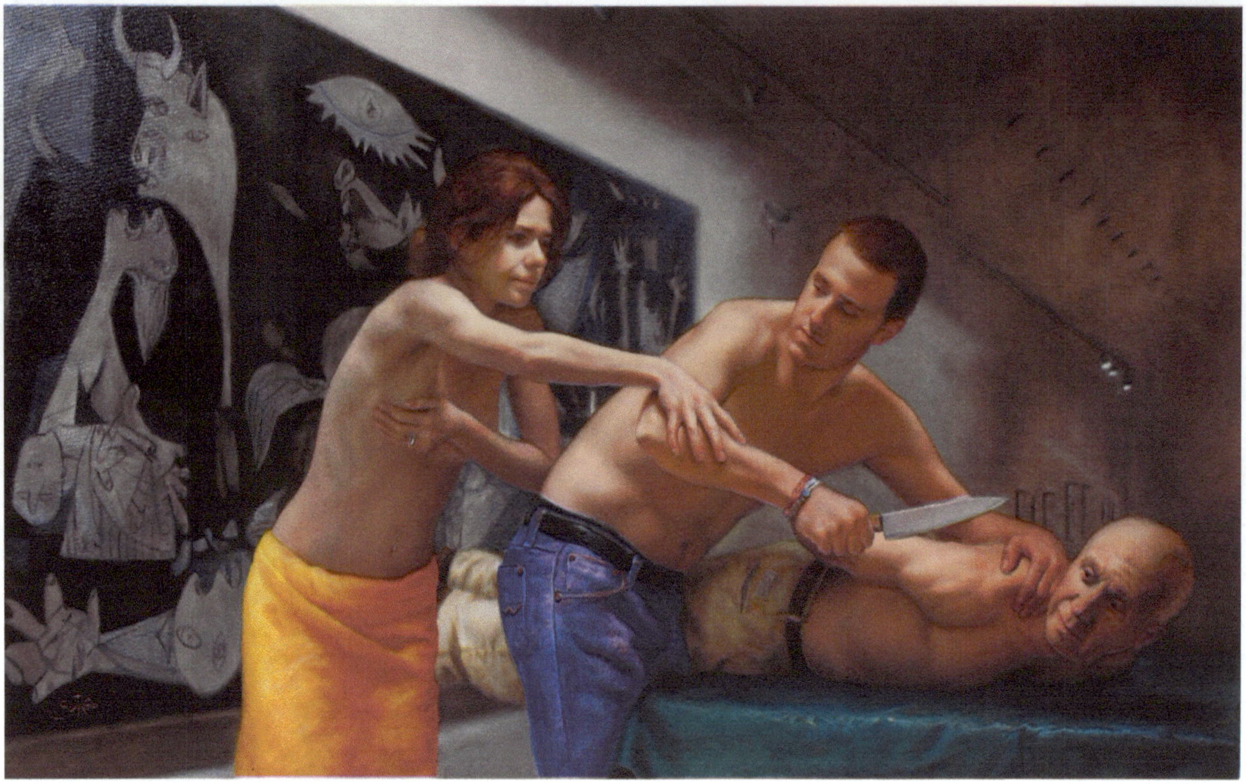

Pablo on the Table, oil on linen, 69 x 122cm

First Tatoo, oil on linen, 71 x 99cm

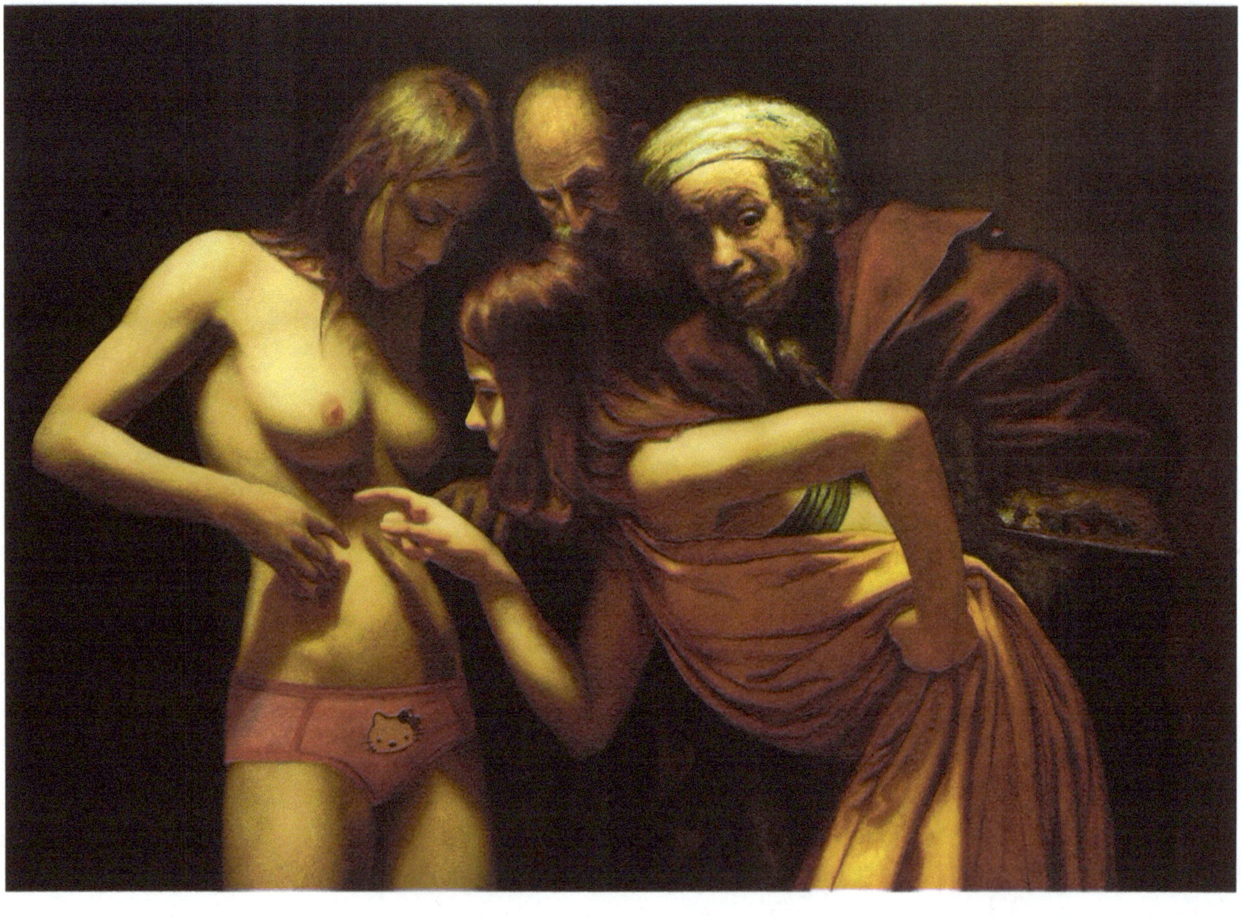

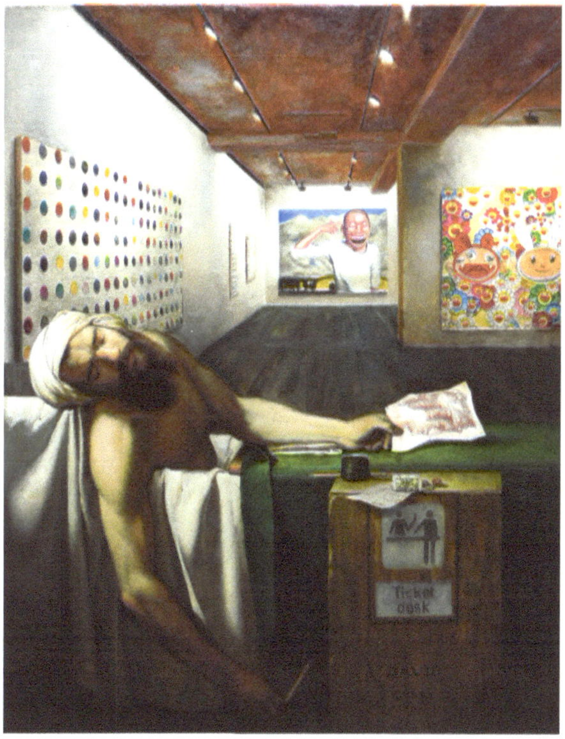

A David, oil on linen, 23 x 97cm

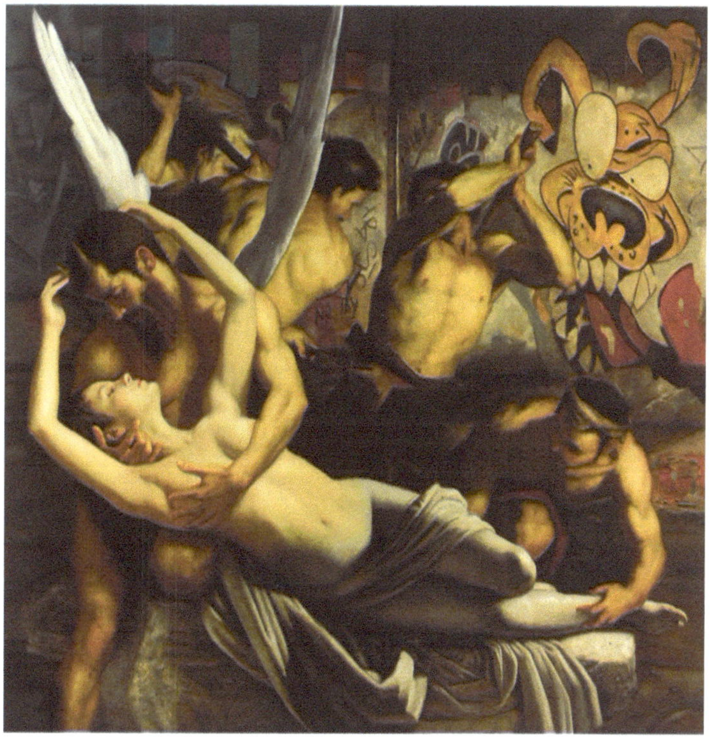

Psyche and I, oil on linen, 142 x 142cm

Aftermath, oil on linen, 94 x 137cm

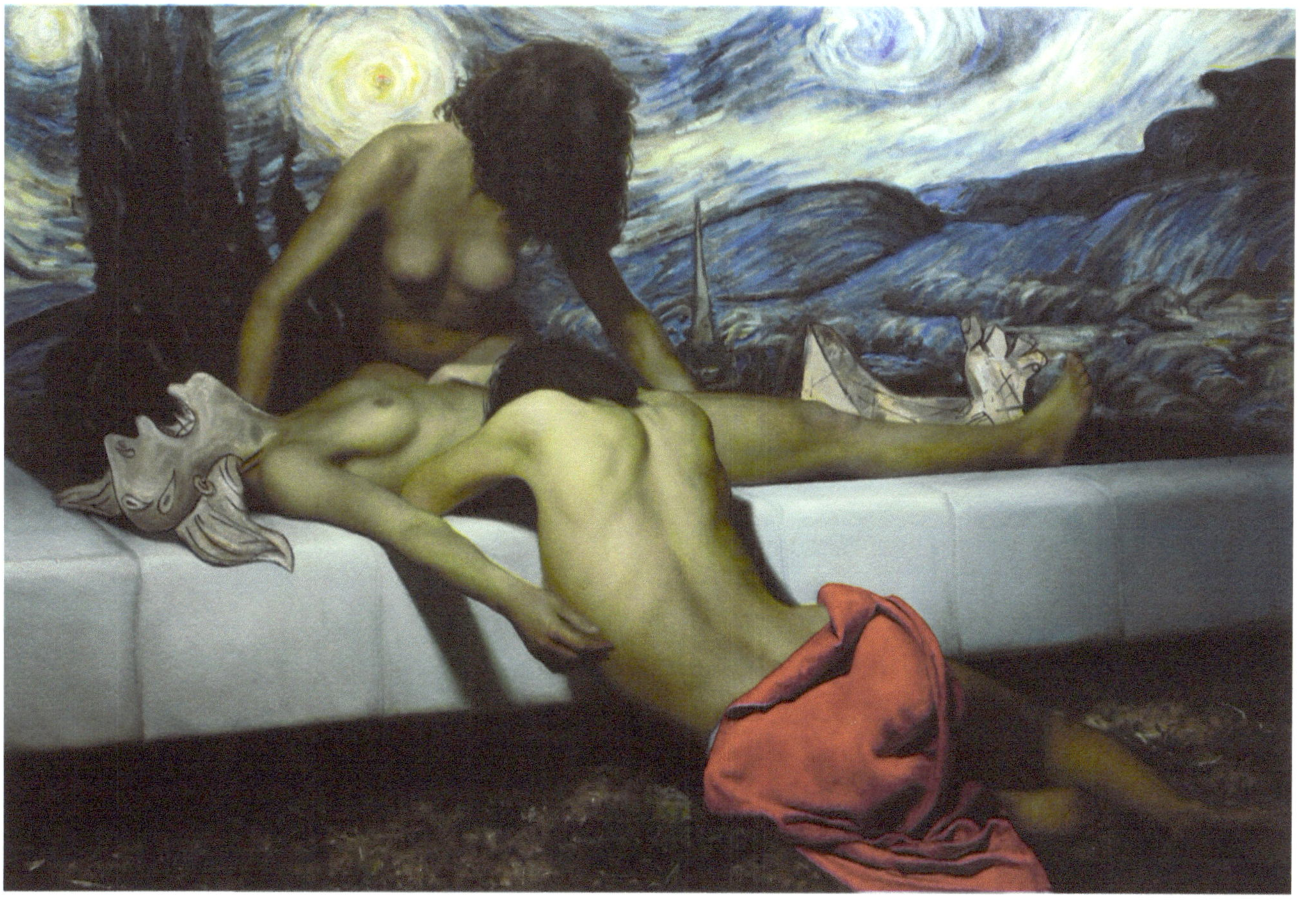

CHRISTOPHE VACHER

PAINTING - FRANCE

www.vacher.com

Christopher Vacher is a French artist whose work has been featured extensively in Hollywood media, including Disney films such as The Hunchback of Notre-Dame, Tarzan, Fantasia 2000, Dinosaur, Treasure Planet, Enchanted , 9, Shark Tale and Despicable Me.

For the last six years, he has served as the Art Director for Hasbro's Transformers TV series, and he is the winner of two Emmy Awards and the nominee for an Annie Award. Since 1989, he has become known as a reliable professional in the film industry, working extensively for Disney, DreamWorks, and Universal Studios.

Christopher today works and lives in California, and he has given lectures at the San Francisco Academy of Arts, the University of California at Berkeley, and California State University at Northridge. His paintings are on display permanently at galleries throughout Europe and the United States.

Drawing influence from old and new artists alike, he is particularly fond of Sandorfi, Berksinski, Ugarte, and Les Visionnaires, as well as such schools as the Hudson River, the American Realists, the Great American Illustrators, the Romantics, and the European Symbolists. In addition, he draws influence from the life that he lives every day, exposing himself to a variety of music and art as he travels all around the world.

Vision at the Lake, oil on canvas, 60.9 x 121.9cm

Right: Norova, oil on canvas, 76.2 x 101.6cm

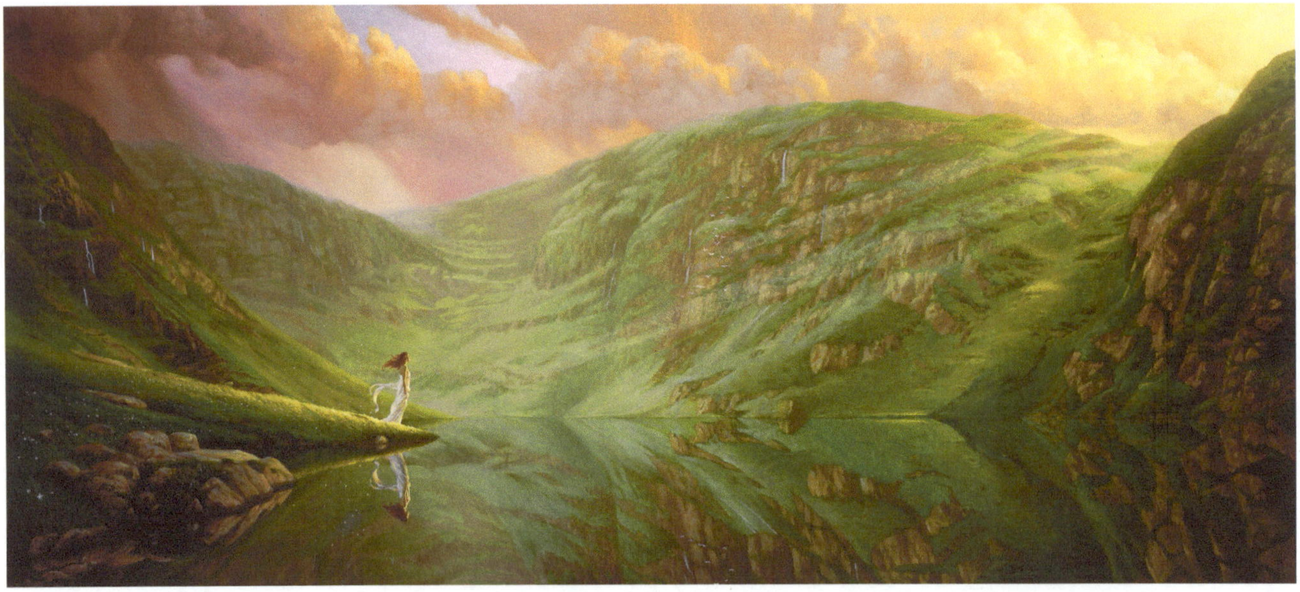

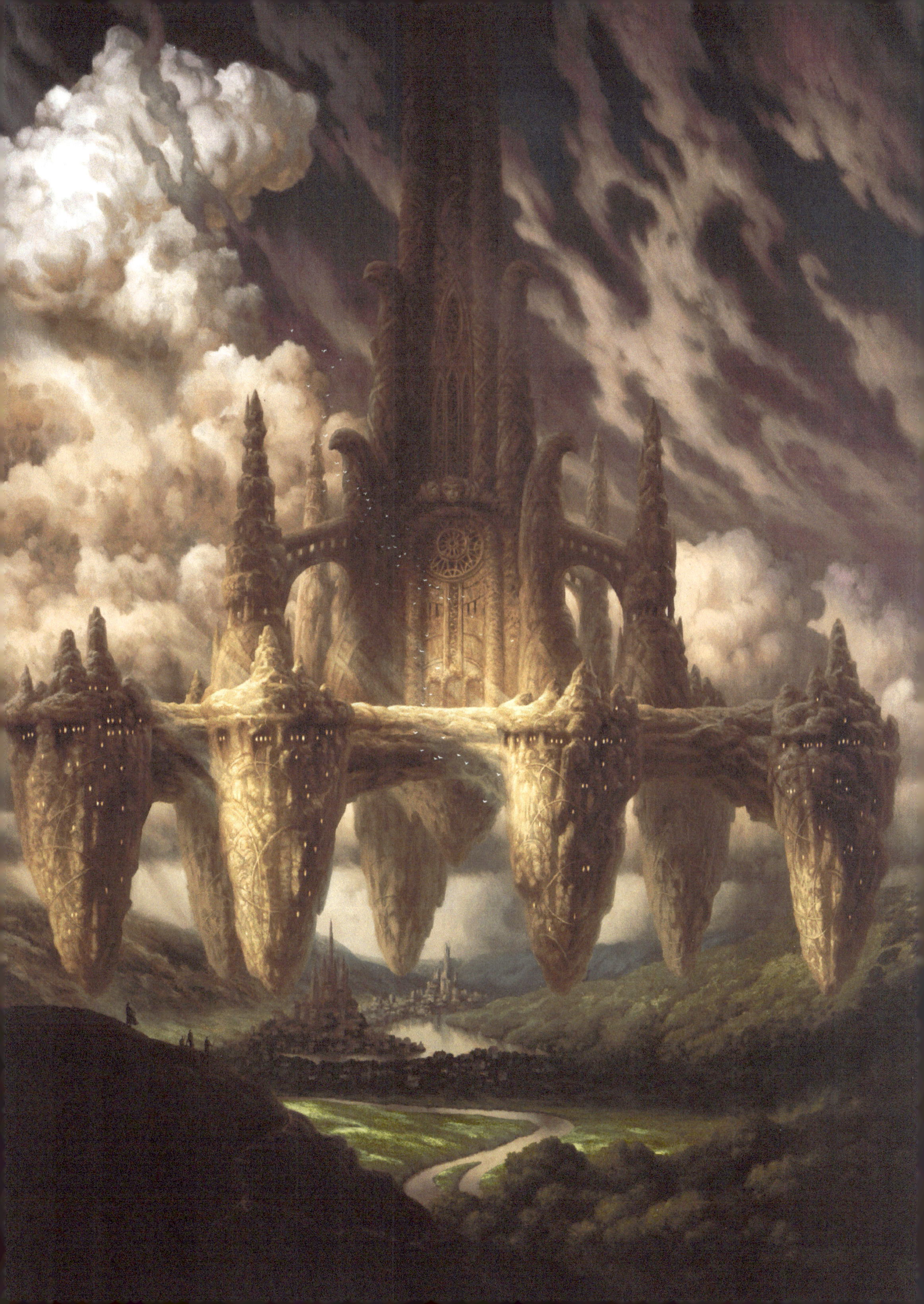

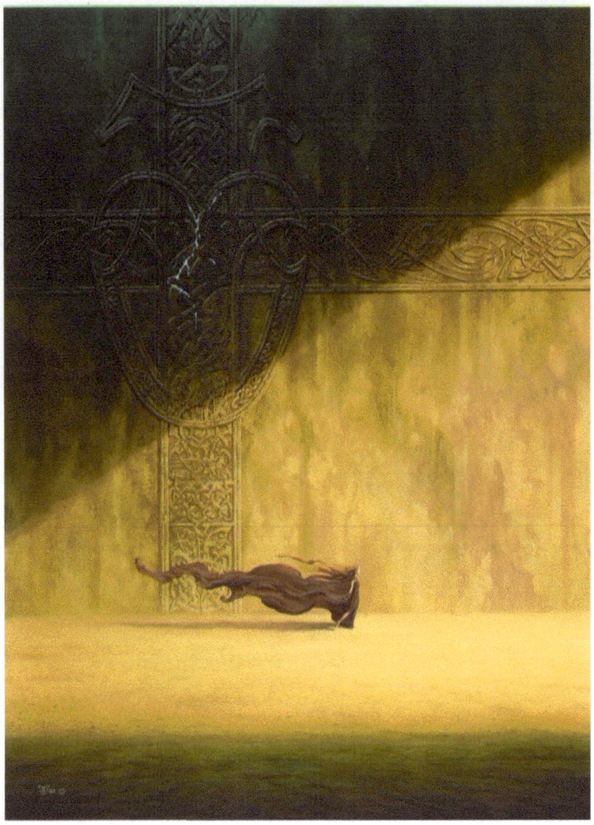

Automne, oil on canavs, 76.2 x 101.6cm

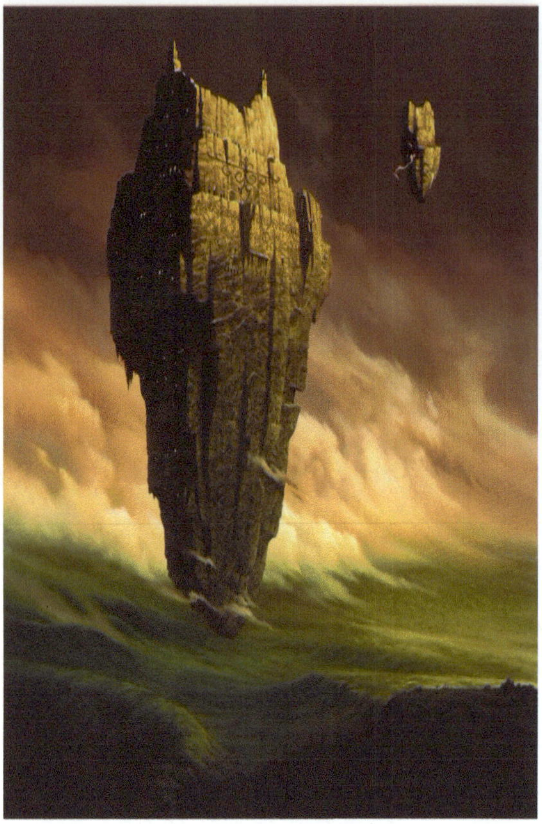

The Guardians, oil on canvas, 60.9 x 76.2cm

Endless Dream, oil on canvas, 45.7 x 60.9cm

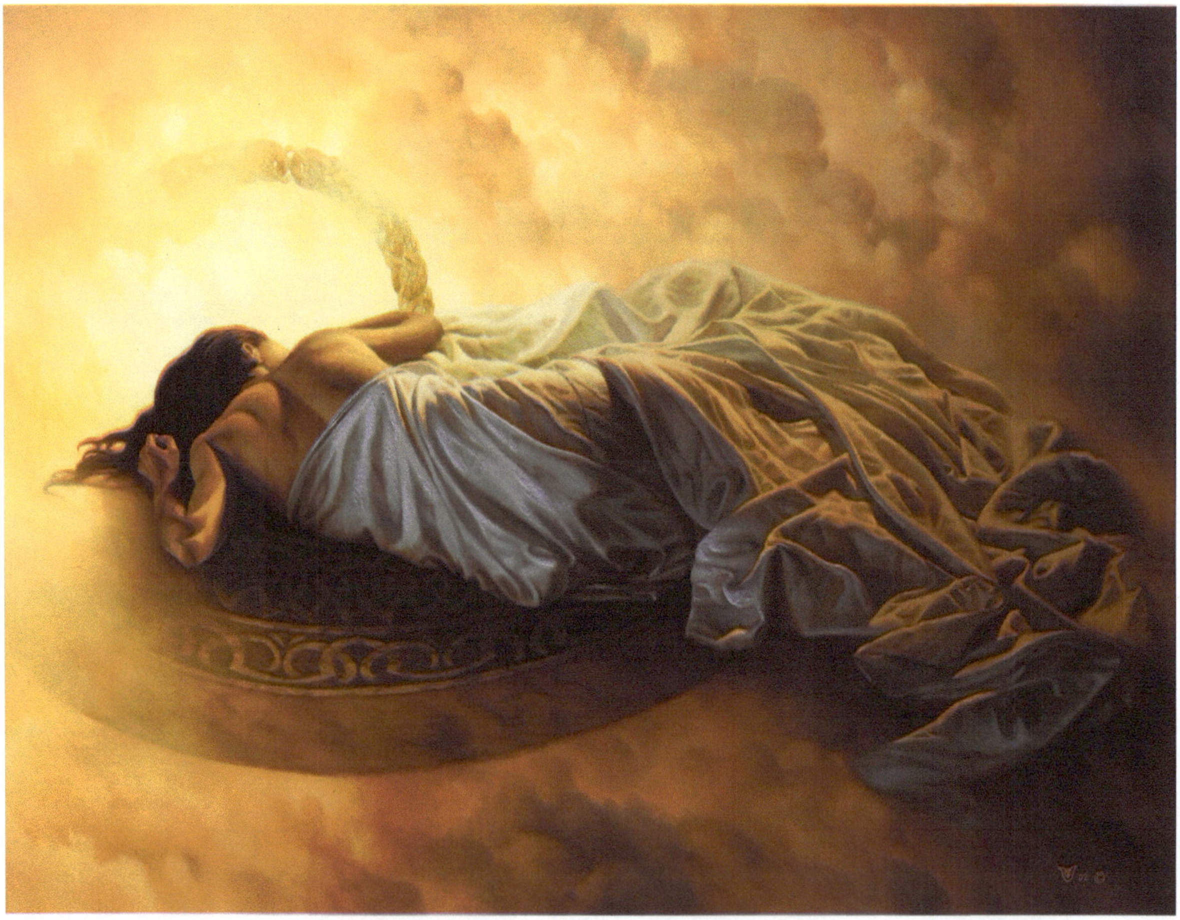

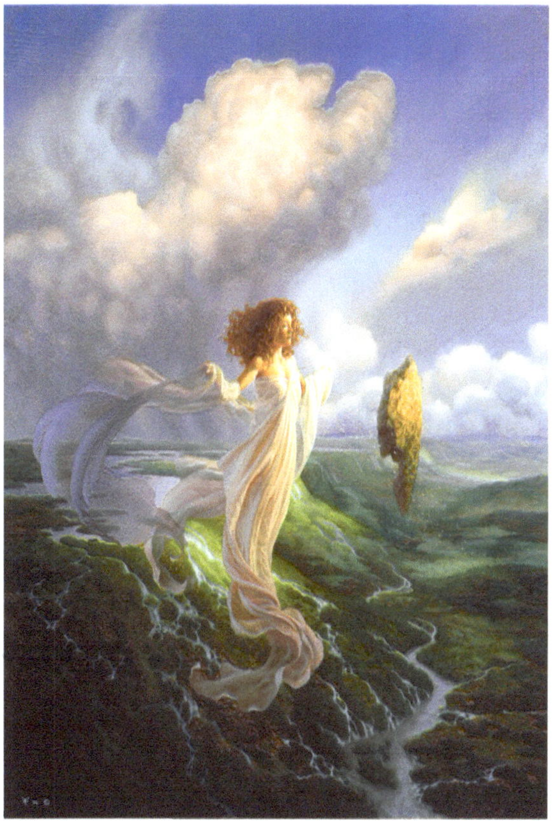

Mistress of the Winds, oil on canvas, 29.8 x 41.9cm

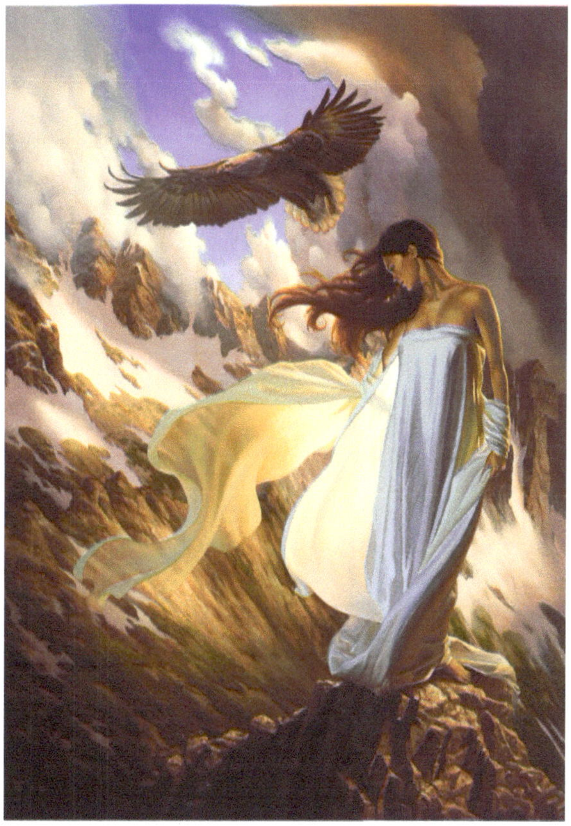

Spirit Rising, oil on canvas, 45.7 x 60.9cm

Untouched Gardens, oil on canvas, 45.7 x 60.9cm

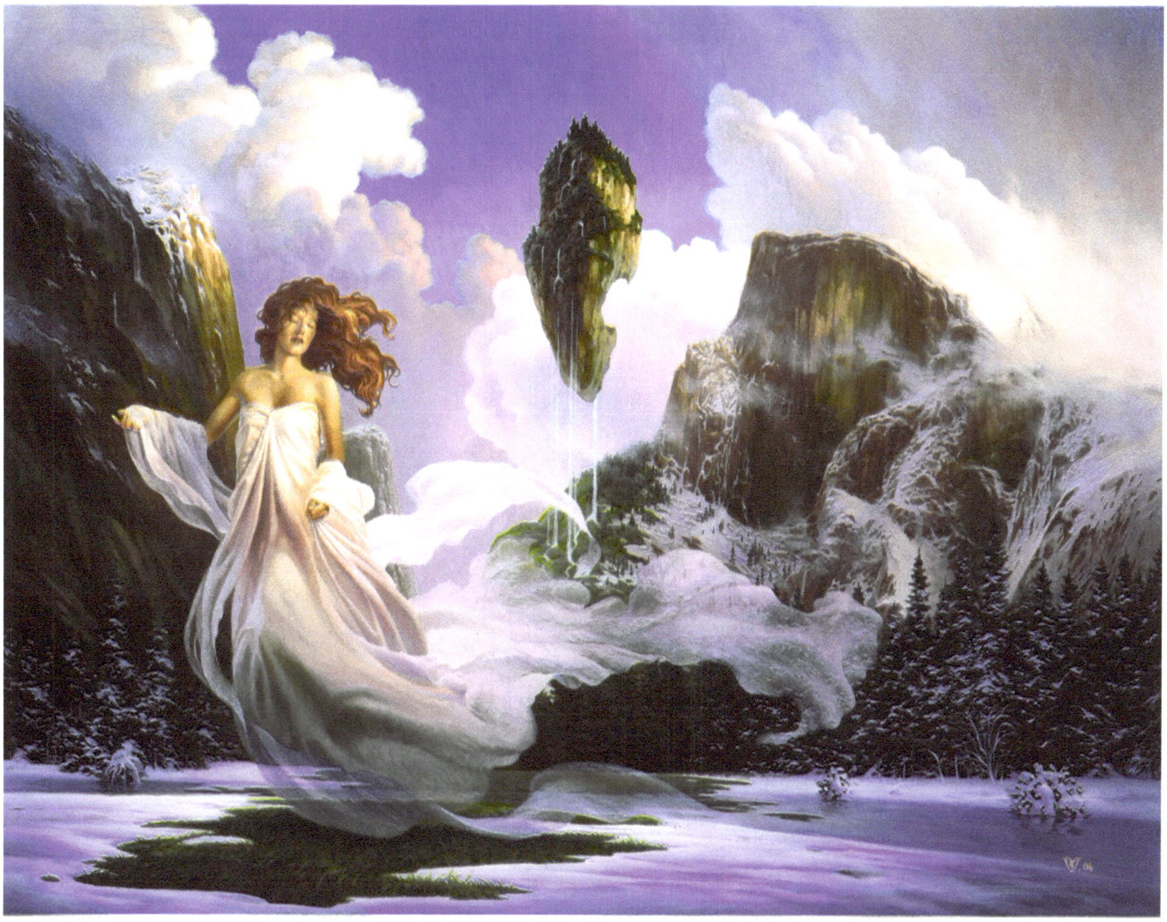

COSTA DVORESKY

PAINTING - RUSSIA

www.dvorezky.com

Costa Dvorezky is a Russian artist who studied at Moscow Secondary School of Art, the Moscow Art College, and Moscow Stroganov Academy of Art.

Known for his blunt, revelatory paintings of the human body, he never errs on the side of bashfulness, illustrating muscle and fat in a way that is true to life without being overly critical. He takes the sensitive nature of his subjects to heart, showing them their due respect and never coming close to making fun of them. He paints with love, expressing his admiration for the human form in all of its variety.

Costa's style vacillates between soft and glimmering, creating a feel that is decidedly smooth, exuding both milky and oily qualities in a way that is firmly sexy, like a freshly made bed that has been strewn with rose petals.

Since 1993, he has served as a member of the International Art Fund of the Young Artists and Critics.

A civic-minded artist, he goes to great lengths not only to see that he is producing a high quality in his own work but also that up-and-comers are presented with the opportunities that they need to establish themselves and succeed.

Right: Party Girl, oil on canvas, 122 x 183cm

Untitled, oil on canvas, 142 x 213cm

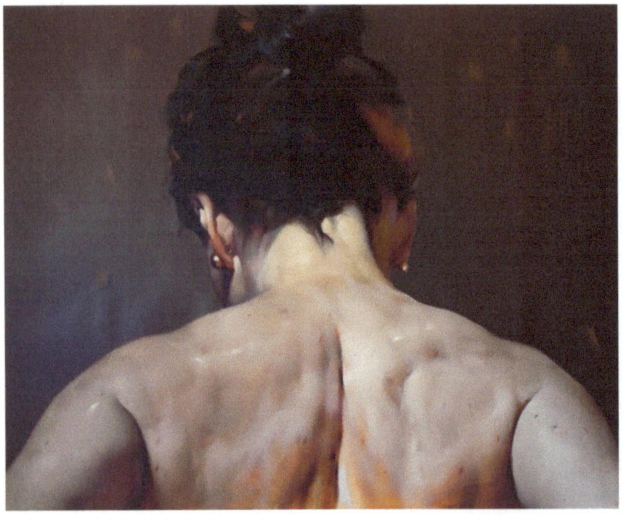

Salsa Teacher, oil on canvas, 152 x 122cm

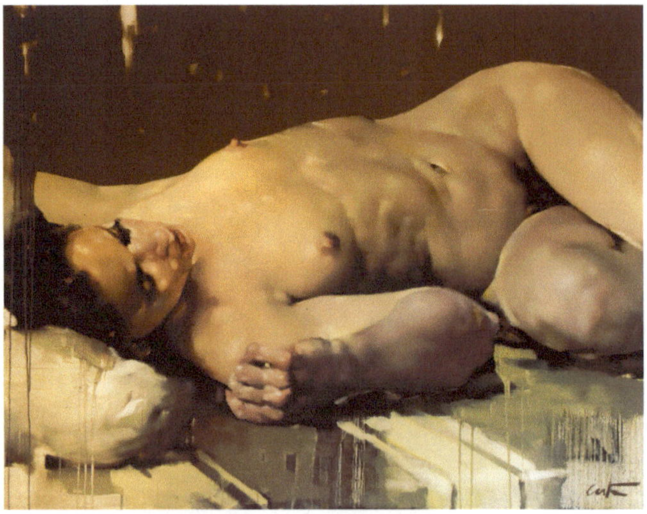

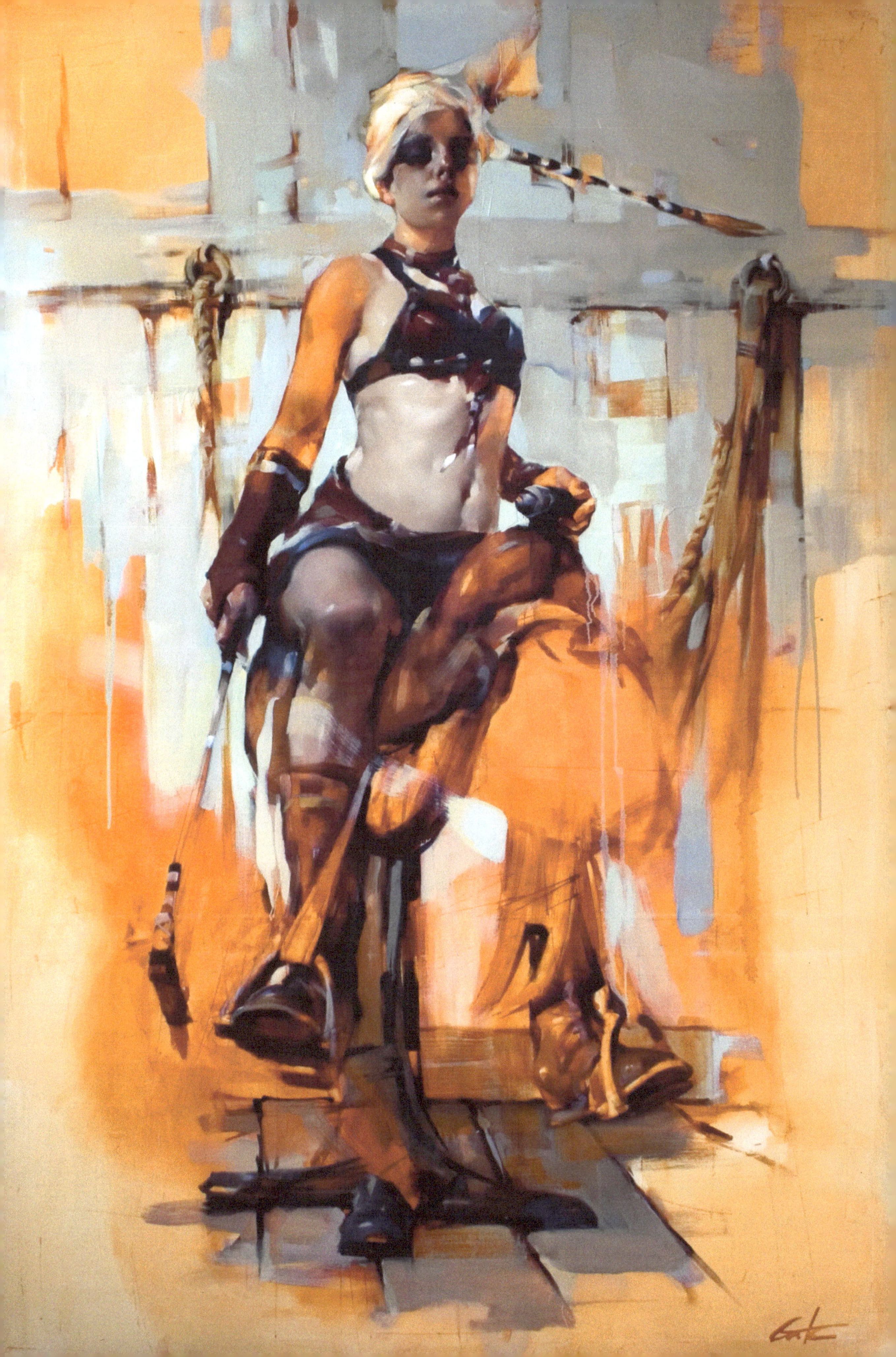

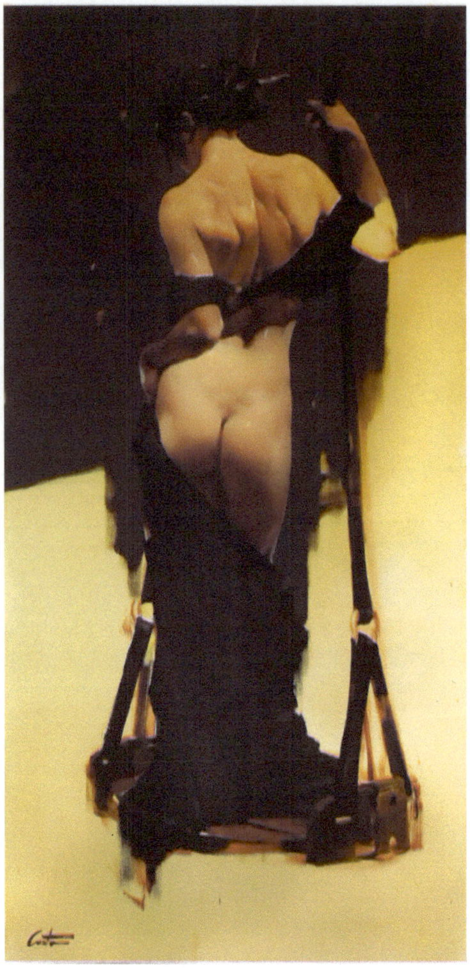

Mermaid, oil on canvas, 104 x 213cm

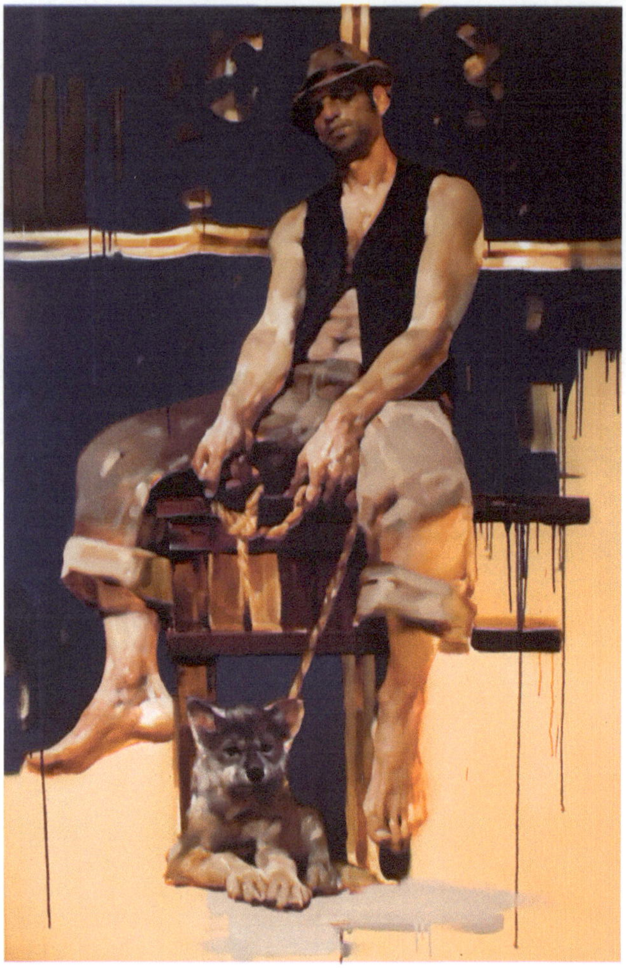

Hash, oil on canvas, 122 x 183cm

In the Studio, oil on canvas, 213 x 142cm

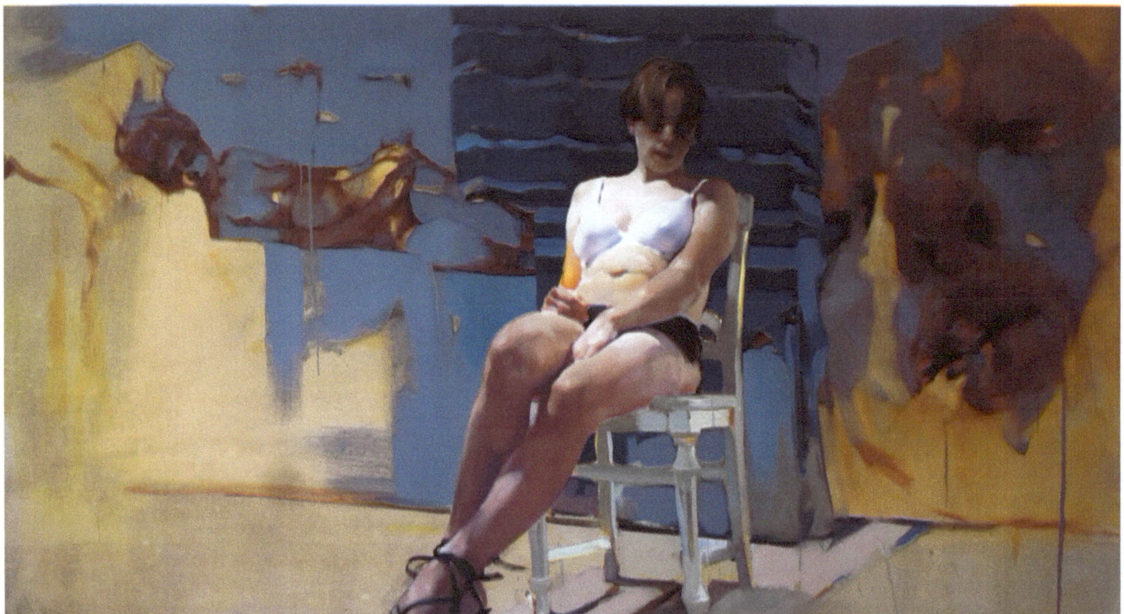

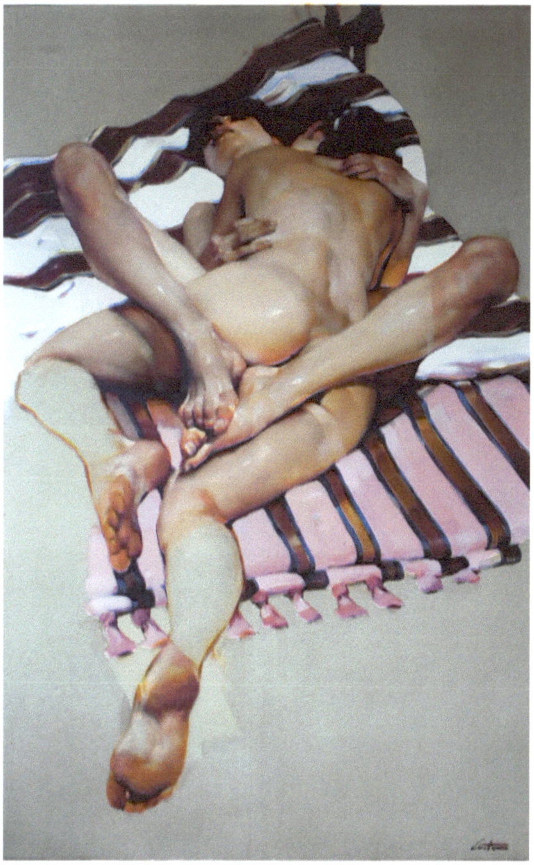

Kiss, oil on canvas, 122 x 183cm

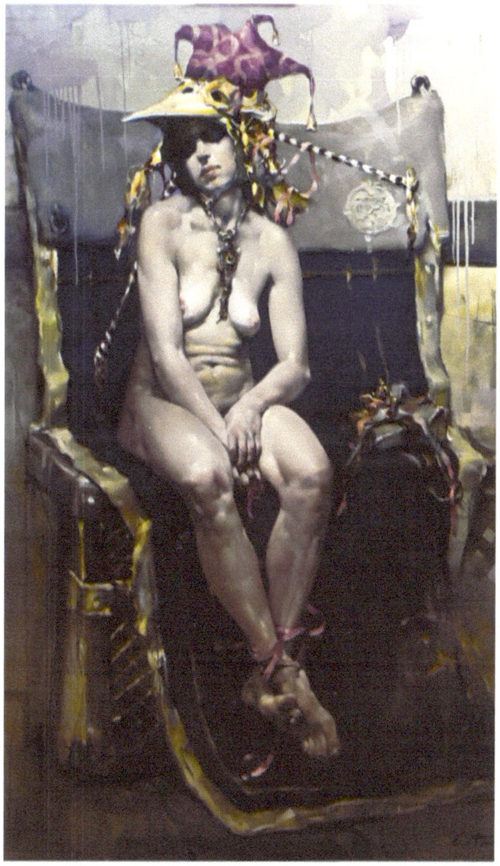

Hide and Seek, oil on canvas, 630 x 183cm

Urban Girl, oil on canvas, 152 x 127cm

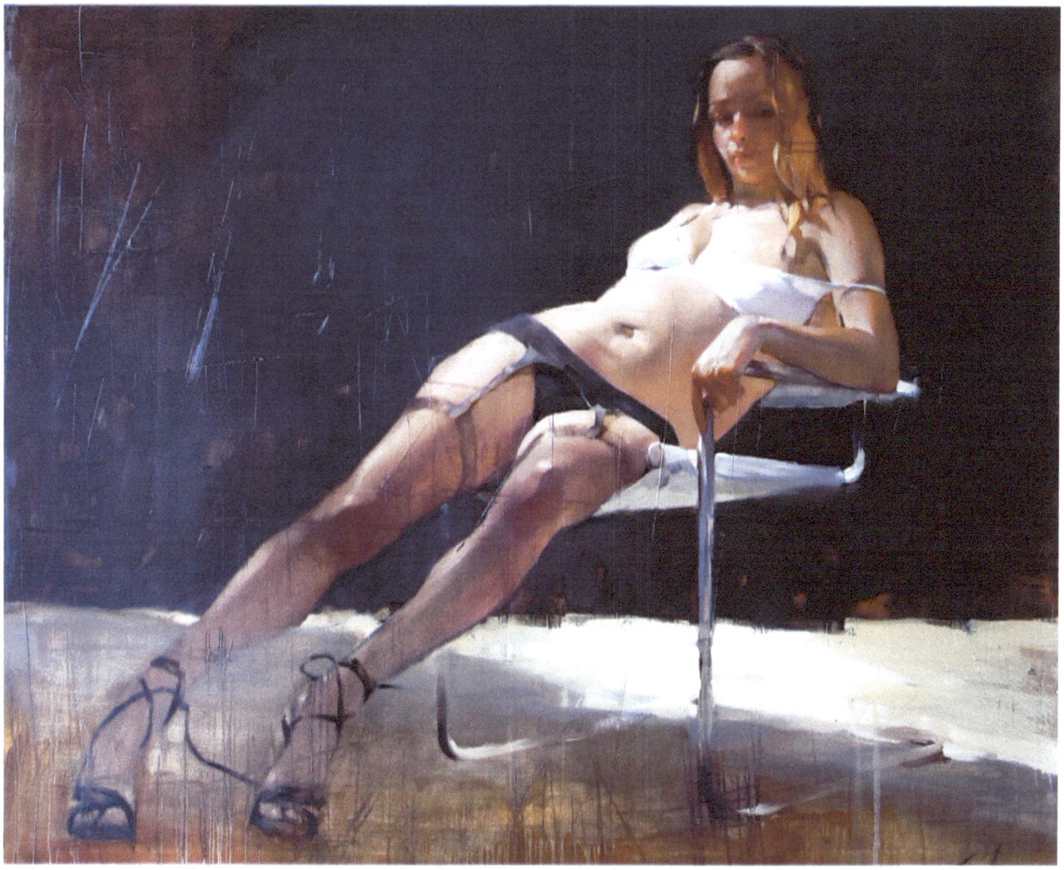

CRISTINA TROUFA

PAINTING - PORTUGAL

www.artgalaxie.com

Cristina Troufa is a Portuguese artist. Based out of Porto, Portugal, she studied painting at the University of Fine Arts of Porto (FBAUP), where she earned her Licentiate Degree in 1998 and her Master's Degree in 2012.

She has been presenting her works globally since 1995, traveling to Italy, Spain, Australia, Canada, Denmark, Taiwan, France and the United States of America.

Known for illustrating herself in her paintings, she communicates spiritual, emotional, and psychological concepts through her paintings, always questioning the assumptions that she is making and exploring her inner world via symbolism.

Cristina has never been content exploring small ideas, taking the meaning of life as one of the overarching themes in her career. She reflects often on her own life, throwing a spotlight on her own beliefs in order to enrich her work for the benefit of her audience.

Operating on the idea that self-knowledge can come only out of self-exploration, she is not afraid to get into the gritty side of the individual, bringing into the conversation the idea of multiple lives.

Right: Old, 2014, acrylic on canvas, 100 x 75cm

Talking to God, 2014, acrylic on canvas, 86 x 100cm

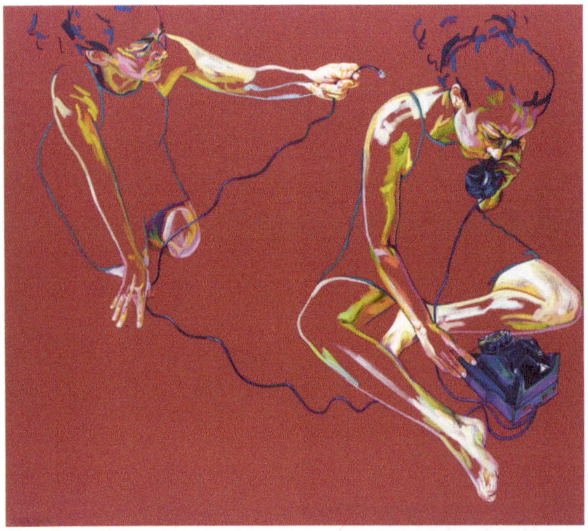

Immune, 2016, acrylic on canvas, 89 x 61cm

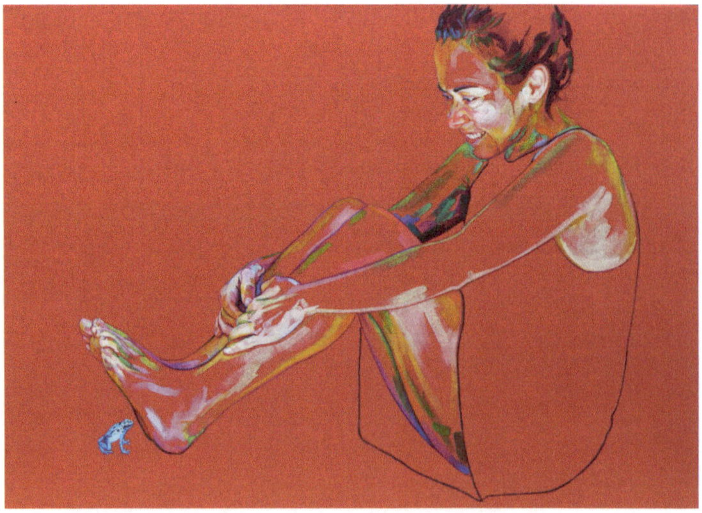

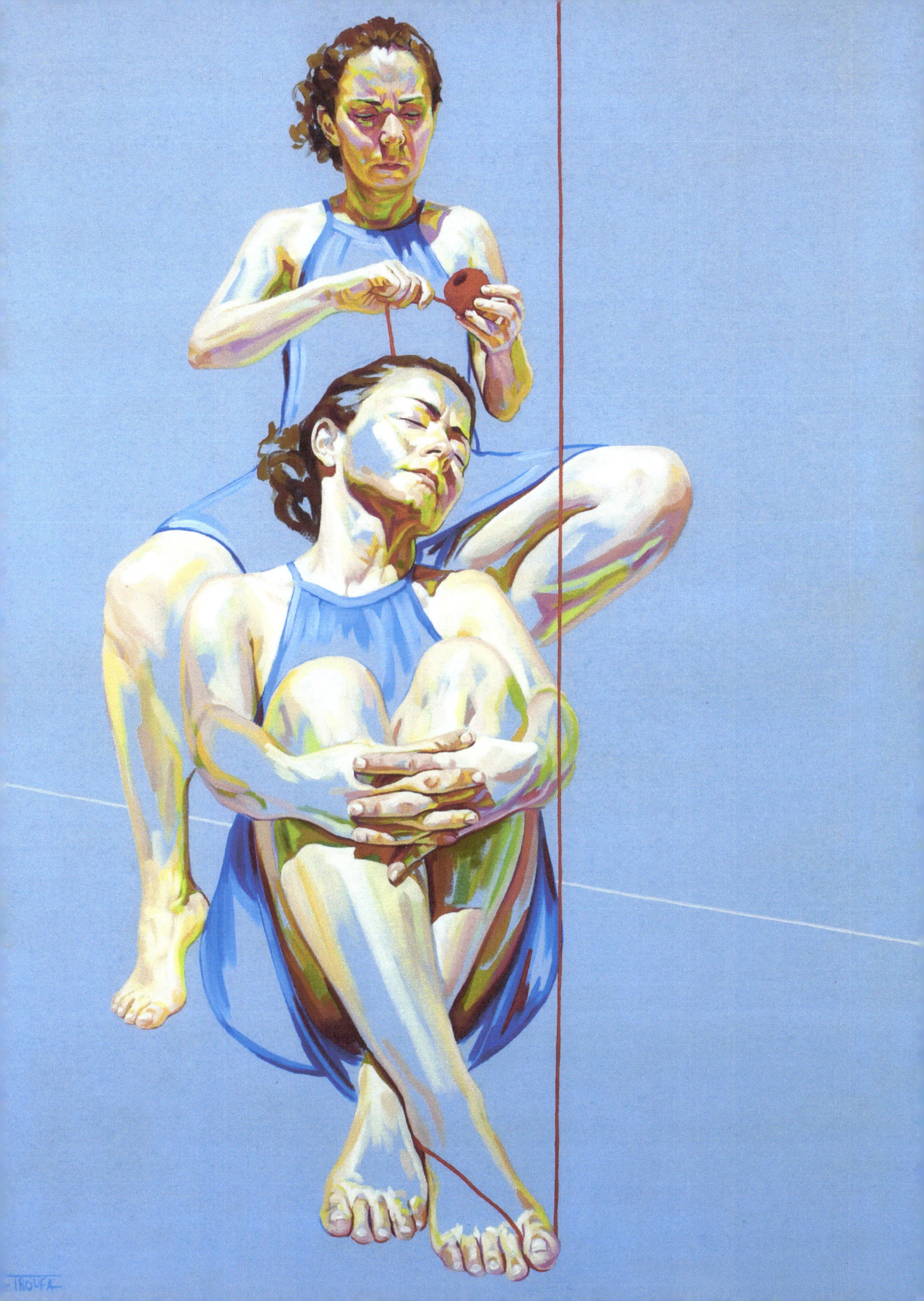
TROUFA

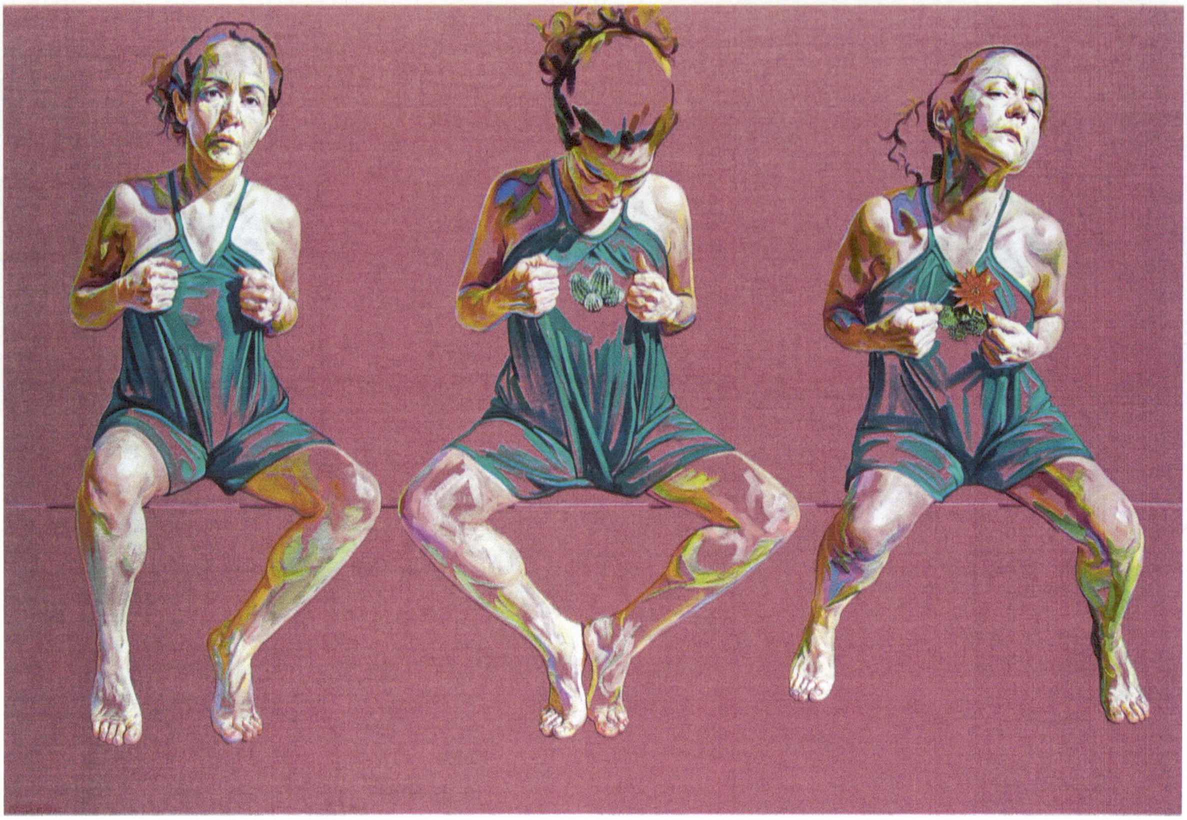

Armor, 2015, acrylic on canvas, 150 x 100cm

Rede ou Teia, 2015, acrylic on canvas, 150 x 100cm

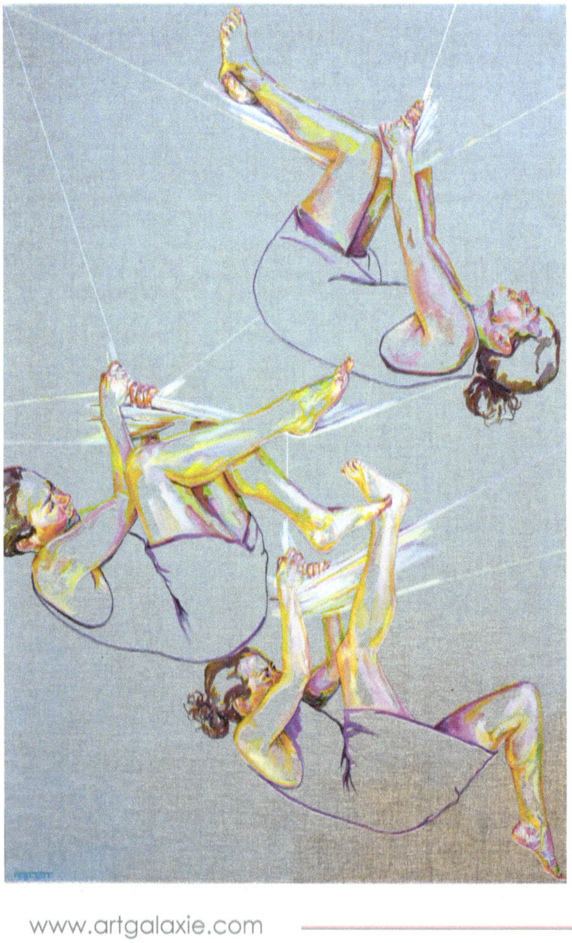

Troféu, 2014, acrylic on canvas, 150 X 100cm

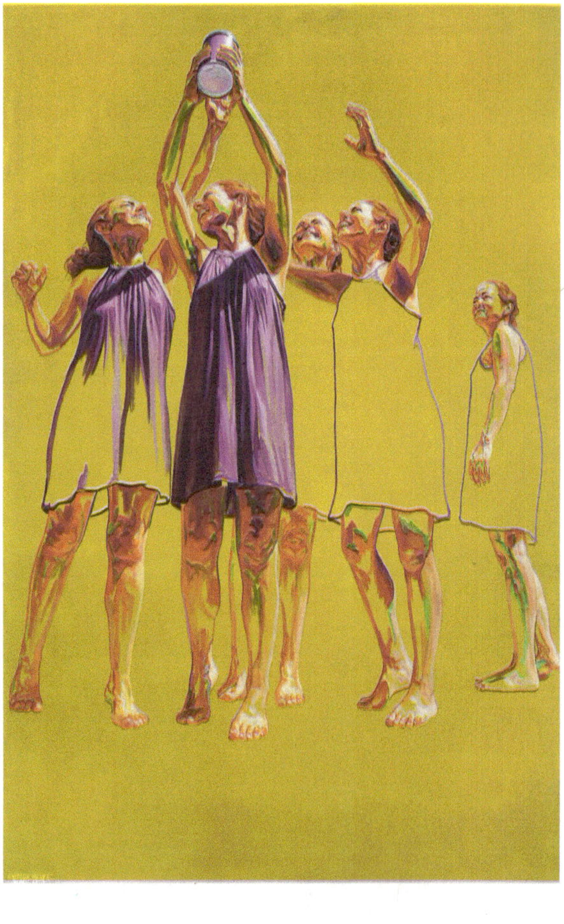

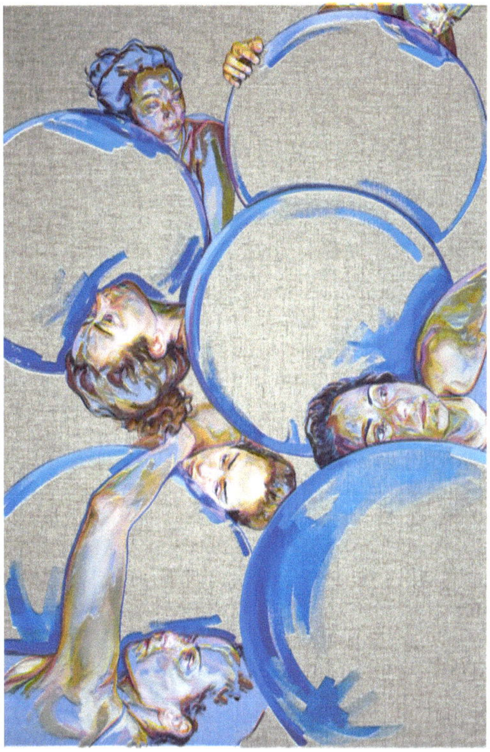

Melancholia, 2014, acrylic on canvas, 150 x 100cm

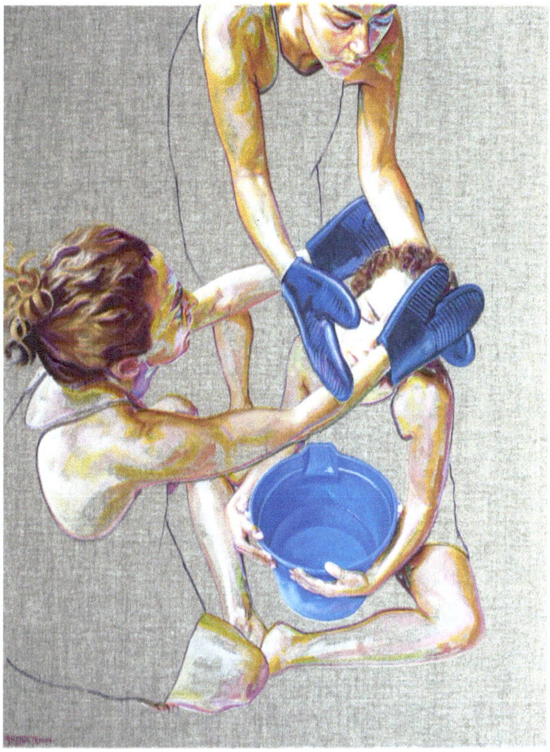

Fever, 2015, acrylic on canvas, 100 x 80cm

Recipiente, 2013, acrylic on canvas, 86 x 100cm

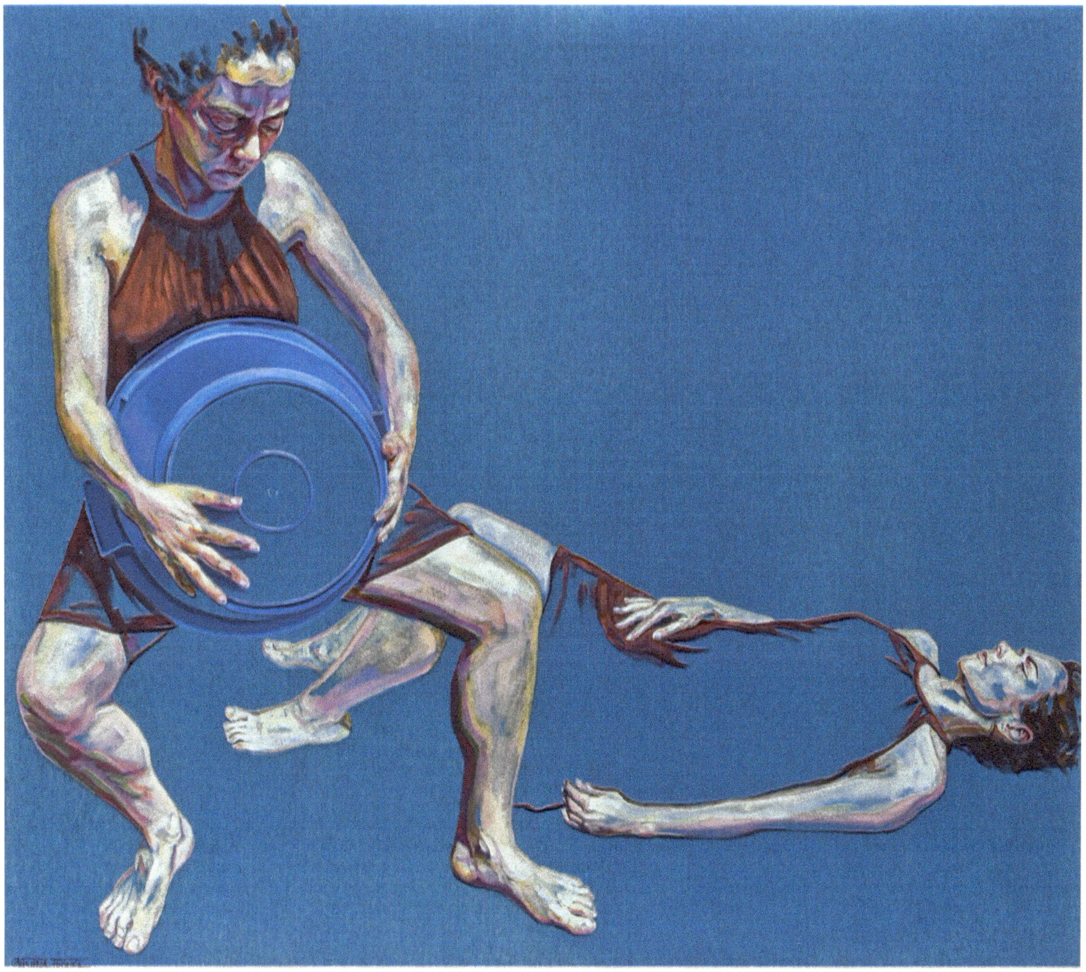

DANILO MARTINIS

PAINTING - ITALY

www.danilomartinis.com

Danilo Martinis is an Italian artist who was born in Milan. Trained formally in Industrial Design and Interior Decorating at the Art Institute of Milan, he got his start in the art world by working for Martinis Design, a family business known for producing high-quality pieces of furniture.

During his time in that role, his work was displayed at furniture fairs in Italy, the United Arab Emirates, Spain, Russia, and Canada, among other places. In the 90s, when he shifted over to painting, he worked first with materials such as stone and enamel, later combining what he had learned with what he knew of design.

Today, Danilo is recognized for the quality and style of his works. He draws influence from Vasarely as well as the Pop movement, incorporating distinctive shapes and playing with the concept of opera in his paintings. Although his work may at a glance seem simple, given the uniformity of its colour, it is actually quite nuanced. He paints in a way that is mathematically precise, building complexity and three-dimensional compositions into visual narratives.

Danilo is fiercely analytical, and yet at the same time, he never fails to put his creativity on display for the world to see. Born to give structure to the abstract, he is always expressing something beautiful in his work, something that can be understood readily and yet felt only with time and patience.

Il Cubo, oil on canvas, 50 x 70cm

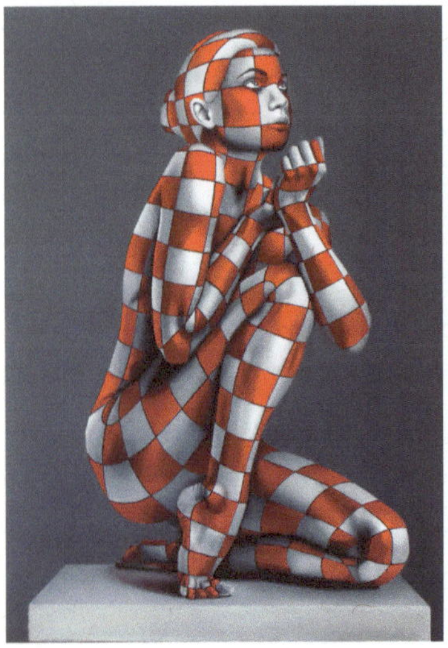

Eros e Pathos, oil on canvas, 80 x 80cm

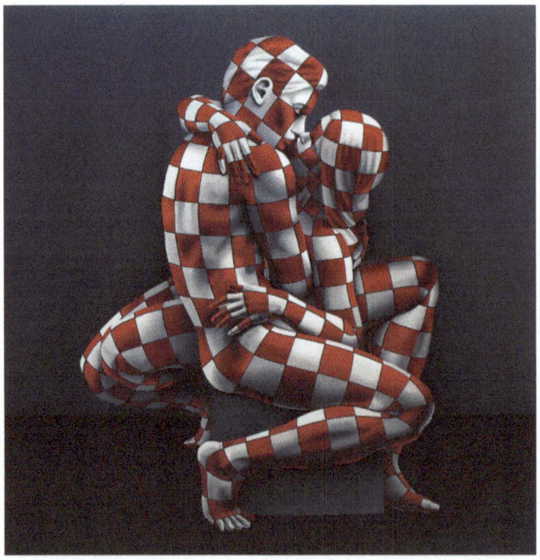

Eros e Pathos,oil on canvas, 100 x 80cm

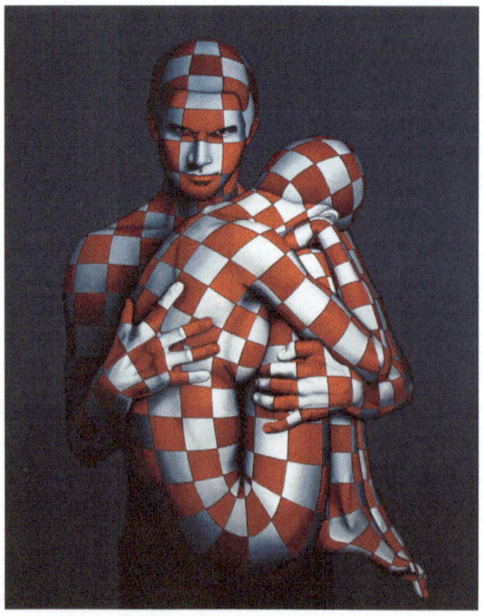

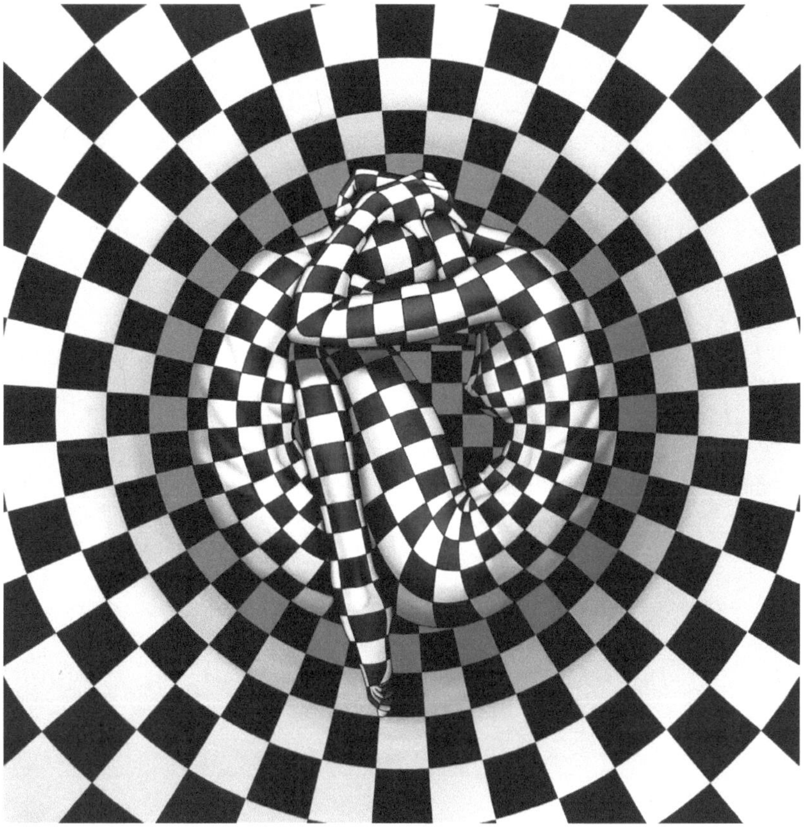

Abbraccio, oil on canvas, 80 x 80cm

L'Unione Divide, oil on canvas, 80 x 100cm

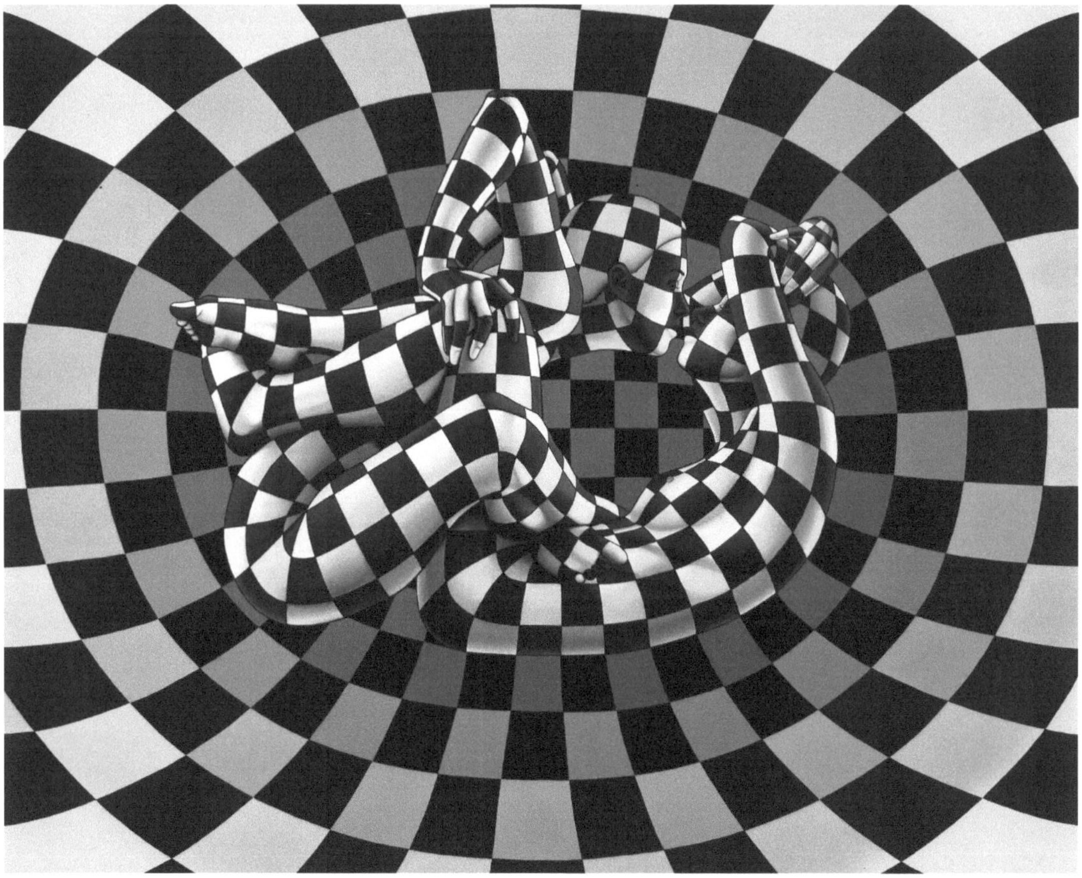

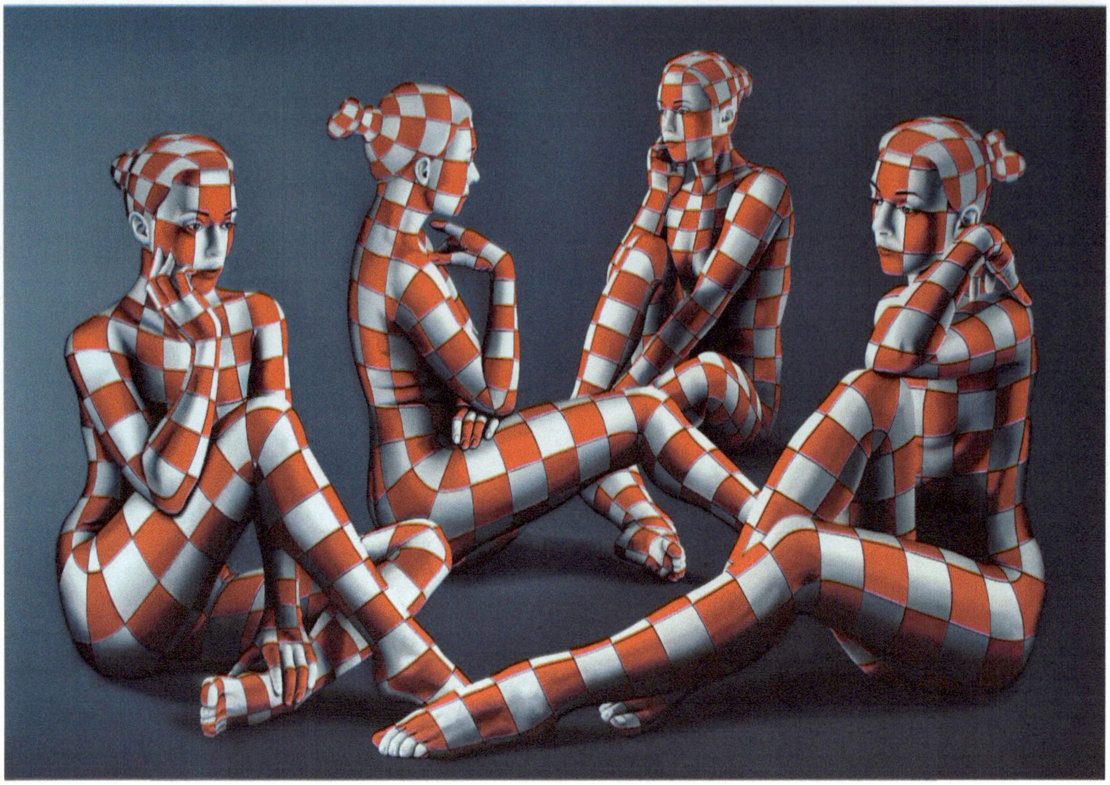

L'Attesa, oil on canvas, 100 x 150cm

Eros e Pathos, oil on canvas, 80 x 100cm

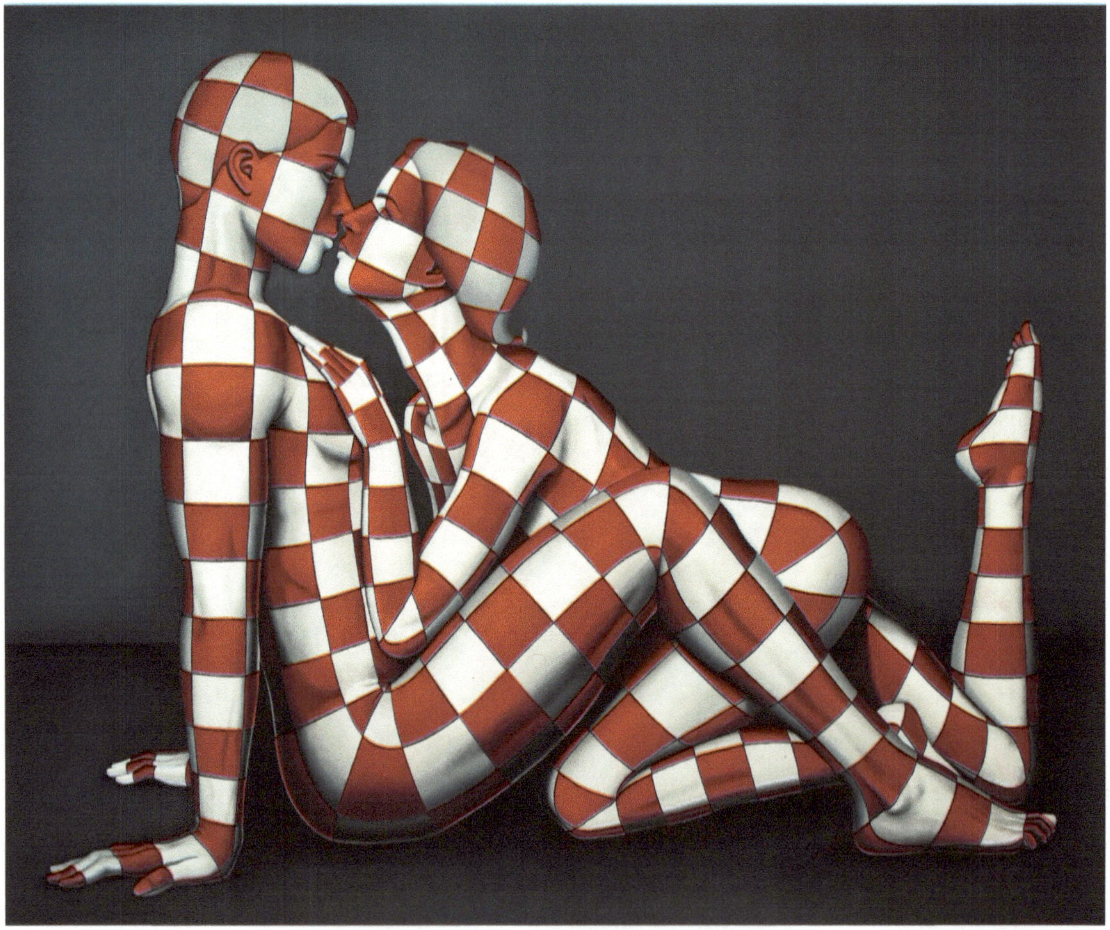

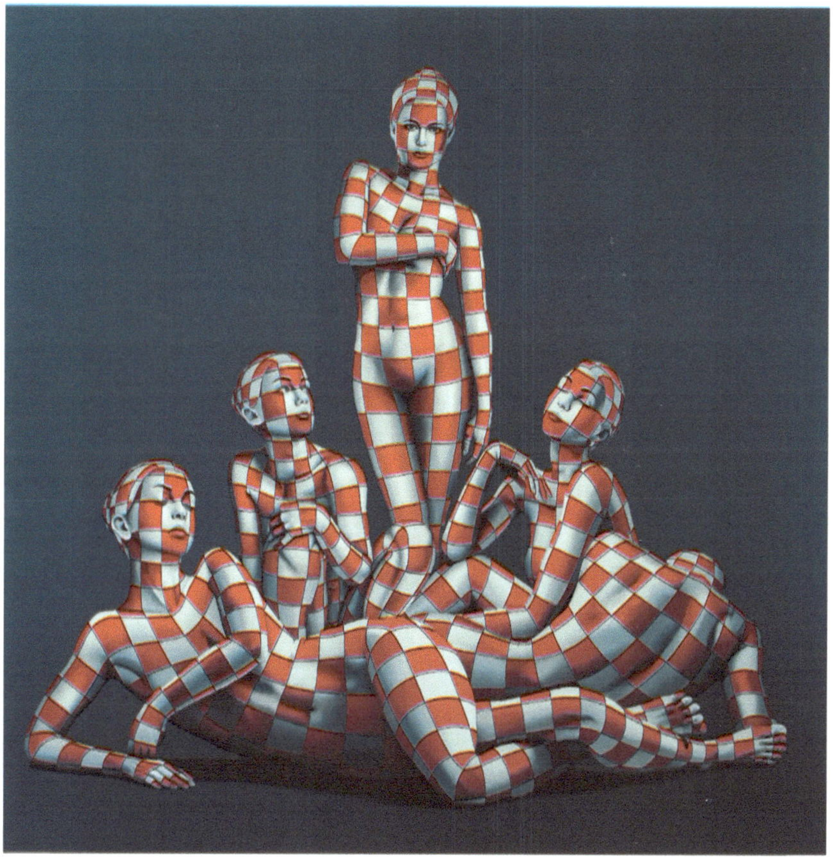

Charme, oil on canvas, 150 x 150cm

Il Guardiano, oil on canvas, 150 x 150cm

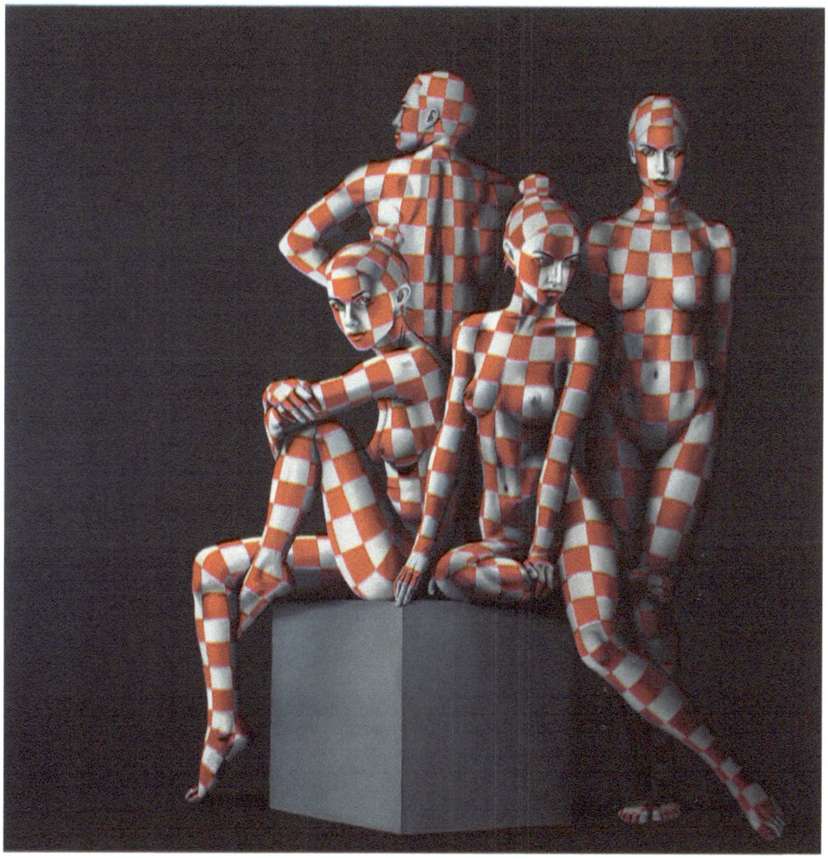

GEORGY KURASOV

PAINTING - RUSSIA

www.kurasov.com

Georgy Kurasov is an artist who is always looking into the future without losing sight of the past to which we are all beholden. He draws influence from such diverse works as Byzantine mosaics, Early Renaissance paintings, Klimt, and Lempicka, speaking through his paintings in a language that is pictorial and precise.

In addition, he is often compared to Constructivists and Cubists, the main difference between him and them being the large number of contrasting features that he pulls into his work. Although his work can be challenging to audiences, he is careful never to complicate any of his compositions unnecessarily. Every part that he includes is included for a specific, immutable reason.

Spectacularly original, Georgy has spent a lifetime working to understand the inner structures of paintings in order to communicate through his work more effectively. The complex geometrical formations in his work can be unsettling, from plastics forms to crossing light rays and beyond, yet throughout his paintings there is the undeniable sense that the subject is natural, that the ideas he is presenting have arisen without force, that he is simply recording some idea, perhaps troubling, in all its splendour.

Georgy works to the point of exhaustion, always finding new ways to demand more of himself for the benefit of his art and those who view it. He is something of a fanatic when it comes to mastering his own style.

Tango, 2014, oil on canvas, gold leaf, 104 x 79cm

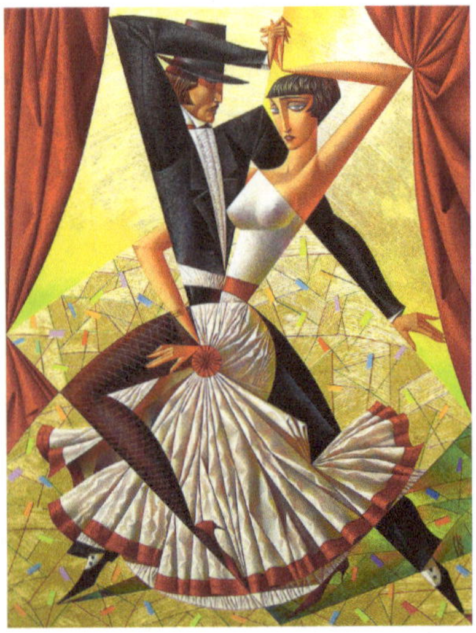

Shadows, 2006, oil on canvas, 152 x 117cm

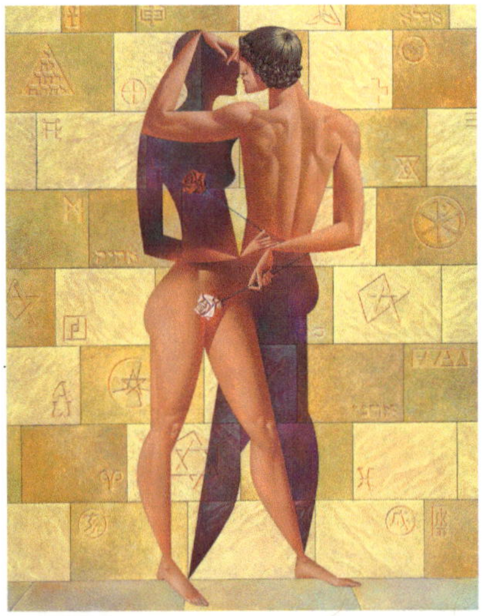

213, 2012, oil on canvas, gold leaf, 105 x 85cm

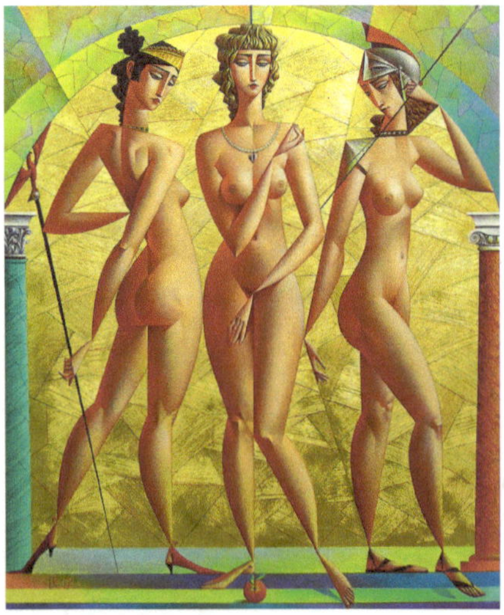

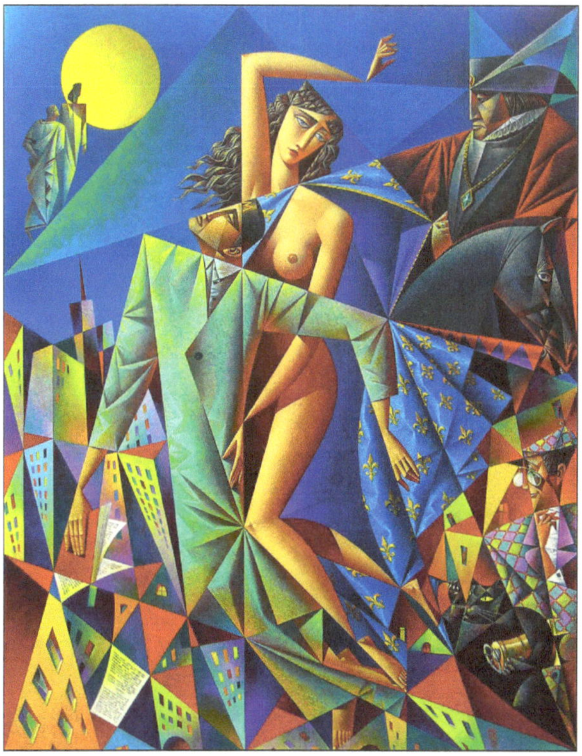
Master and Margarita, 2012, oil on canvas,120 x 94cm

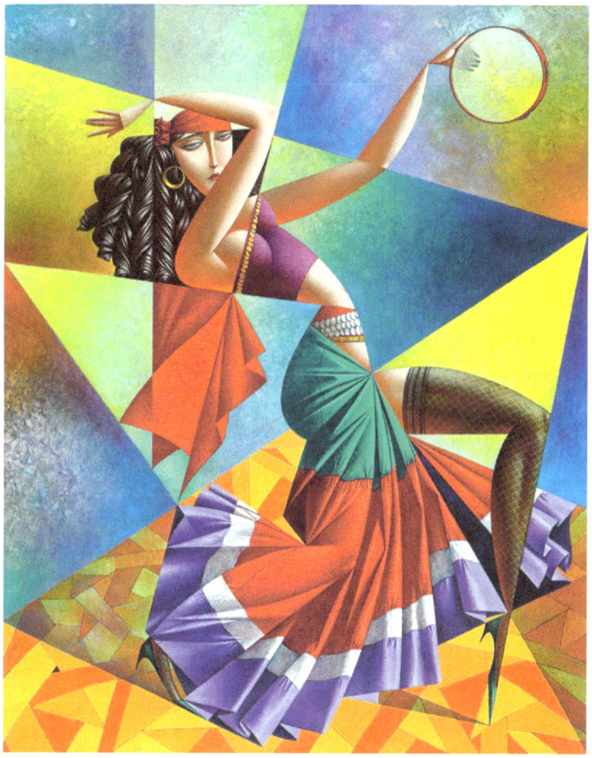
The Gypsy Dancer, 2005, oil on canvas, 102 x 81cm

The Battle of Amazon and Centaurs, 2013, oil on canvas, 178 x 228cm

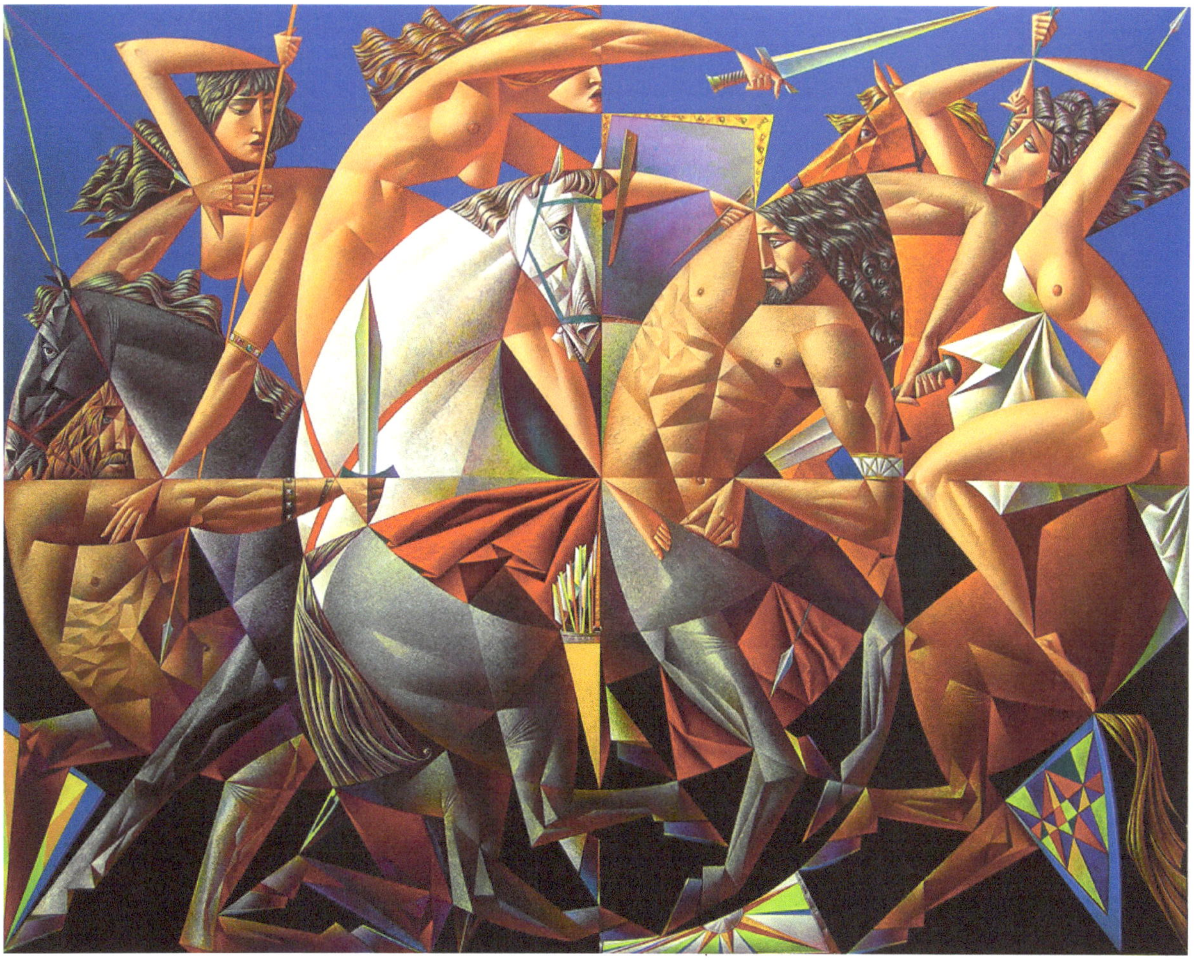

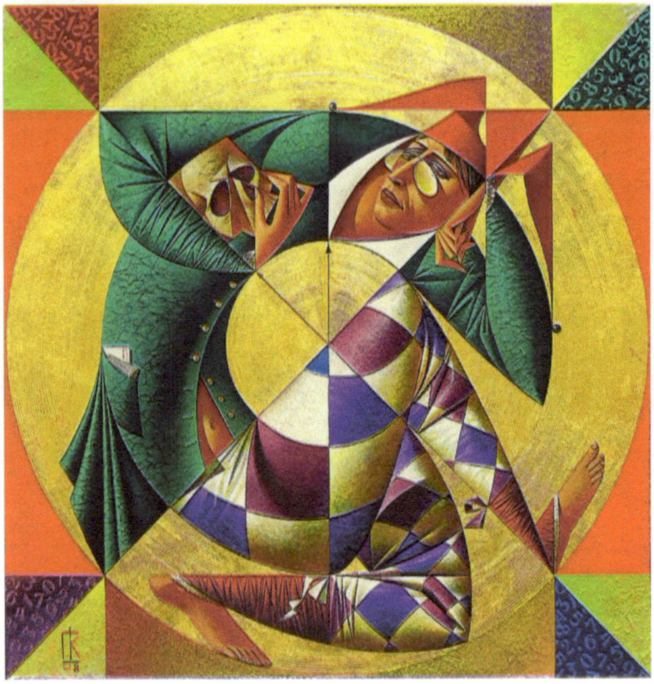

Yorick, 2008, oil on canvas, gold leaf, 62 x 62cm

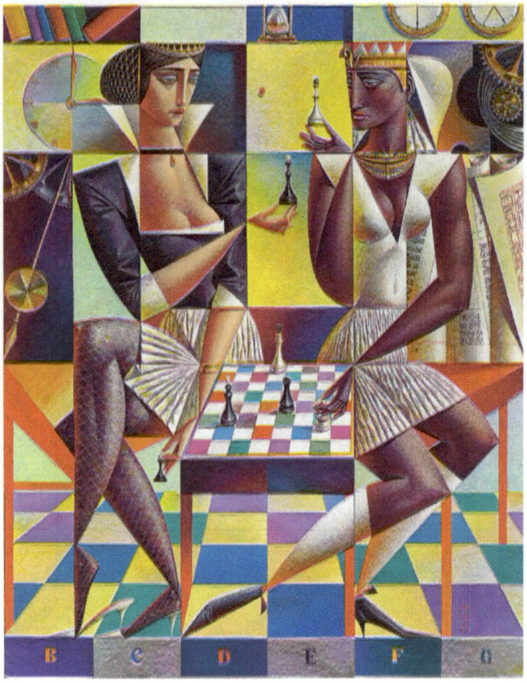

Chess, 2015, oil on canvas, 100 x 80cm

Sunny Dreams, 2015, oil on canvas, 100 x 80cm

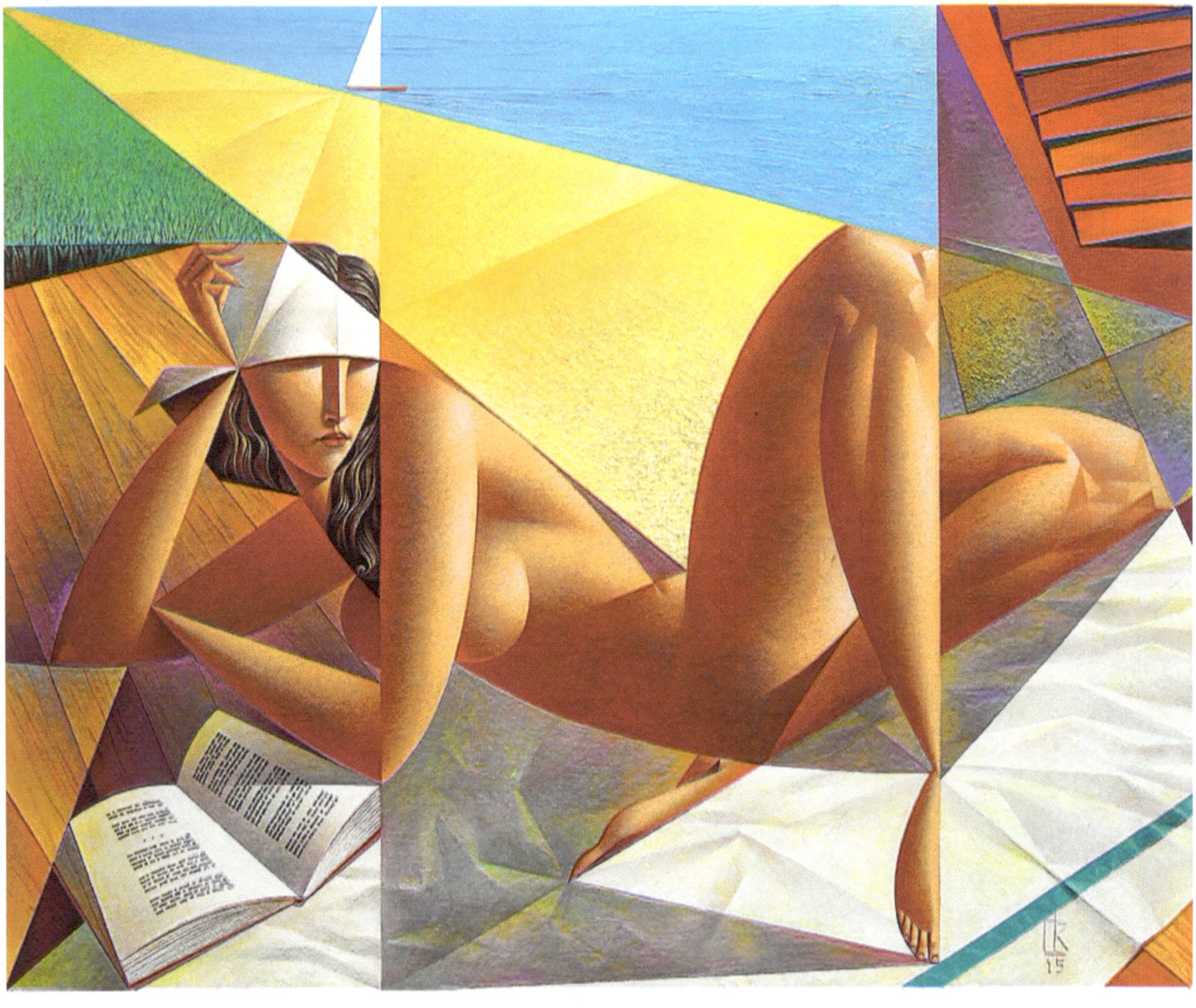

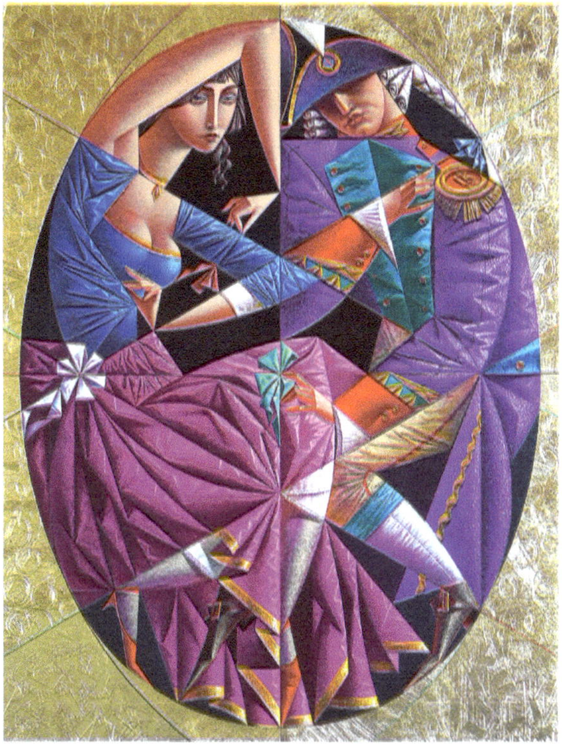
Analytic research of building Baroque's composition, 2014, oil on canvas, gold leaf, 89 x 69cm

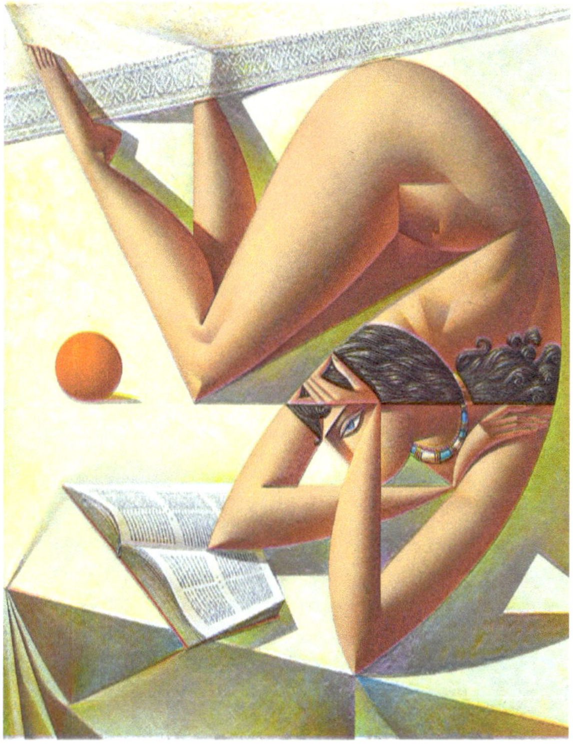
194, 2009, oil on canvas, 74 x 64cm

The Rape of Europe, 2015, oil on canvas, 100 x 80cm
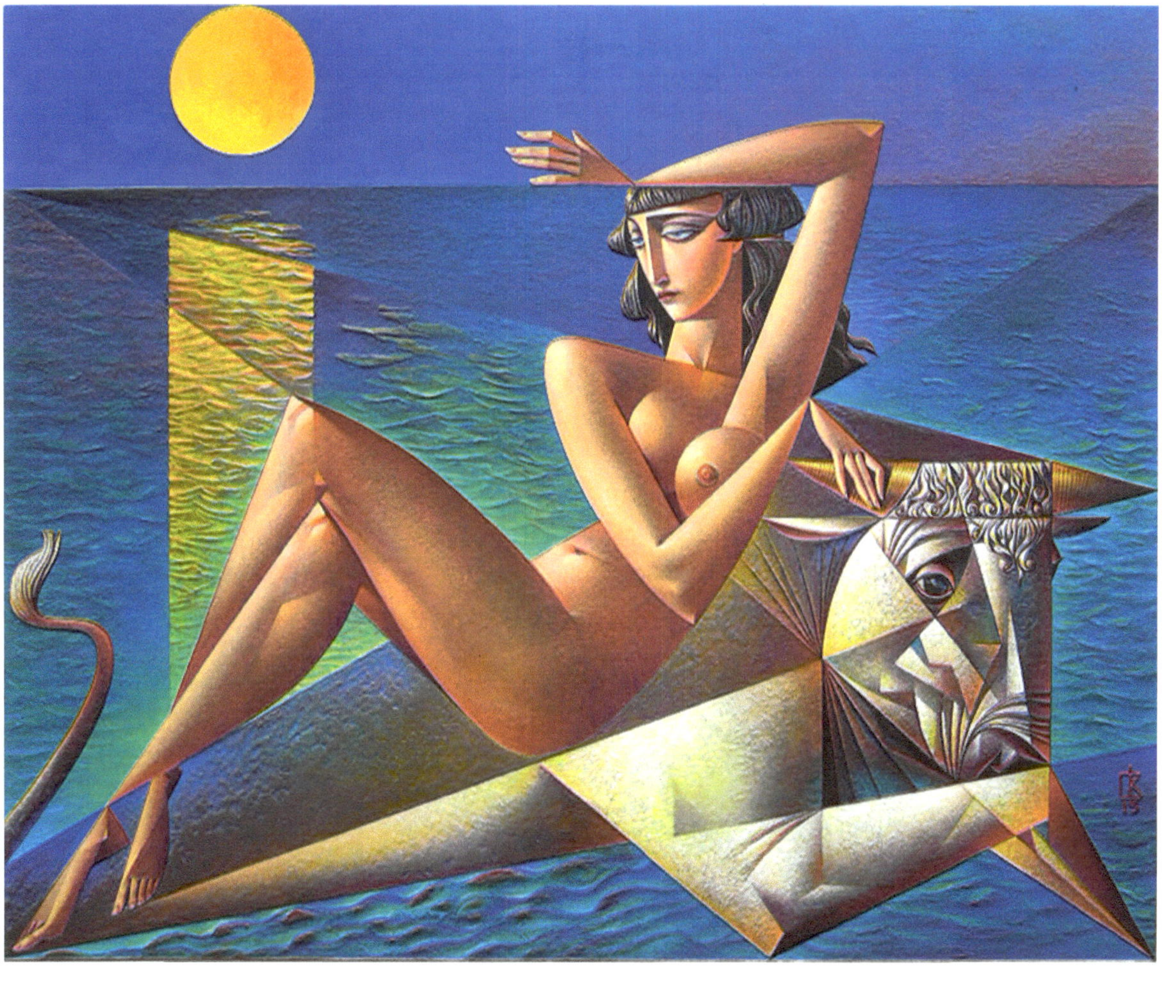

GISELA BANZER

PAINTING - ARGENTINA

www.giselabanzer.wordpress.com

Gisela Banzer is an Argentinian artist. After studying Visual and Communication Design, she decided to shift into Fine Arts. An autodidact, she trained herself in drawing and painting, coming to master these techniques over a period of several years. From a young age, she had been drawn to visual media, attracted to the clarity that it offered.

As an artist, she focuses a large amount of her energy on crafting atmospheres and character personalities, trying to illustrate what reality may look like in an unreal world. She is a dreamer at heart, sure to find the fantastic parts of everyday life. Perceptive perhaps to a fault, she picks up on the details that other people miss and then incorporates what she sees into her work.

Splendidly imaginative, Gisela sees a world in which animals are heroes. She is a storyteller, and the stories that she tells flow in a way not often seen in visual art. Her work is influenced deeply by Edwardian aesthetics and photographs from the early part of the 20th century, so any time you see something reminiscent of an antique photo in her works, there is a huge level of intentionality present. She seeks to evoke the past that the influence holds over the present by placing its shadow within our line of sight.

Gisela is a one-of-a-kind artist whose work manages to call back to other works while still standing on its own two feet.

Right: Estrella, 2015, acrylic on canvas, 100 x 120cm

Joven Espíritu Alóctono 2, 2016, acrylic on canvas, 140 x100cm

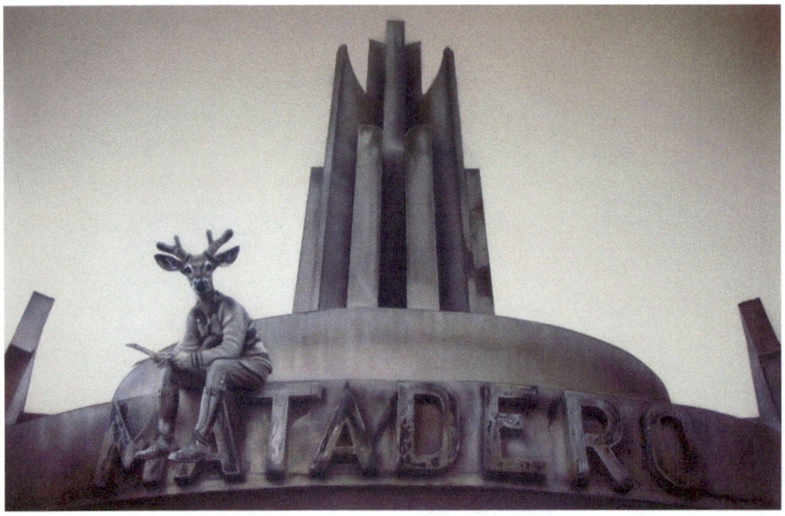

Espíritu Autóctono, 2015, acrylic on canvas, 80 x100cm

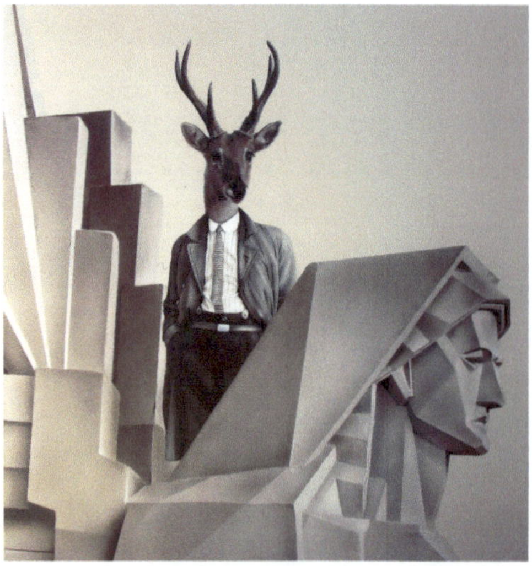

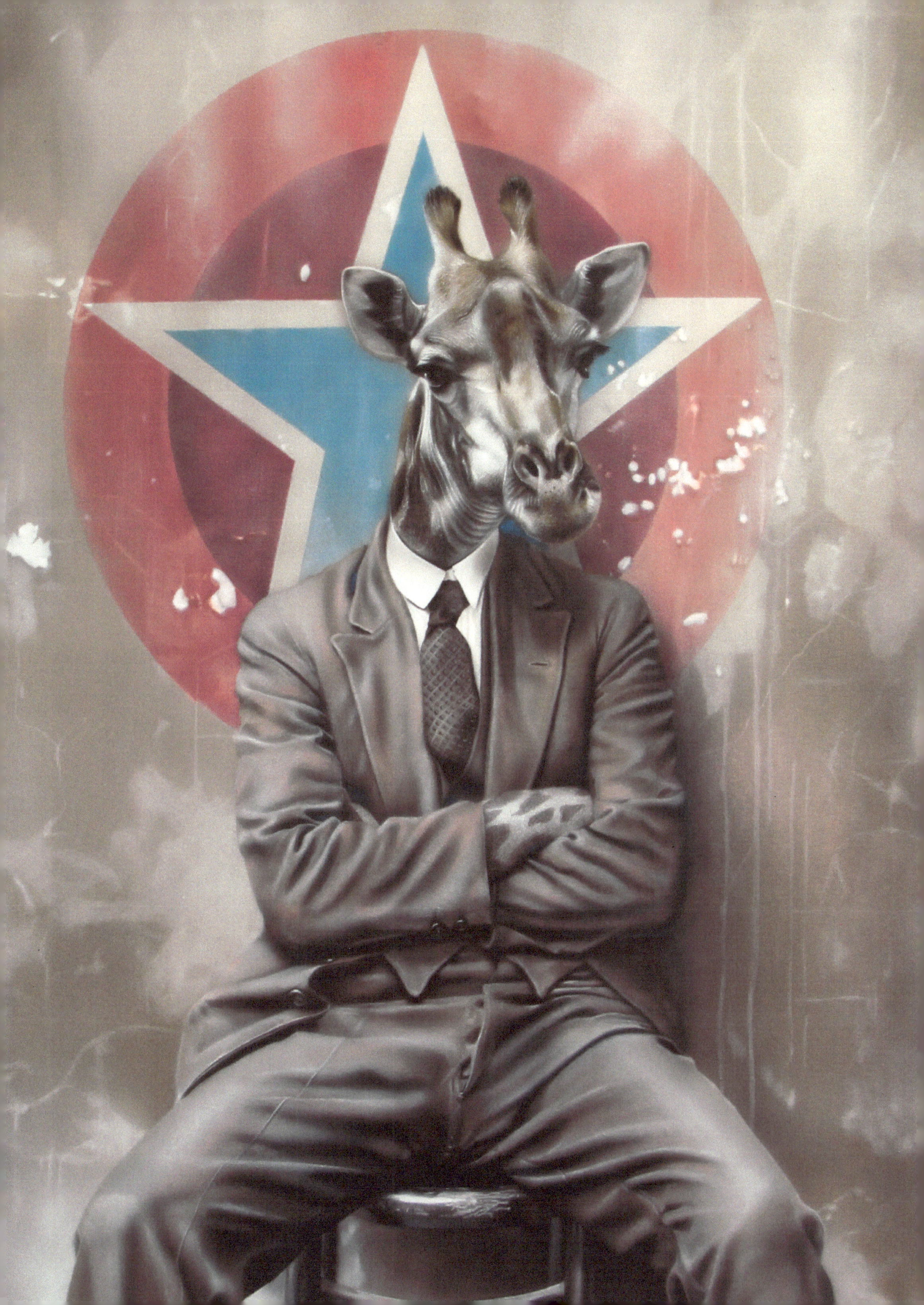

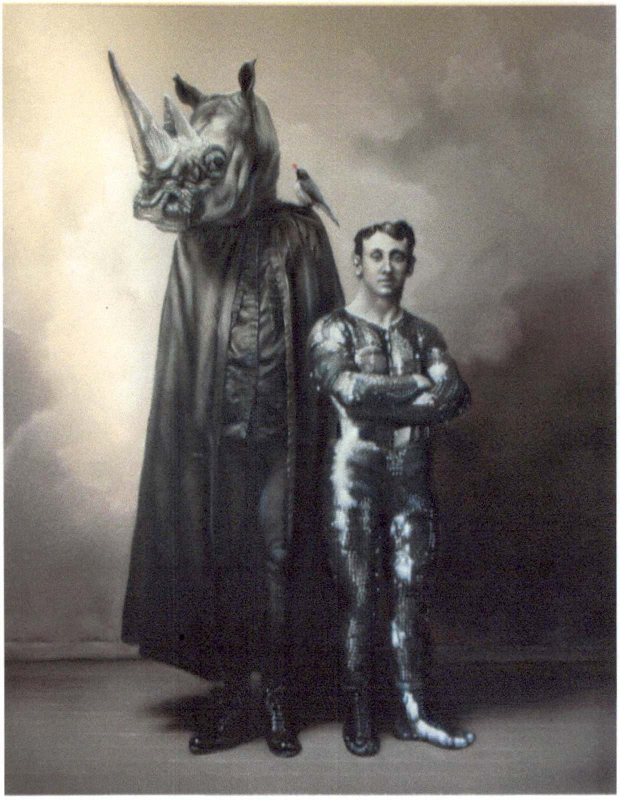

El Ilusionista y el Hombre Pez, 2015, acrylic on canvas, 100 x 120cm

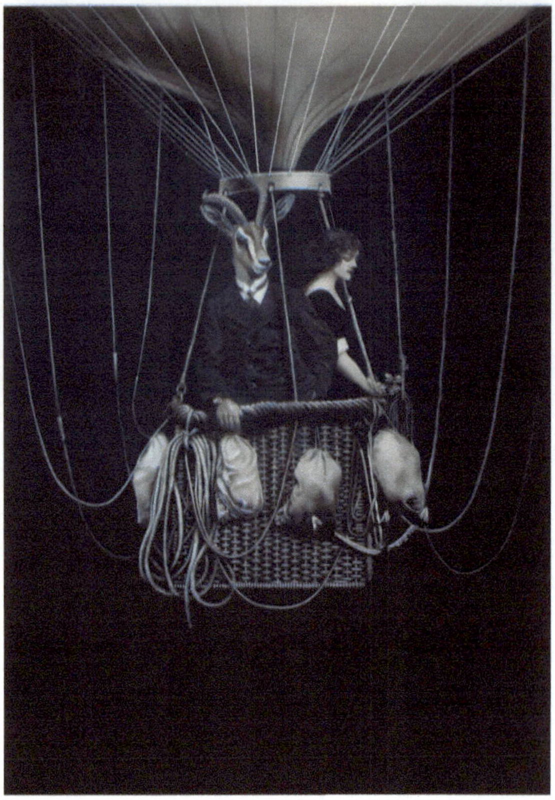

El Paseador Nocturno, 2015, acrylic on canvas, 70 x 100cm

El Gremio, 2015, acrylic on canvas, 200 x 150cm

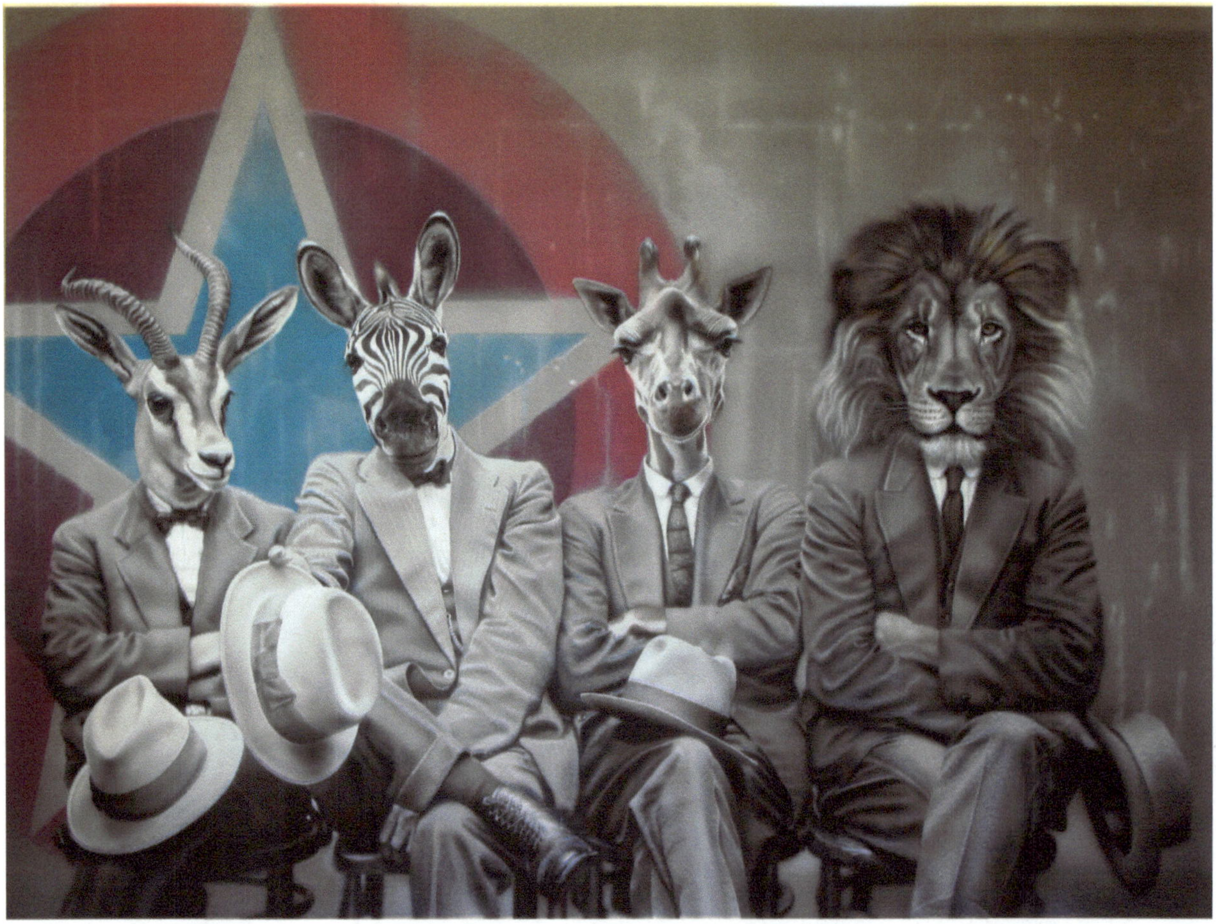

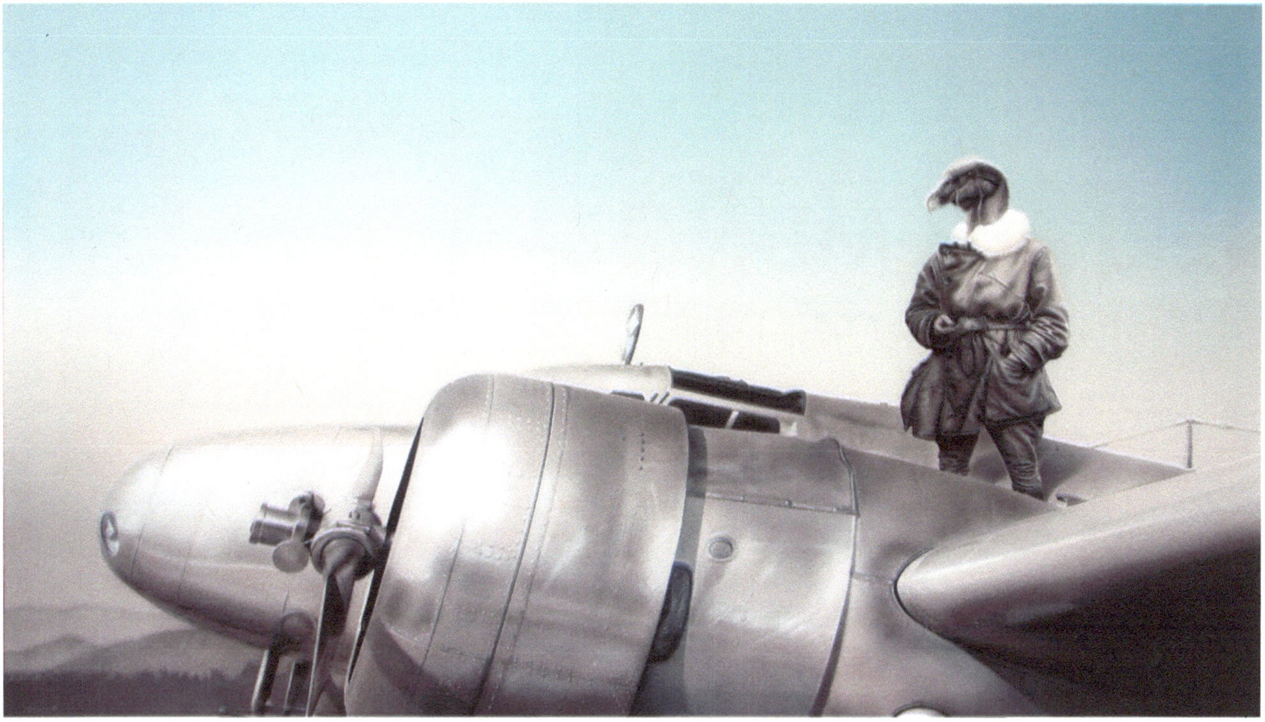

Espíritu Andino, 2016, acrylic on canvas, 150 x 100cm

El Arca, 2015, acylic on canvas, 200 x 100cm

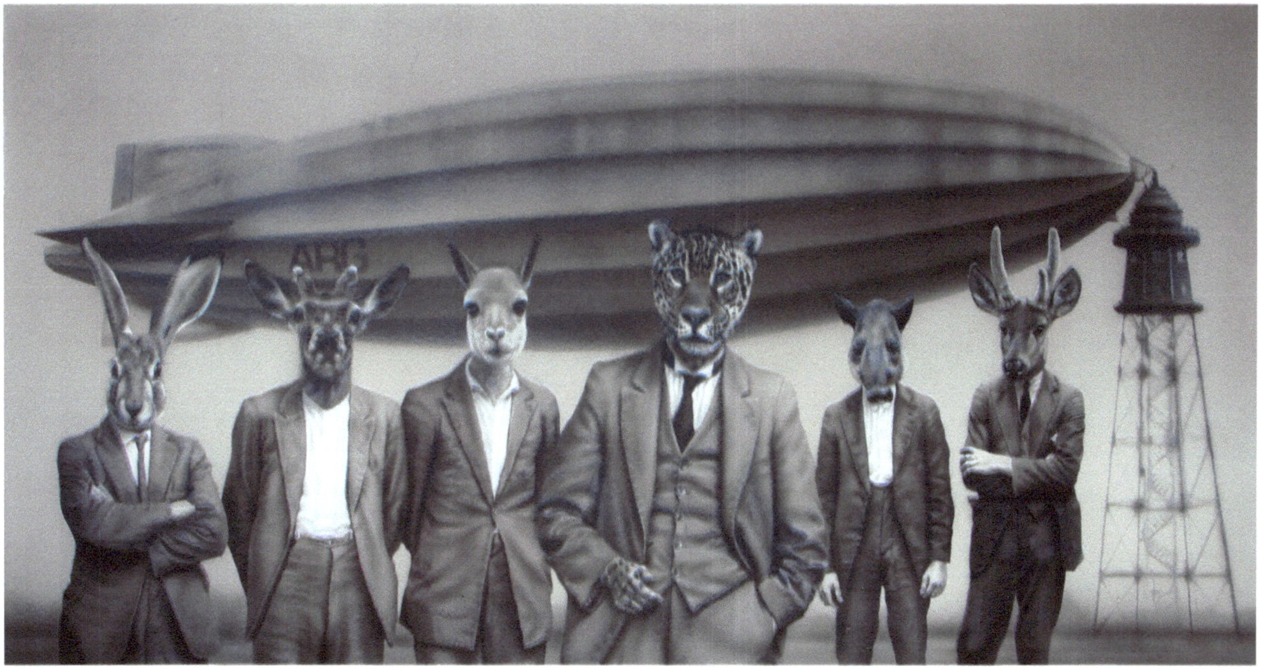

HERNAN MUÑOZ

PAINTING - ARGENTINA

www.artgalaxie.com

Hernan Muñoz is an Argentinian artist who was something of a child prodigy in drawing. As a child, he was placed in an art school. However, he did not take his studies seriously at that time, blowing off his schoolwork and failing to impress any of his professors. After high school, he struggled to make ends meet, taking any job that he could find, even jobs that had nothing to do with art. A couple years after that, when he was twenty, he became immersed in the work of William-Adolphe Bourguereau and began spending much of his time at the Museum of Fine Arts. His passion for art became greater than it ever had been before.

Hernan made use of what he had, painting with pigments and linseed oil. He studied the paintings of the old masters vigorously, and at age thirty-three today, he works in his own studio in Buenos Airos. Known for the slick way in which he melds reality and dreams, he is intent on pouring his heart, soul, and mind into all of his output.

He works within the genre of Fantastic Realism, although his paintings are completely of himself, unique in the way that he himself is. Once a prodigy, he himself is now a master. He has passed on from the merely impressive to the wildly expressive and made a name for himself that stands apart from any talent with which he was born.

Right: Hamingja Curiosa ante la Disolución de las Palabras, oil on canvas, 170 x 120cm

Anima noi Fissando, oil on canvas, 90 x 100cm

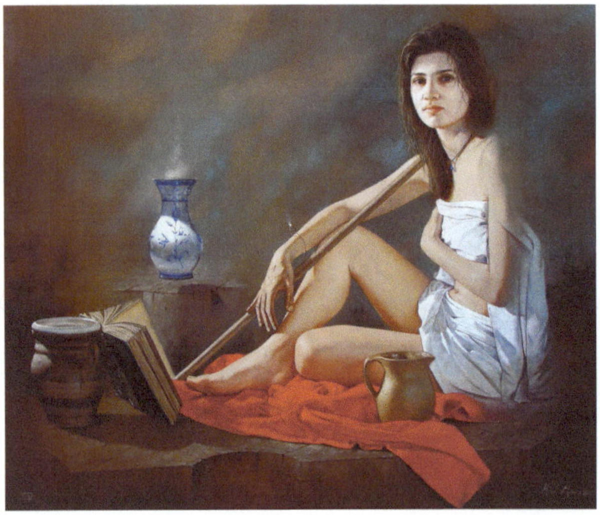

Sonata Cuántica, oil on canvas, 95 x 95cm

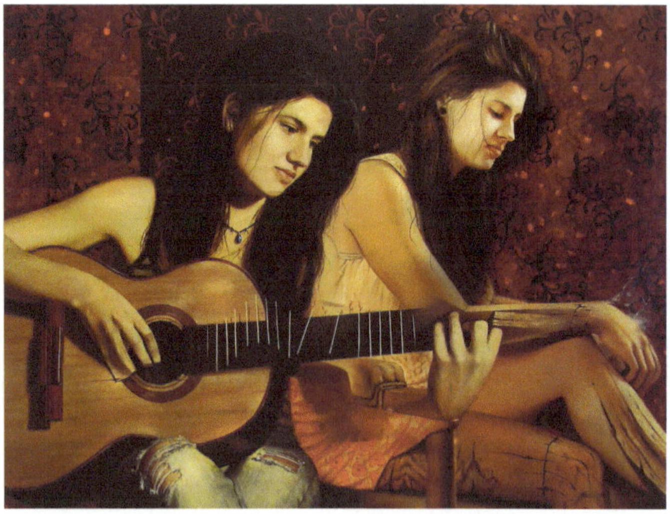

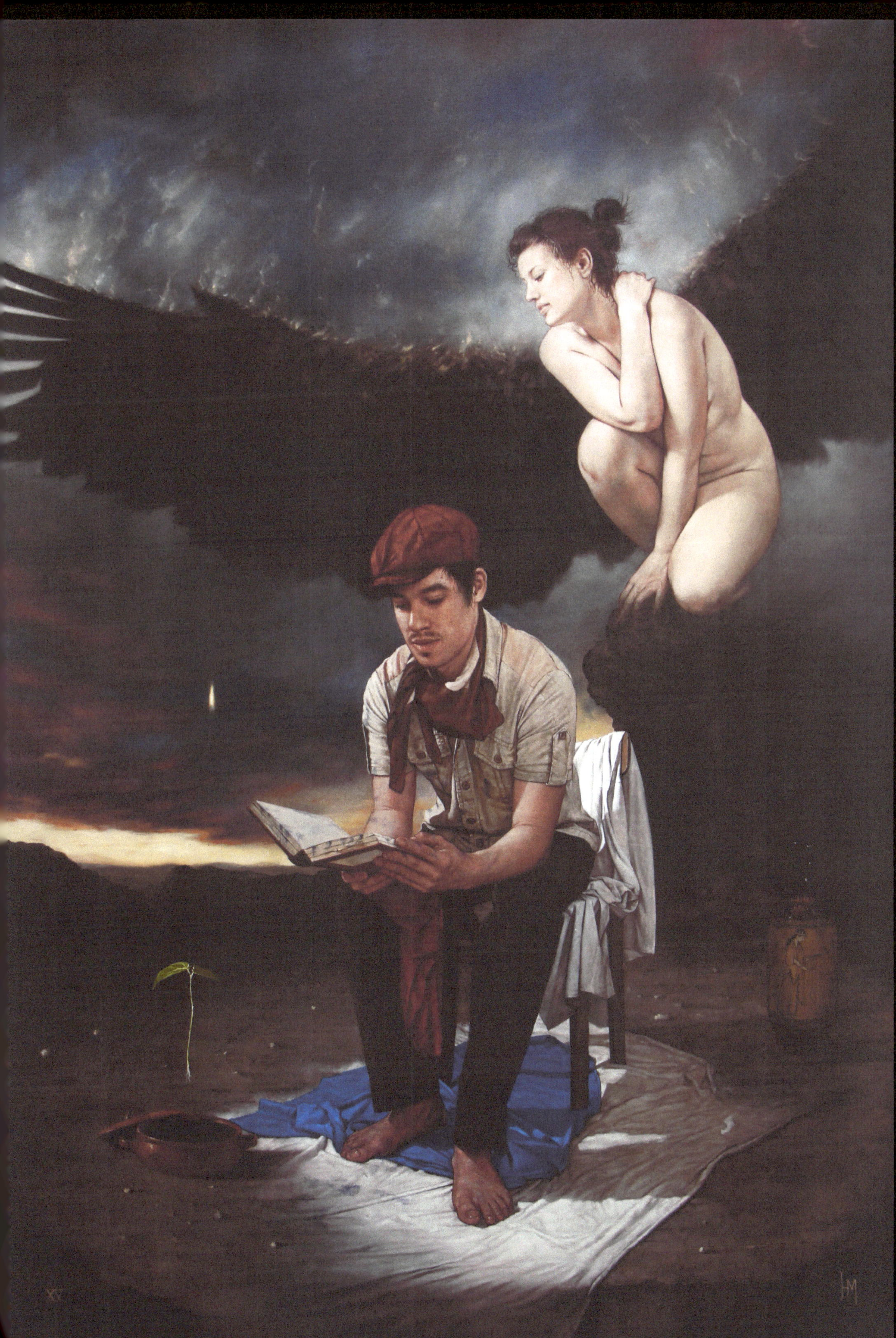

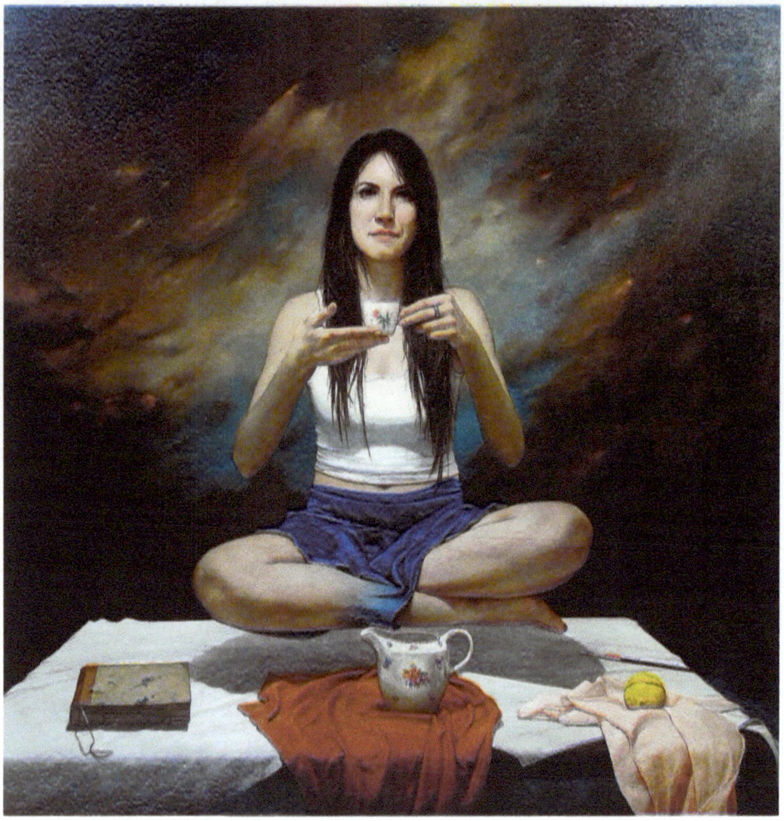

Afternoon Tea, oil on canvas,100 x 120cm

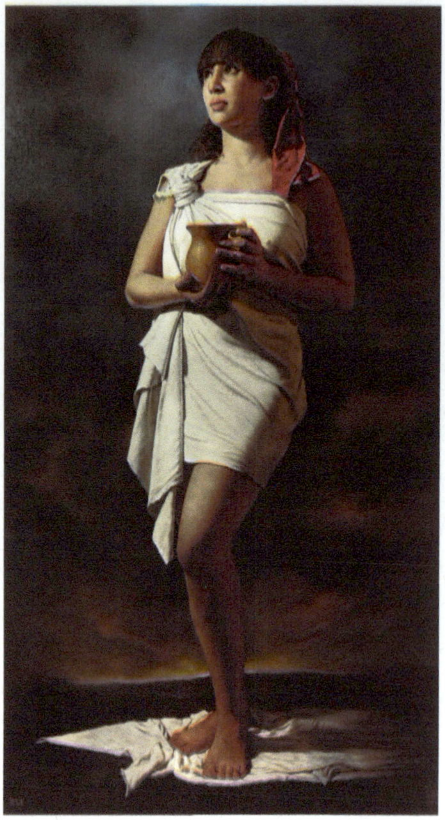

La Primer Gota, oil on canvas, 88 x 140cm

Surrealismo del Descanso, oil on canvas, 90 x 100cm

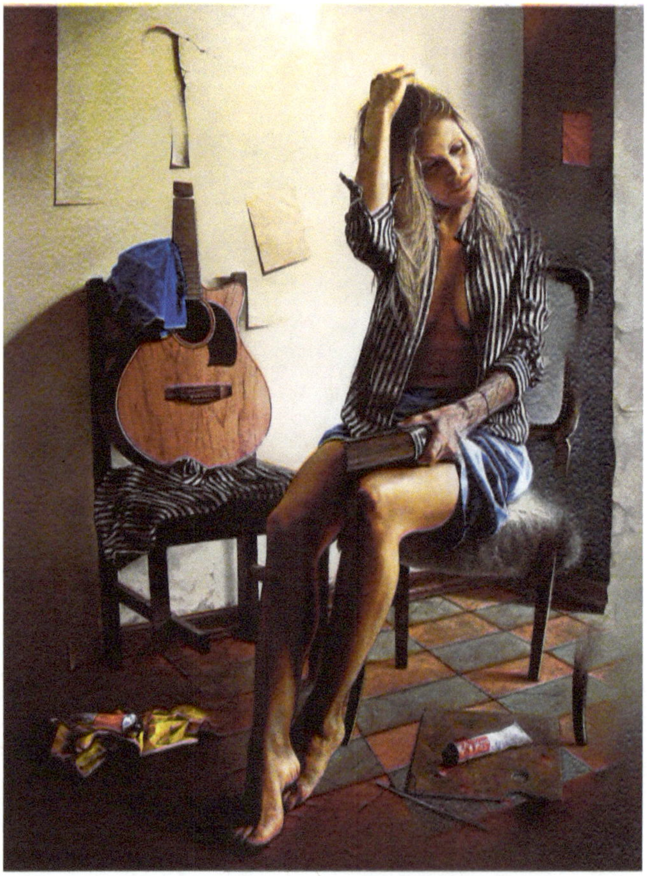

El Secreto del Renacimiento de Afrodita, oil on canvas, 160 x 120cm

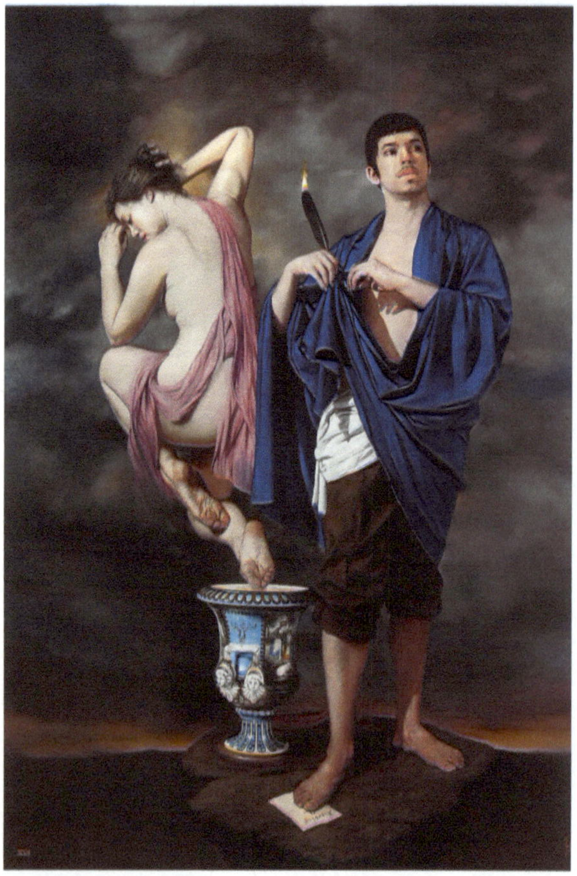

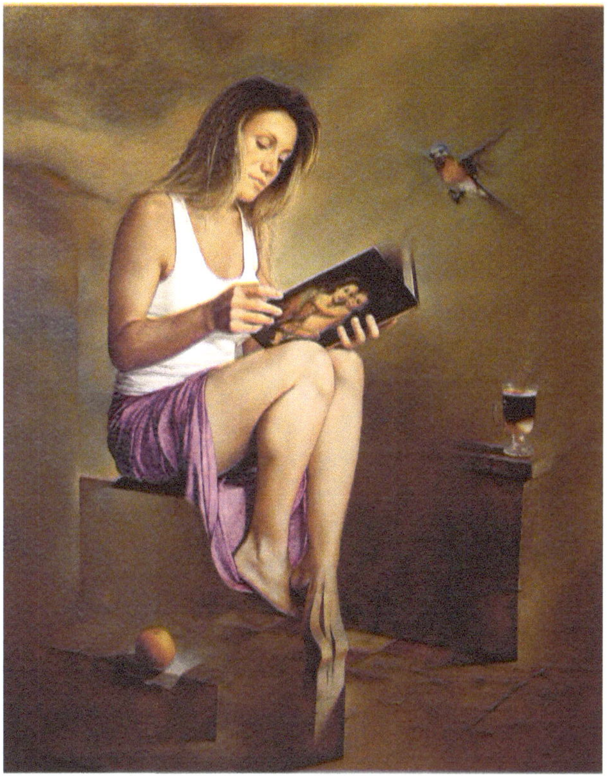

Dama Merendando con Murillo, oil on canvas, 90cm x 100cm

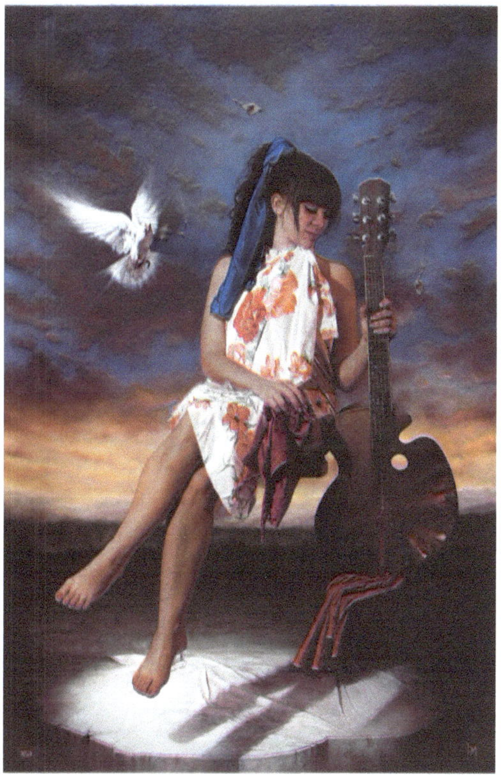

Inspiration, oil on canvas, 100 x 150cm

Metafora del Alma en Piedra, oil on canvas, 130 x 100cm

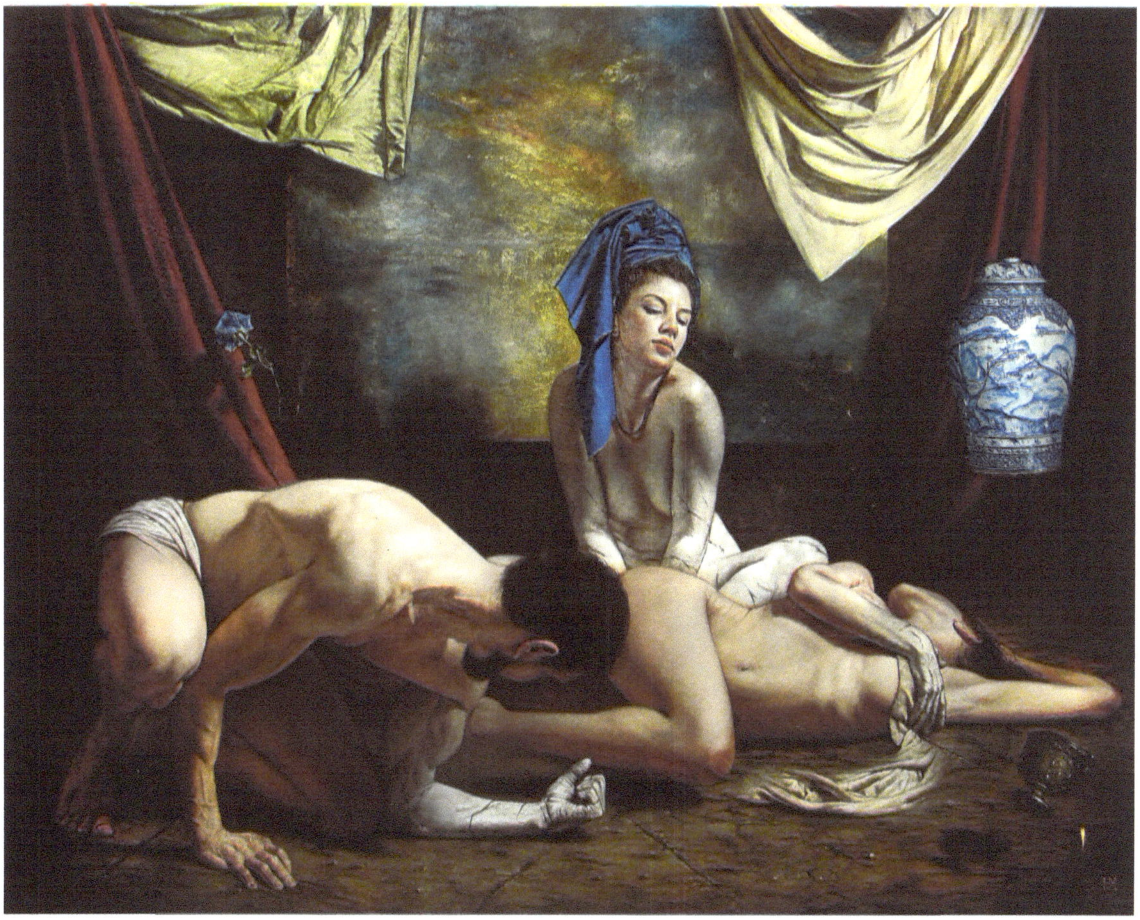

JUAN MEDINA

PAINTING - MEXICO

www.medinajuan.com

Juan Medina is a Mexican artist whose career has spanned more than 35 years. He got his start in painting with watercolours, and by the time he had shifted over to oils, he was using advanced techniques and incorporating complex themes and ideas into his work.

Seeking to portray a universe other than our own, a universe that is in a way a mirror of ours, he paints from a point-of-view that is nothing if not distinct. As he shows space dissolving and recalls memories of times past, he takes his audience on a journey through existence to which they would otherwise have no access. In this way, he is like a guide out of this world and into a world of his own making.

Juan is a structuralist at heart, composing out of his memories countless dimensions.

Most recently, he has shifted his attention even more to the idea of visual perception. By blurring the lines between hyperrealism and surrealism, he has positioned himself as a leader among contemporary Latin American painters.

When Juan sits down to paint, he sits down not only with his brushes and his oil paints but also with his vision of a world that could be. In an apple, he may see the entire universe, and in the sky, the inside of an apple.

It is in the cracks of what actually is that he sees what he wants to share with all of us.

Open Dimensions, oil on linen, 100 x 160cm

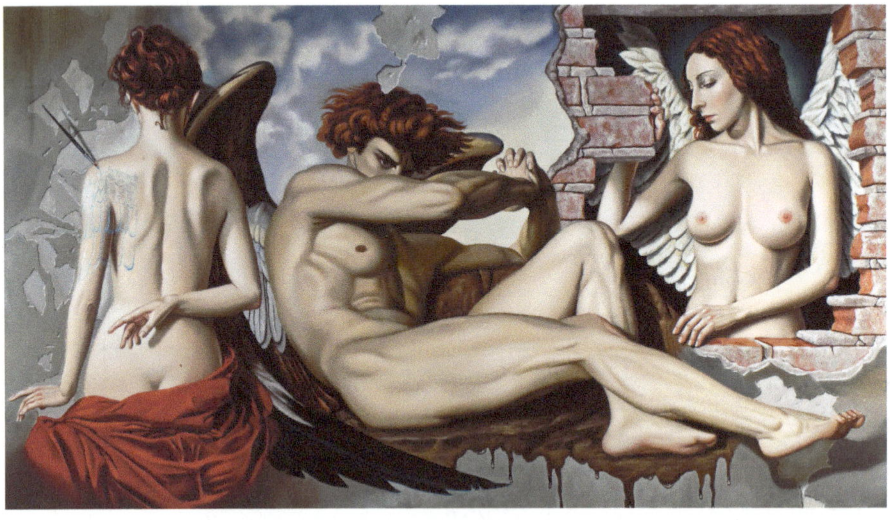

Miroir, oil on linen, 127 x 86cm

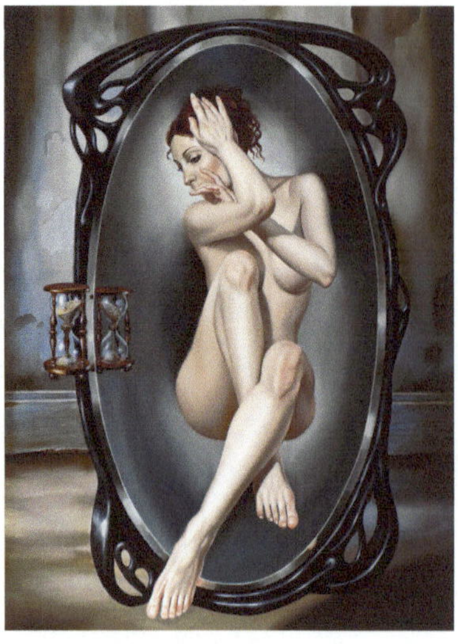

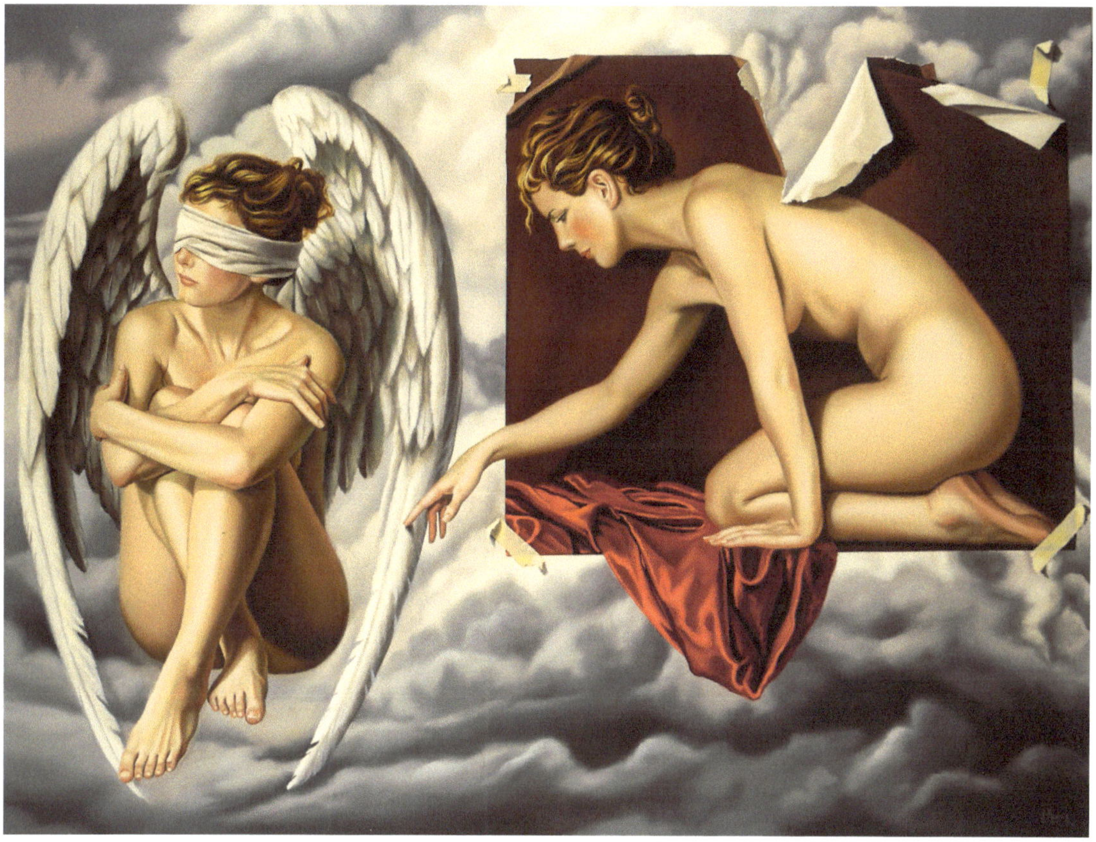

Enticing, oil on linen, 90 x 120cm

Haunting Duties, oil on linen, 90 x 120cm

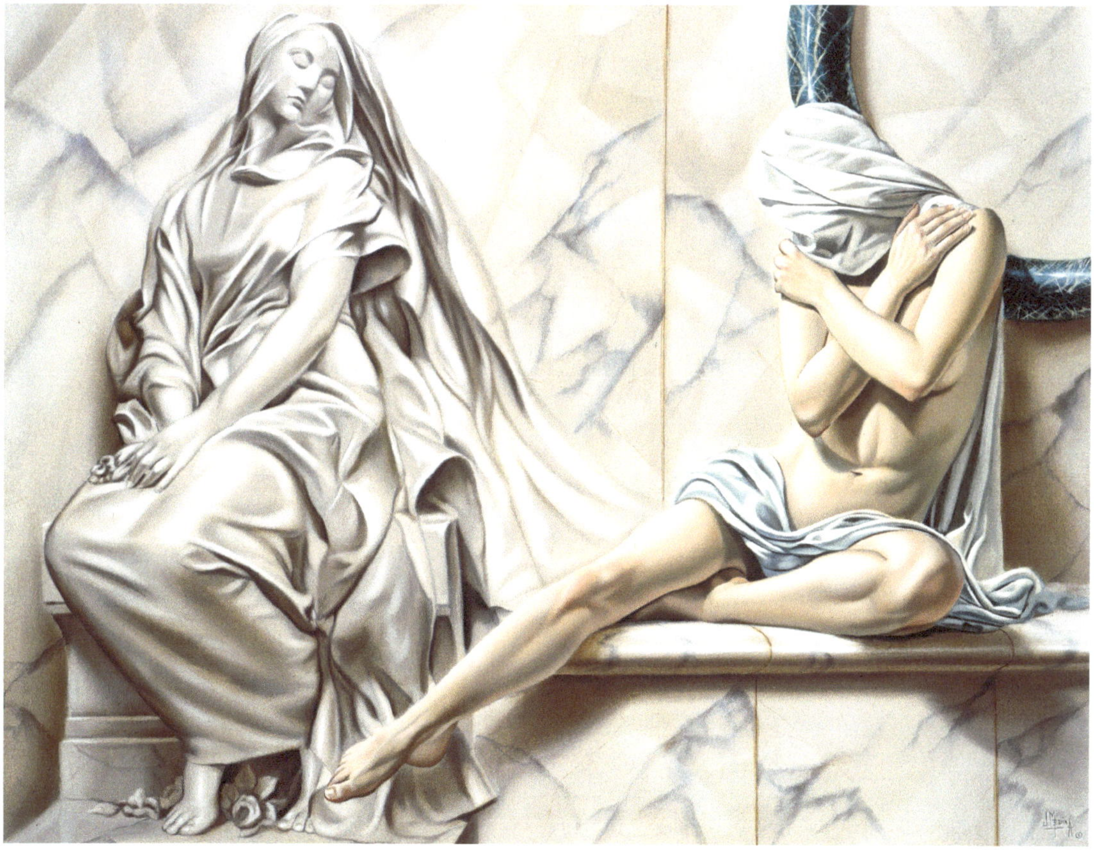

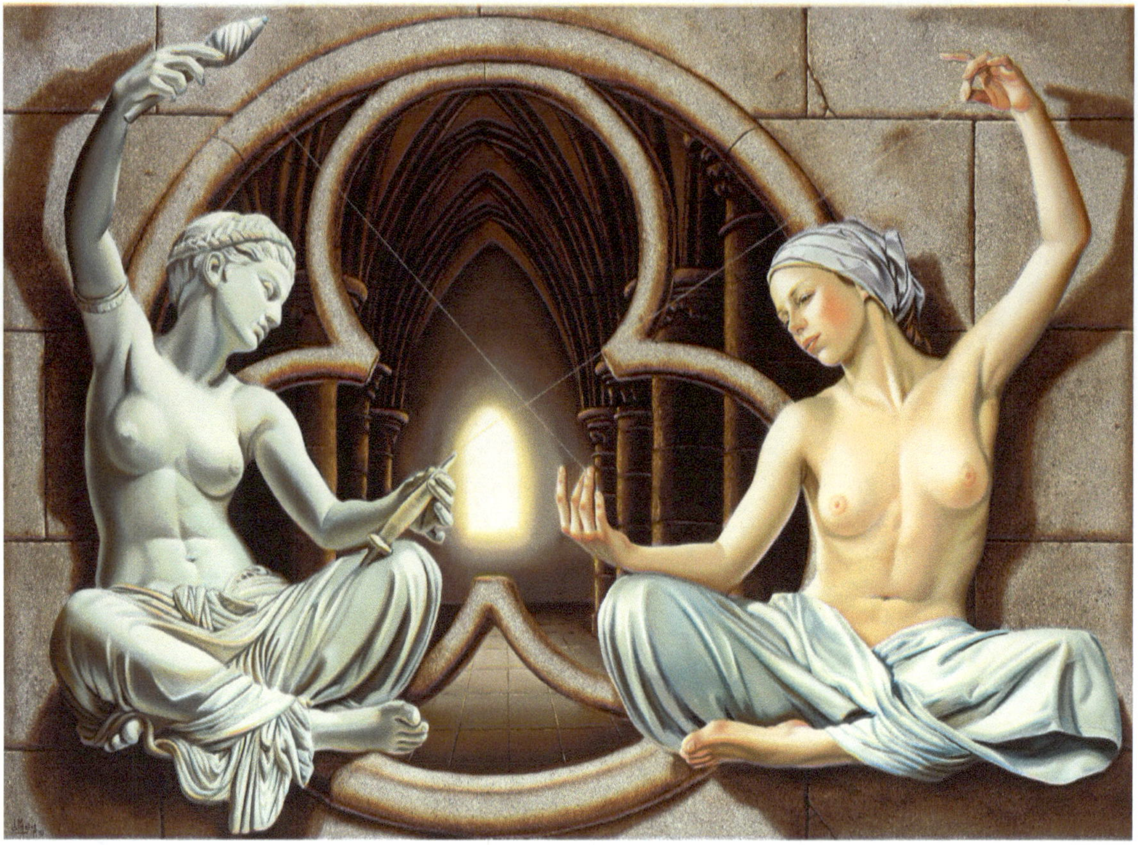

The Moiras, oil on linen, 99 x 140cm

Shrouded and Broken, oil on linen, 99 x 140cm

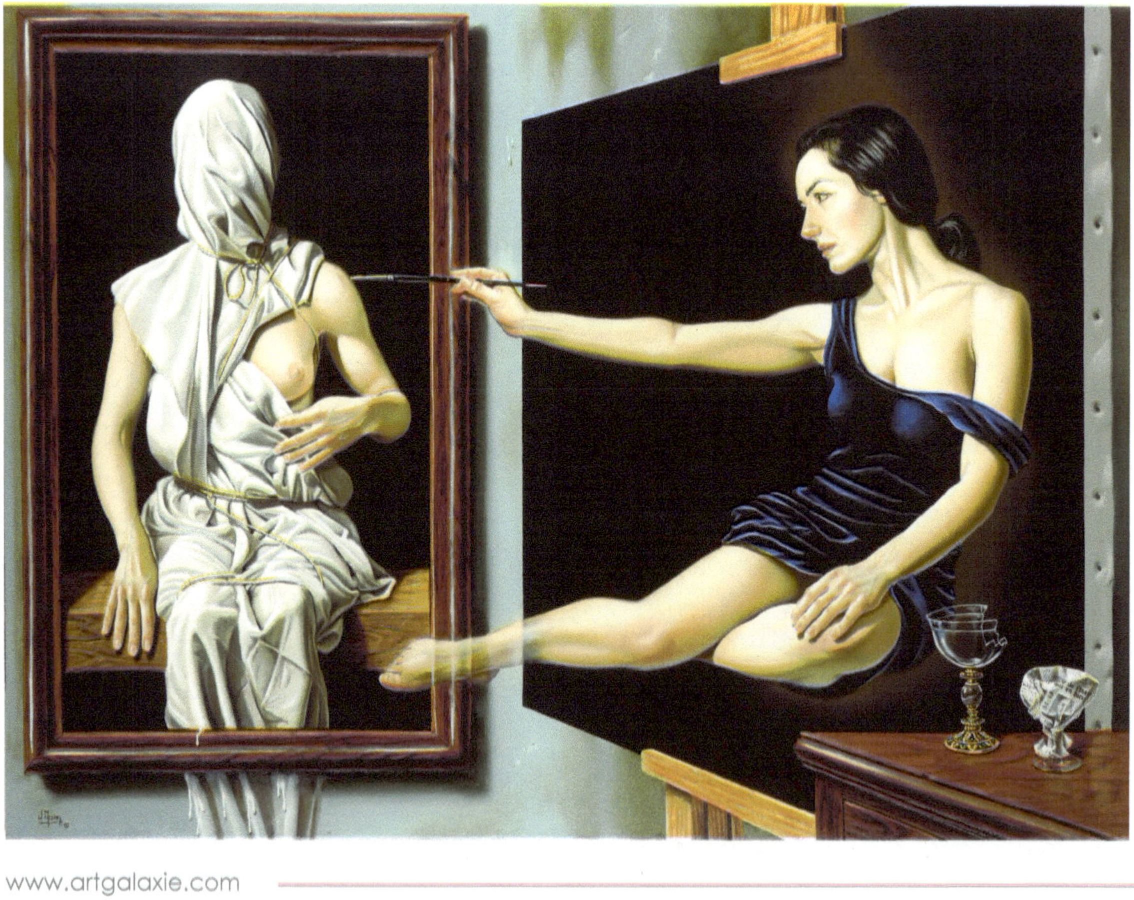

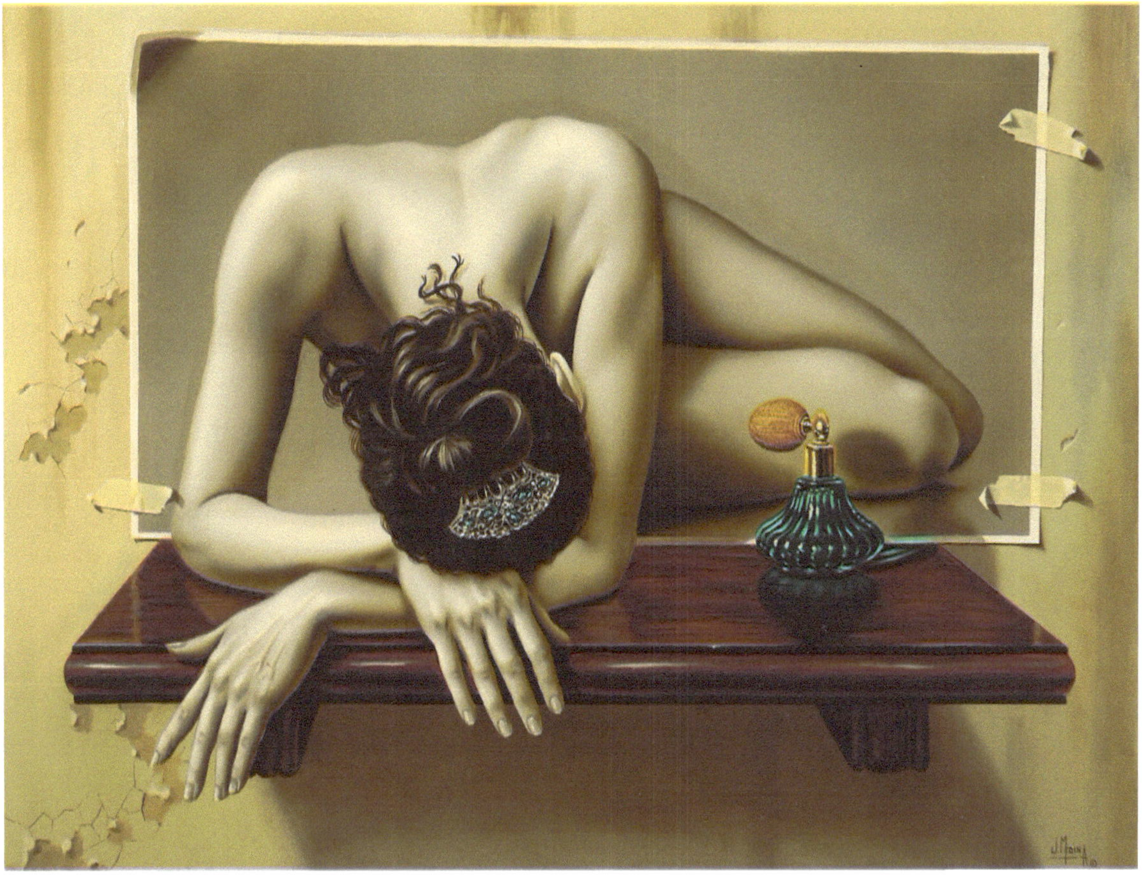

Nostalgia, oil on linen, 60 x 81cm

Fake Real, oil on linen, 86 x 127cm

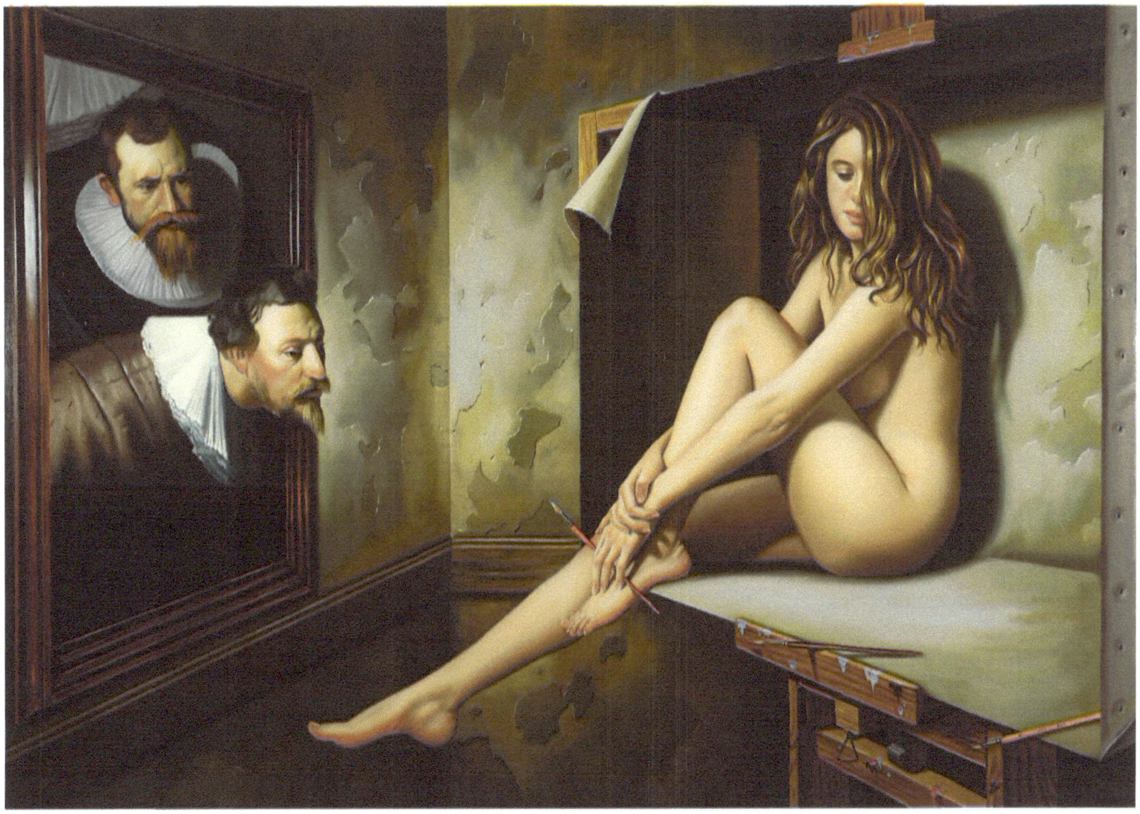

KONSTANTIN KACEV

PAINTING - MACEDONIA

www.konstantinkacev.com

Konstantin Kacev is a Russian artist. He was born in 1967 in Taschent, where he remained until 1983. After that, he studied in Skopje, and he then graduated from the Faculty of Fine Arts at Skopje in 1995. There, he learned all of the ins and outs of painting, conservation, and restoration, He was for a long time an unknown artist, but in the late 90s, his profile began to rise.

During that time, he worked at the Republic's Department of Culture and Conservation, working as a freelance wall painting conservator. The responsibilities of that job were to him an opportunity to hone his skills and become a more efficient artist. His hard work paid off in 1999 when he started to exhibit his work throughout Macedonia.

In 2005, Konstanin did several independent exhibitions in Paris and New York. He continues to live and work in Skopje, feeling deeply connected to this place where he first discovered himself and where he first came into his own as an artist.

A small-town artist with a big-city talent, he is renowned for the wonder of his still life paintings, which are said to be vibrant without being lucid and reserved without being dull. He strikes a balance between colour and lack of colour, painting paintings that to many people reflect life better than anyone else. A connoisseur of reality, he considers these presentations to be his calling.

Right: Sophie, 2014, oil on canvas, 90 x 120cm

Still Life Portrait, 2014, oil on canvas, 100 x 100cm

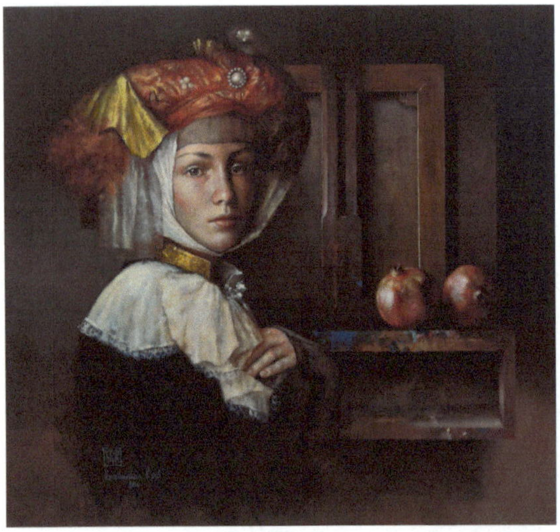

Magyc, 2013, oil on canvas, 120 x 90cm

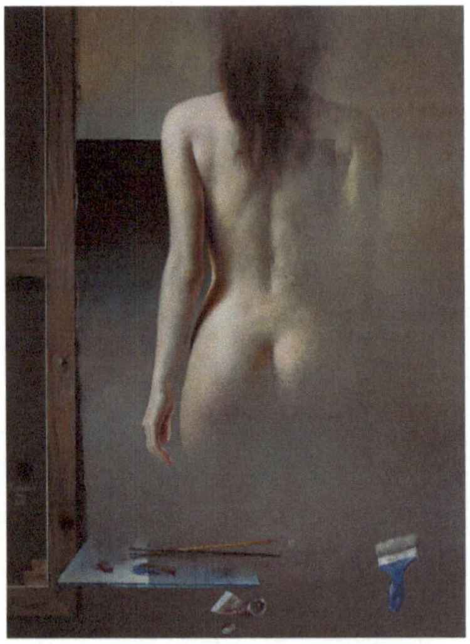

The Picture, 2014, oil on canvas, 80 x 50cm

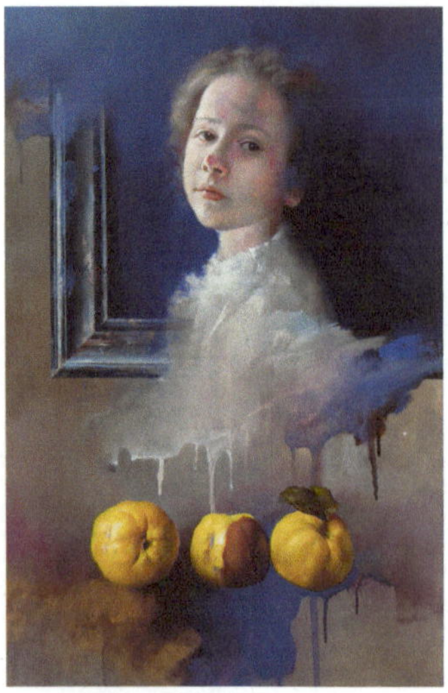

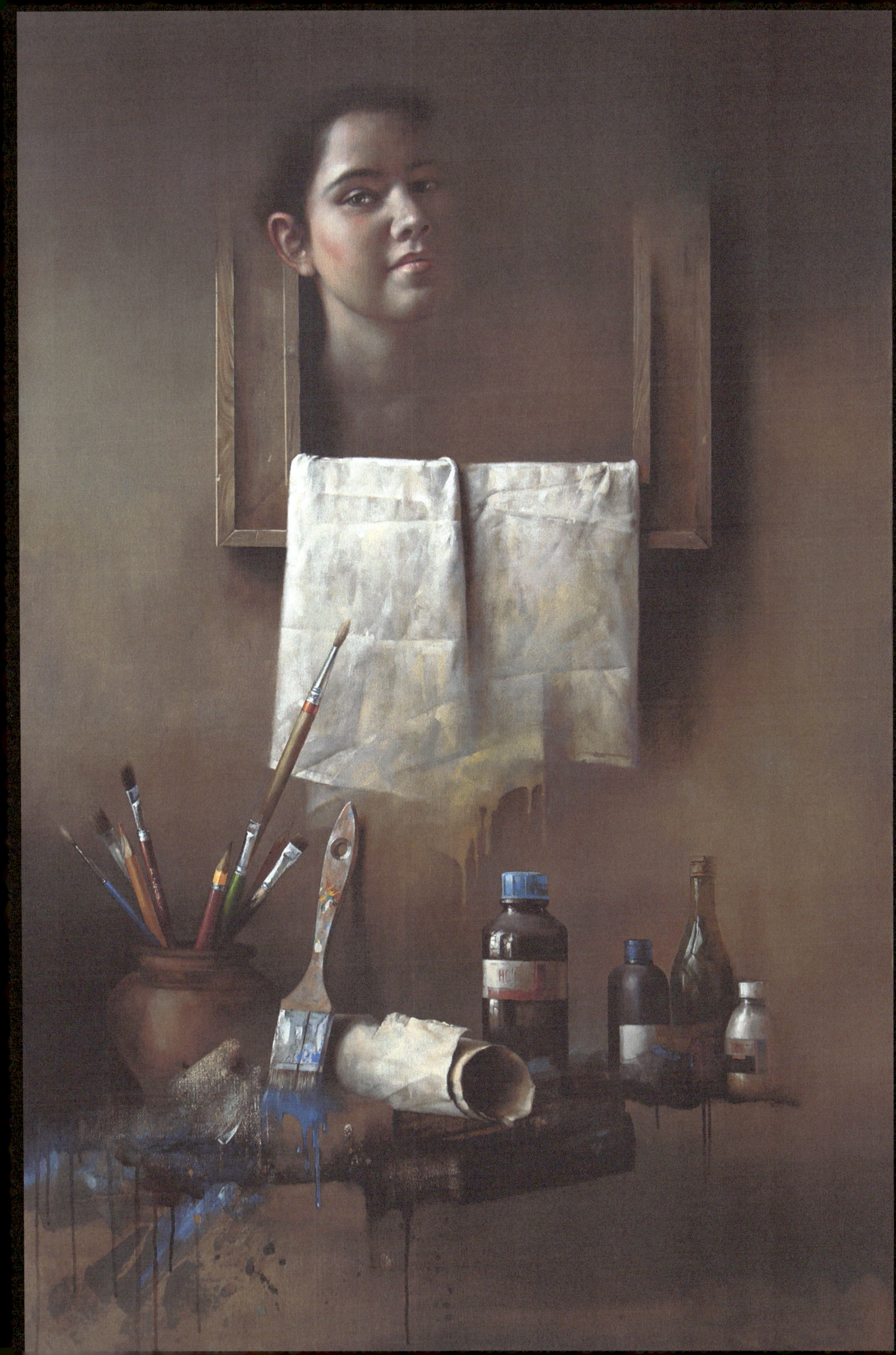

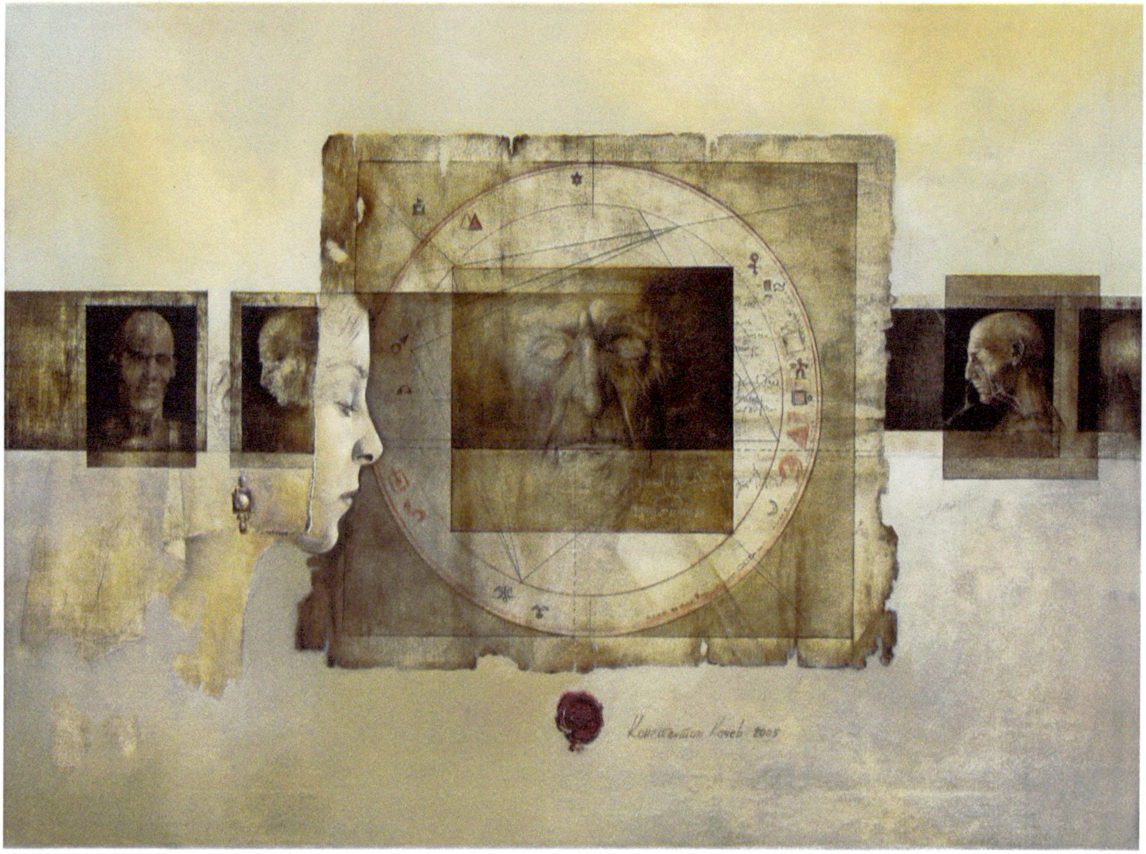

The Horoscope, 2004, oil on canvas, 70 x 90cm

Diary of a Mad Man, 2006, oil on canvas, 72 x 90cm

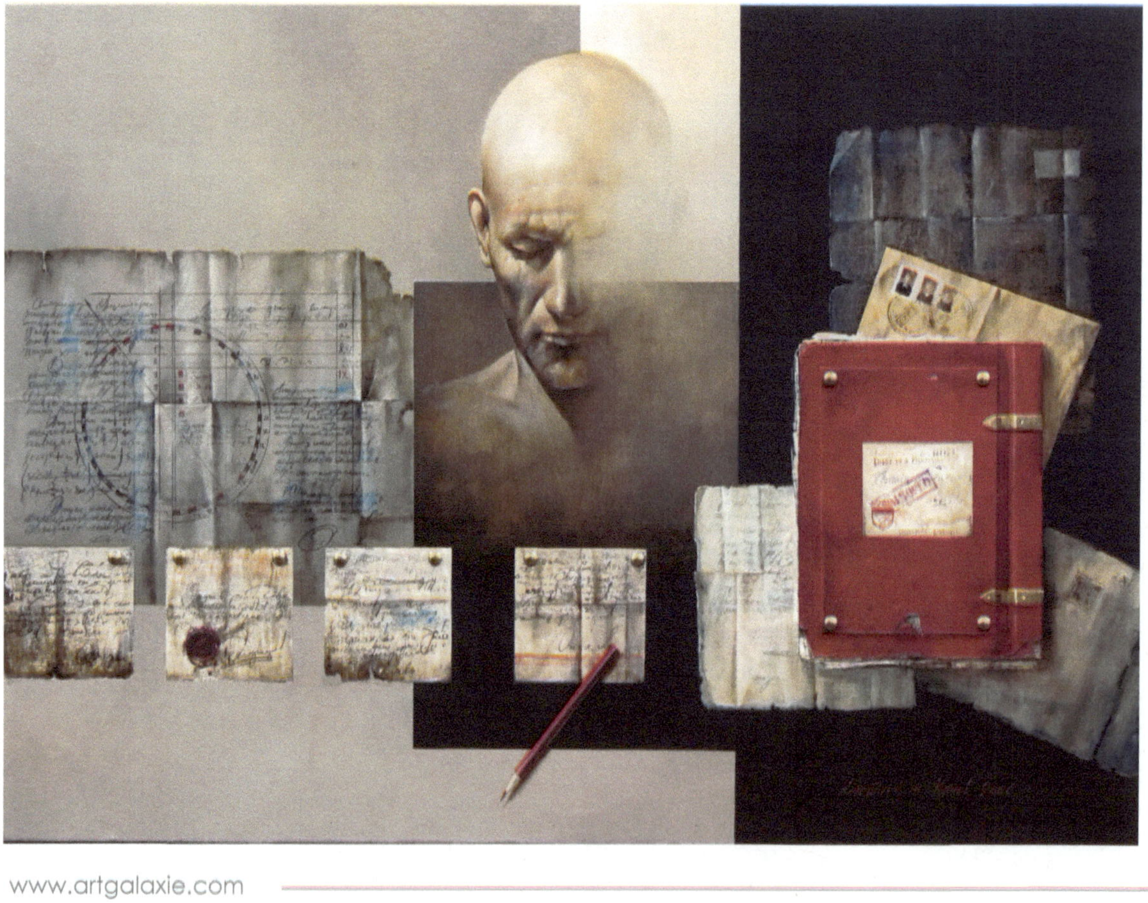

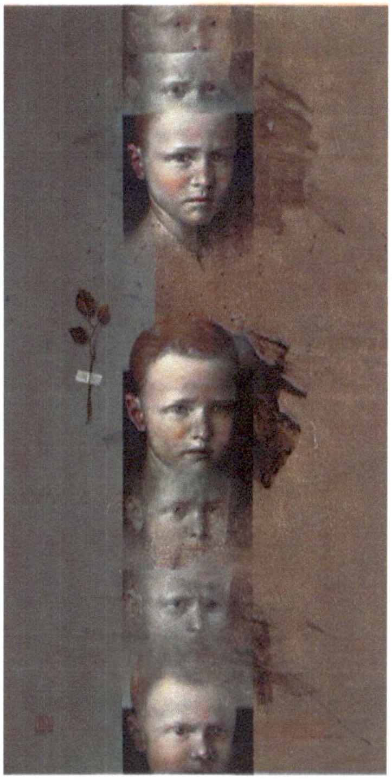

Out of the Capture, 2011, oil on canvas, 55 x 120cm

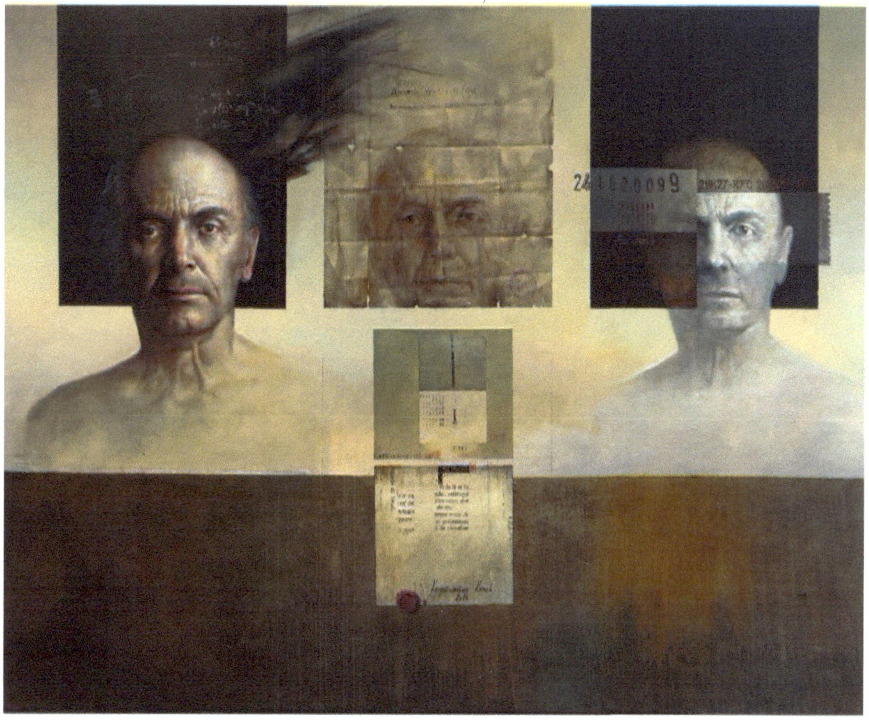

Trilogy of Life, 2014, oil on canvas, 120 x 90cm

The Templars's Secret, 2006, oil on canvas, 60 x 120cm

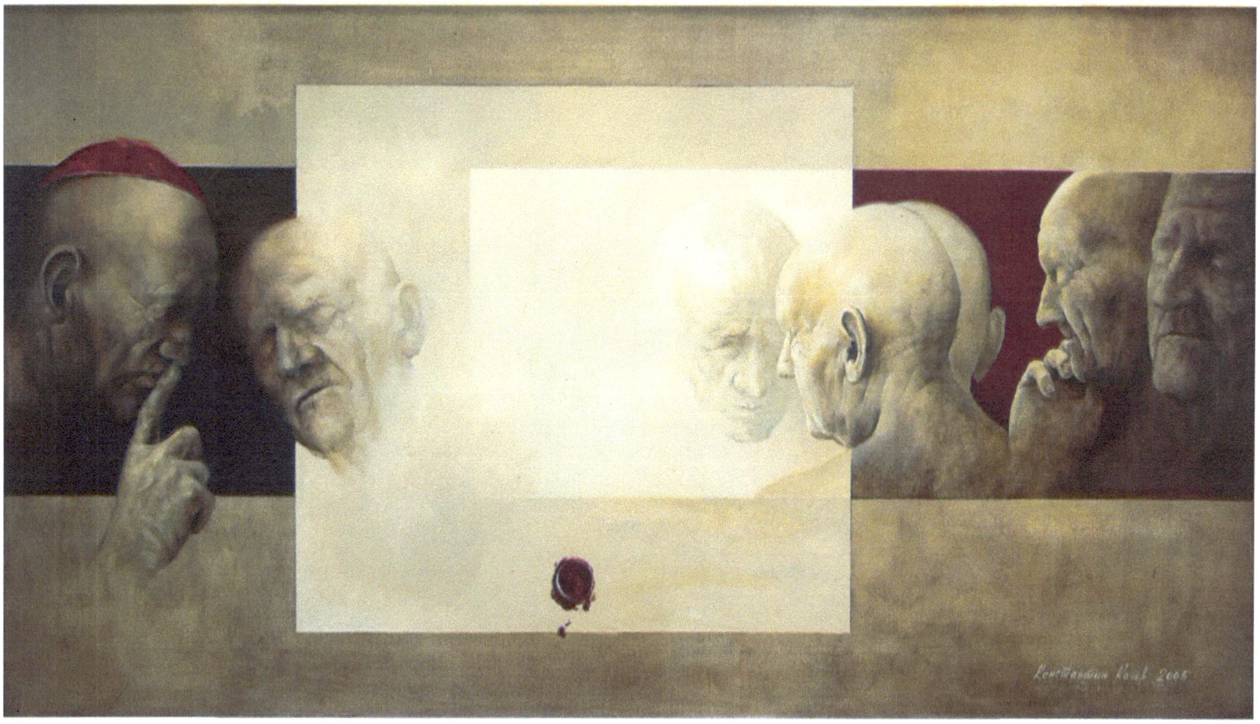

LARISSA MORAIS

PAINTING - RUSSIA

www.larissamorais.com

Larissa Morais was born and raised in Moscow. She has been painting since she was in high school, however her first love was not the brush but the keys of a piano. The replacement of a teacher changed her vision from music and into the world of art. While helping her sister one afternoon with her art homework something sparked her passion for painting and perhaps she stumbled upon her destiny.

Larissa became a graduate from BFA, Moscow Theatrical Arts Institute, and attended the Graduate School of Restoration and conservation where throughout the years she took courses in conservation and restoration of 15th and 16th century paintings. "When you restore a painting, you can paint your own strokes into history". Larissa is influenced by everything in her life. Her brush creates a realistic impression as if it couldn't possibly be anything but a photo. She views her subject matter as architecture. She sees the subject and presents it in a way that is usually not seen from the naked eye. Her favourite subject to paint is the human figure from which she brings a reality to the paintings where attention to detail is as strong as attention to the character of the model. In her artwork, we are in the company of beautiful men and women, intimately poised and positioned. All her artwork is conceived from a sketch, which she later paints onto a large black canvas. Her delicate technique is with very thin layers of oil paint, while using the black background for shadowing. She captures every detail of her subject. For her it is all there, she just uncovers it. Her favourite painting is always the one she is working on and the most difficult thing is to part with her art. She usually falls in love while painting, and she describes it as "it is always bittersweet when parting with a painting however it's always validating".

Right: Solace, 2014, oil on panel, 40 x 30cm

Promotion, 2010, oil on canvas, 36 x 36cm

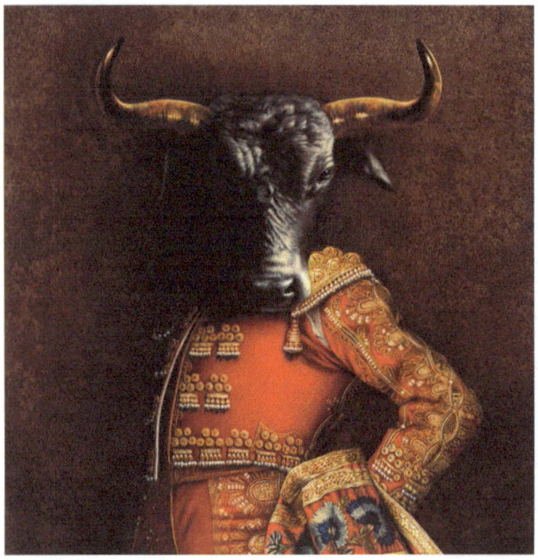

Sleight, 2014, oil on wood, 48 x 30cm

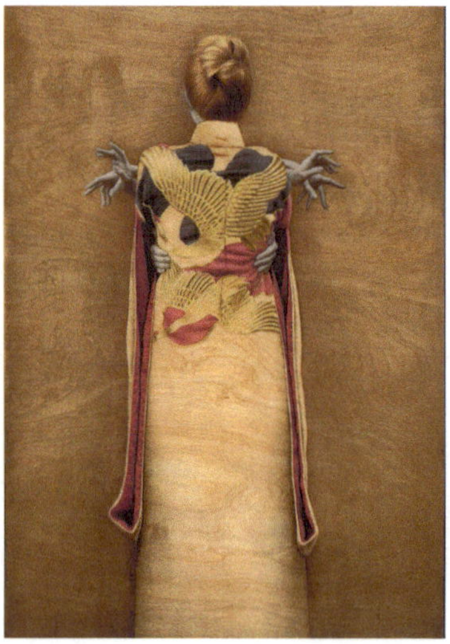

Head Study I, 2013, oil on wood, 20 x 16cm

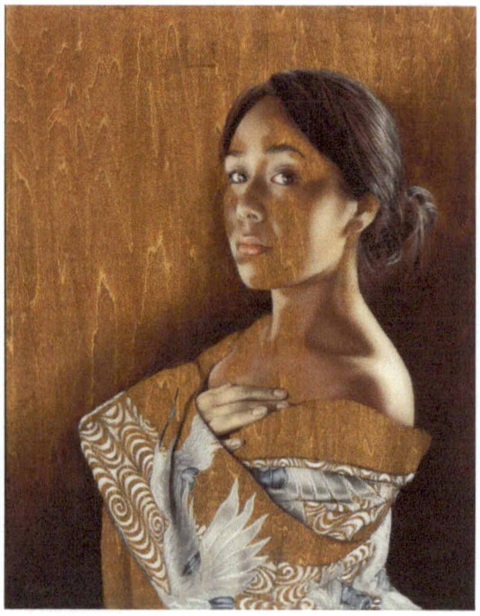

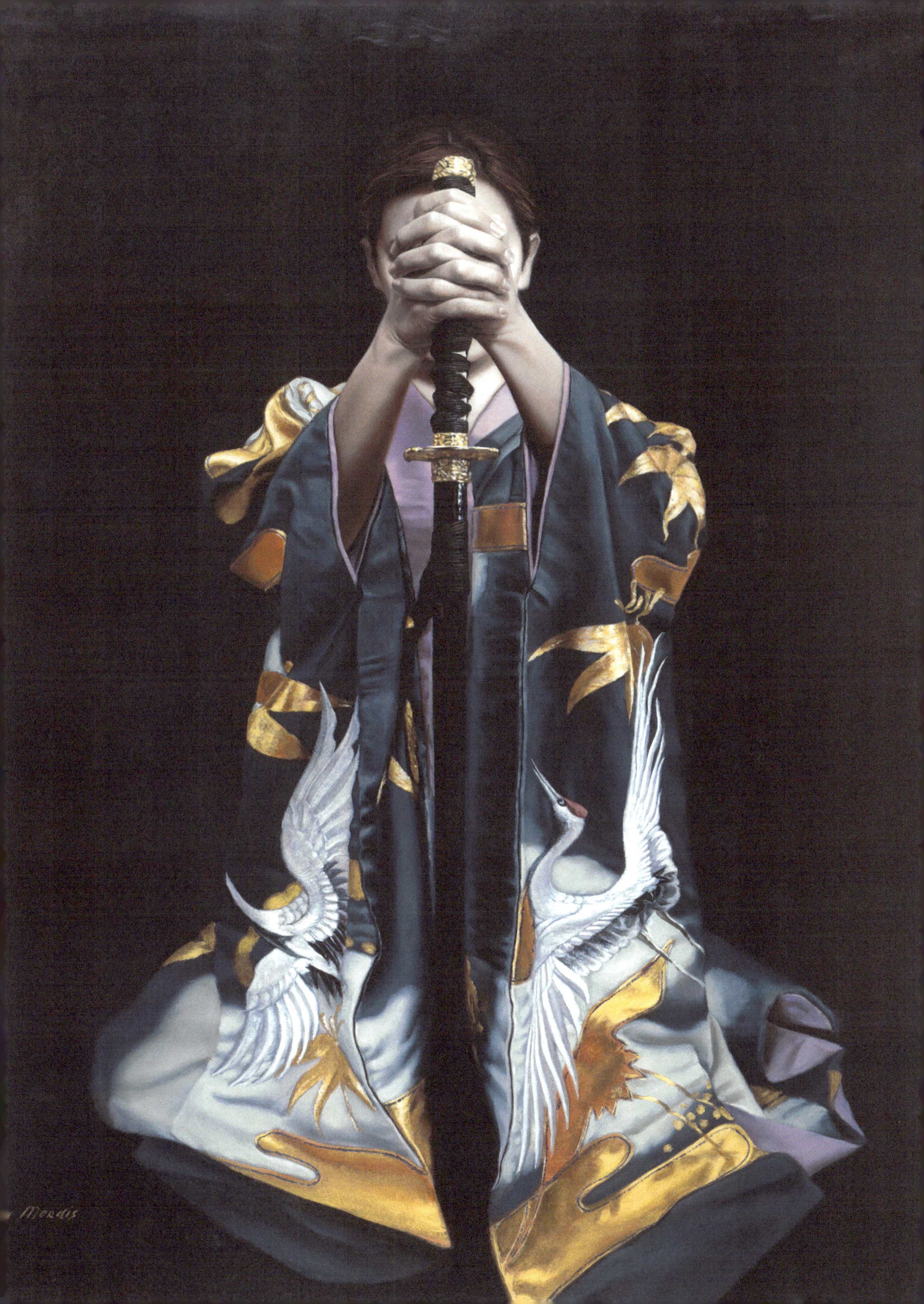

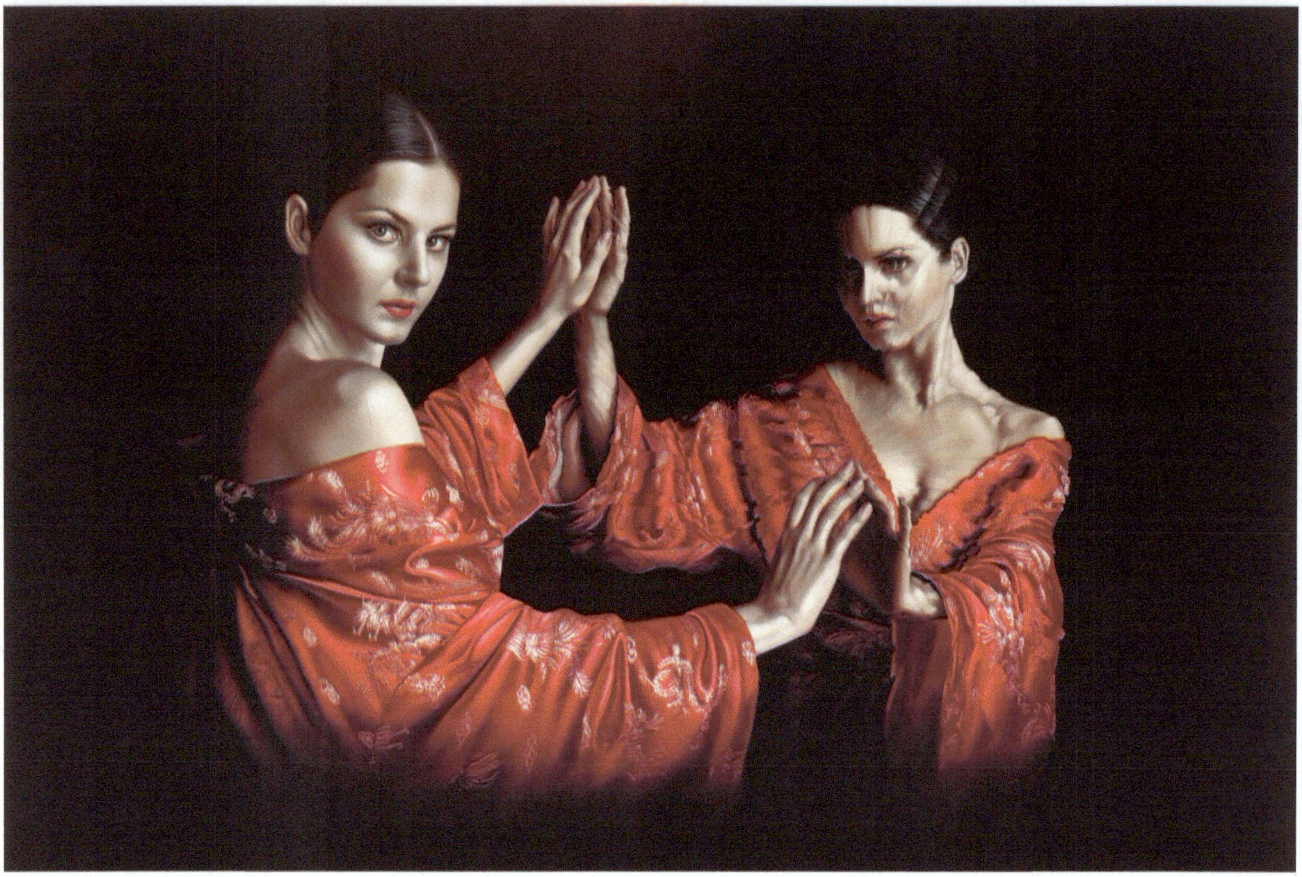

Through the Looking Glass, 2012, oil on board, 36 x 48cm

Offerings, 2012, oil on panel, 30 x 48cm

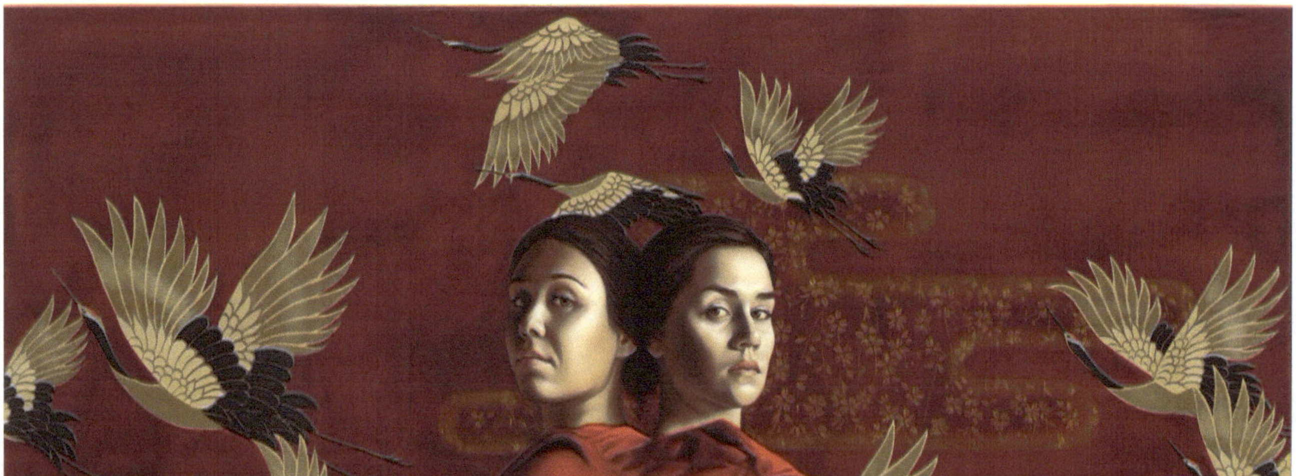

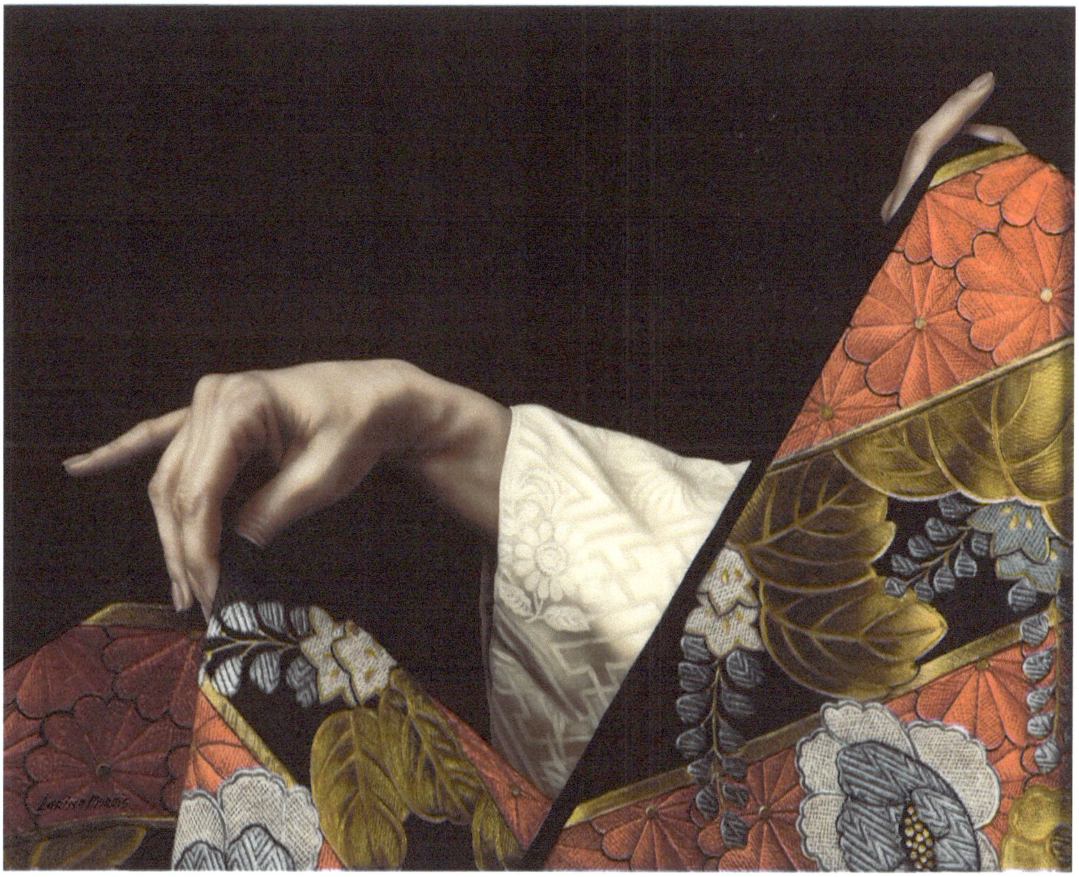
Obi Dance, 2014, oil on board, 18 x 24cm

Mother of Three, 2012, oil on panel, 36 x 48cm
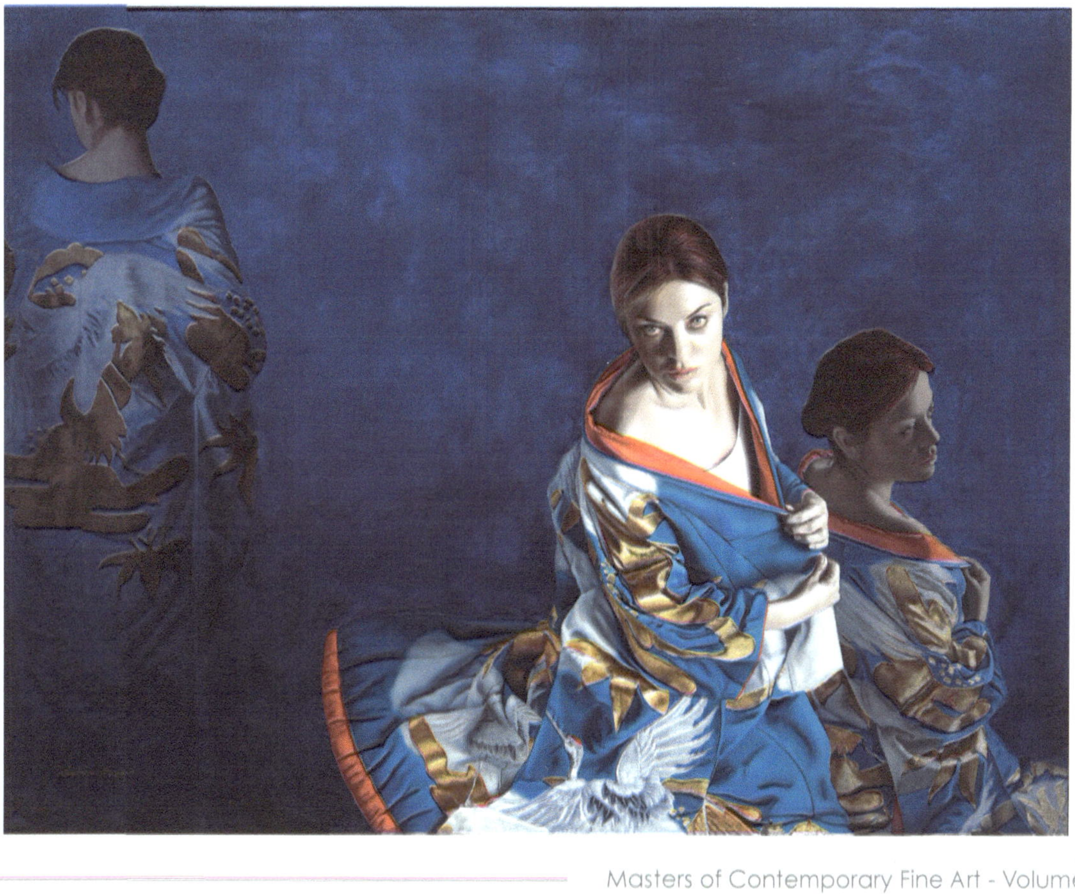

MICHAEL HUTTER

PAINTING - GERMANY

www.kunstkrake.de

Michael Hutter is a German artist who first became immersed in religion after attending a Catholic primary schools in the 1970s. He learned all about the Last Judgement and Eternal Damnation, and although he lost his faith while he was still young, he remained fascinated by the demons that he had learned about, demons that have tortured his mind ever since. Upon discovering Hieronymus Bosch and the Surrealists in 1976, he felt that he had found something truly worthwhile. From then on, he was committed to art, living his life with it always on his mind. He drifted during the 1980s, first experimenting with occult practices and then attending the Kunsthochschule in Cologne for a few semesters.

Michael has spent long periods of time in isolation, working manically and studying on his own. Between 2000 and 2001, he studied in the library of a monastery in the Eifel. That time inspired him to write and illustrate is first books, The Melchior Gruen Tales. His life came to an abrupt halt in 2006 when his father died, and for the first time, he shed himself of all spiritual teachings and declared himself an agnostic.

Michael continues to live and work in Cologne, still working manically at times and just as devoted to art as he has ever been. A fascinating figure, he has stayed on the same path for a very long time, making great strides in a style to which he is one of only a few heirs.

The triumph of flesh, oil on wood panel, 120 x 60cm

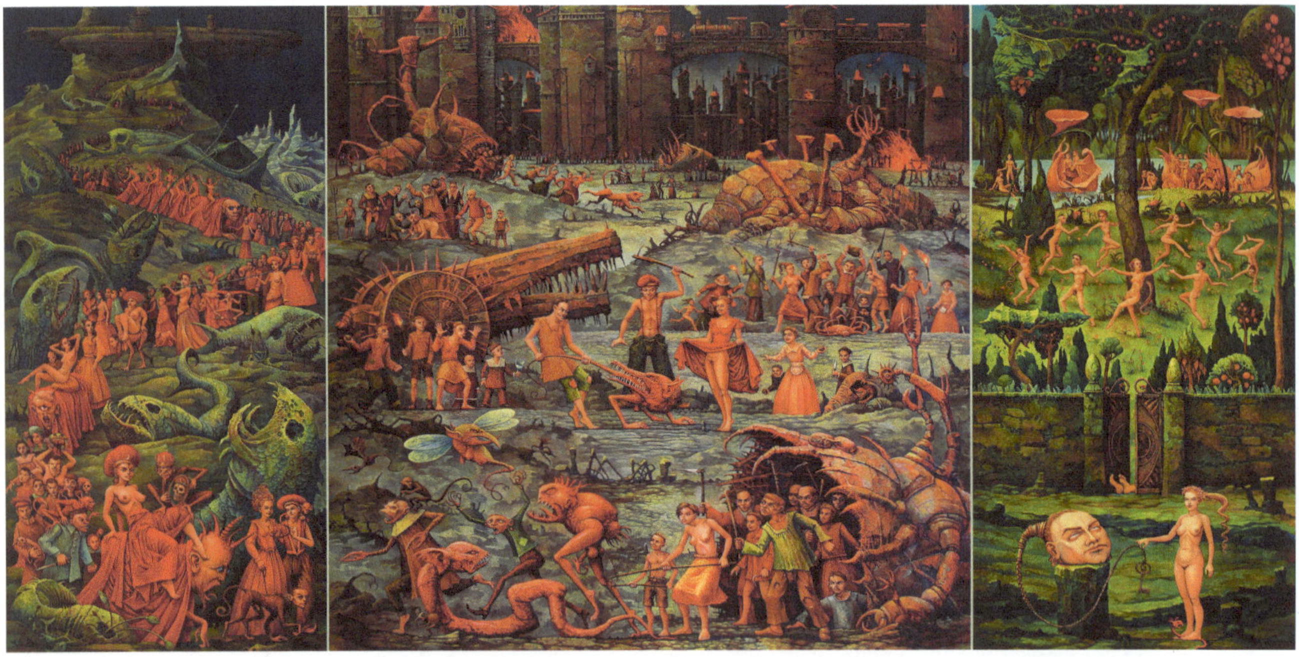

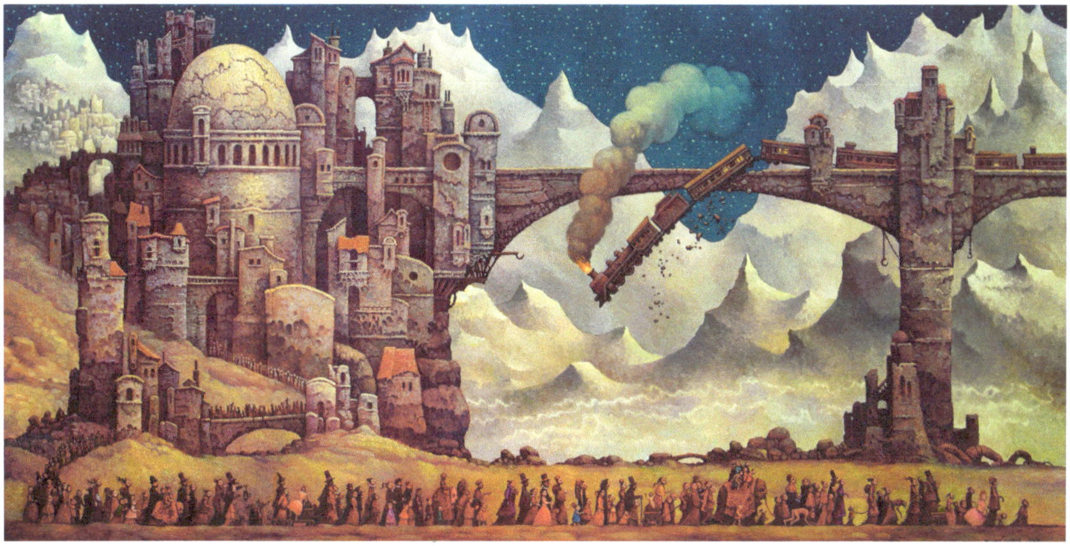

Exodus, oil on wood panel, 60 x 120cm

Lot Presenting his Daughters to the Citizens of Sodom, oil on wood panel, 110 x 220cm

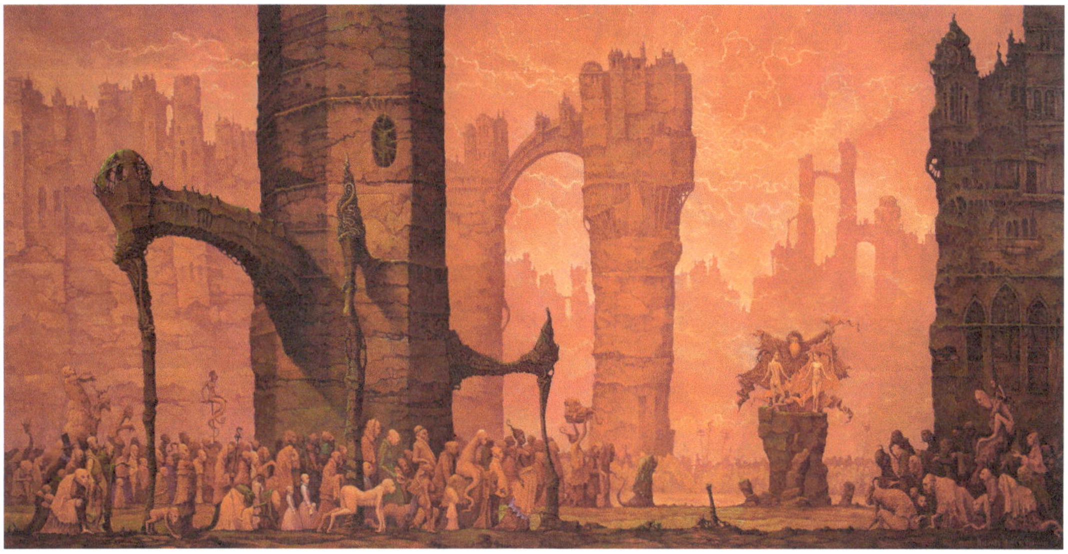

The Feast of the Great Worm, oil on canvas, 100 x 200cm

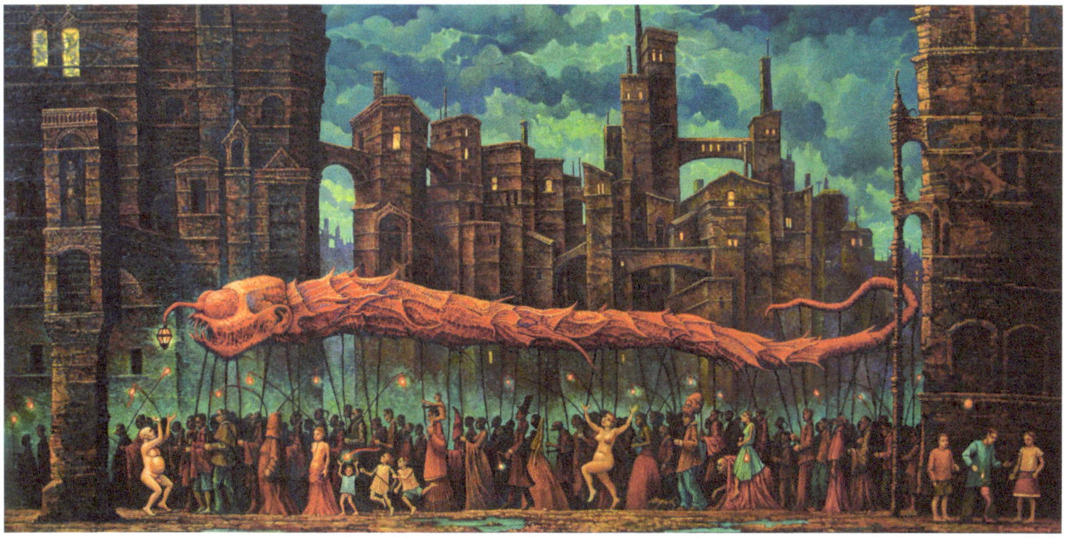

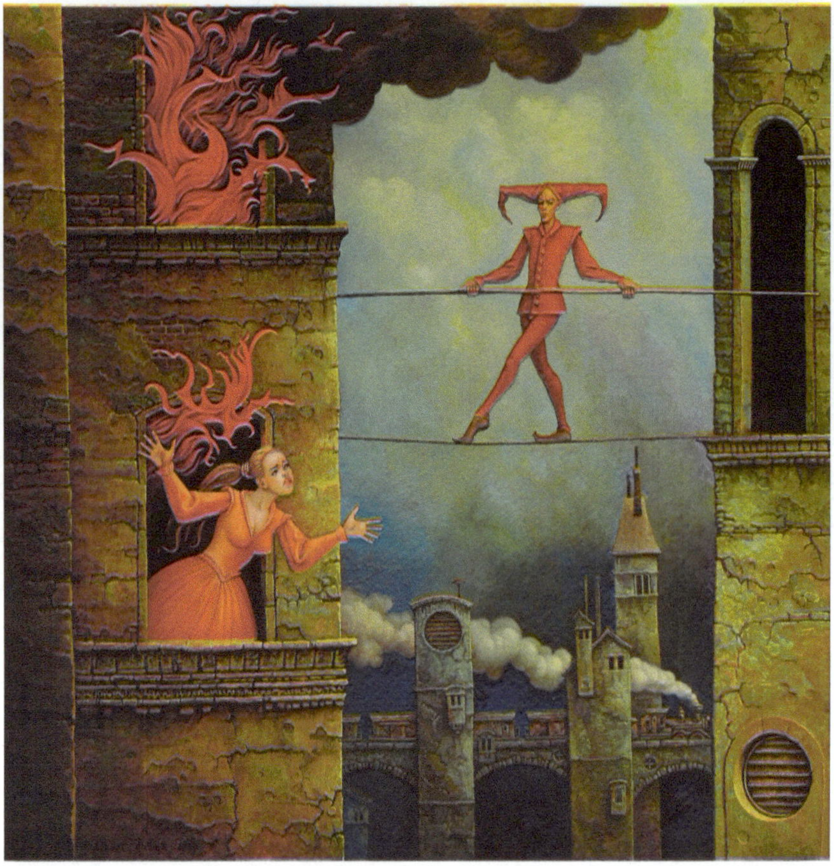

The Last tTain, oil on wood panel, 60 x 60cm

The Weigher of Head and Heart, oil on wood panel, 60 x 60cm

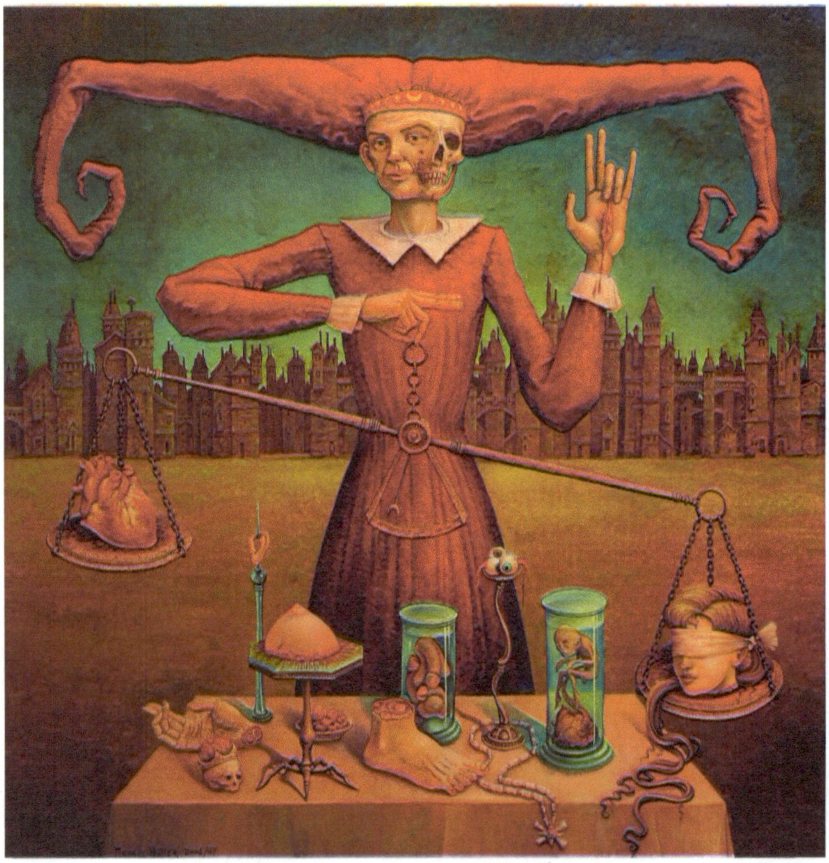

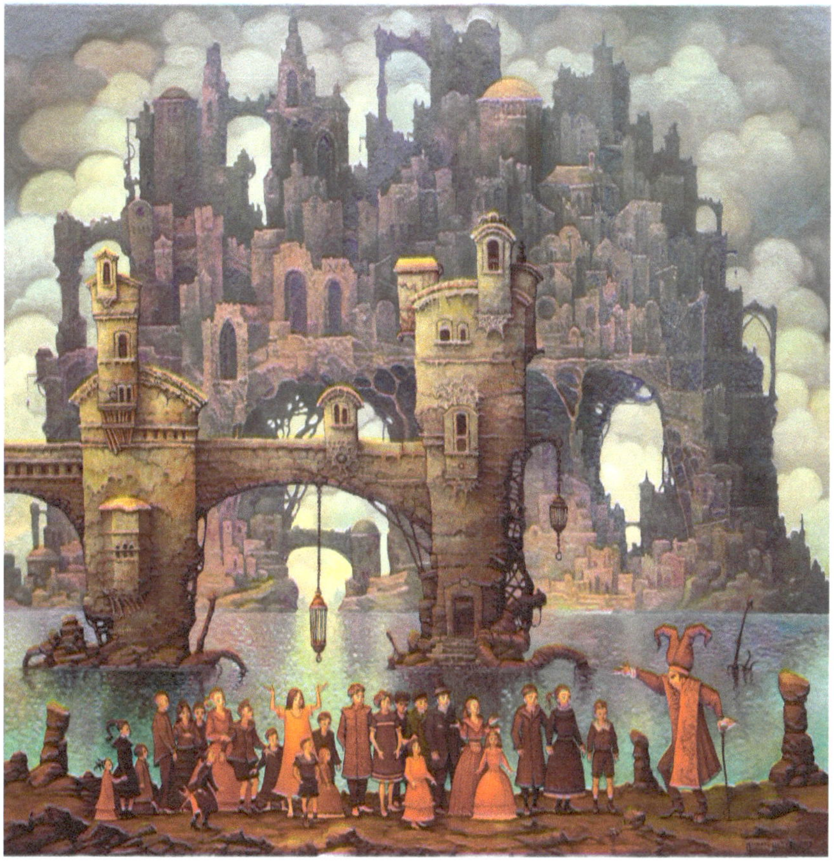

Satan showing his City to the Children, oil on wood panel, 90 x 90cm

Games in Purgatory, oil on wood panel, 60 x 60cm

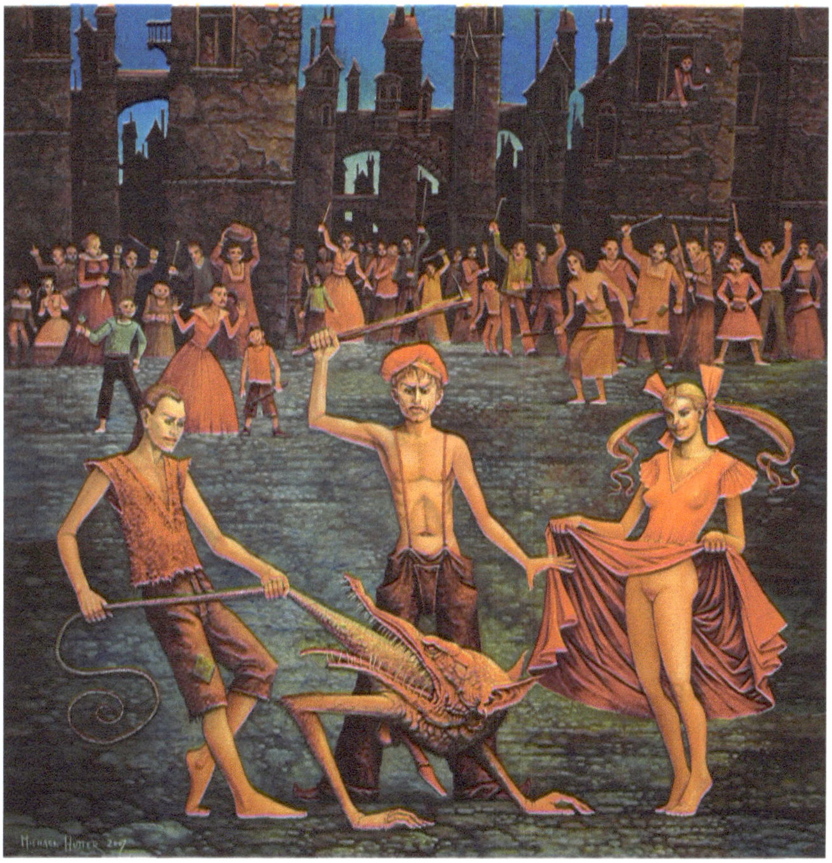

MYRIAM FEUILLOLEY

PAINTING - FRANCE

www.feuilloley.com

Myriam Feuilloley is a french artist living and working by the sea in Normandy. Graduated from the Decorative Arts school Paris in 1982, her early career saw her work extensive as a graphic designer and director of CGI films. Since 1990, she has concentrated her attention exclusively on painting.

The narraratives and characters portrayed in her work are easily recognised. Often bearing a hallmark, they are naked, hairless, and the bodies shapes freed from the classic image what is "the norm". Common themes include people bathing, couples, family portraits, totems, crosses, the Tower of Babel, puppets, and meeting with angels. All captured in her unique style. In 2006, Honfleur Library commissioned her to produce a series of illustrations based on her own interpretation of La Fontaine's Fables.

Myriam's work has been exhibited at the Museum of Villa Carlotta by Como Lake, Montivilliers Abbey, the Museum of Terre Neuvas in Fécamp, Maison des Arts in Conches, as well at the Tristan Bernard theater in Paris. In 2016, she was invited to exhibit her work as part of the World Day of Art at the United Nations Office in Geneva. Her work regularly features in exhibitions across France and internationally. She has published two books on her work, the first a retrospective, « Feuilloley, 20 years of painting » (2006), the second « 20 fables La Fontaine illustrated by Feuilloley » (2012).

Theme after theme again Feuilloley prompts us to reimagine the human soul thought the naked body.

Right: Reaching the Open Sea, 2009, oil on canvas 160 x 110cm

Shadow Theater, 2005, oil on canvas, 100 x 73cm

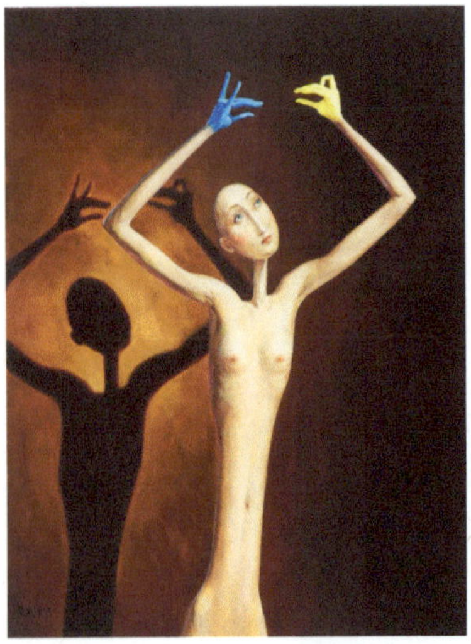

Soaring, 2000, oil on canvas, 80 x 40cm

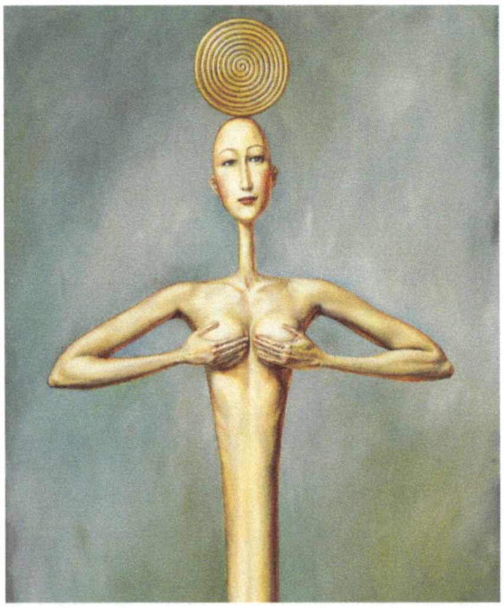

Swan Language, 2012, oil on canvas, 100 x 73cm

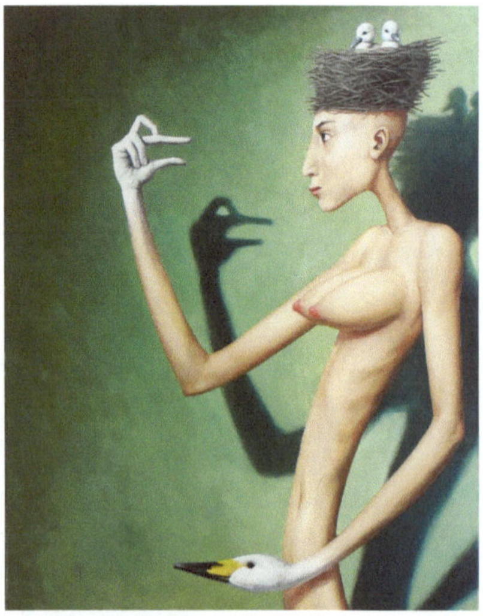

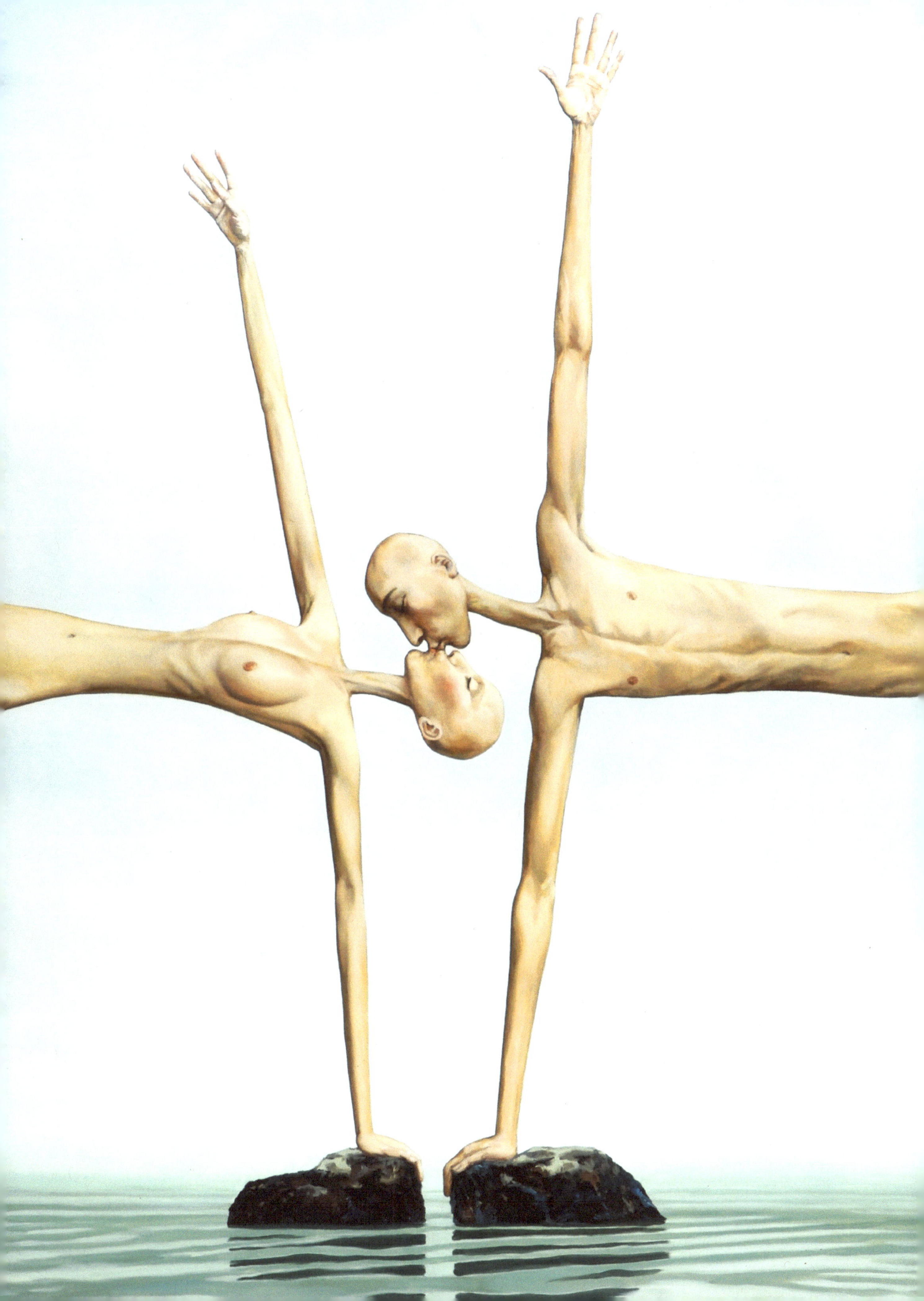

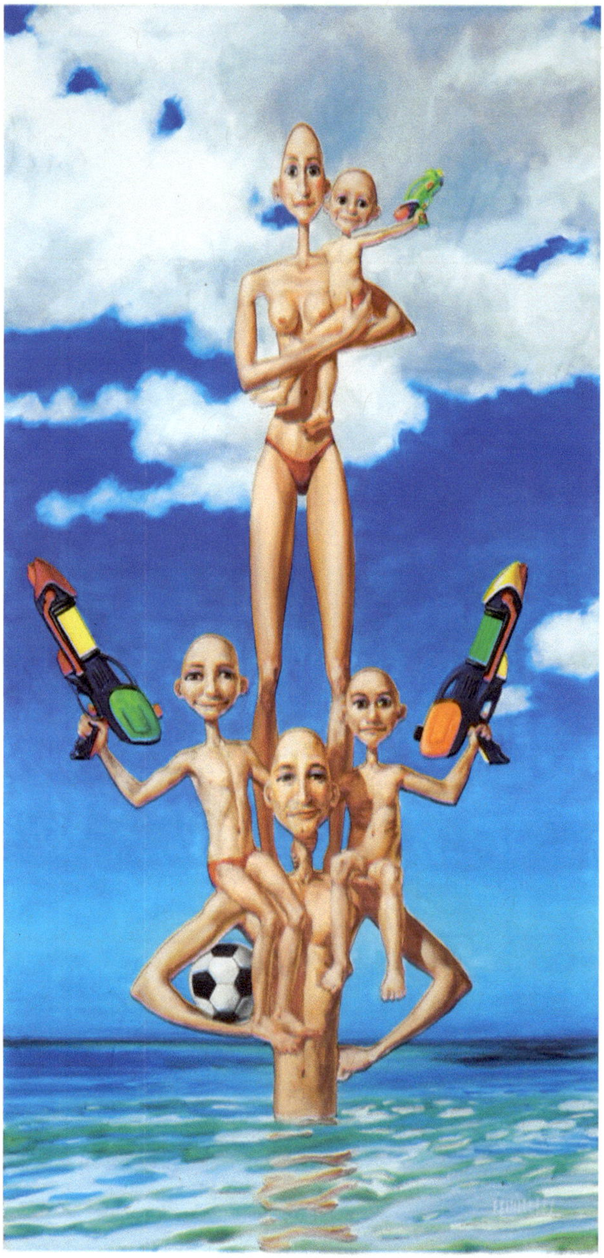

Family Portrait, 2006, oil on canvas, 80 x 40cm

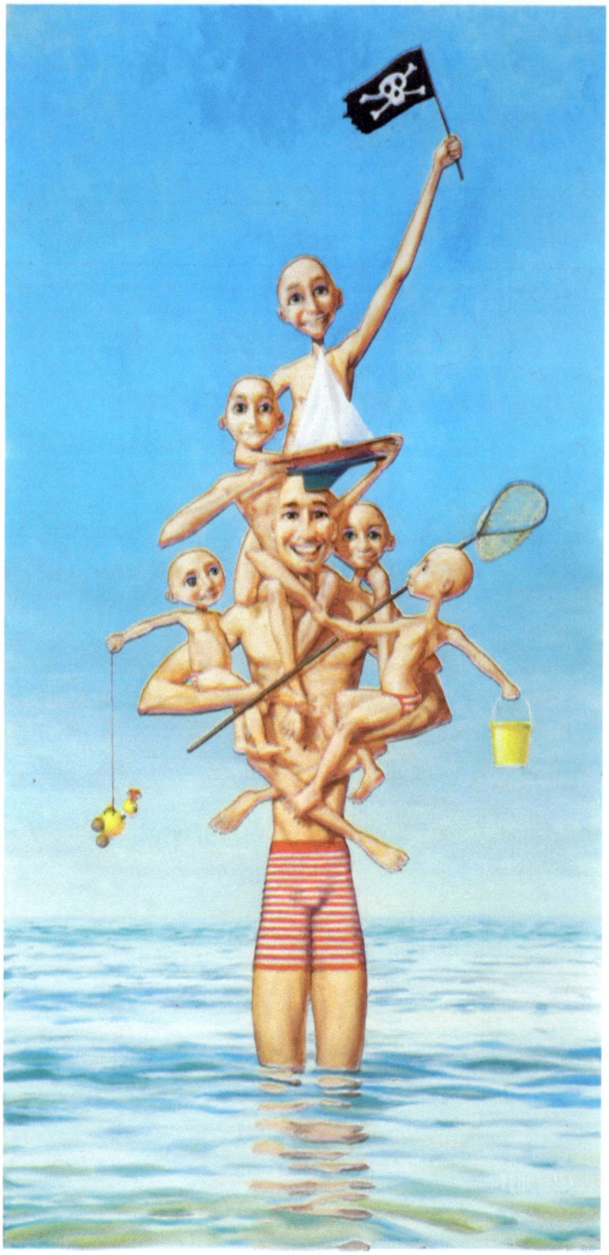

Family Support, 2006, oil on canvas, 80 x 40cm

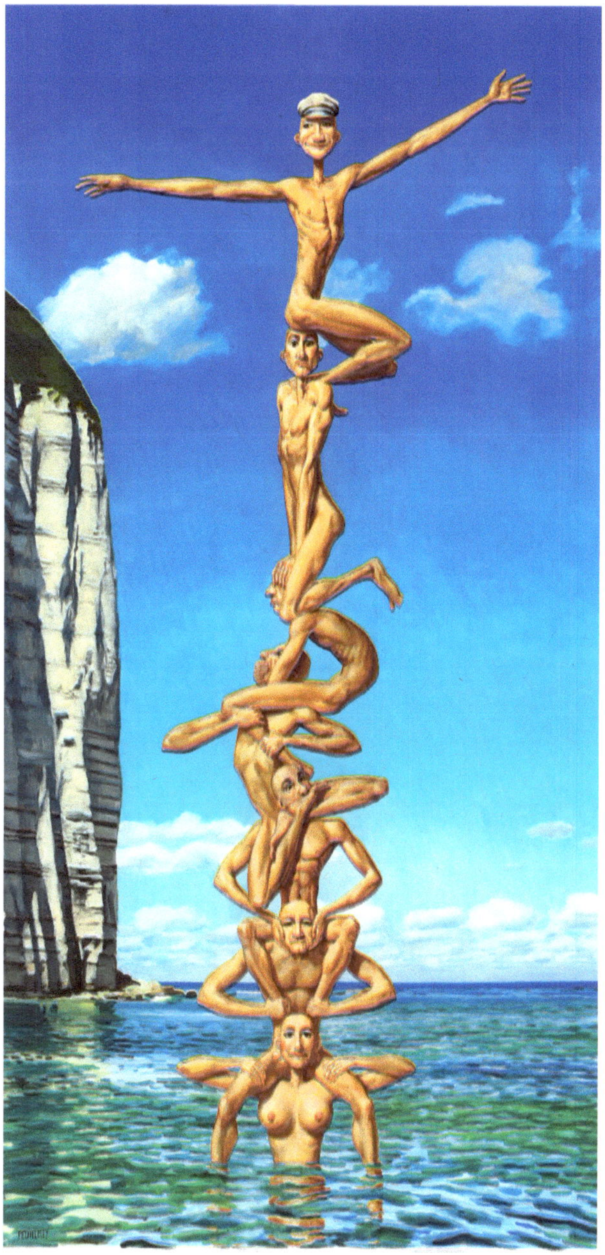

Tower of Babel I, 2008, oil on canvas, 195 x 120cm

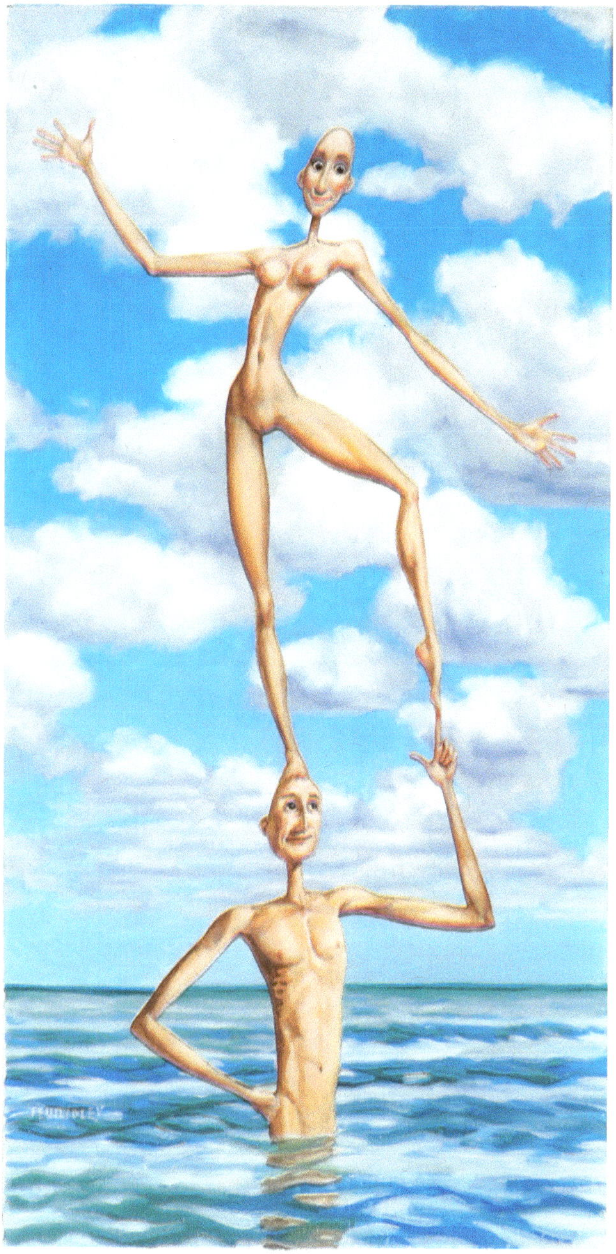

Equilibrium, 2009, oil on canvas, 60 x 30cm

PATRICIA VAN LUBECK

PAINTING - THE NETHERLANDS

www.vanlubeck.com

Patricia Van Lubeck is a Dutch painter. Born in Amsterdam, she now lives and works in New Zealand. Most recently, she is known for her oil paintings, which express most fiercely the concept of "individualism." A series of landscapes, these oil paintings are unlike anything else that she has done over the course of her career, sending a message that is at once demanding and inviting.

Striving never to be preachy or even to teach anyone anything about life, she is content simply by making people aware of their individualism and also bringing to light the pressures that society puts on that trait of ours.

Inspired by a lifetime of dreams and experiences, Patricia is someone who sees every life as a gift. The trees that she paints often speak to people on a personal level, and many people even identify with these trees as reflections of themselves. Her work "The Brave One" is reminiscent of a moment that many of us share, when we stood up to a crowd, expressing our individualism despite the risks and dangers that we faced. "The Lucky One", on the other hand, is an illustration of multiple possible leaders within a group, perhaps taking as its subject the concept that each of us is a leader in our own life.

Inspirational without ever being disconnected from reality, Patricia is an artist whose work is therapeutic to the people who view it.

The Happy One, 2012, oil on canvas, 101 x 51cm

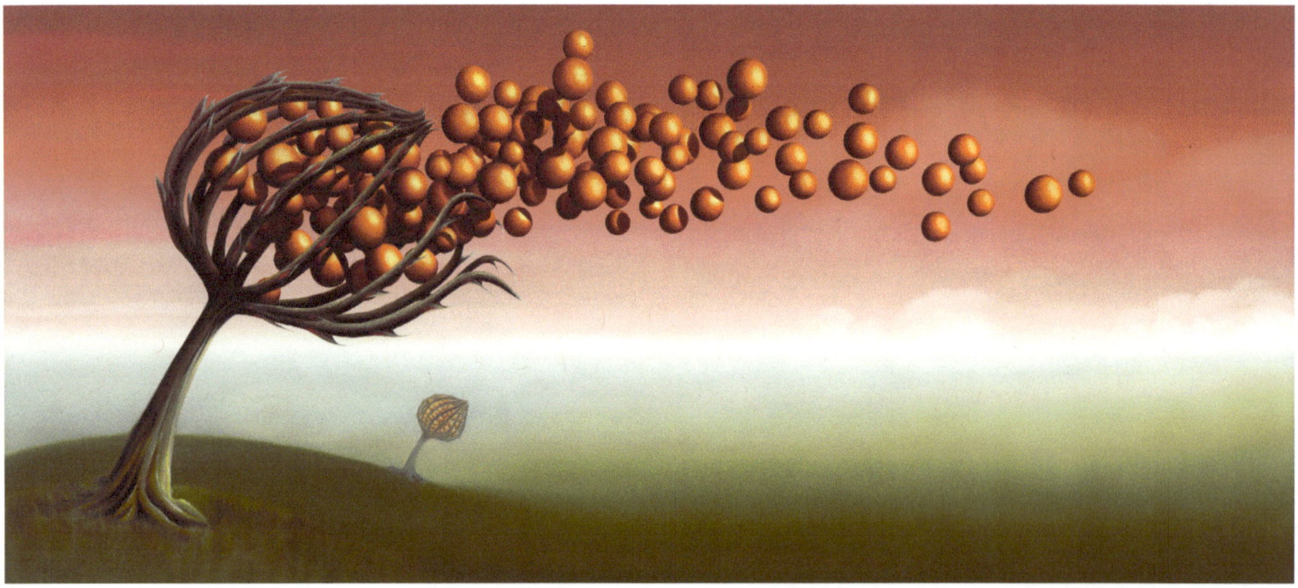

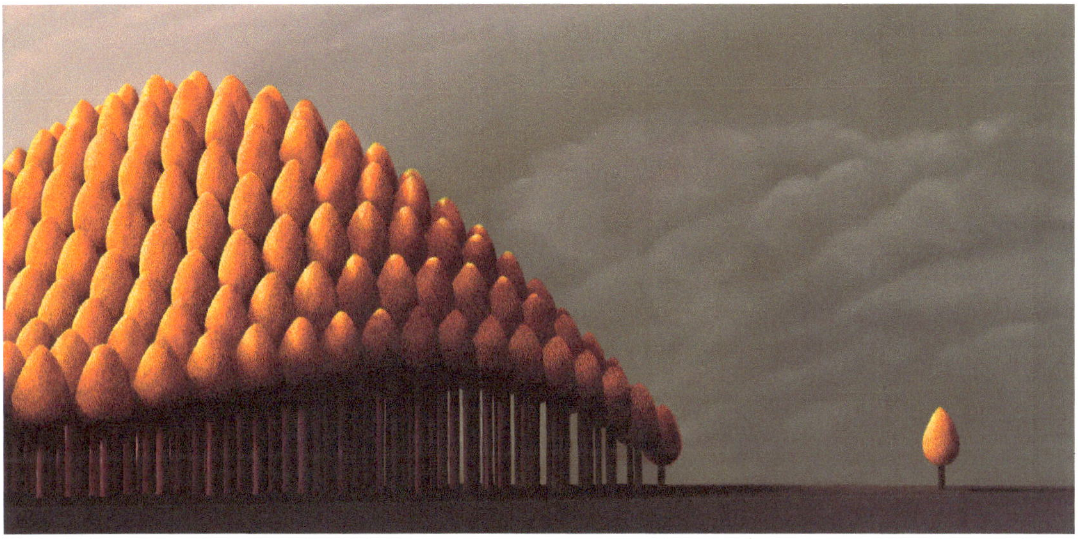

The Brave One, 2012, oil on canvas, 101 x 51cm

The Famous One, 2013, oil on canvas, 101 x 51cm

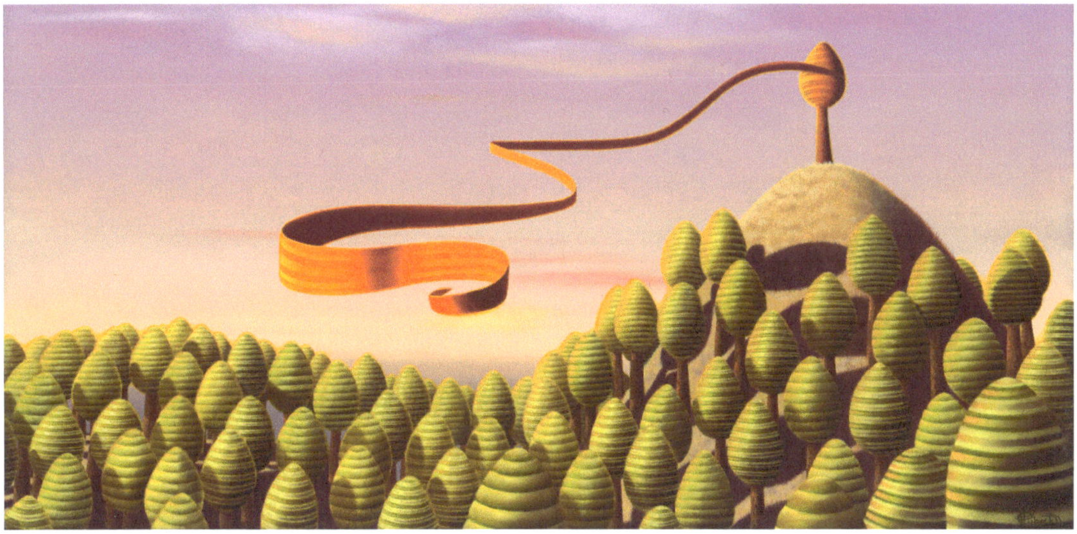

The Same One, 2013, oil on canvas, 101 x 51cm

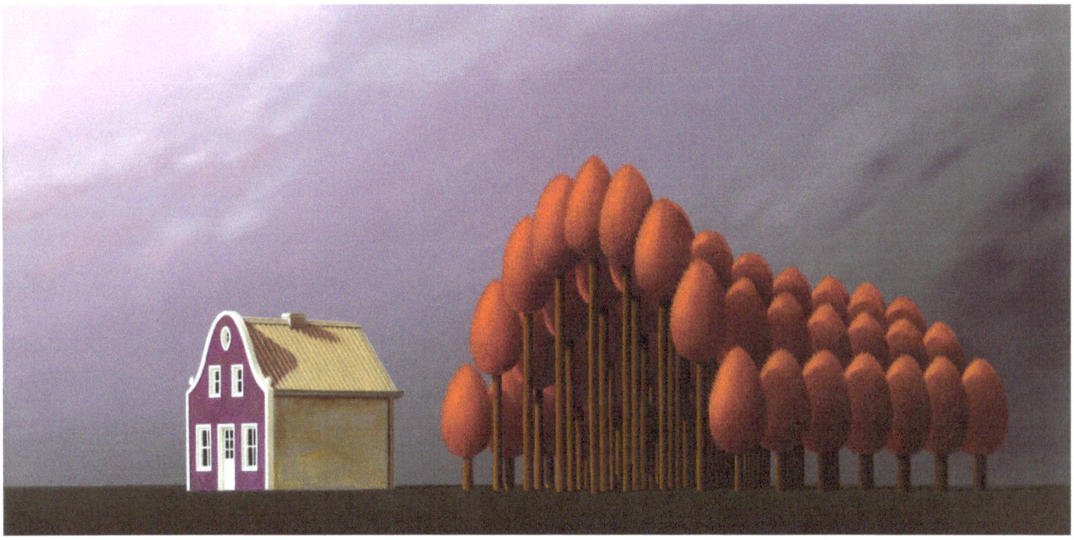

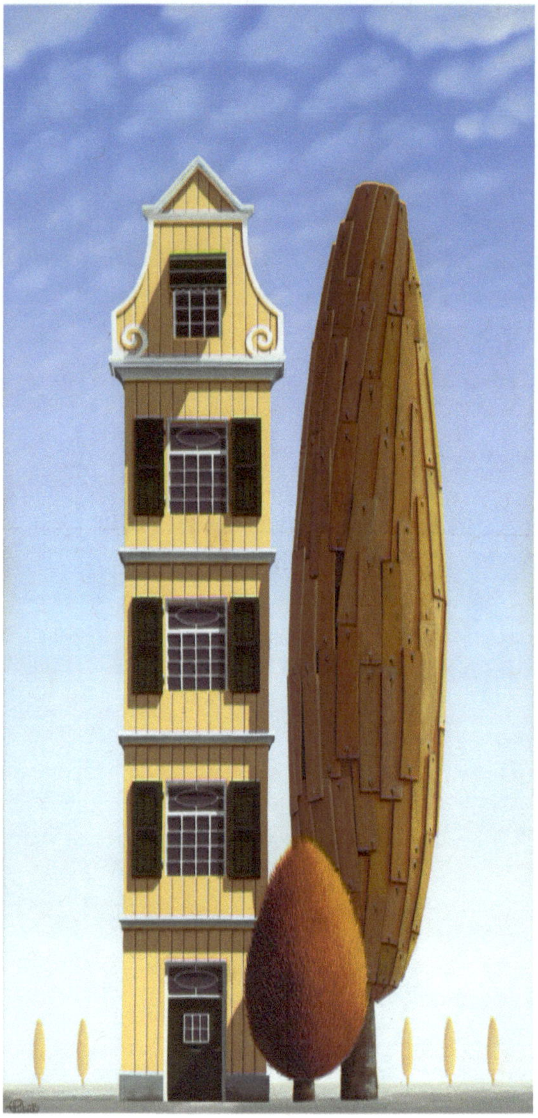
The Loyal One, 2014, oil on canvas, 51 x 101cm

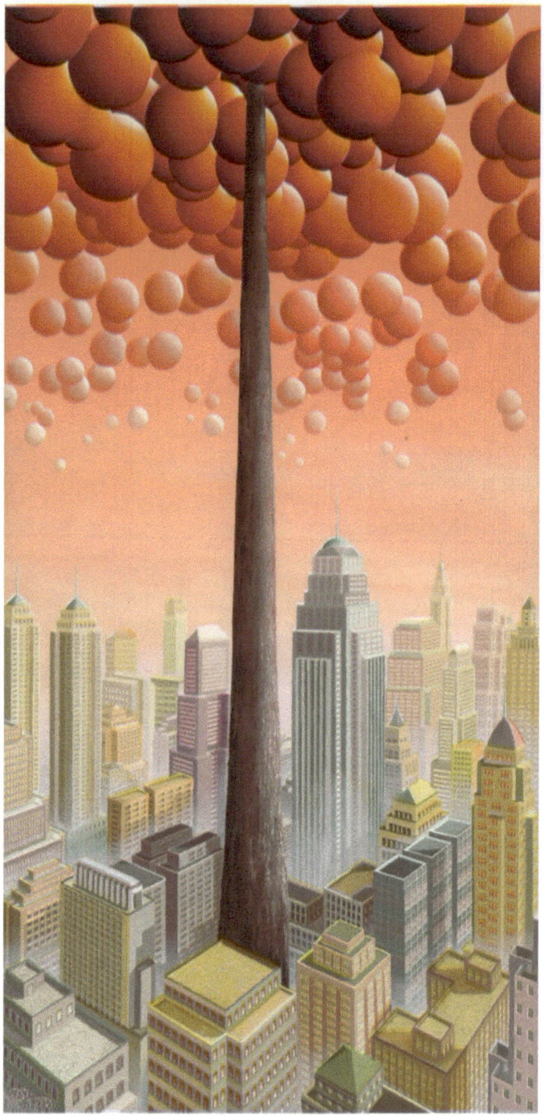
The Persistent One, 2014, oil on canvas, 51 x 101cm

The Cheeky One, 2013, oil on canvas, 101 x 51cm
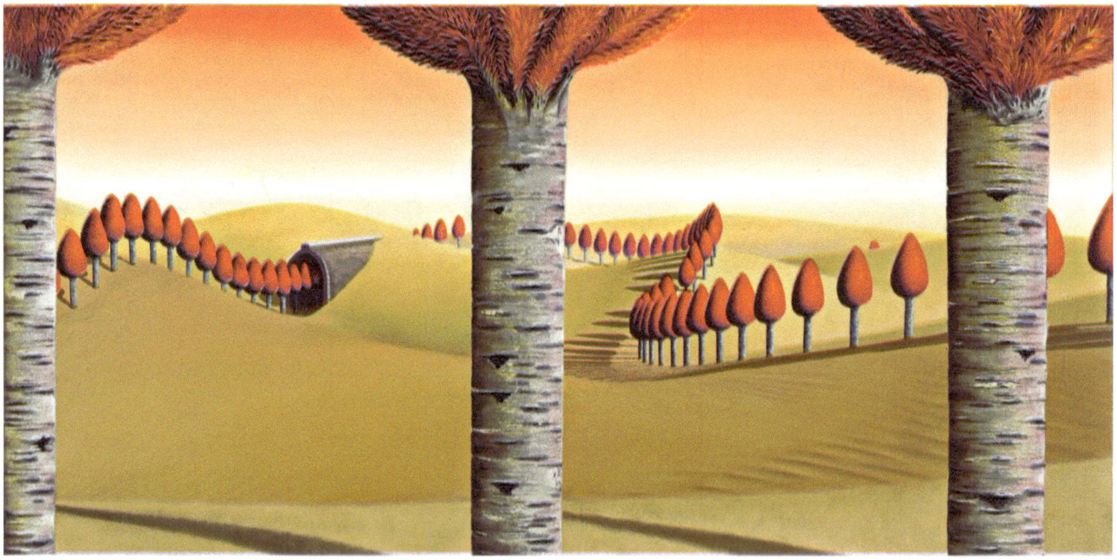

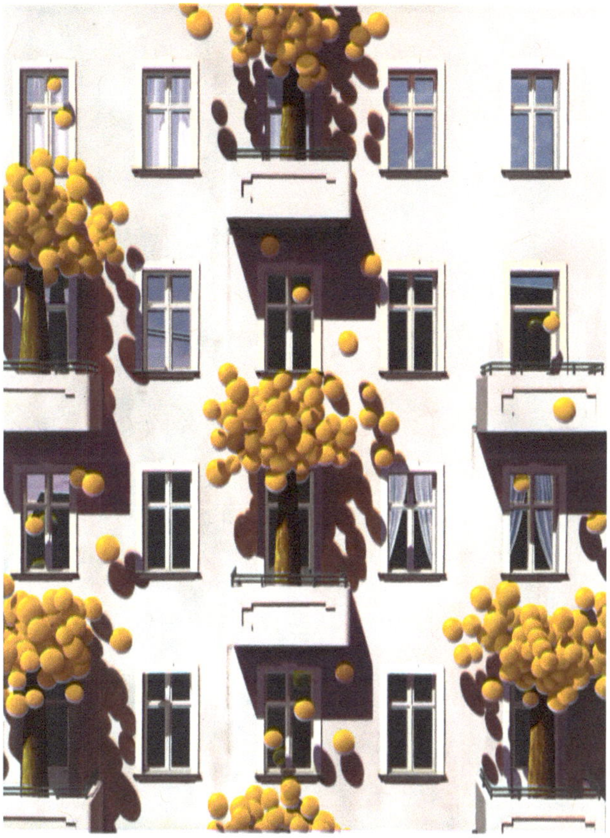

The Shy One, 2013, oil on canvas, 61 x 81cm

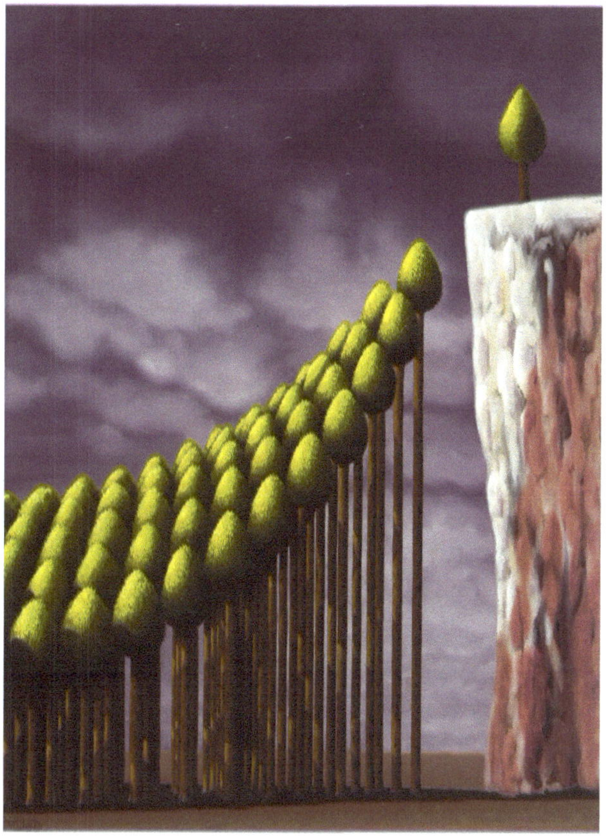

The Lucky One, 2013, oil on canvas, 61 x 81cm

The Free One, 2014, oil on canvas, 61 x 101cm

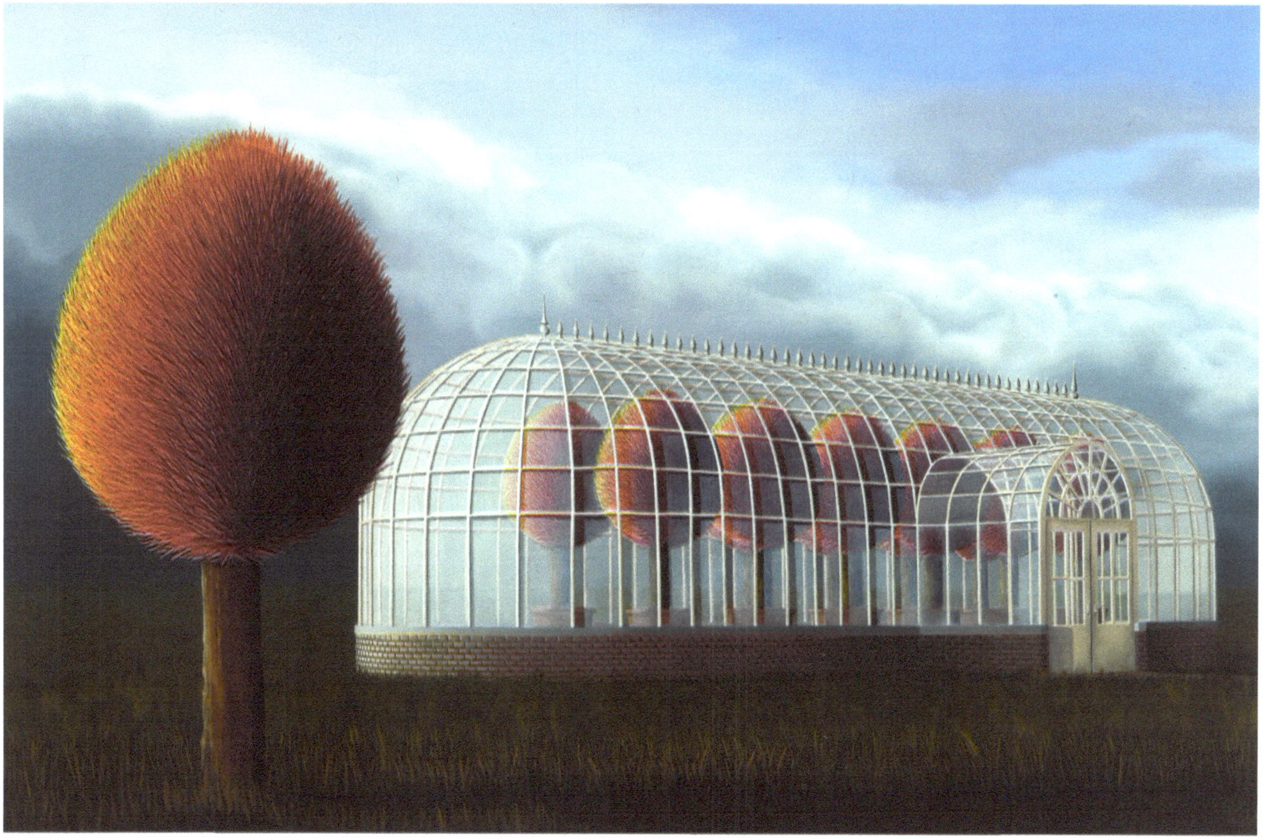

PEDRO BOAVENTURA

PAINTING - PORTUGAL

www.boaventura.com.pt

Pedro Boaventura is a Portuguese artist, filmmaker, curator, and entrepreneur. As the founder of Art Galaxie, he has dedicated himself to popularizing art and artists in a variety of forms. This is only the most recent of many incredible projects and initiatives that he has been involved in through the years, bringing a breath of fresh air to the world of contemporary arts through his passion, dedication and commitment to the artists who are brave and equally as passionate when it comes to creating emotional and forward-thinking work.

He first became interested in art while he was still a child, and by his teenage years, he had become obsessed with drawing. After graduating in Audiovisual Communication at the Antonio Arroio School of Arts, he went into business for himself and continued to hone his skills as an artist. Serving as a TV Director, Director of Photography, and Technical Supervisor, he has become known for his practical skills almost as much as he has become known for his creative abilities. Right now, he is directing a series of art documentary films under the Art Galaxie banner.

Pedro draws and paints in a variety of artistic styles. Always seeking to push his own boundaries in order to grow, he tries out new techniques, themes, and motifs regularly. Colour plays a primary role in his work, and each movement is integral to the message that he is trying to communicate. At times called an Expressionist, at other times an Impressionist or even a Cubist, Pedro operates in a school that is completely his own.

Right: Triple Bass, oil on canvas, 80 x 120cm

Untitled, oil on canvas, 60 x 90cm

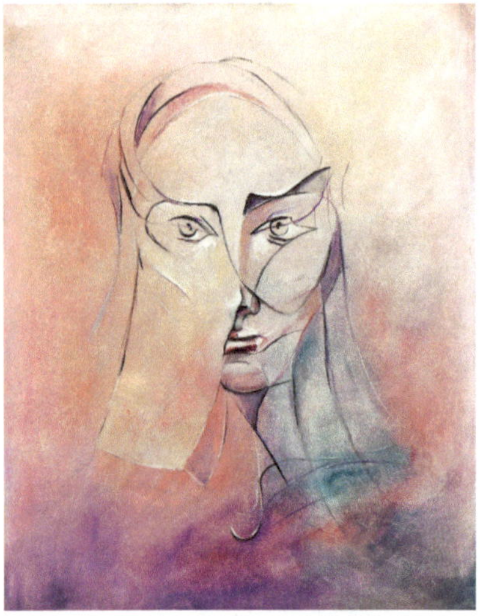

Musical Fusion, oil on canvas, 40 x 50cm

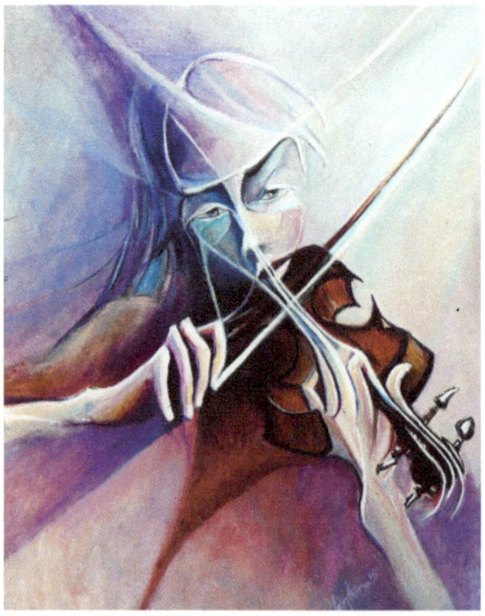

We Only Live Twice, oil on canvas, 60 x 90cm

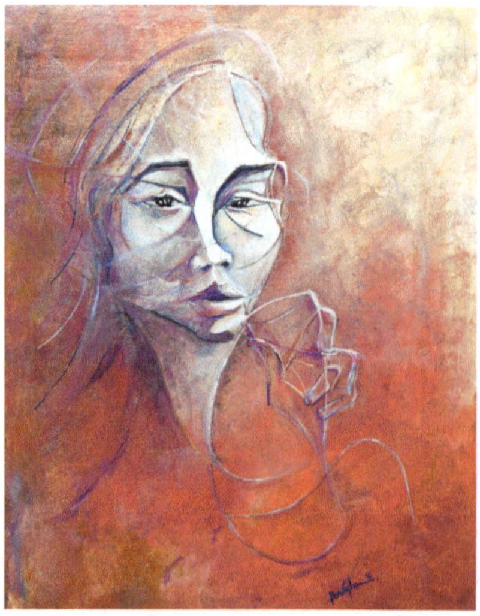

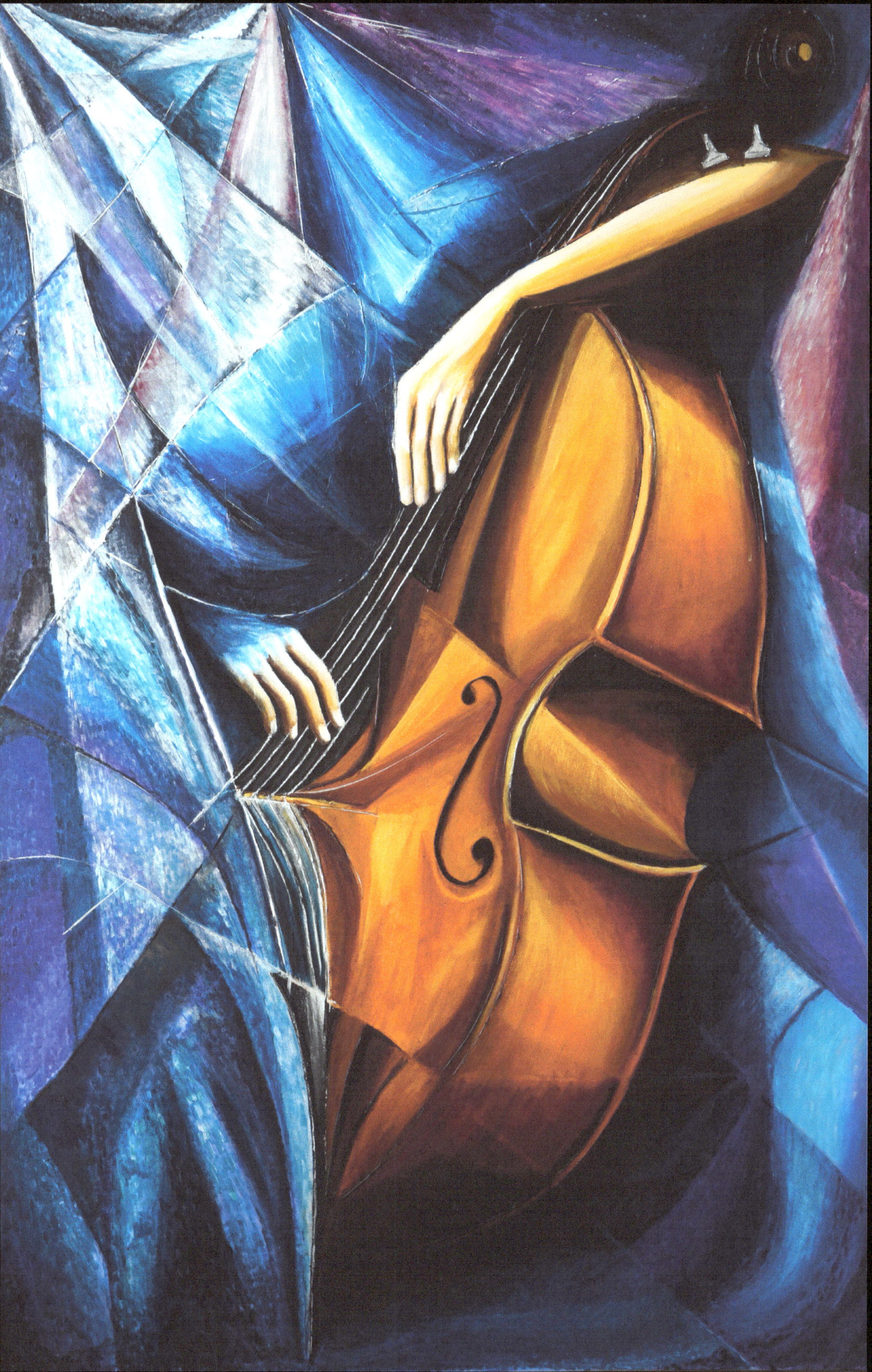

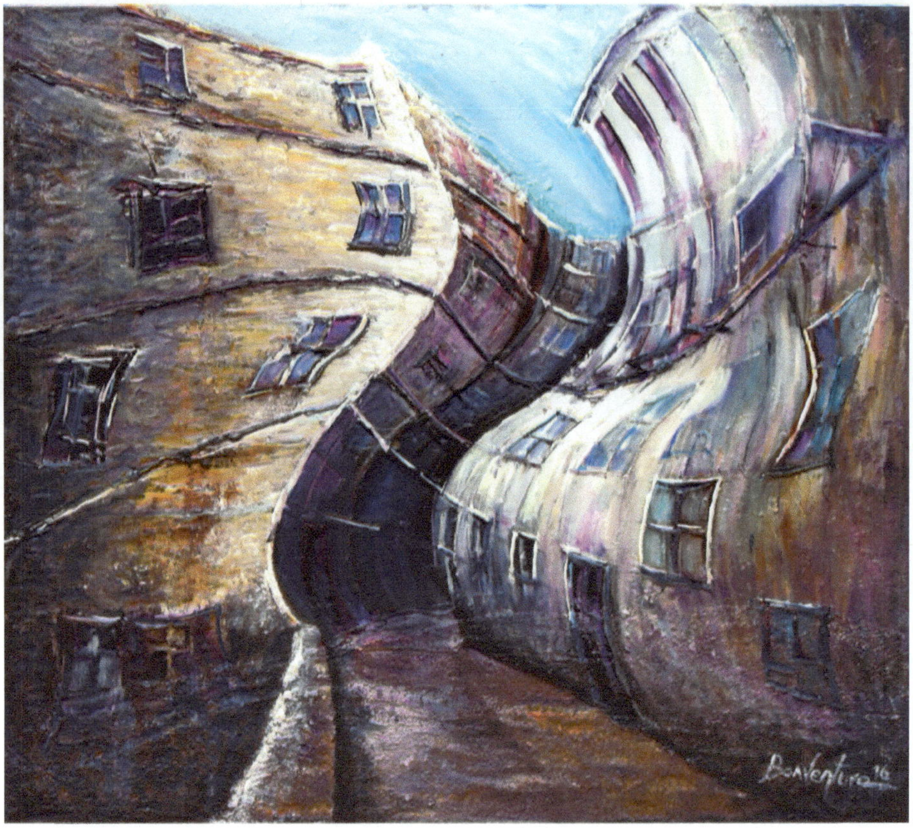

Around the Corner, oil on canvas, 40 x 60cm

A Moment in Time, oil on canvas, 40 x 60cm

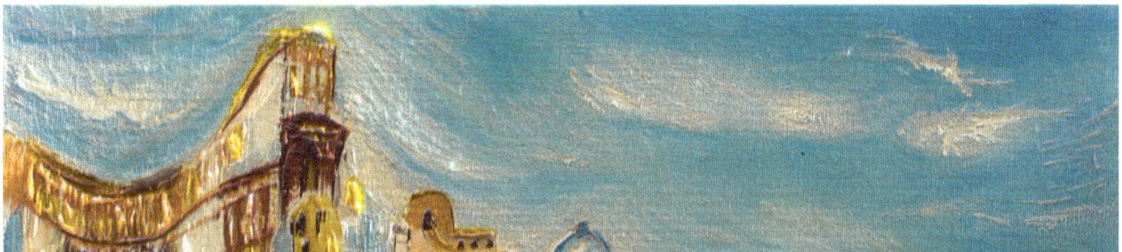

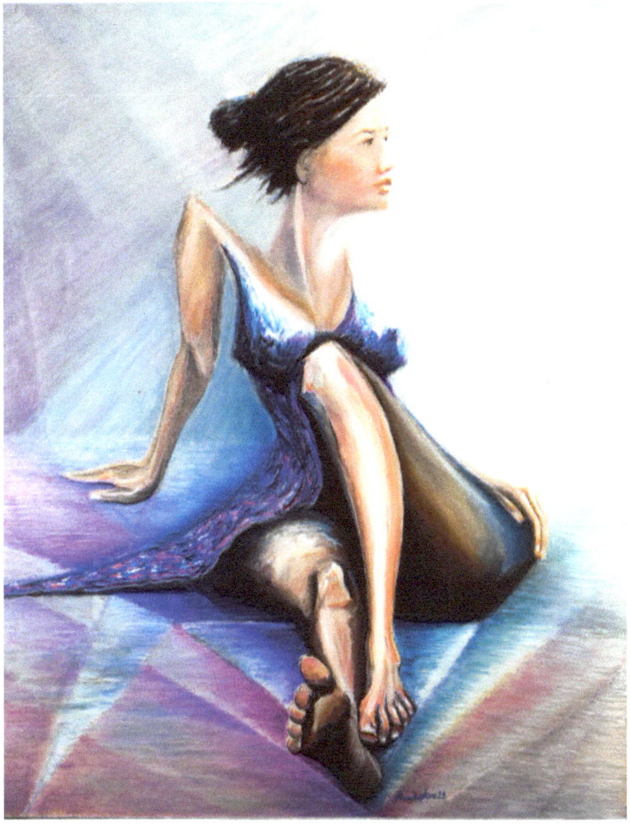
The Lady in Blue, oil on canvas, 80 x 100cm

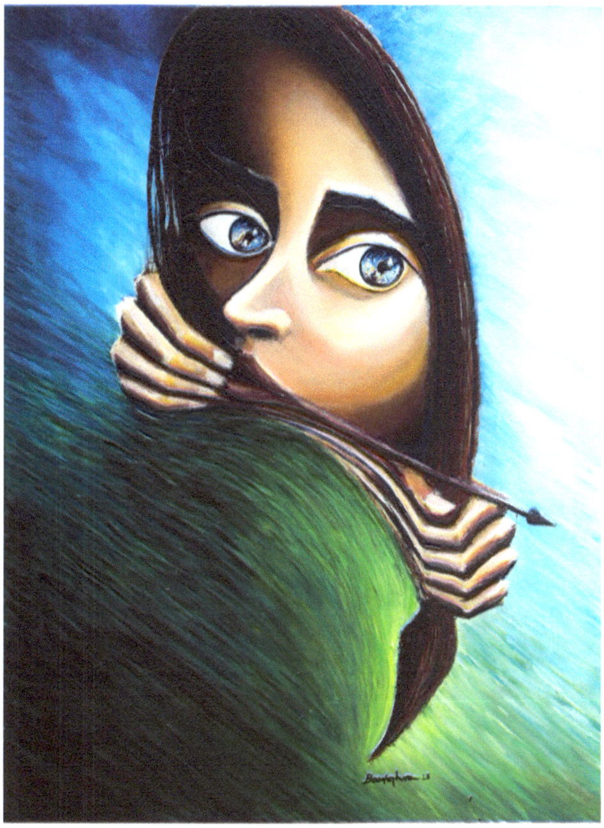
Cupid's Kiss, oil on canvas, 60 x 80cm

A Moment in Time II, oil on canvas, 60 x 90cm

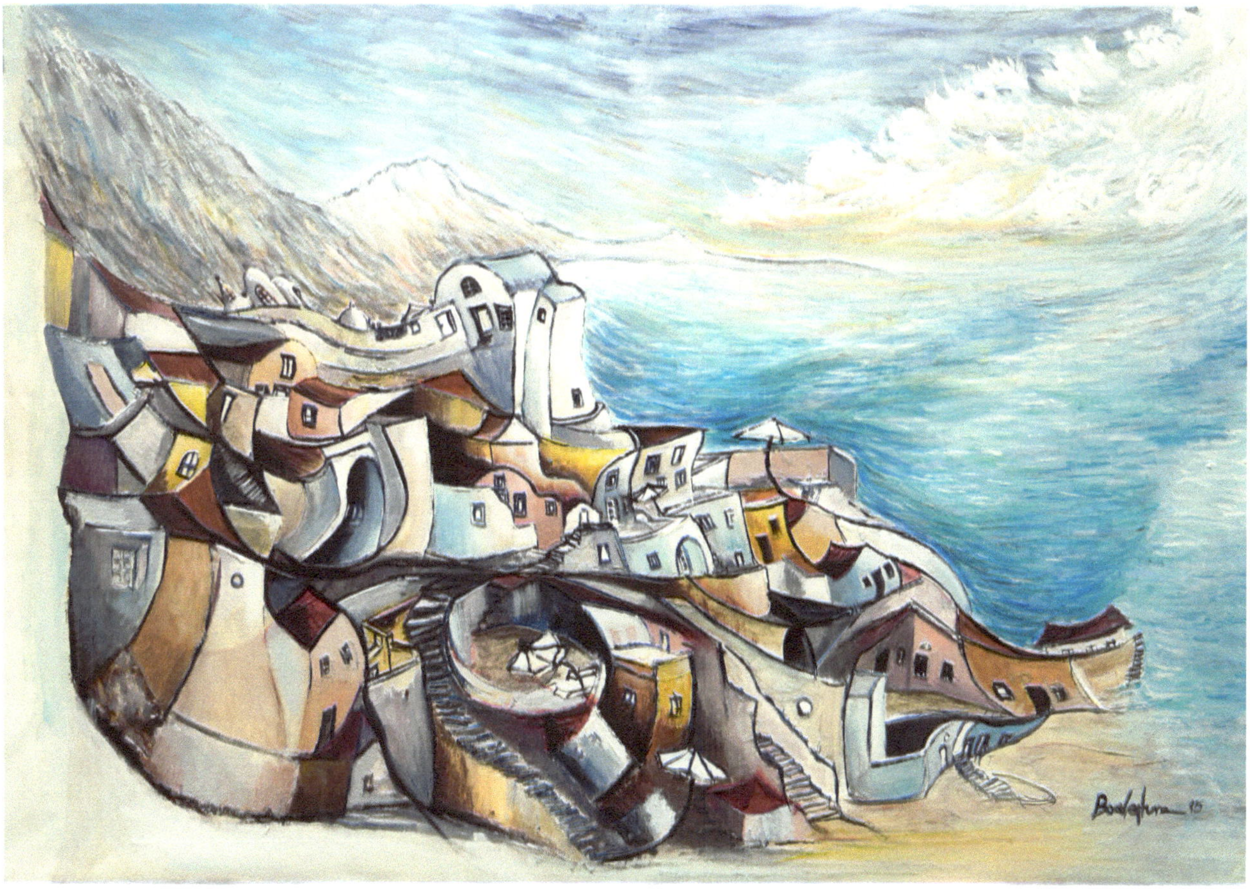

PETER MITCHEV

PAINTING - BULGARIA

www.petermitchev.com

Peter Mitchev is a Bulgarian master visual artist. Self-taught, he first got into painting when he was 15. From his twenties into his mid-thirties, he worked almost exclusively in Bulgaria due to travel restrictions that were put in place by the Communist administration.

In 1990, when these restrictions became looser, he started to exhibit his work internationally. His work was displayed at Gallerie L'angle aigu in Bruxelles, Belgium, and he has won a major following throughout Belgium, France, Germany, Switzerland, Luxembourg, and Denmark. Known for the emotional power of his work, he is a huge proponent of embracing ones feelings.

Peter's work can in one moment express joy and in the next express inconsolable sadness. Despite this volatility, there is an undeniable stillness in his work, a stillness in which history is unified.

He is sending a clear message of love and beauty through his painting, and it is his chief mission to inspire mankind toward more positive vibrations and energy levels.

Since 2005, Peter has lived and worked in his hometown, Pleven, Bulgaria, and for five years prior to that, he lived and worked in Tampa, Florida.

Right: Untitled, oil on canvas

Dreams, oil on canvas, 65.5 x 54.5cm

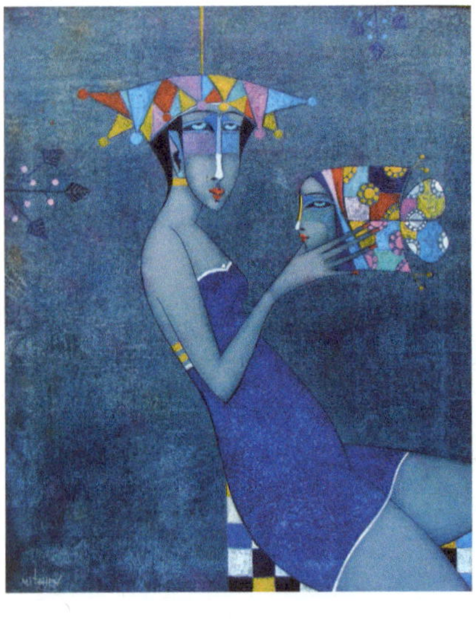

Reverie, oil on canvas, 60 x 50cm

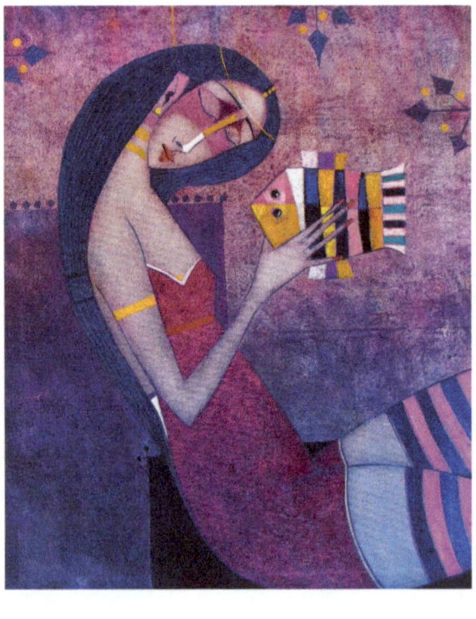

Dream with White Dove, oil on canvas, 60 x 50cm

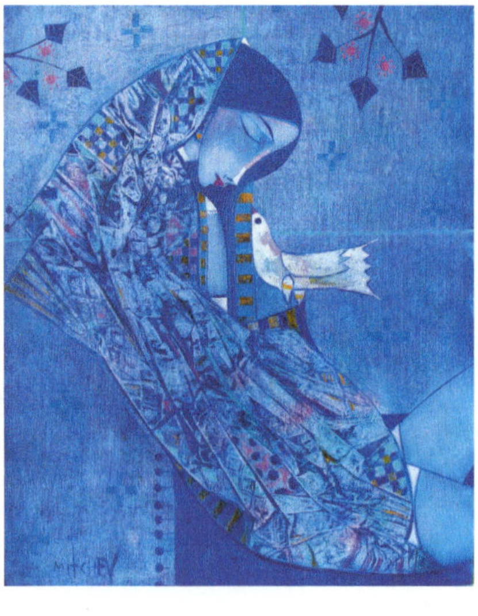

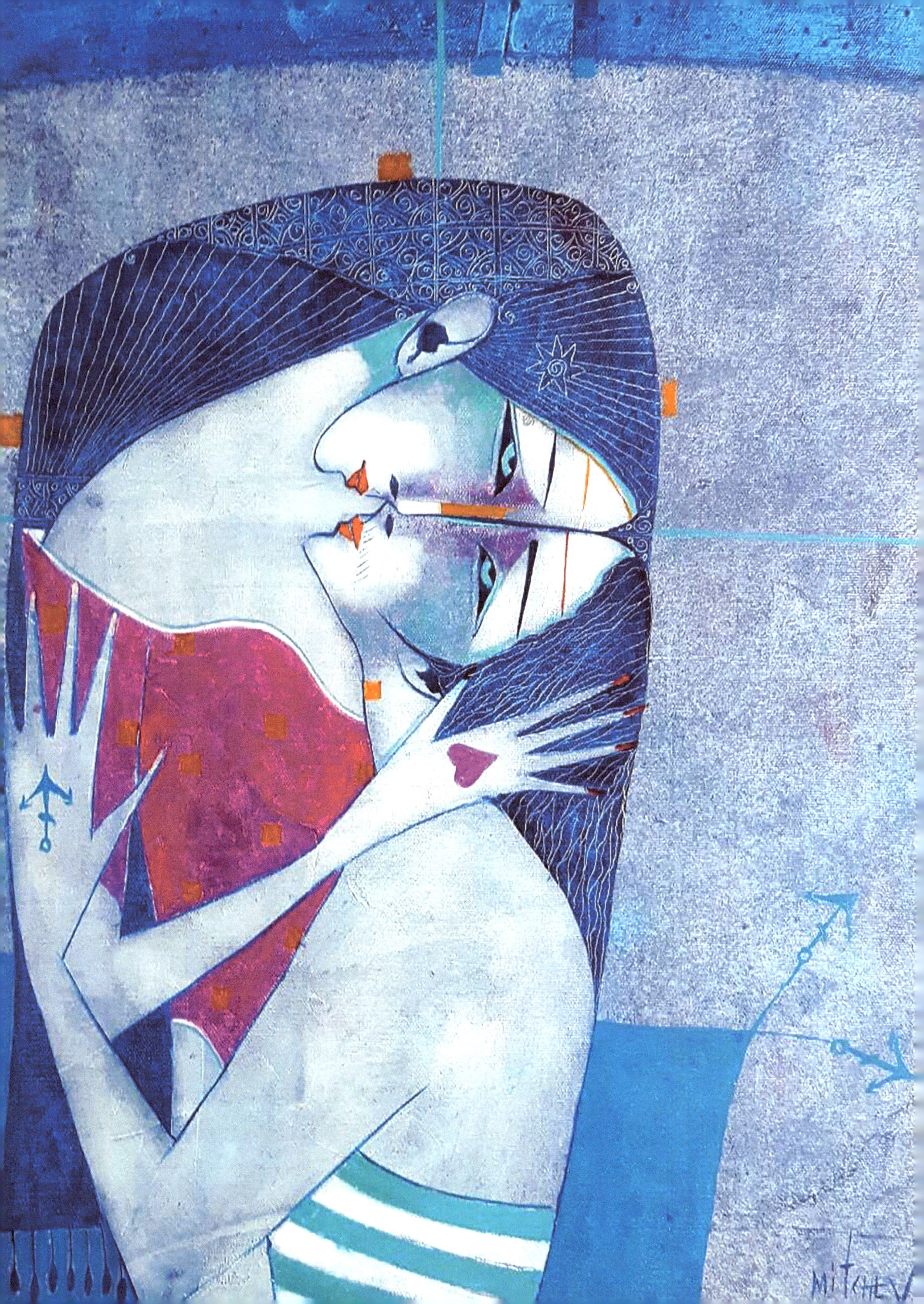
MITCHEV

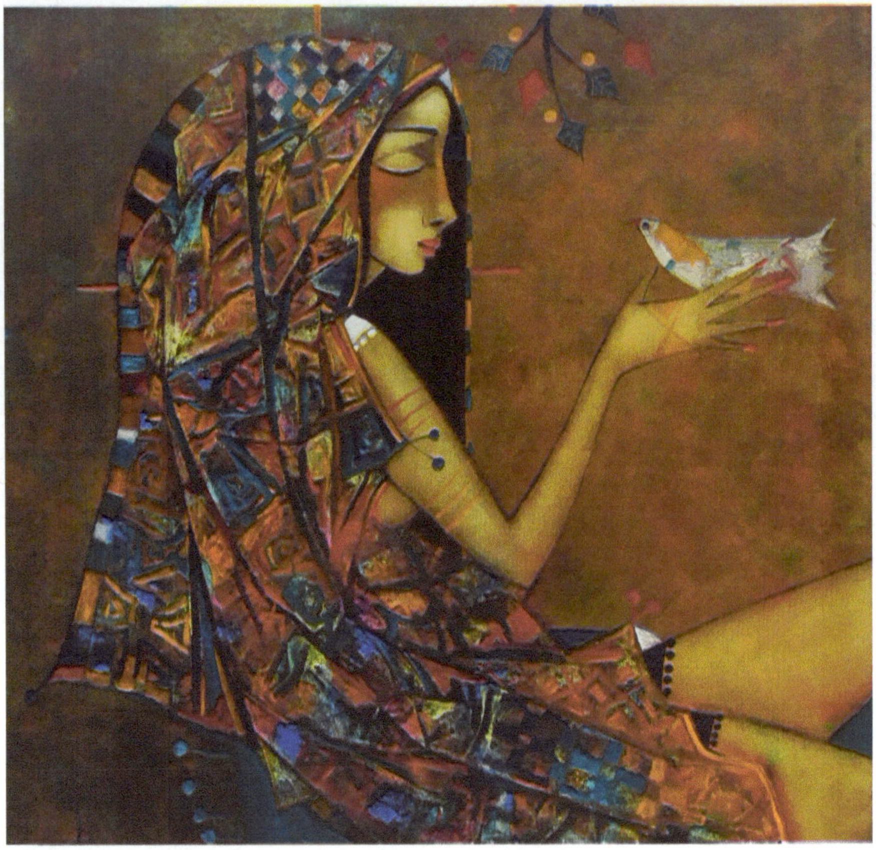

Reviere, oil on canvas, 60 x 60cm

Dreamszzzz, oil on canvas, 40 x 40cm

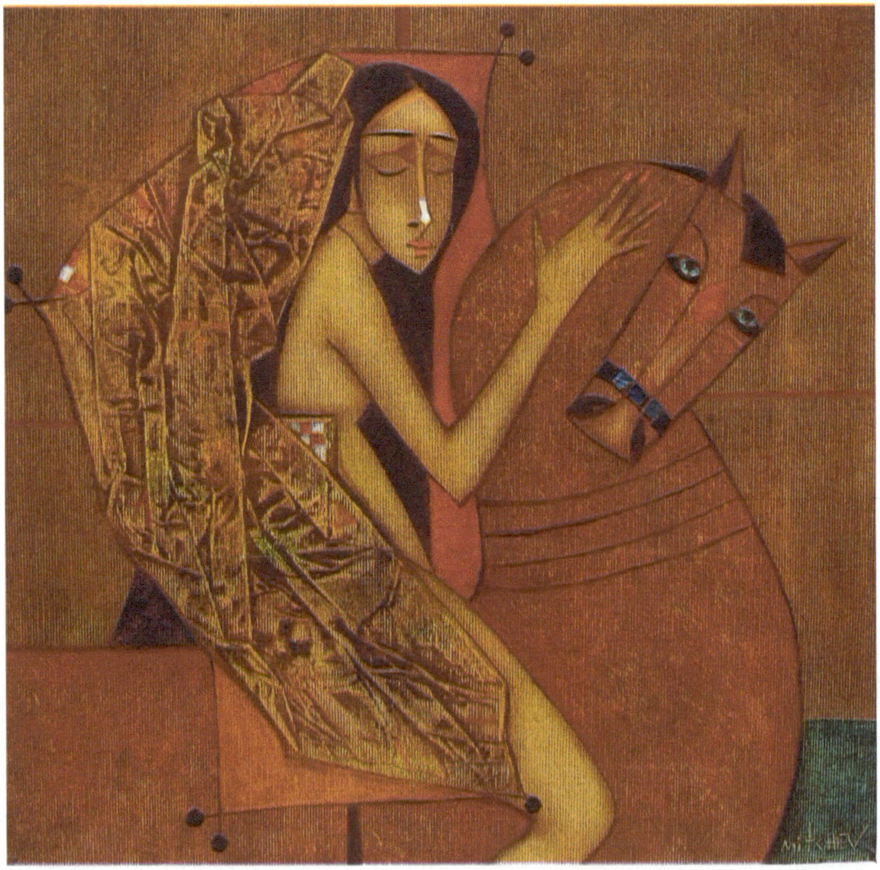

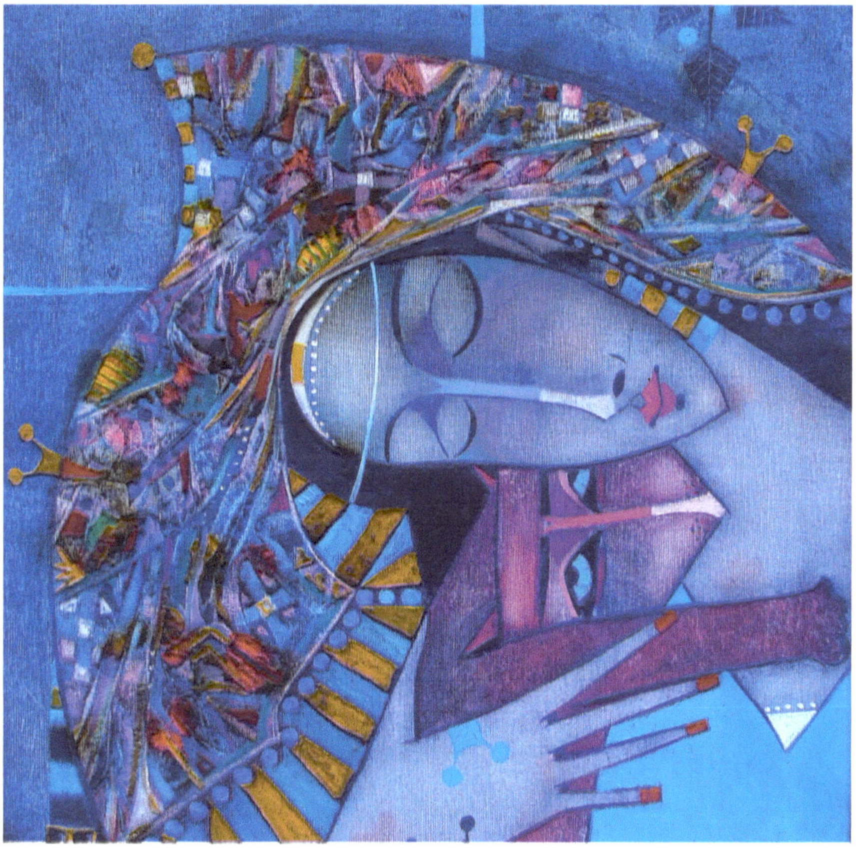
Dream with Cat, oil on canvas, 40 x 40cm

Butterfly, oil on canvas, 60 x 40cm
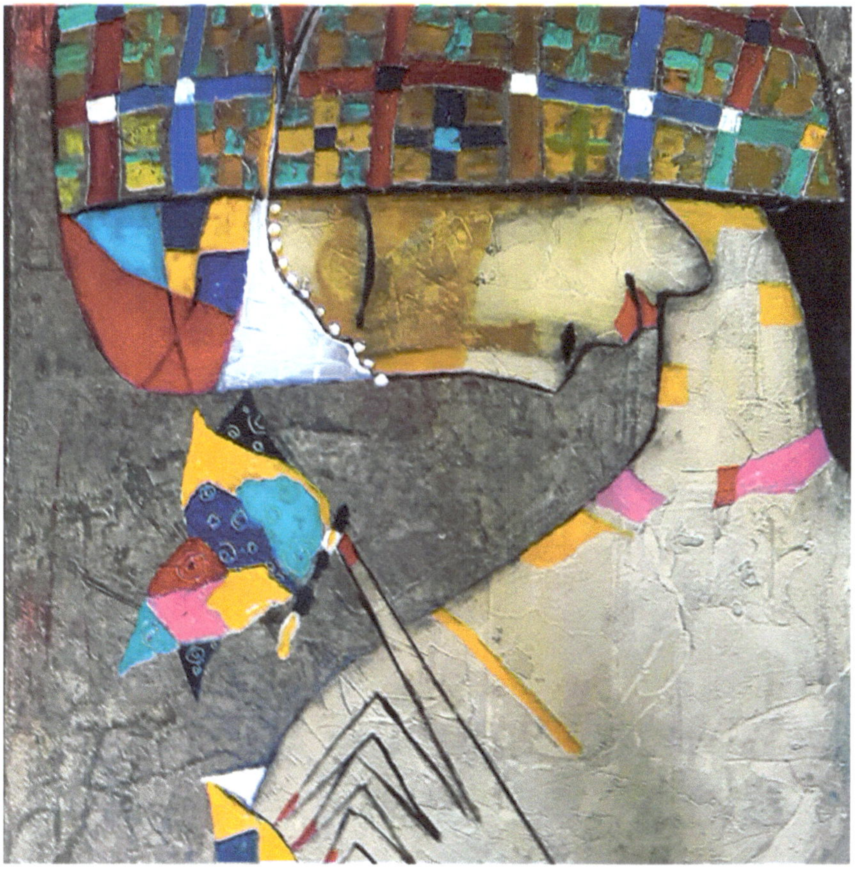

R. M. KAVANAGH

PAINTING - IRELAND

www.rmkavanagh.ie

RM Kavanagh was born in 1977. He lives and works in Wicklow, Ireland. He has exhibited continuously from 1996-2016 in Ireland, Los Angeles, New York, London and Edinburgh. In 2005 he was commissioned by The Irish Drinks Distillery - Jameson Whiskey to create four unique paintings for their private collection.

Kavanagh has continued to work on a large number of private commissions throughout his career. In 2015 he accepted the honour of Invited Artist to the Royal Hibernian Academy Annual Show. Most recently, a piece of Kavanagh's resides in the Imago Mundi Collection and has also been chosen as a finalist in ARC Salon 2017 competition.

RM Kavanagh's work captures that instant moment of when tragedy and beauty collide, which leaves him to contemplate the grey areas of life. His work explores the realms of the birth of an idea, it's existence and it's demise. Does it morph and evolve into something more manipulative, complex and beautiful in order to deceive?

We strive for harmony in everyday routine but sometimes the mundane cycle of life drags us down into a subtle emotional abyss. With Kavanagh's work we see the familiar and strange, the disturbing yet illuminating manifestations of an inquisitive and provocative mind. As an artist he delves into the areas of life which are uncomfortable to ponder and creates those ideas onto canvas leaving an everlasting stain on the viewers mind.

Right: Merda D'Artista, 2015, oil on linen, 76 x 122cm

A Gentle Breeze, 2015, oil on linen, 66 x 86cm

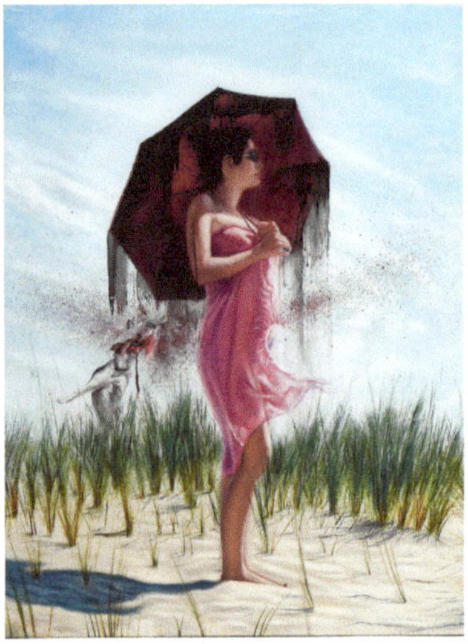

The Ark's On Fire, 2015, oil on linen, 92 x 87cm

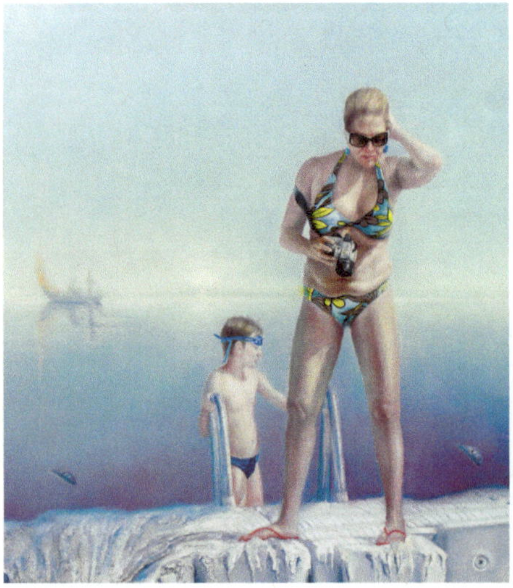

Queen O The South, 2015, oil on linen, 92 x 87cm

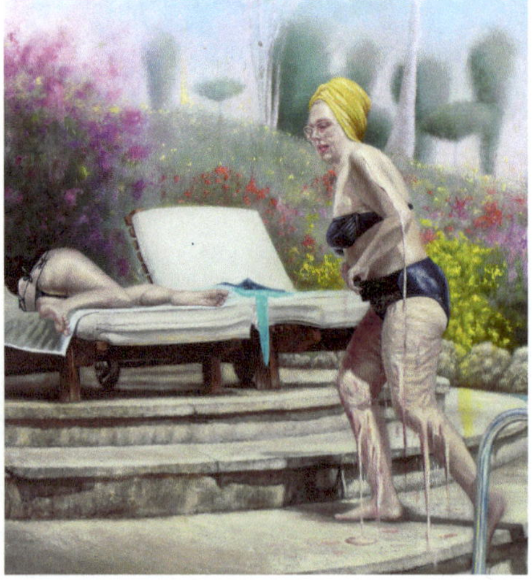

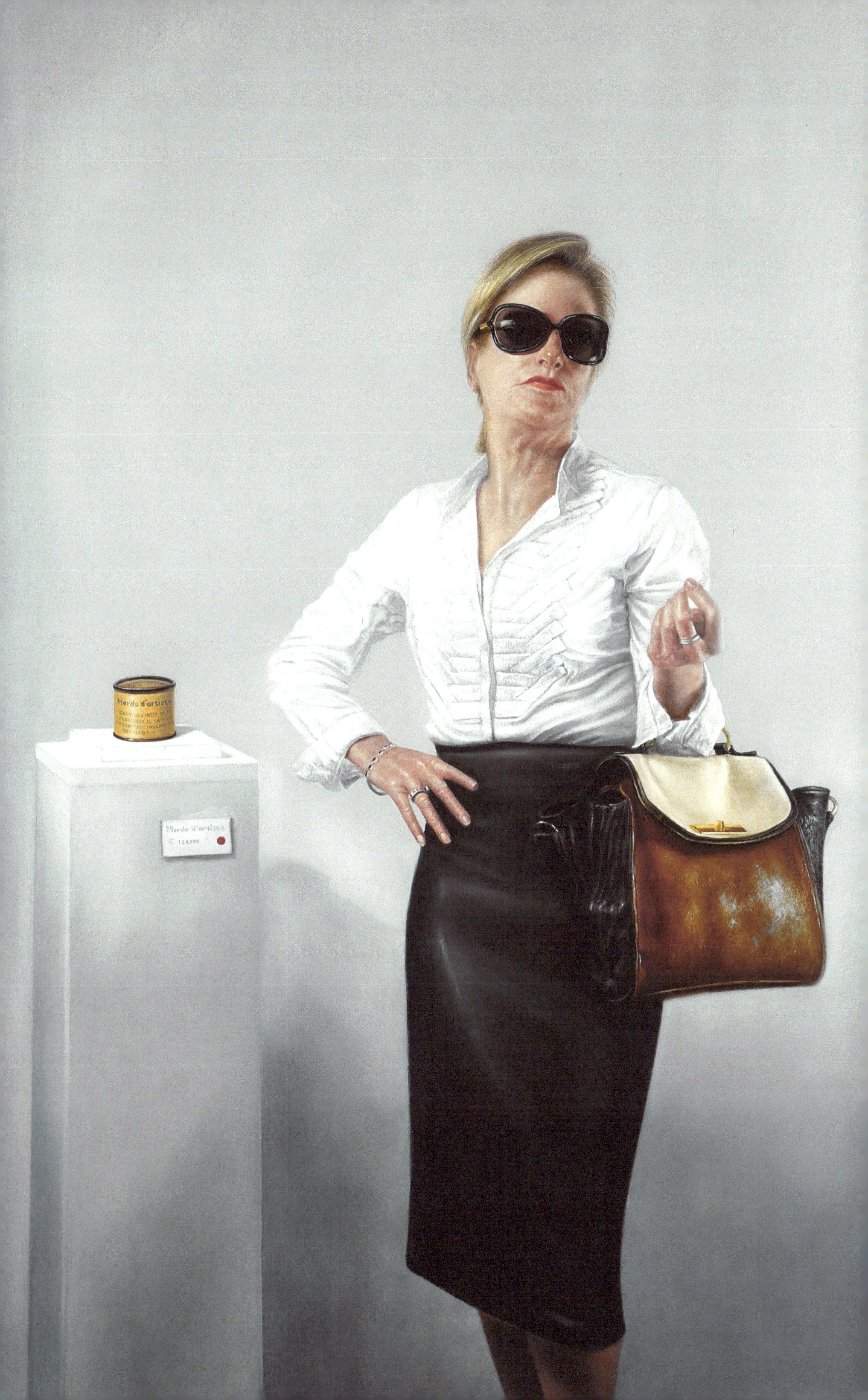
Merda d'artista
Merda d'artista
€ 124,000

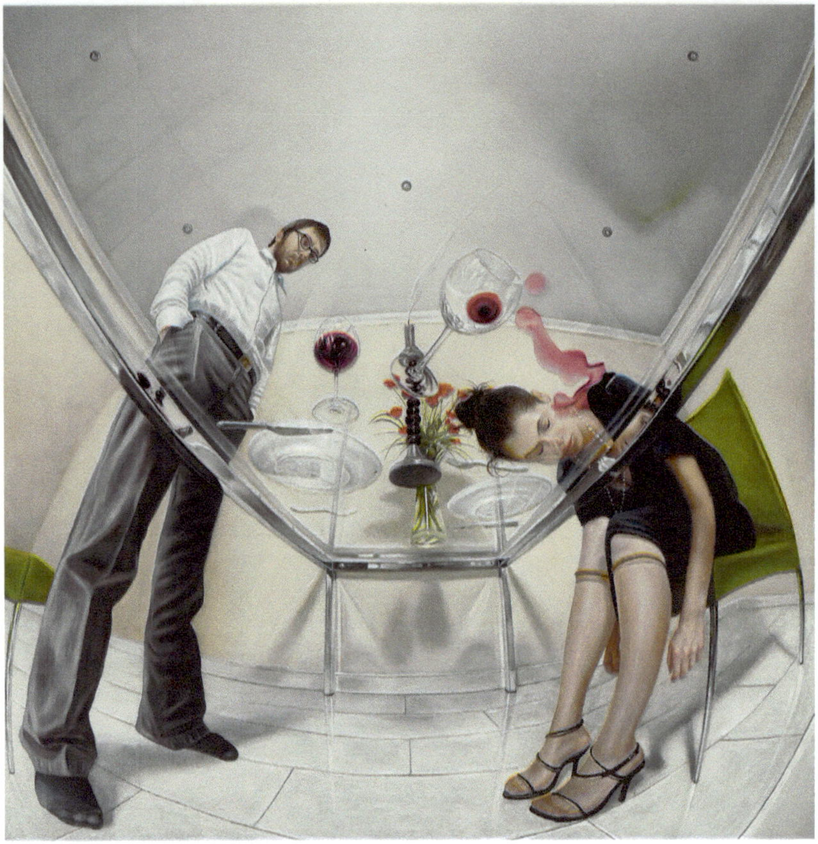

Comfortably Numb, 2015, oil on linen, 76 x 76cm

Groundhog Day, 2015, oil on linen, 64 x 64cm

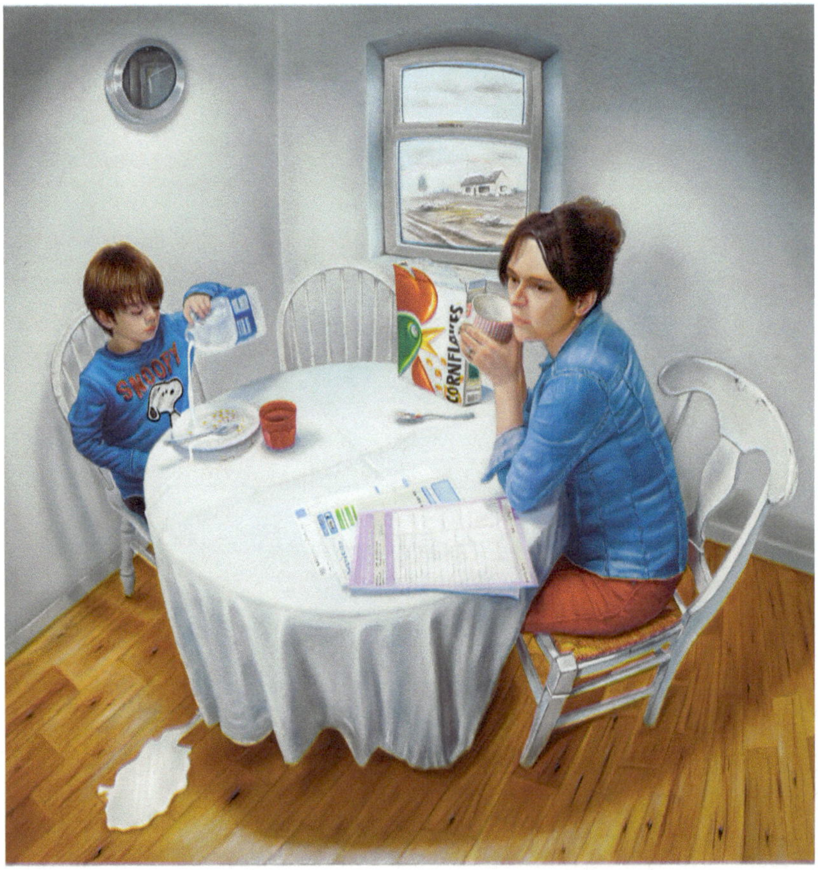

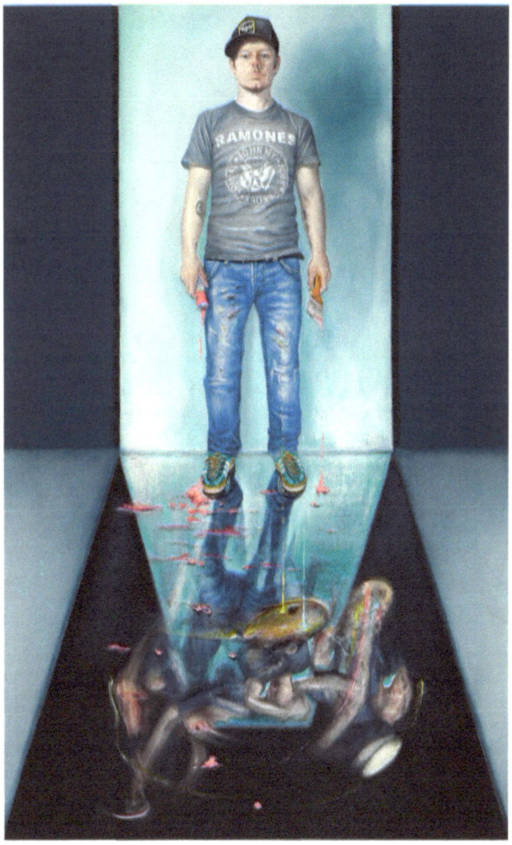

Where From Here, 2015, oil on linen, 76 x 122cm

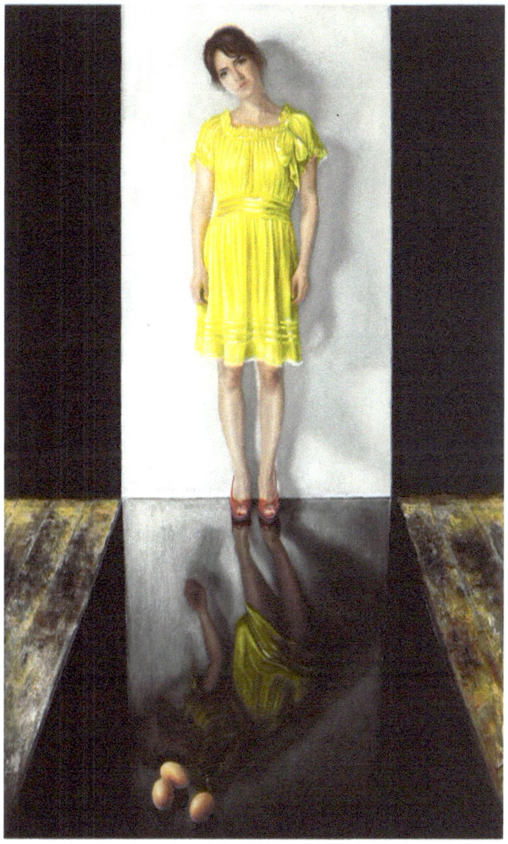

Sombre In Yellow, 2015, oil on linen, 76 x 122cm

Lilac Lust And Silky Milk, 2015, oil on linen, 76 x 76cm

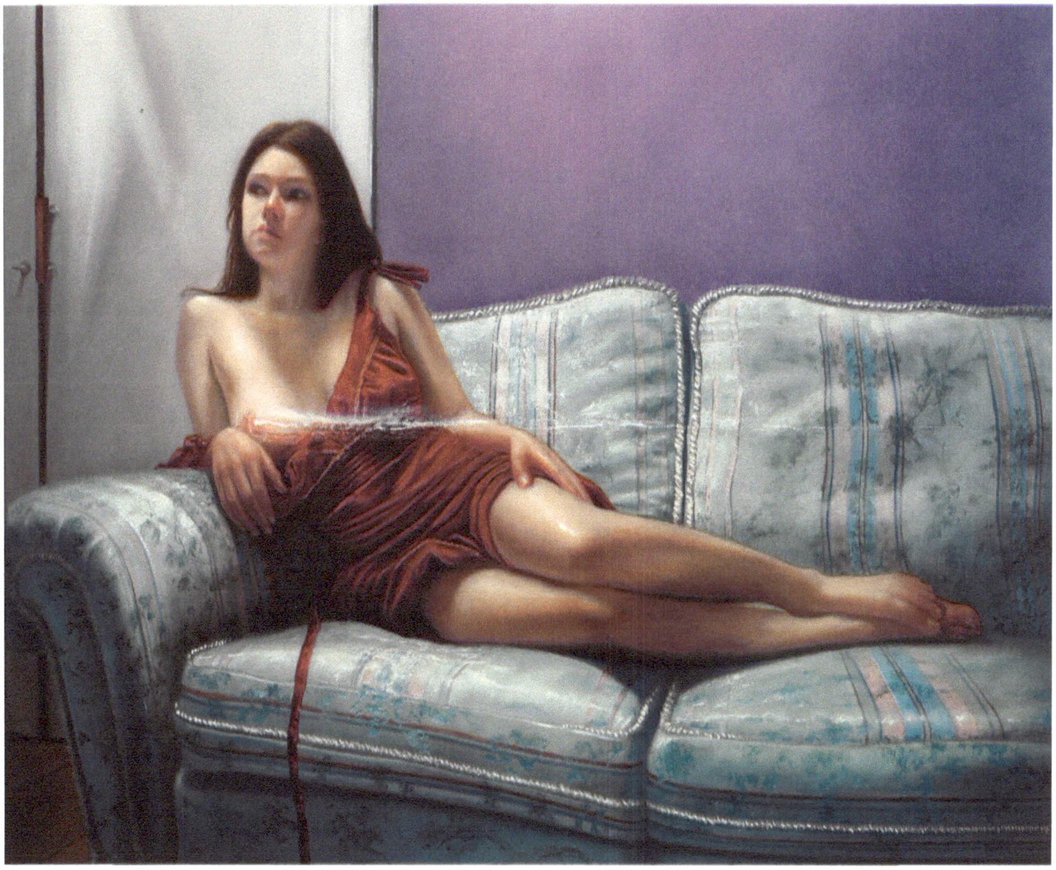

SALMAN AL MALIK

PAINTING - QATAR

www.salmanalmalik.com

Salman Al Malik is an artist who is driven to achieve originality. Tired of the same old techniques and styles, he has devoted his life to creating paintings that are undeniably his own. He draws influence from the world around him, observing closely politicians, leaders, artists, and regular people in order to illustrate their personalities and their roles in the world as accurately as he can.

Although his work could be called abstract, it is also not without its firm messages. In addition to painting, he also works as a photographer, caricaturist, printing director, designer, and inventor. He thinks of himself as a dreamer before all else, someone who sees images in his mind and then tries to share those images with others. Fiercely opposed to what he considers the "plastic arts," he wants his art to ooze spirit, experience, and discovery.

Salman is dedicated immensely to his work, spending long hours on getting a single piece just right. He is always willing to fight on behalf of truth and on behalf of his right to express truth as he perceives it.

His work is at times solitary, his mission at times lonely, but he is not someone who is easily discouraged. Rather, he is an artist who is invigorated by hardship and goaded on by difficulty. He is an artist who finds in failure new ways to succeed, and that is why he is such an exciting figure to behold.

Right: Untitled, acrylic on canvas

Untitled, acrylic on canvas, 160cm x 100cm

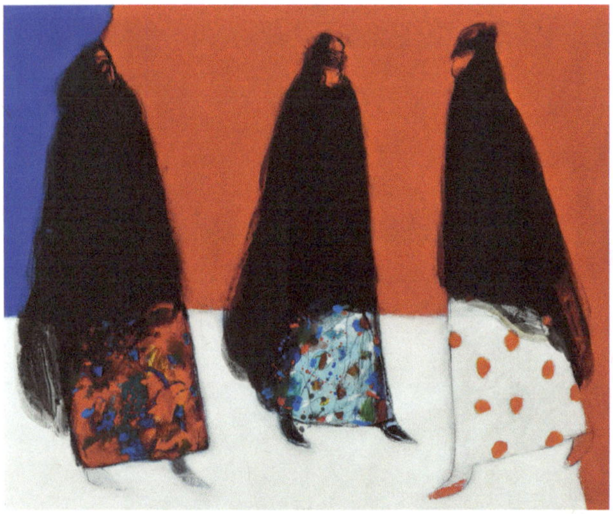

Untitled, acrylic on canvas

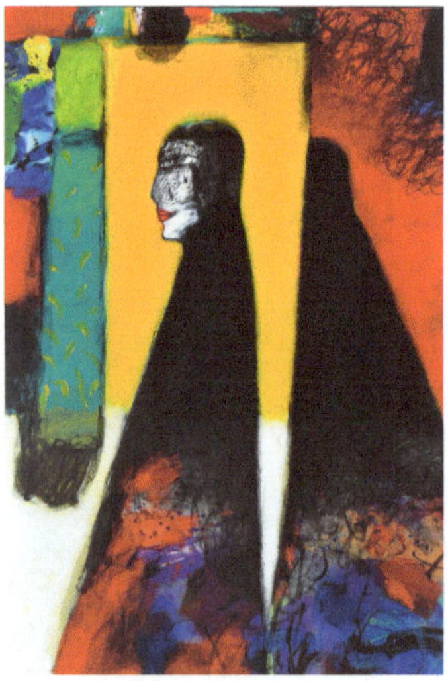

Untitled, acrylic on canvas

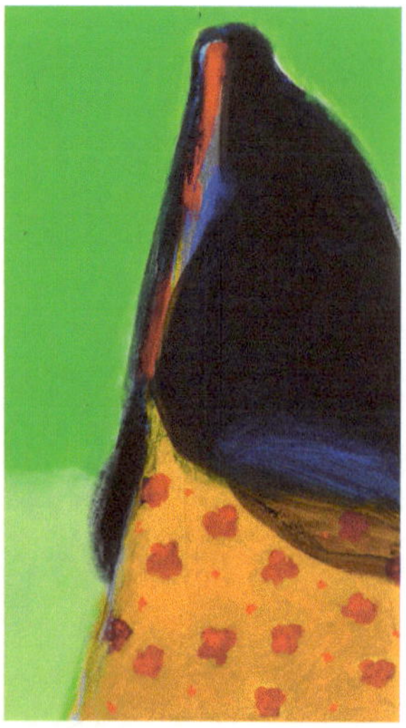

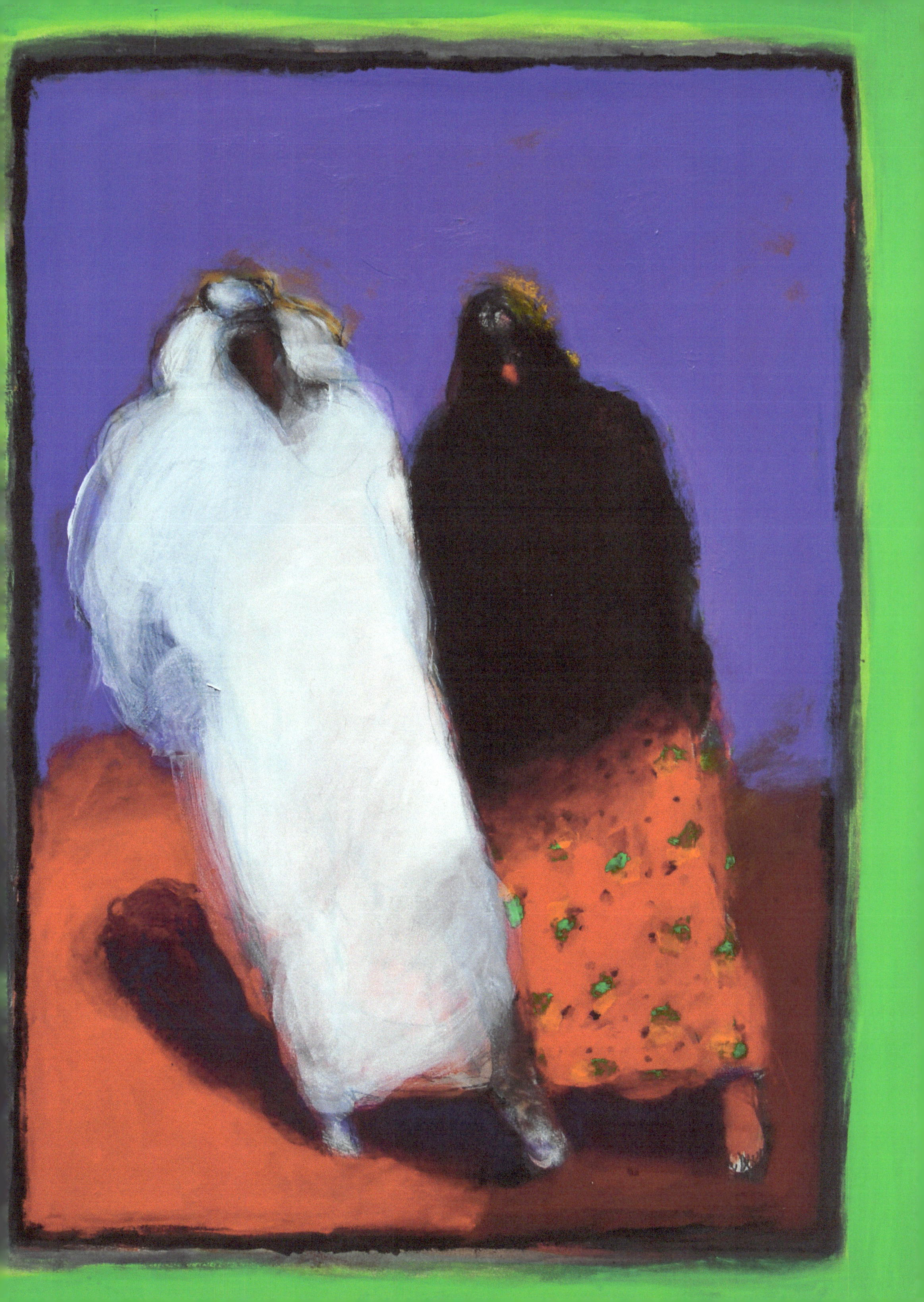

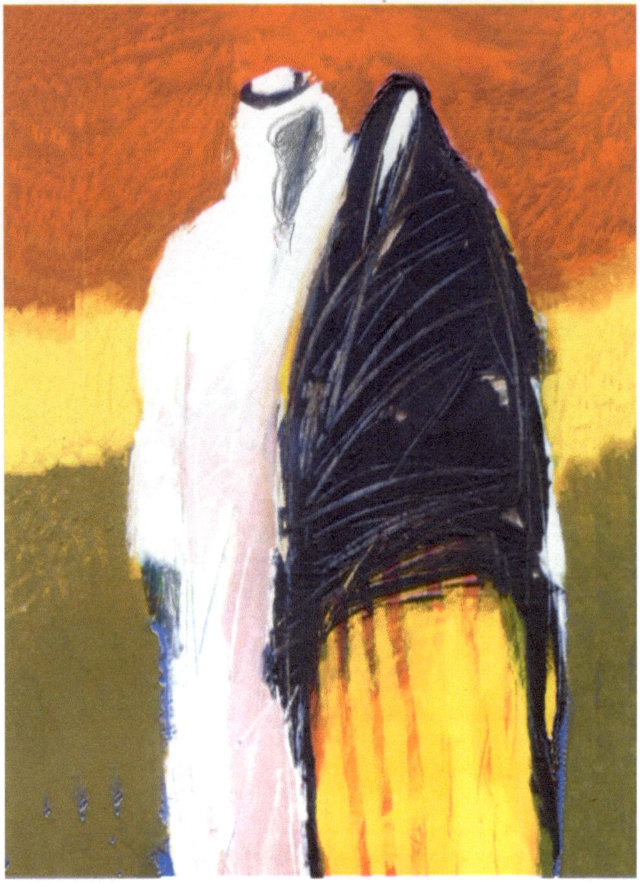

Untitled, acrylic on canvas

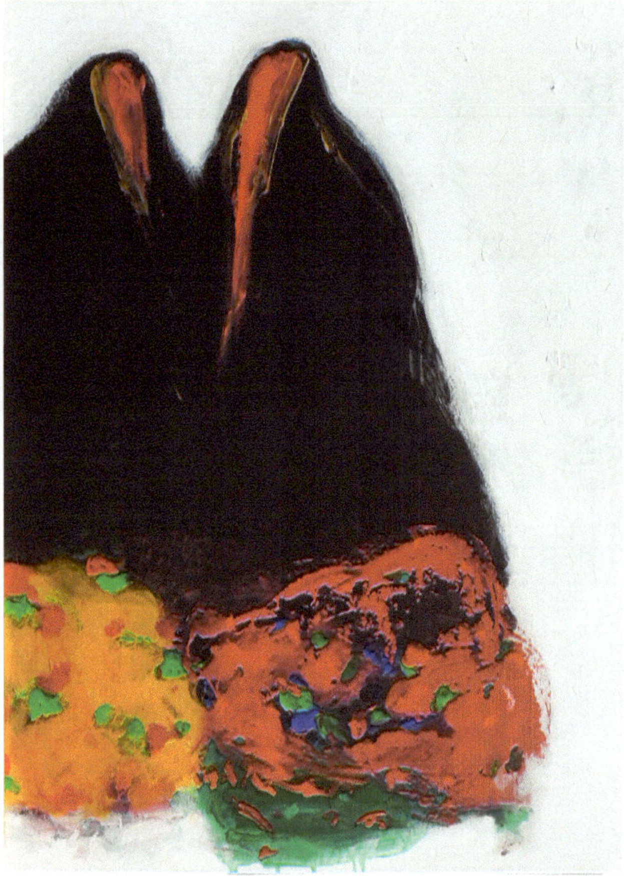

Untitled, acrylic on canvas

Untitled, acrylic on canvas

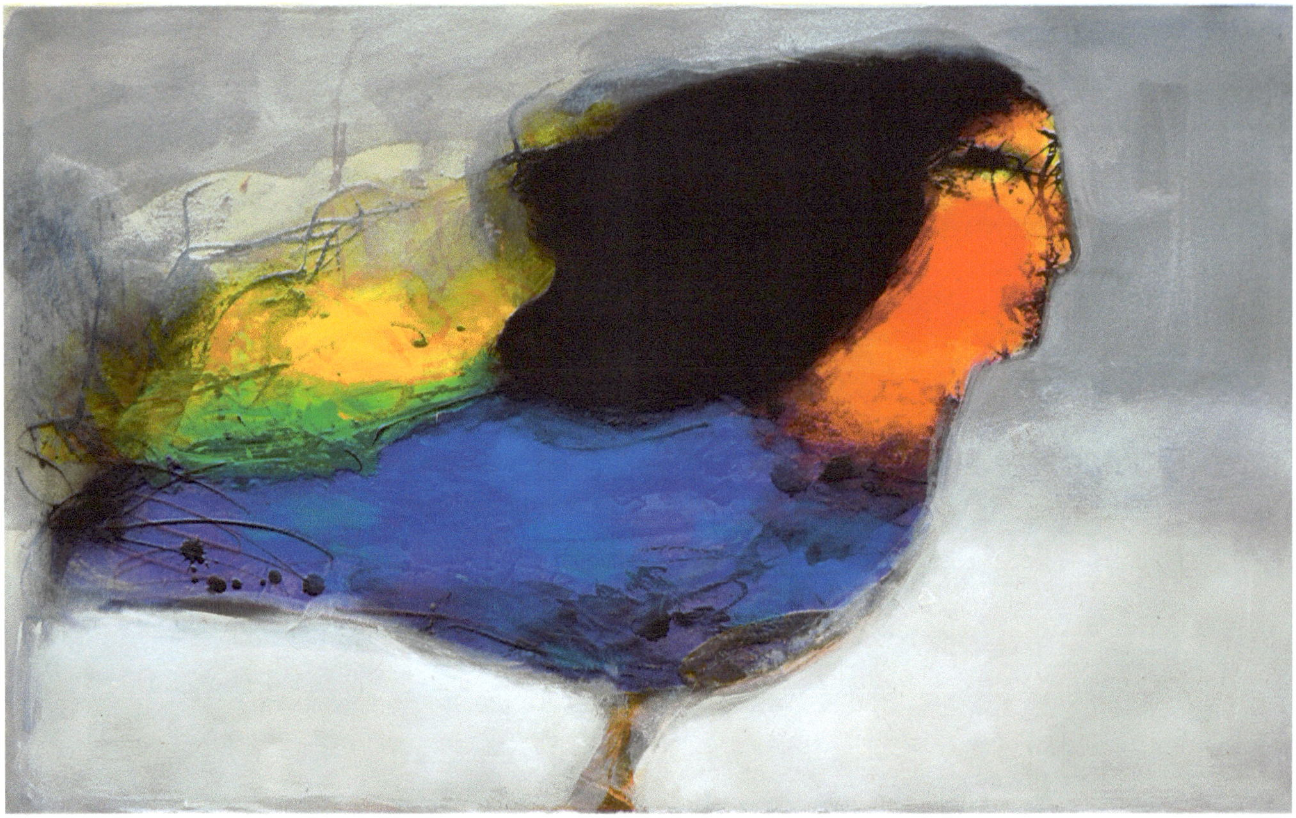

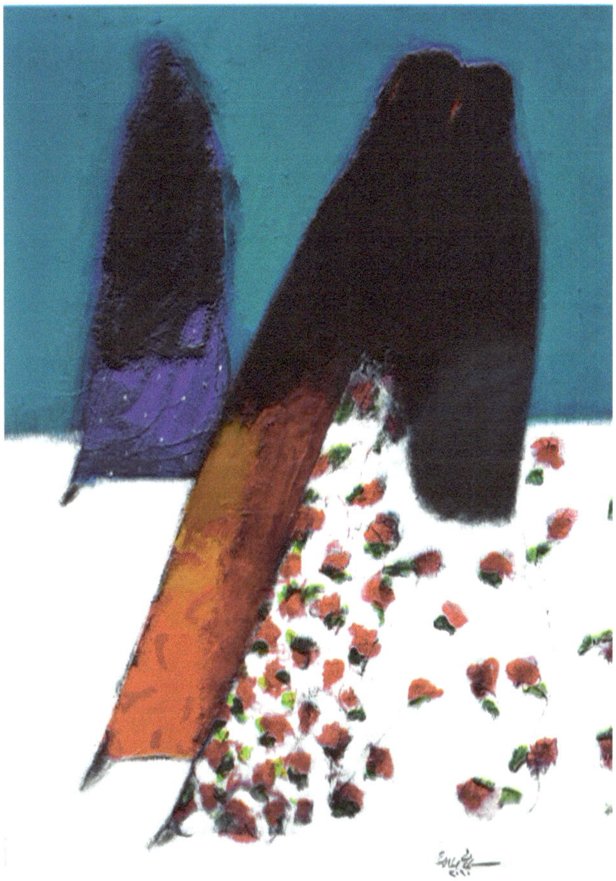

Untitled, acrylic on canvas, 100 x 80cm

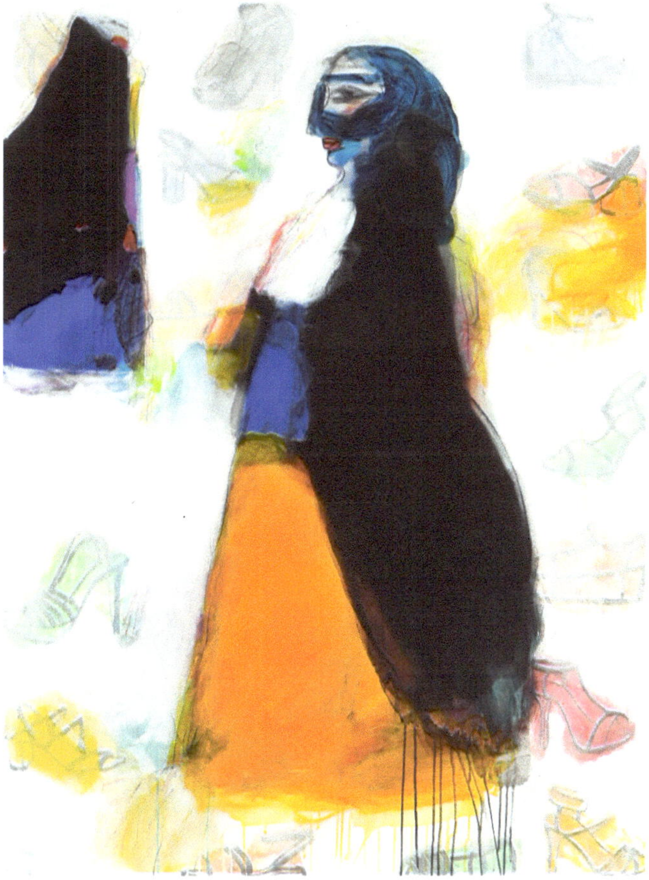

Untitled, acrylic on canvas

Untitled, acrylic on canvas

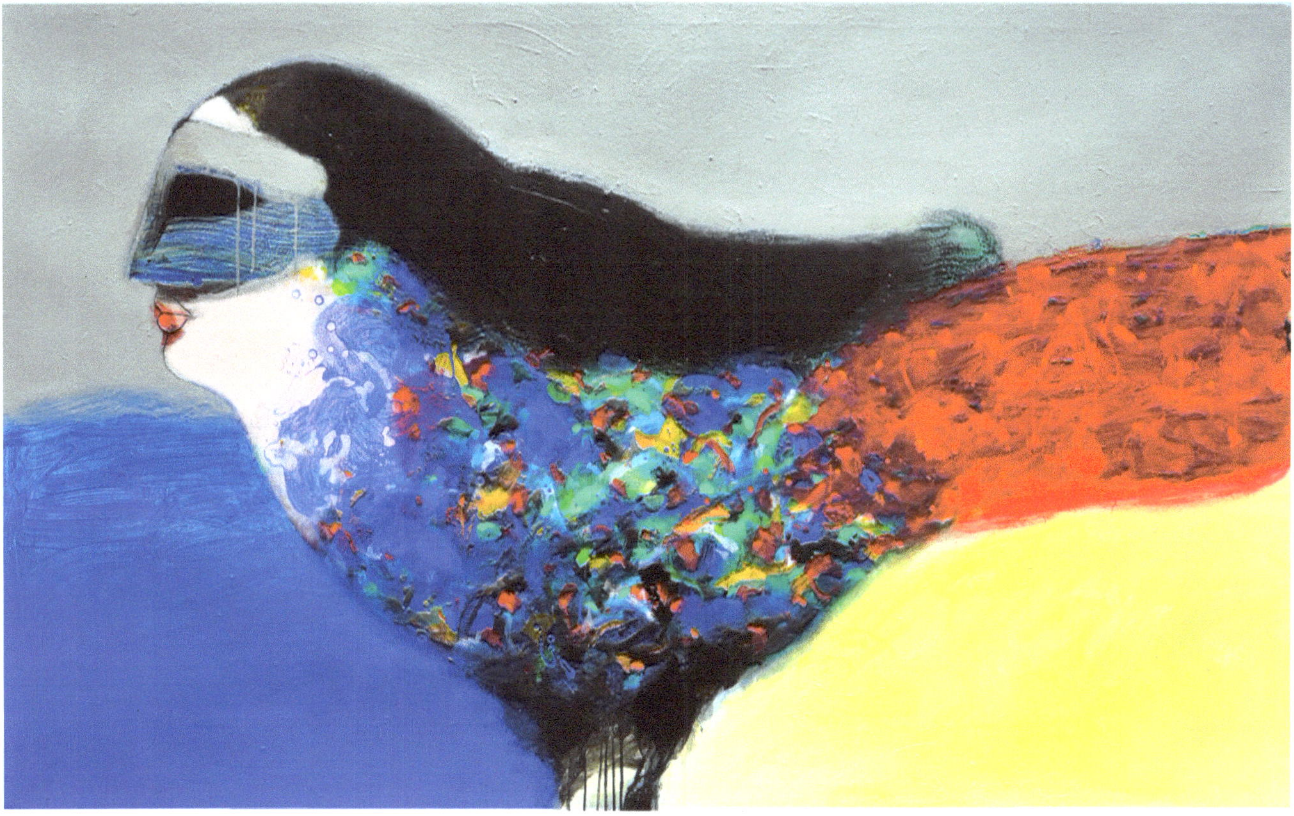

TOMASZ ALEN KOPERA

PAINTING - POLAND

www.alenkopera.com

Tomasz Alen Kopera is a Polish artist. Recognized as a budding talent from a very young age, he spent his adolescence discovering the breadth of his abilities. Since earning his degree in Construction Engineering at the University of Technology in Wroclaw, he has gone on to earn a reputation as a painter.

Working with oil paints, he is clearly in close touch with his emotions, paying attention to the details of his work in order to express himself clearly and form a connection with his audience. He relocated in 2005 to Northern Ireland, and he continues to live and work there today. In 2012, he joined the Libellule Group, which was founded by Lukas Kandl.

There is in Tomasz's work an innate sense of the subconscious. He tries to redirect eyes away from the most obvious details if his work and toward the subtleties. It is his goal to elicit self-reflection and even epiphanies through his work. Fire, a recurring theme, could be seen as magnifying this concept, because fire is something that purifies whatever it touches, transforming it into its most basic components.

Tomasz is an artist whose work is never simple and yet never inaccessible either. He is saying something, of course, and if it is not immediately clear what that thing is, then perhaps his distraction is working and your attention ought to shift somewhere else in the piece.

Right: P15, 2015, oil on canvas, 122 x 91cm

K14 , 2014, oil on canvas, 71 x 56cm

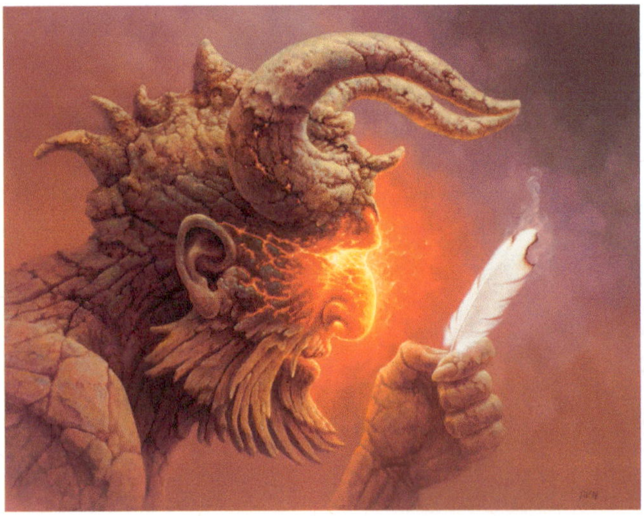

G15, 2015, oil on canvas, 76 x 60cm

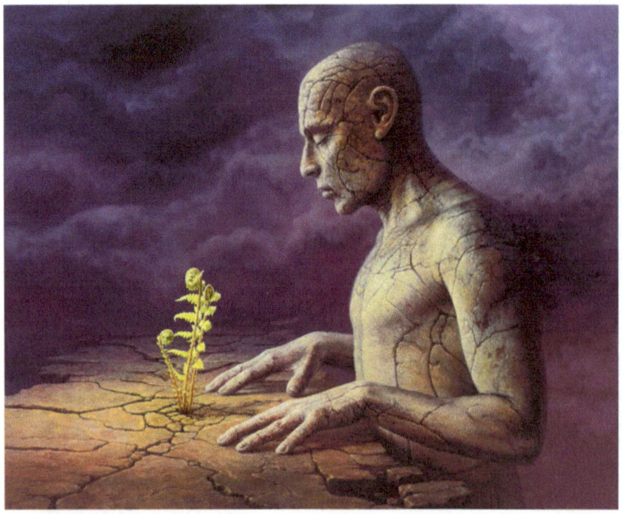

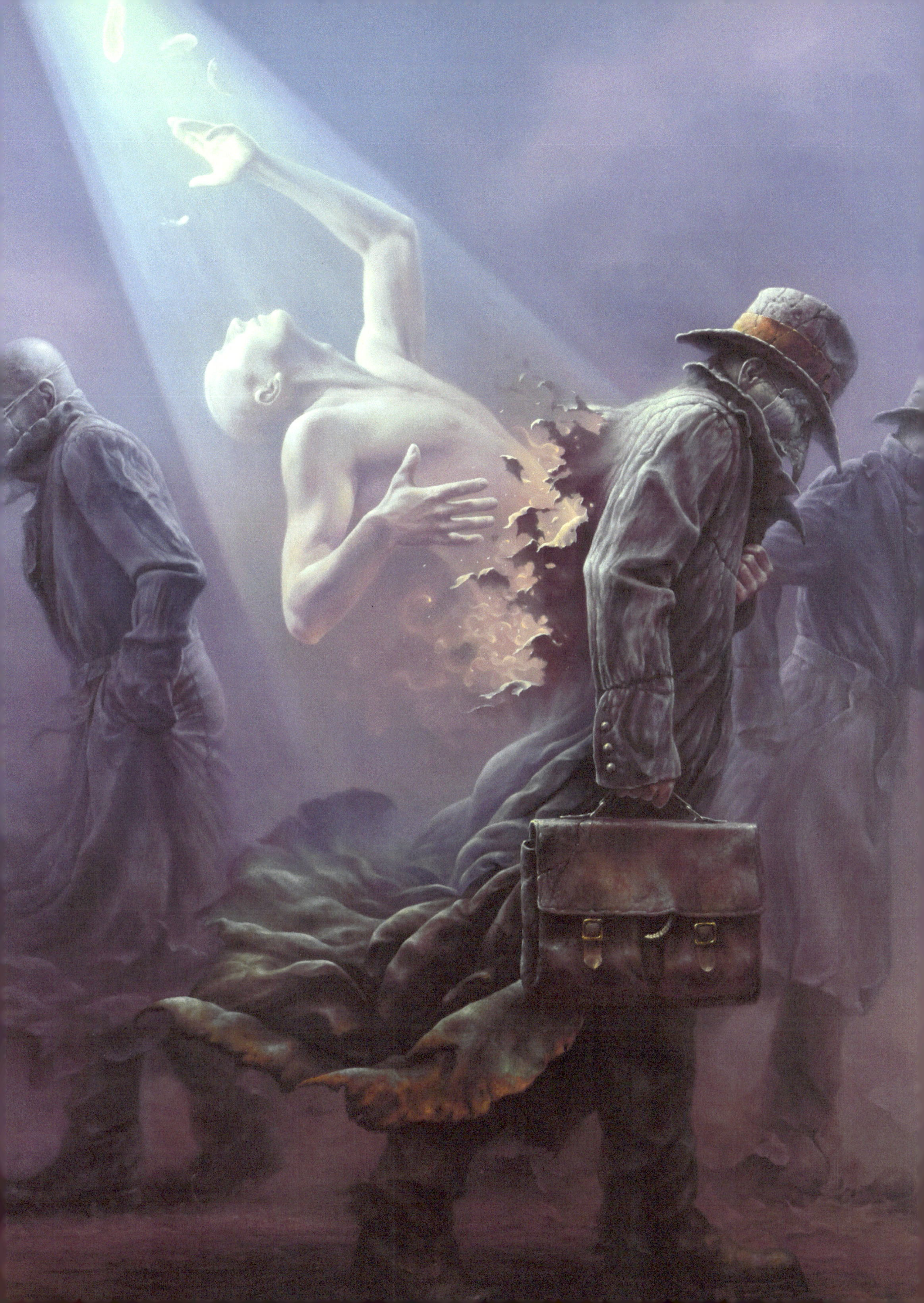

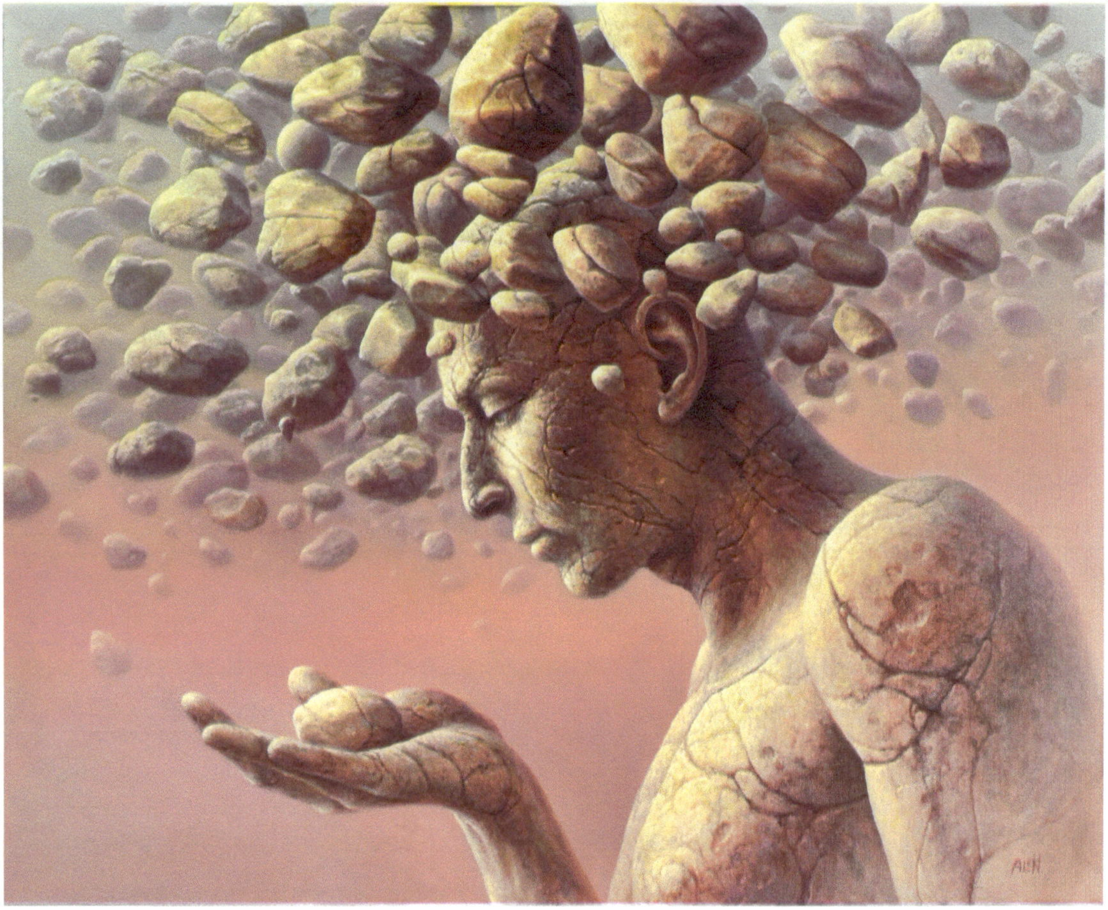

J15, 2015, oil on canvas, 56 x 71cm

K13, 2013, oil on canvas, 66 x 46cm

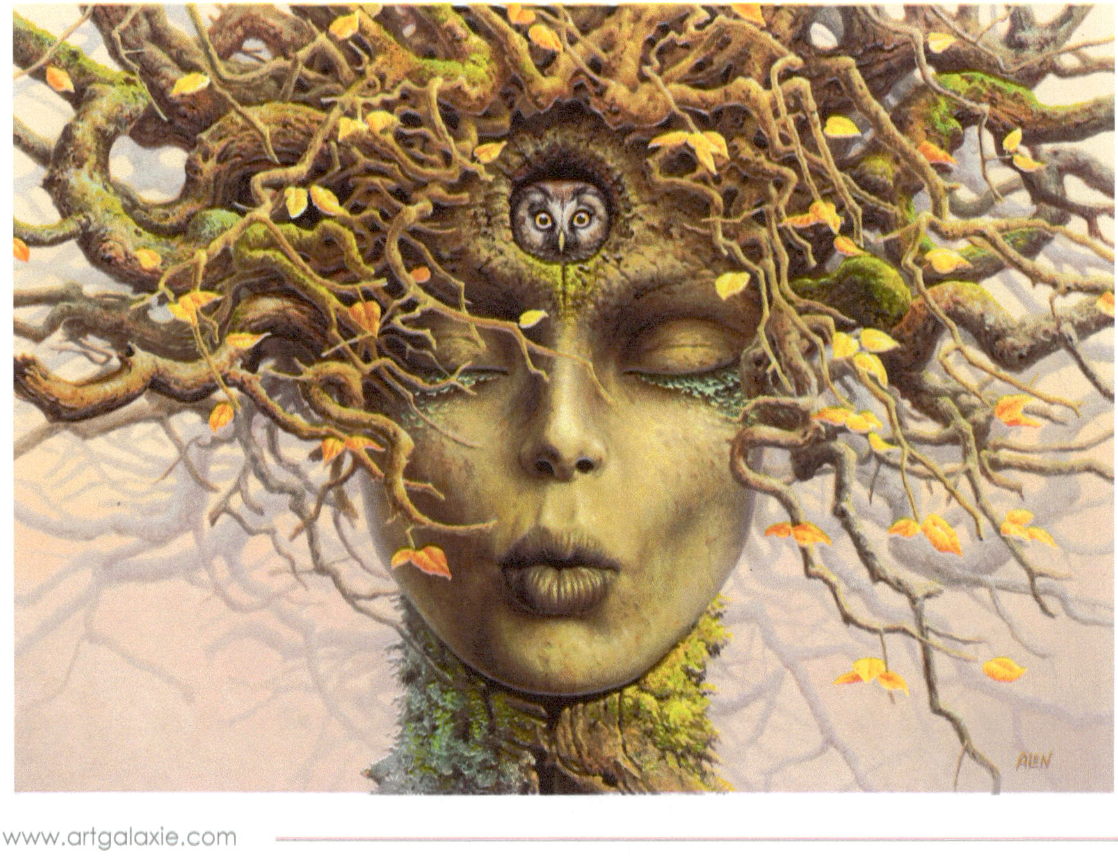

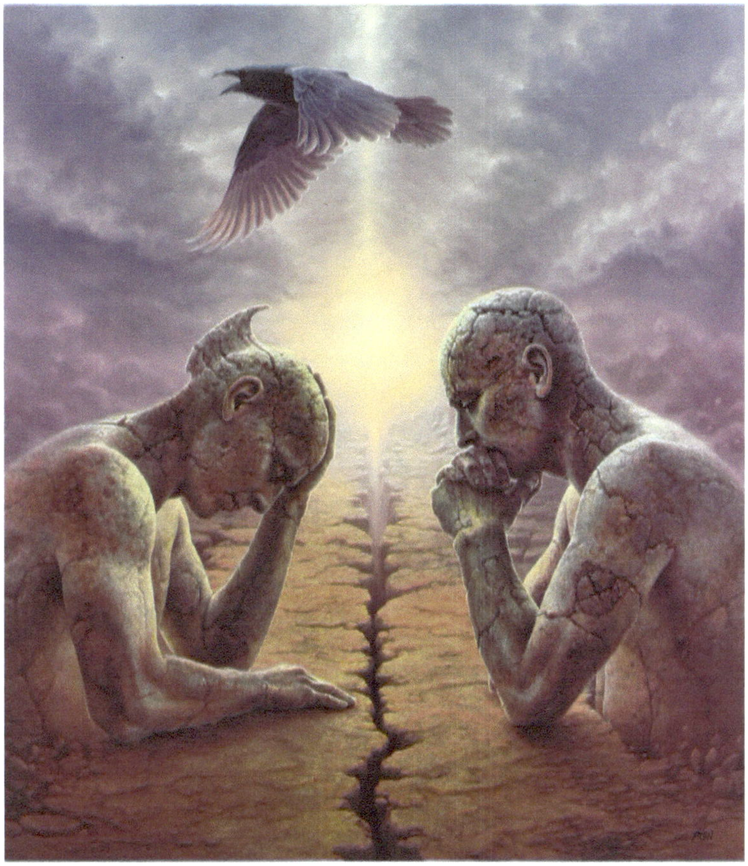

Kopera I16, 2016, oil on canvas, 90 x 80cm

Kopera H15, 2015, oil on canvas. 91 x 102cm

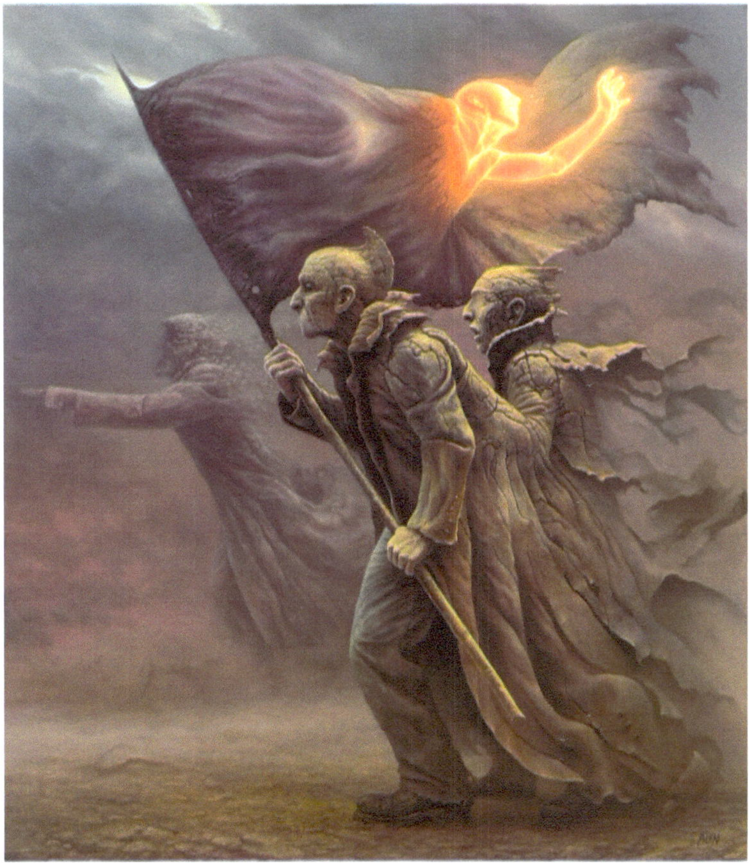

VLADIMIR PETRAN

PAINTING - BELARUS

www.artgalaxie.com

Vladimir Petran is a Belarusian artist. A seeker in life, he sees his art at meeting his audience at the crossroads of the universe. Rather than working logically, he aims to work figuratively, pouring the breadth of his soul into every one of his works. Always blunt with himself, he doubts himself in order to produce work that is a more accurate reflection of reality and truth. His style has been described as "figurative surrealism," although this label falls apart from one work to the next. Taking together themes and techniques that are not often associated with one another, he produces paintings that have a quality of being sculpted or embossed.

Vladimir earned his degree in Design at Bobruisk Art College. Deformity, rhythm, and movement are recurring concepts in his work, connecting his early structural-analytical roots with his professional emphasis on the less-readily understood. He began to exhibit his works internationally in 1988, appearing in galleries and collections throughout Russia, Poland, Germany, Switzerland, Great Britain, the United States, the former Soviet Republics, and his own home country.

An artist who is never content to accept the world at face value, Vladimir tries to push his audience to see past that which seems simple and to accept a little more uncertainty in their lives. What he is expressing is universal, although at the same time, it is almost universally overlooked. He is bringing these overlooked parts of existence to the foreground.

Right: Aquarium, 2013, oil on canvas, 100 x 70cm

Untitled, 2007, oil on canvas, 90 x 90cm

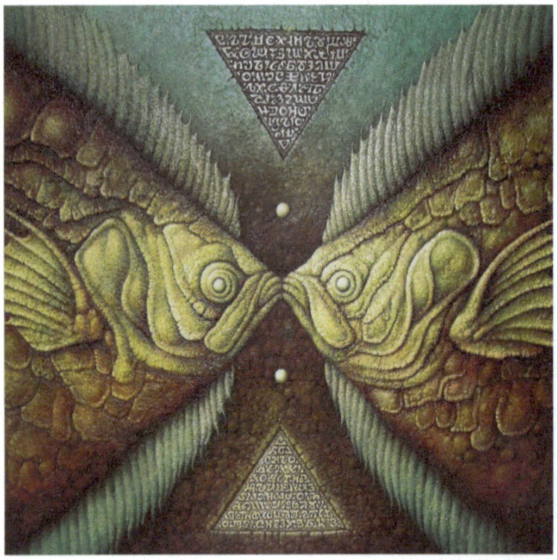

Untitled, 2016, oil on canvas, 80 x 100cm

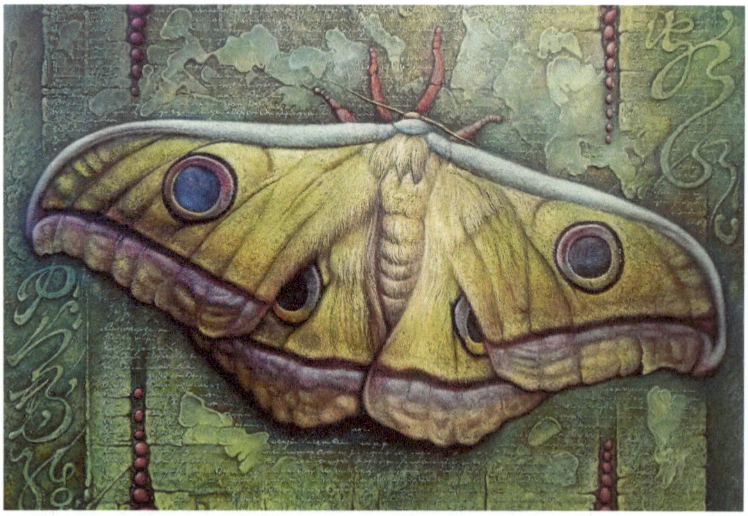

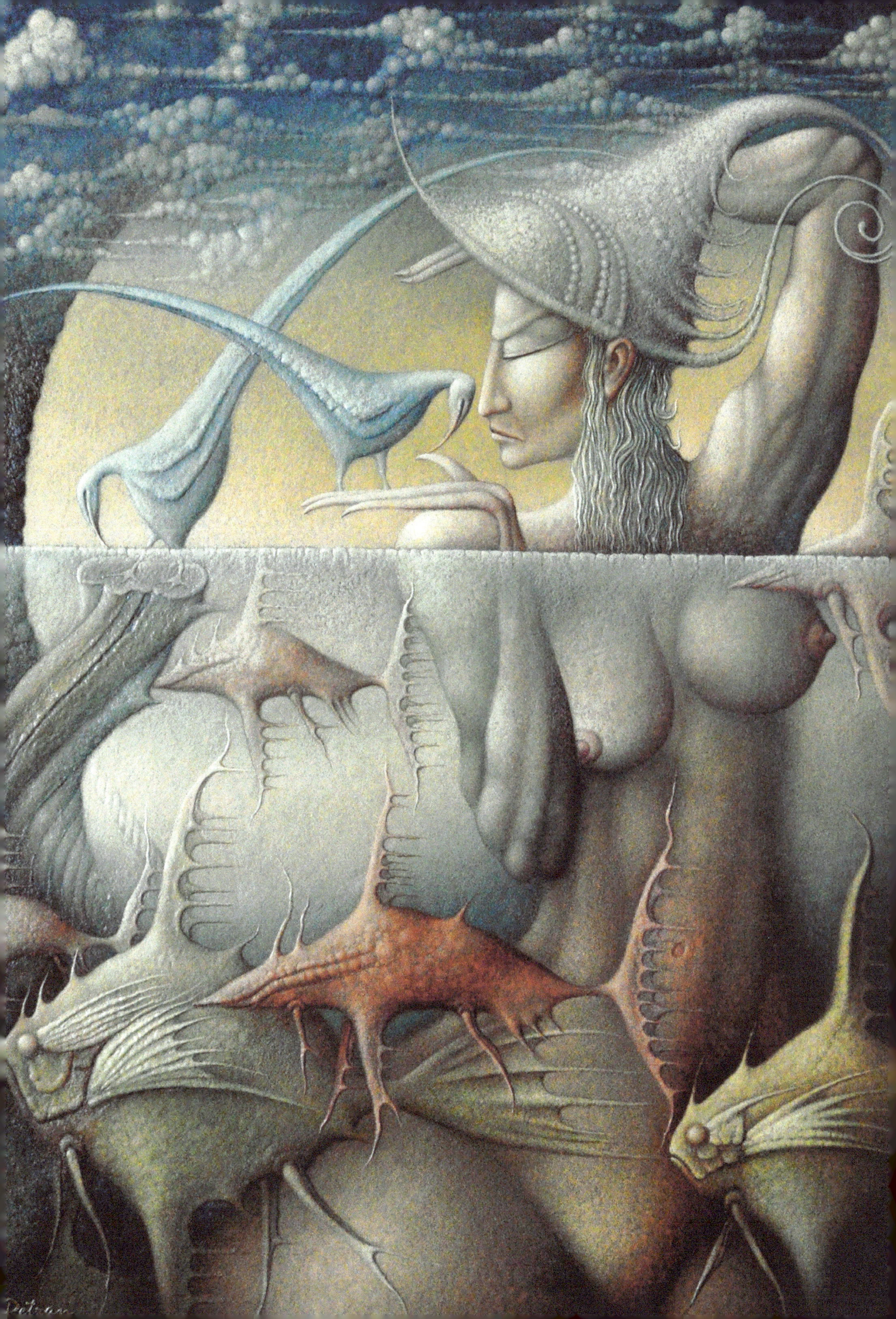

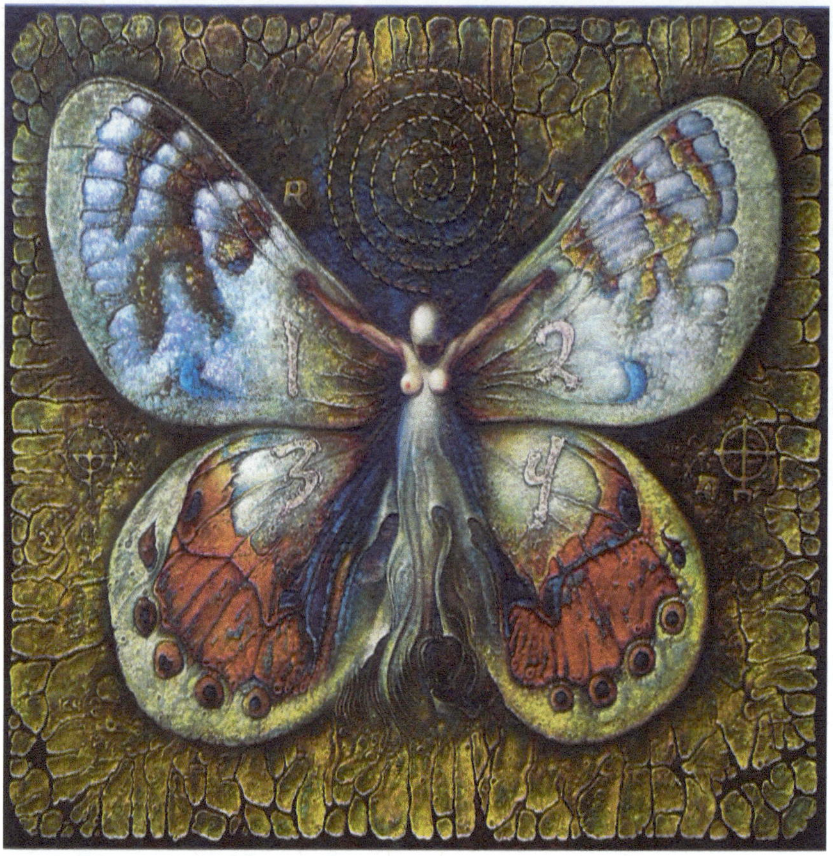

Untitled, 2014, oil on canvas, 80 x 80cm

Yellow Dog with its Tail Cut Off in Two Places, 2015, oil on canvas, 80 x 80cm

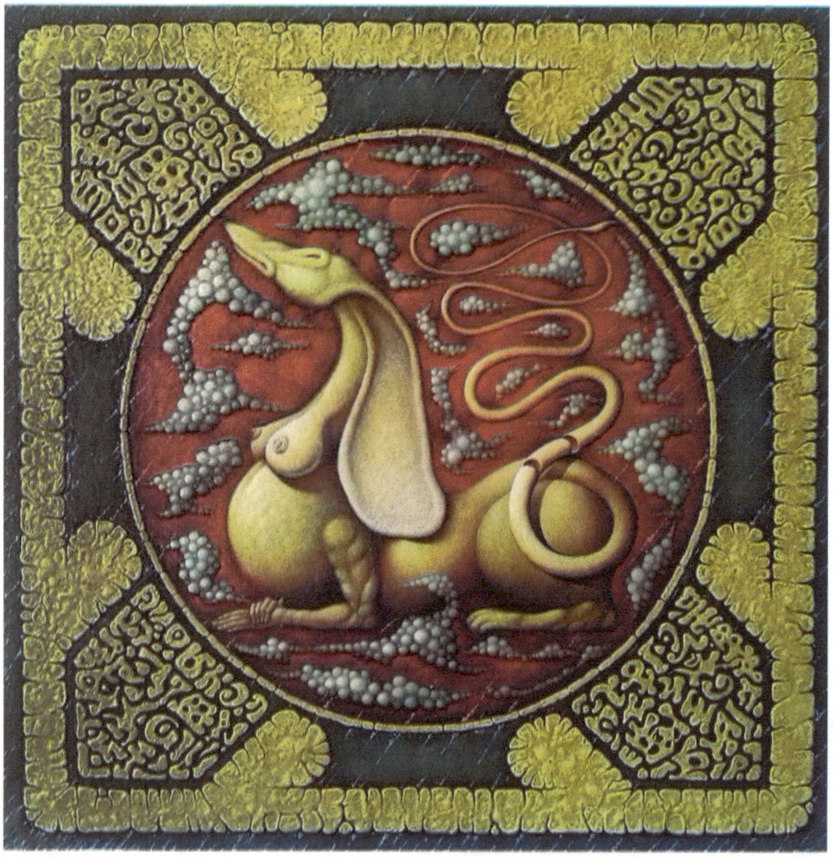

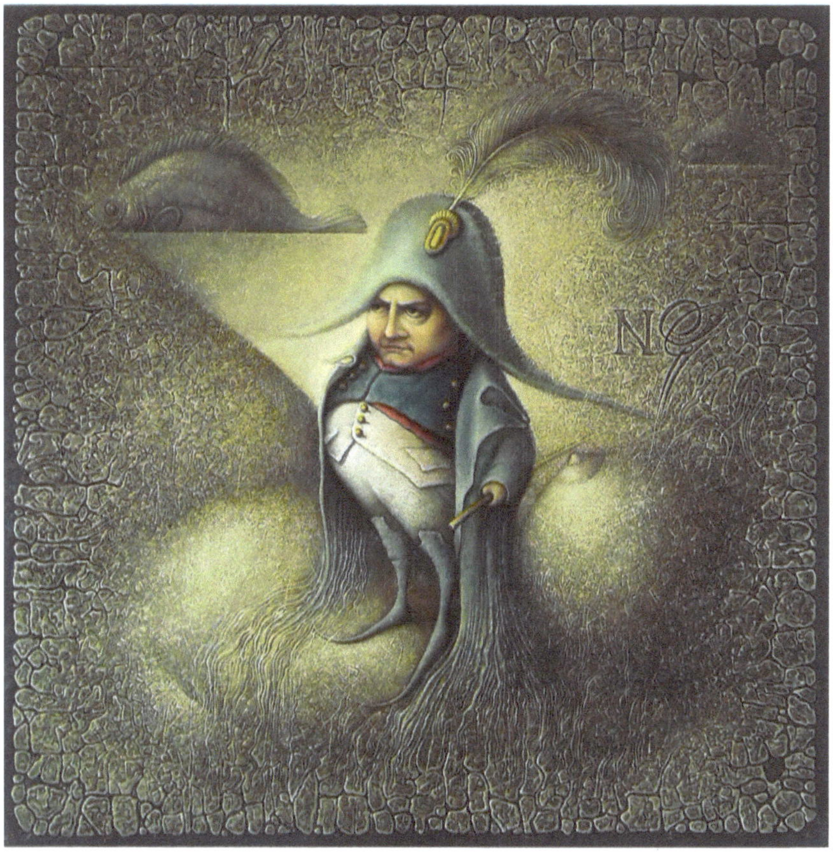

On the Island of Saint Helena, 2012, oil on canvas, 80 x 80cm

Two and a White Dog, 2013, oil on canvas, 80 x 80cm

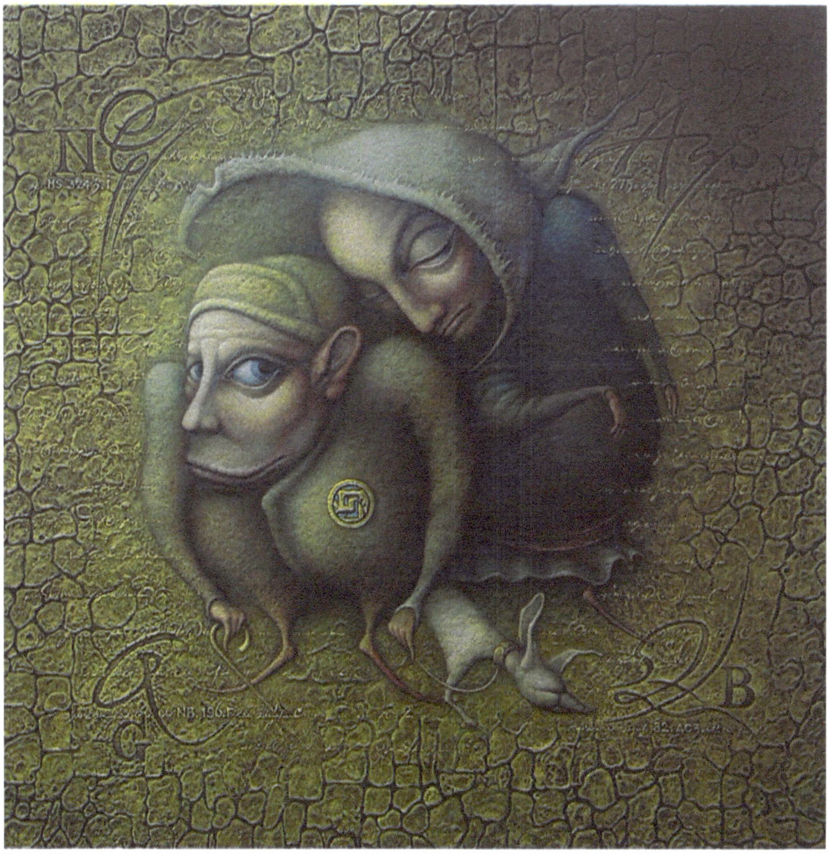

IGOR GRECHANYK

SCULPTURE - UKRAINE

www.grechanyk.com

Born in Kiev, Ukraine and being raised in an artistic family, it was from a young age that he took great interest in art and drawing. He attended the Republican Art School and later graduated from the State Art Institute in Kiev. Presently, Igor Grechanyk's work and talent have made him an integral part of the pleiad of renowned Contemporary Artists. Numerous exhibitions of his work, all over the world, have invariably enjoyed success. His style is well recognized on the global level.

As Art Historian Gerrit Ludinga wrote, "Igor Grechanyk is mesmerized by the mystery of the universe and regards it as his mission to make visible what is concealed beneath the surface of the phenomena, thus creating new worlds, so that spiritual energy is released.

In fact, Igor Grechanyk's sculptures may be seen as symbols of a spiritual entity. His art shows a strong affinity with Symbolism, which, as a reaction to the realism that dominated the arts around 1850, focused attention on the power of imagination, fantastic images and intuition".

His sculpture titled "4th Dimension" depicts the path to the discovery of new dimensions, and the expansion of the boundaries of perception, which goes through the inner world of a man. Creativity is an opening of one self. Through creativity, an artist is able to discover a new unique world and make it visible to others.

Right: Mirror, 2014, bronze, 77cm tall

Hunting Season, 2015, bronze, 124cm tall

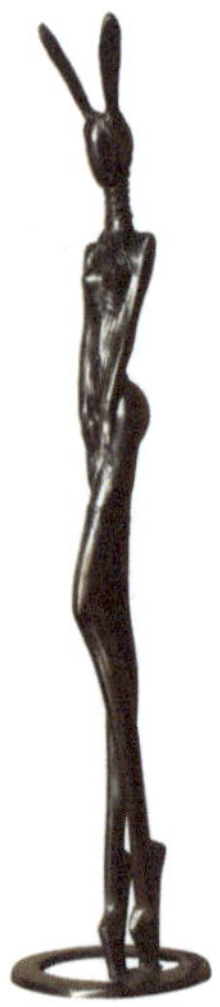

Orange, 2015, bronze, 111cm tall

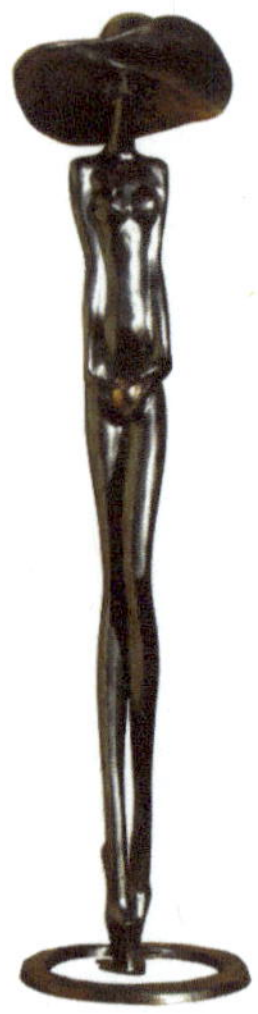

Course of the Queen, 2015, bronze, 77cm tall

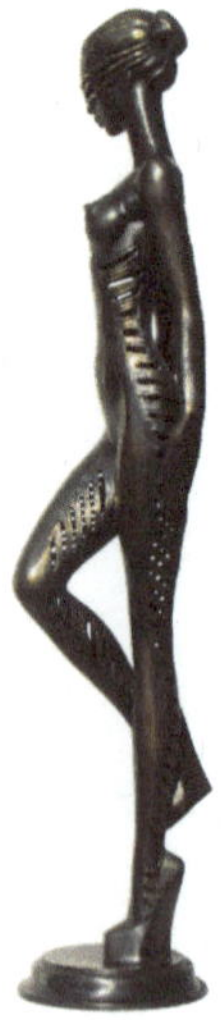

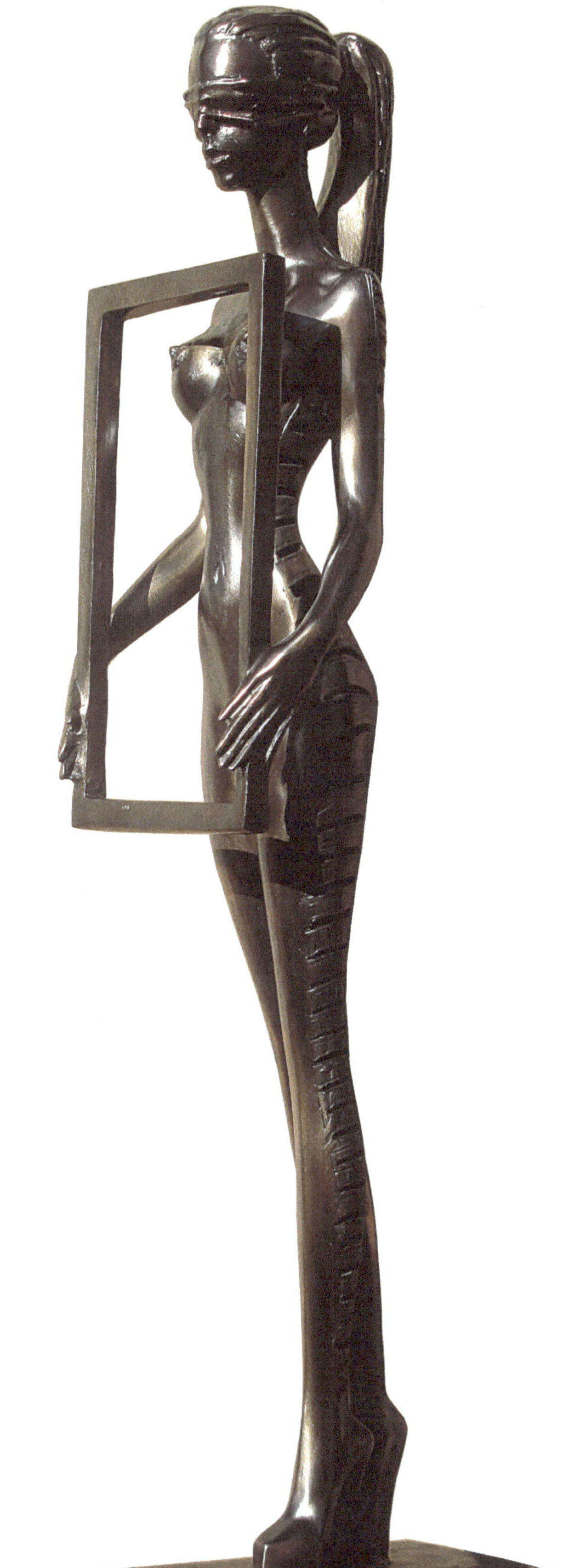

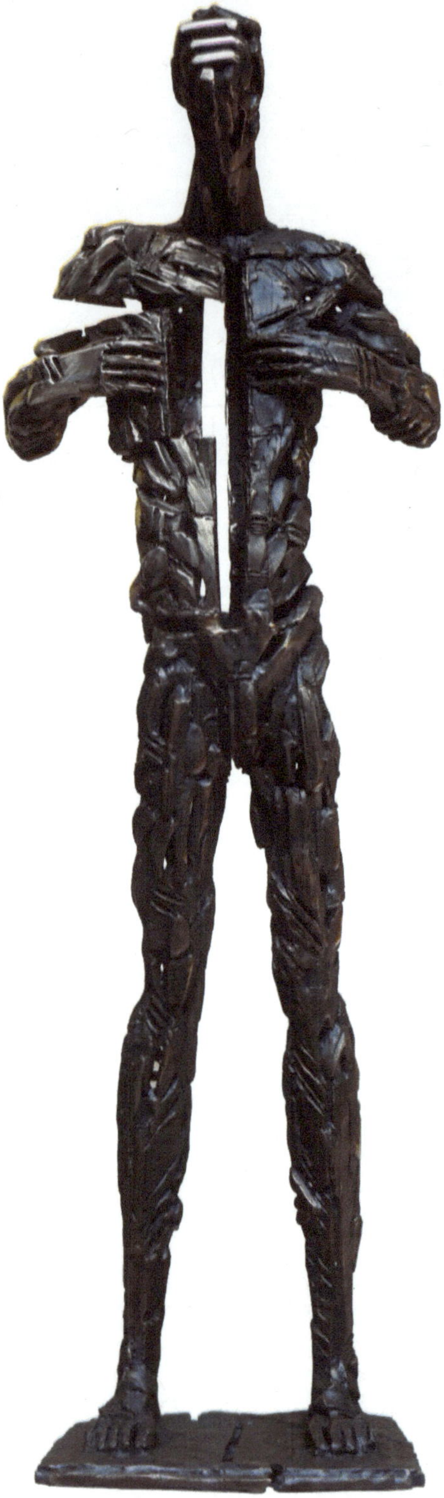

4th Dimension, 2016, bronze, 72cm tall

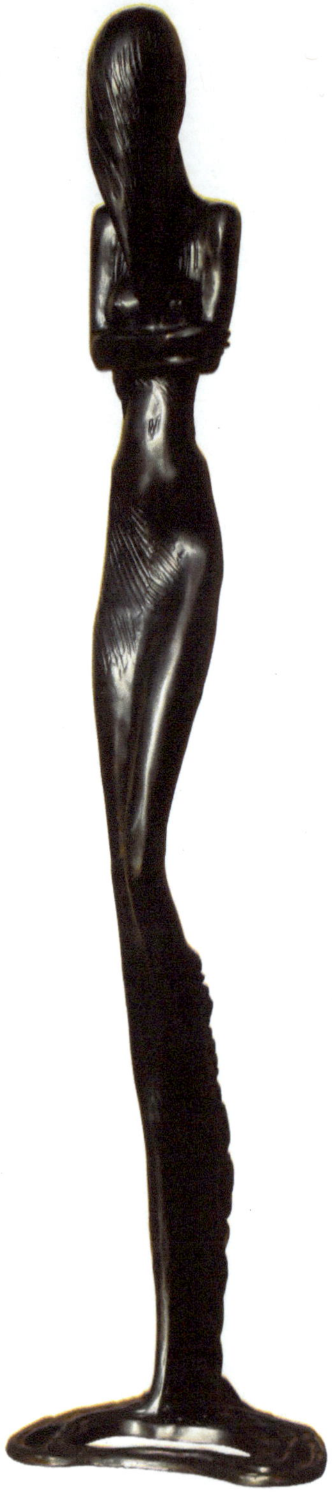

Waterfall, 2015, bronze, 146cm tall

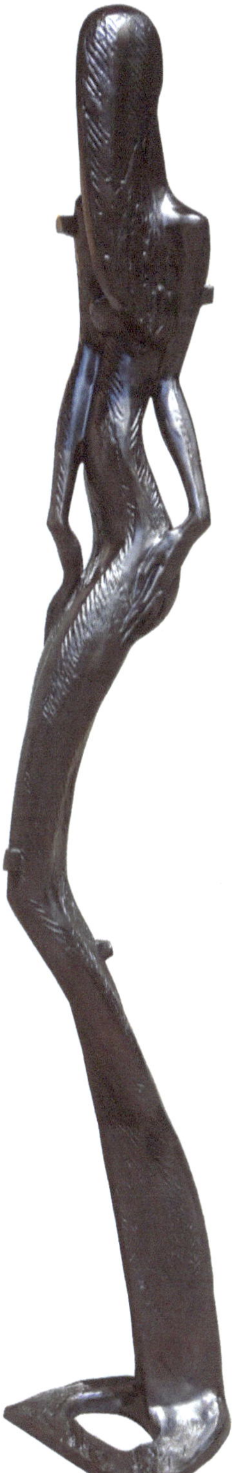

Line of Life, 2016, bronze, 172cm tall

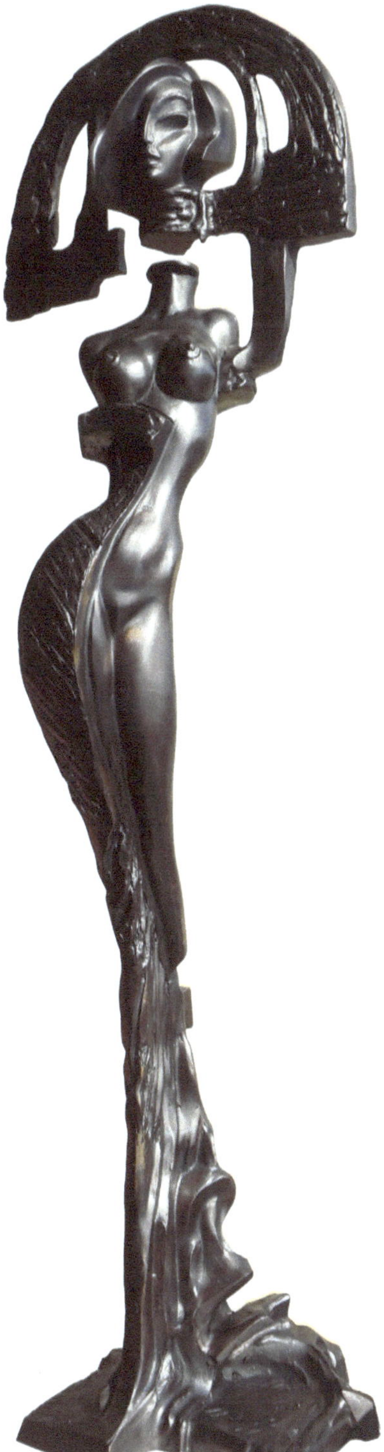

Queen, 2016, bronze, 94cm tall

JEFFRO UITTO

SCULPTURE - UNITED STATES OF AMERICA

www.jeffrouitto.com

Born in 1982, Jeffro Uitto was raised in a small coastal town of Tokeland Washington, where he still resides.

Growing up on the ocean with the mountains nearby, there was plenty of inspiration for his creations. It was in high school where he realized he had large potential in what he could create. A close family friend encouraged him to step in the world of organic furniture which soon led into the endless possibiltiy of sculpture.

The artist breathes new life into the salvaged wood and nature's leftovers by transforming them into incredible sculptures. The pieces discovered and rescued from the shores of Tokeland, the banks of Smith Creek and the valleys between the Willapa Hills, serve as the construction material for his artwork. Every finished creation shows Jeffro's creativity and his fascination for wood and its organic forms which he has had since his childhood.

His now own a shop which is situated near the historic Tokeland Hotel where one can find him carving and sawing with his own hand made tools and working on his projects.

His sculptures are displayed and collected throughout the US and found in publications across the world.

Right: Rhino Bust, mixed salvaged woods, 122cm tall x 102cm deep x 91cm wide (photo by Marcy Merrill)

Flow of the Throne, mixed salvaged woods, 244cm tall x 91cm deep x 81cm wide

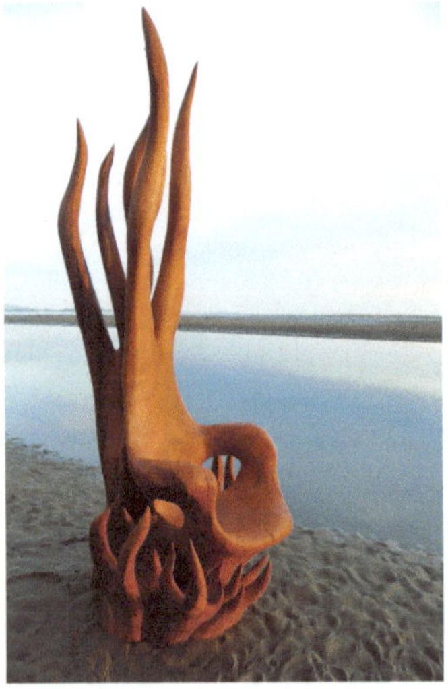

Free Form, mixed salvaged woods, 249cm tall x 66cm deep x 71cm wide (photo by Marcy Merrill)

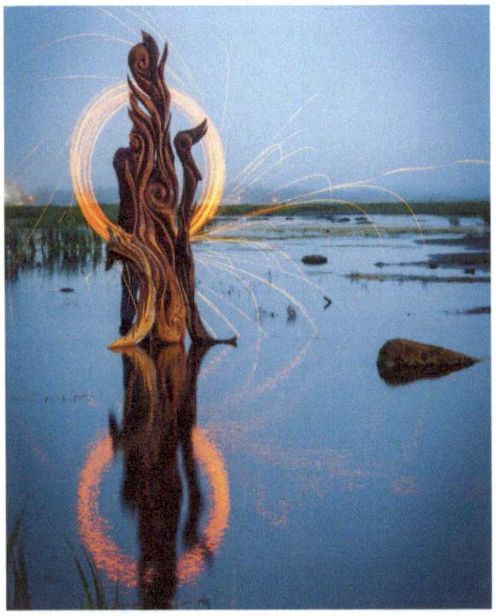

Heron, mixed salvaged woods, 163cm wide x 46cm deep x 66cm wide

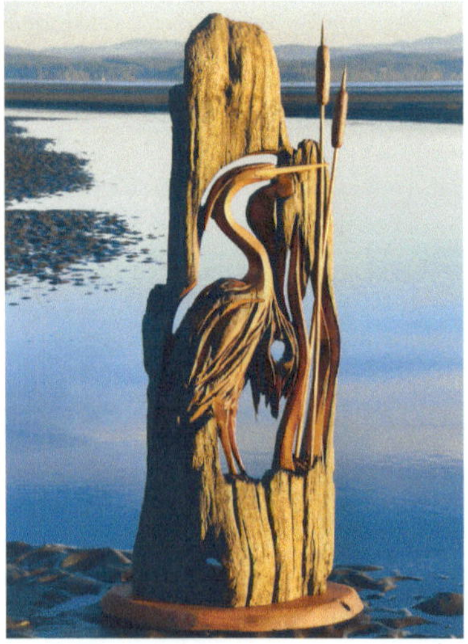

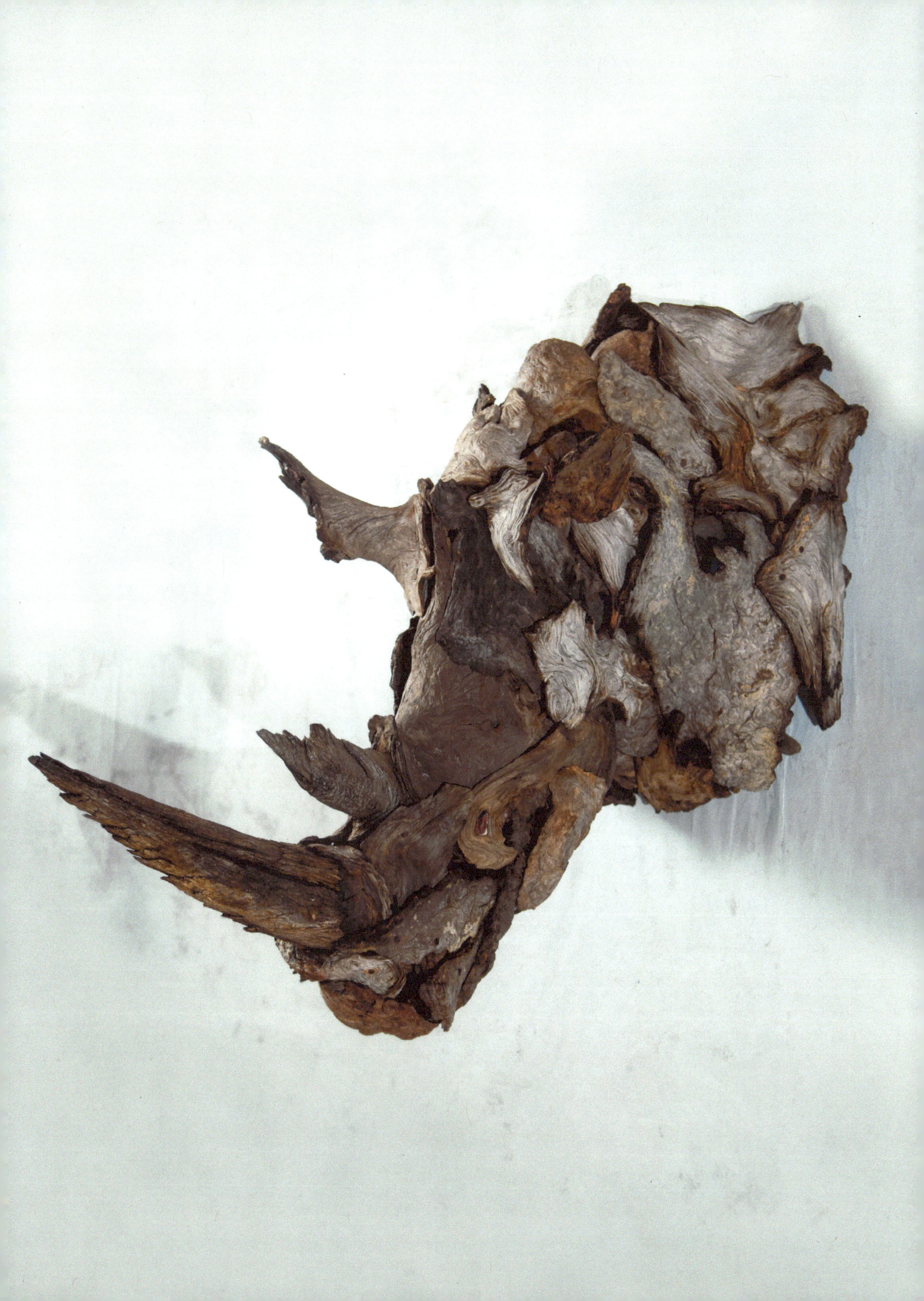

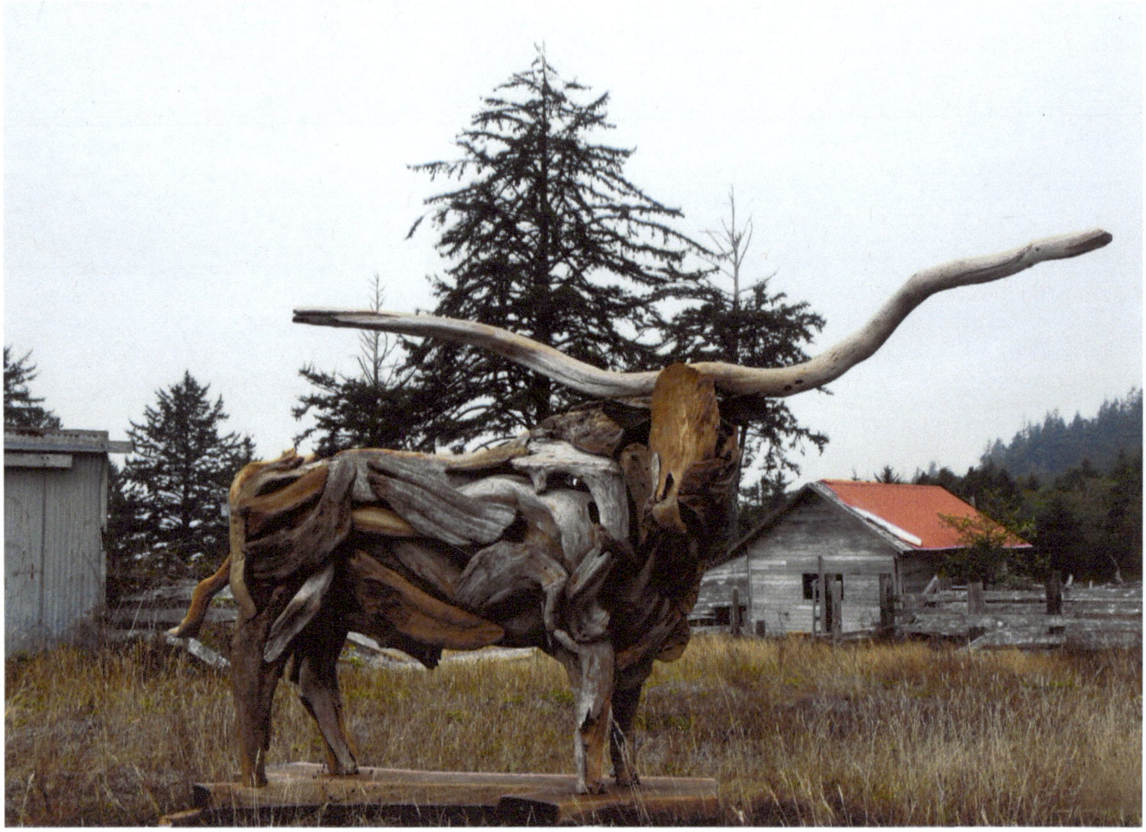

Longhorn Bull, mixed salvaged woods, 193cm tall x 427cm deep x 122cm wide

Giraffe, mixed salvaged woods,304cm tall x 229cm long x 81cm wide

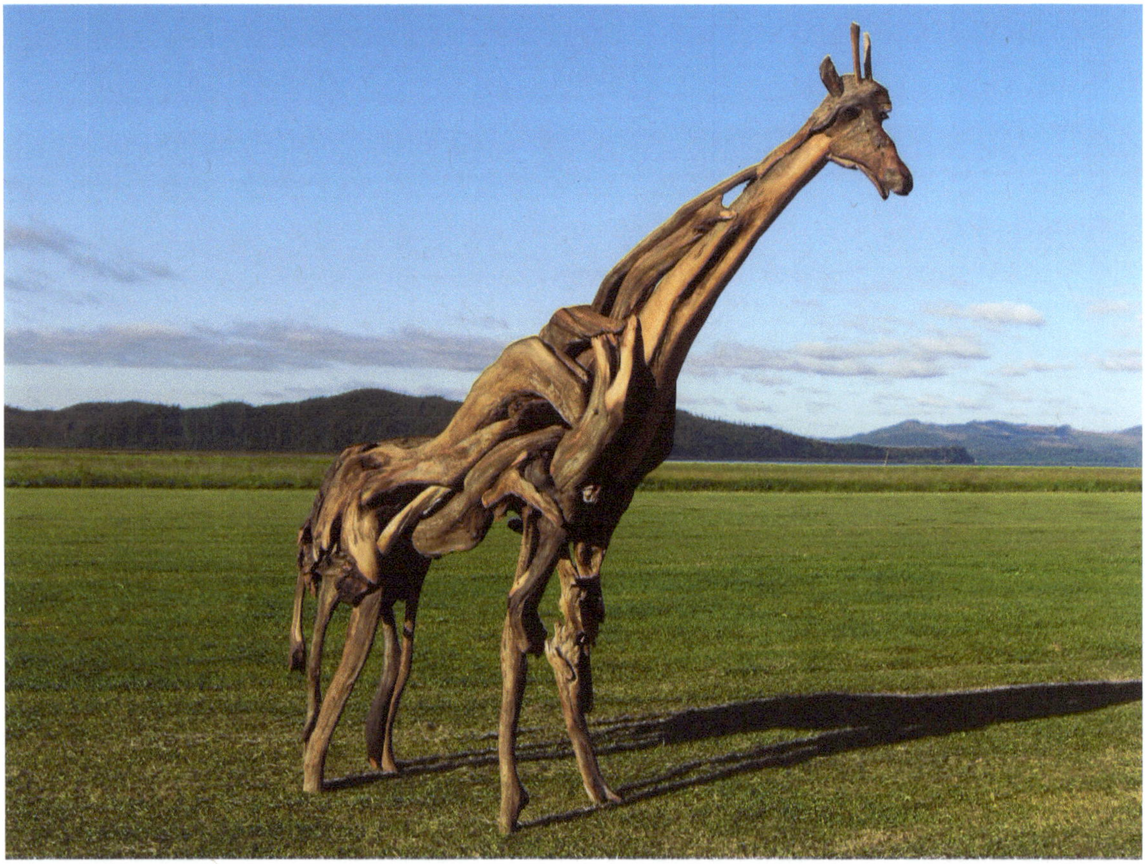

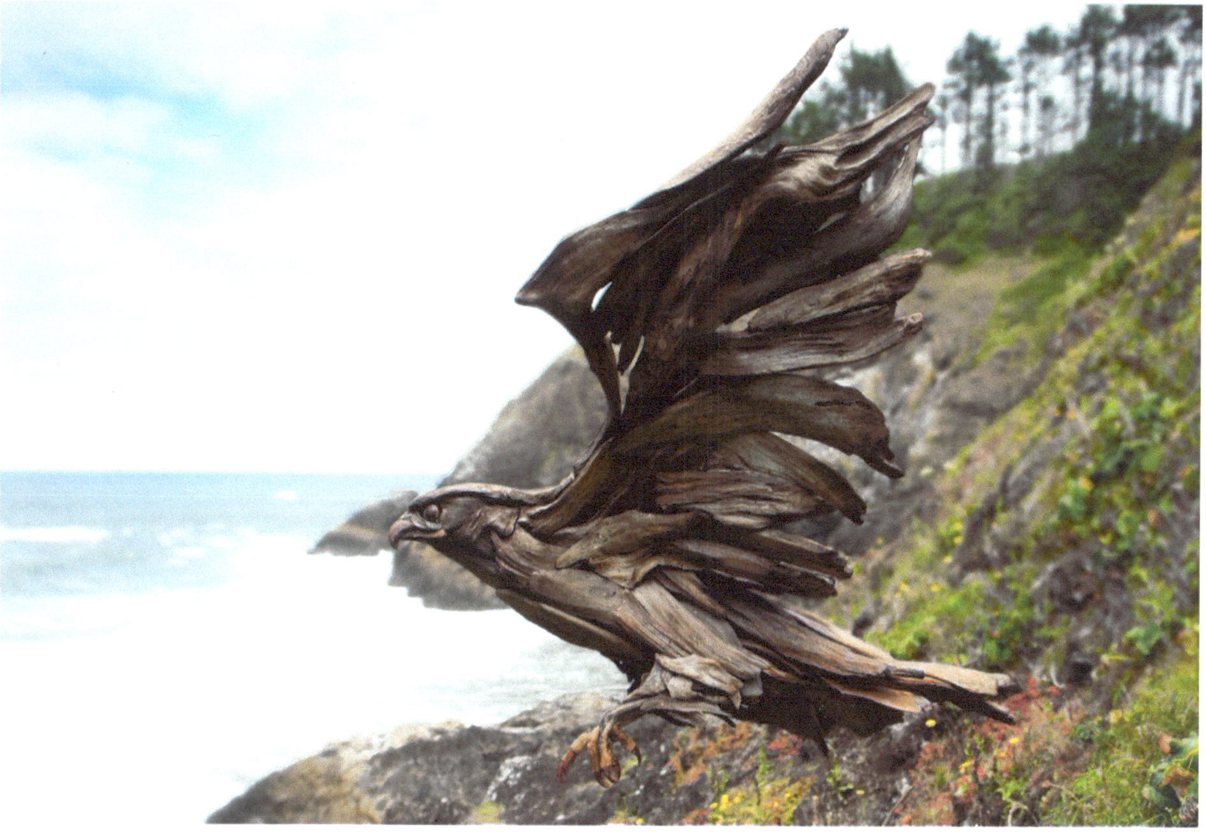

Red Tailed Hawk, mixed salvaged woods, 51cm tall x 71cm deep x 102cm wide (photo by Marcy Merrill)

Arching Horse Bust, mixed salvaged woods, 234cm tall x 107cm deep x 56cm wide

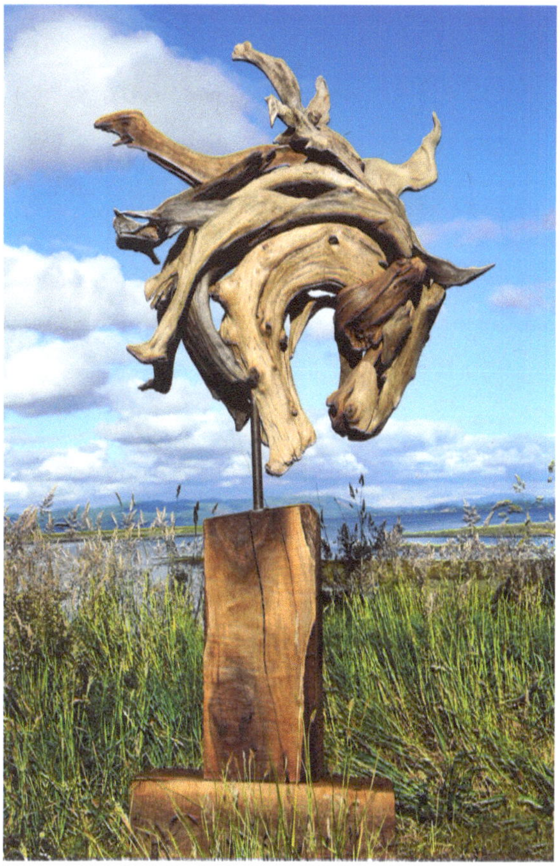

Arabian Horse Bust, mixed salvaged woods, 229cm tall x 107cm deep x 56cm wide

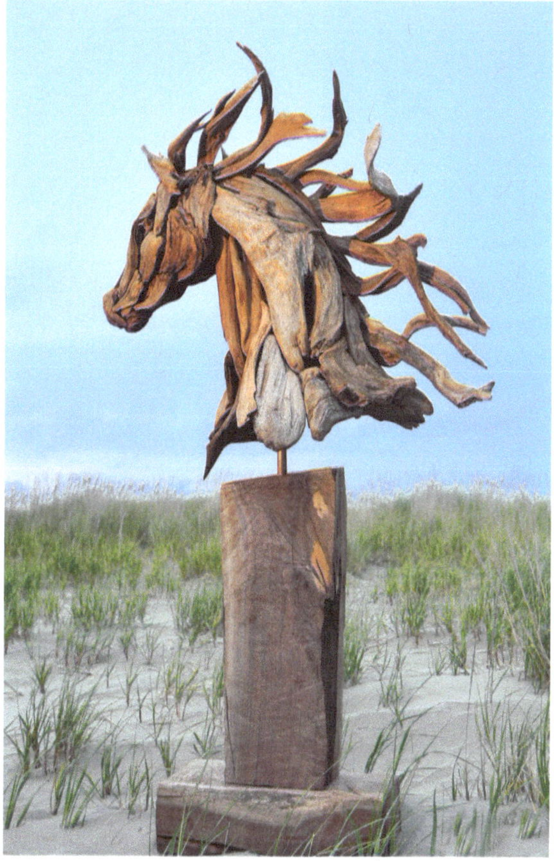

JOHNSON TSANG

SCULPTURE - CHINA

www.johnsontsang.wordpress.com

Johnson Tsang was born in Hong Kong in 1960. His artwork mostly employ realist sculptural techniques accompanied by surrealist imagination. He integrates the human form and objects to create interesting and creative themes.

Tsang started to represent versatile splashes with ceramics in 2002. He called this the "Yuanyang series", which were then collected by the Hong Kong Museum of Art and the Yingge Ceramics Museum of Taiwan.

In 2009, Tsang received "The Secretary for Home Affairs' Commendation" from the Government of Hong Kong Special Administrative Region for his outstanding achievements in international art events.

He has also been awarded the 2011 Korea Gyeonggi International Ceramix Biennale and the 2012 Taiwan International Ceramics Biennale, making him the first Chinese to receive these 2 prestigious international awards.

Since 1993, Tsang's works have been exhibited in Hong Kong, Taiwan, Korea, Spain and Switzerland and collected by local and overseas museums and collectors.

Right: Quarantine (Lucid Dream Series), 2016, porcelain, 50 x 14 x 11cm

The Backup(Lucid Dream Series), 2016, 25 x 18.5 x 10cmporcelain,

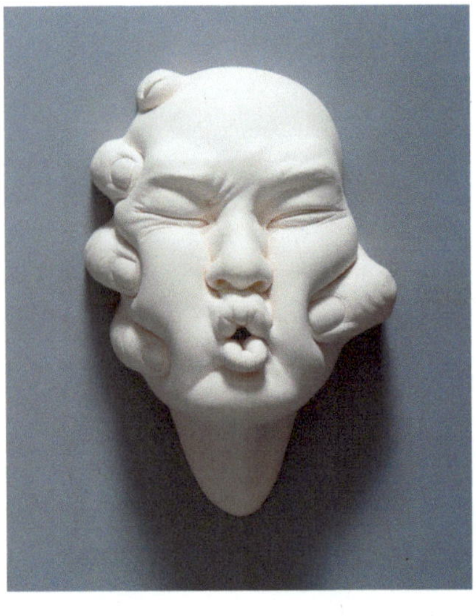

Two in One (Lucid Dream Series), 2016, porcelain, 29 x 14 x 10cm

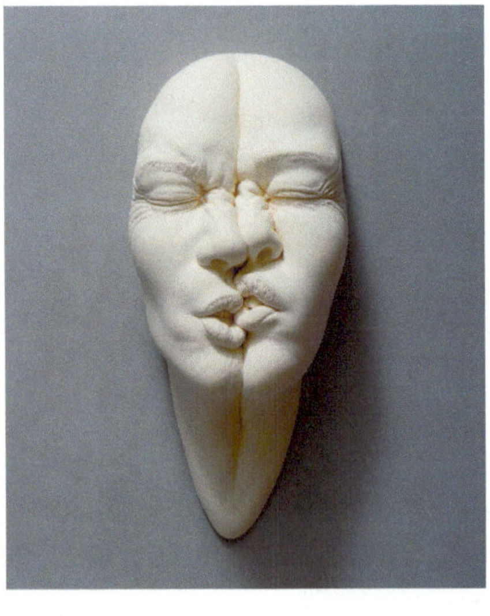

The Comfort (Lucid Dream Series), 2016, porcelain, 23 x 13 x 11cm

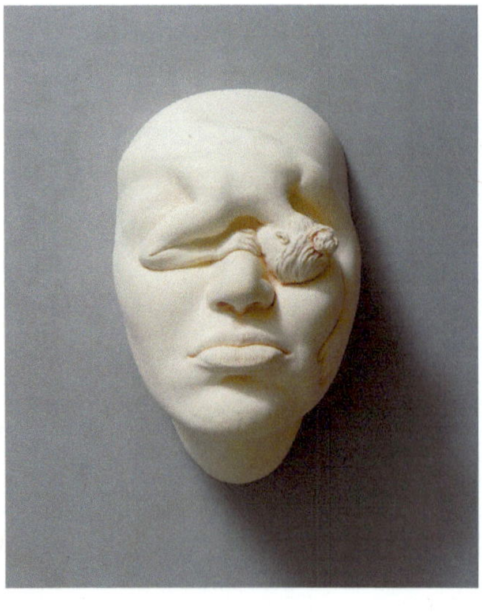

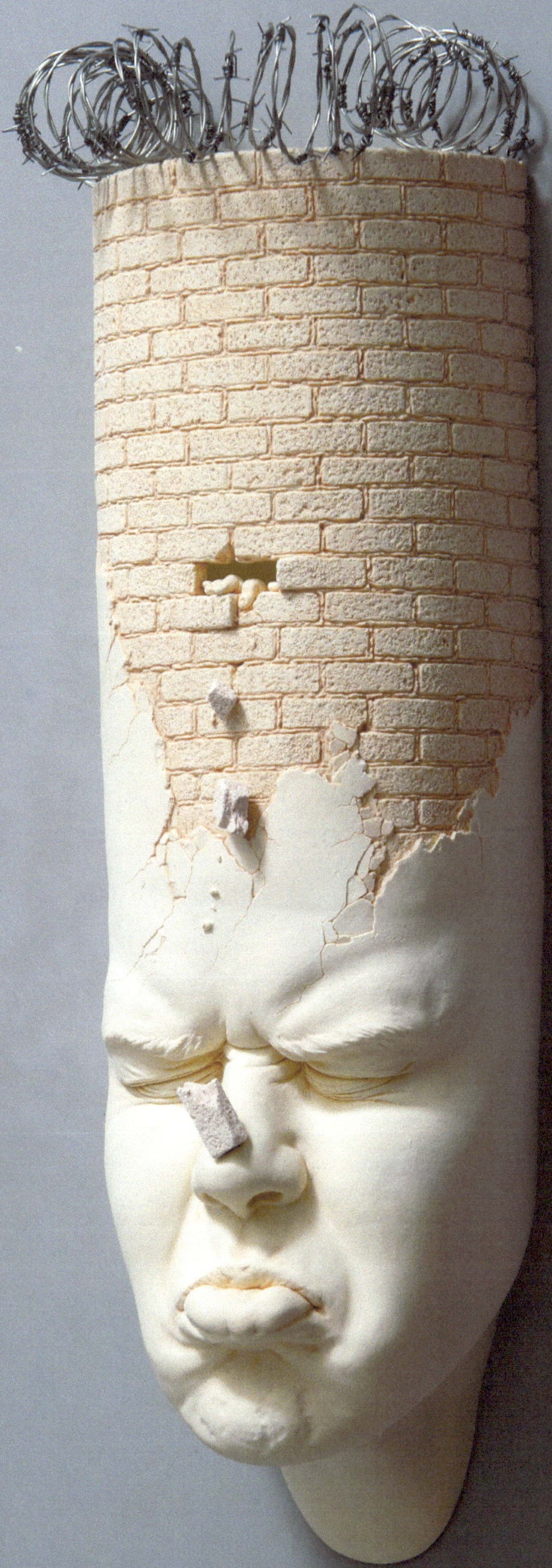

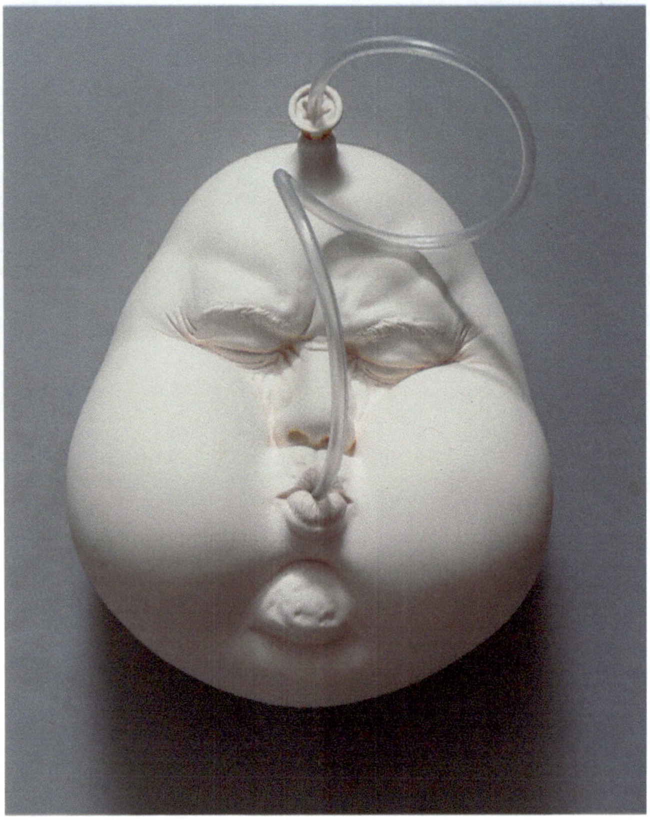

Re-mind (Lucid Dream Series), 2016, porcelain, 27 x 22 x 22cm

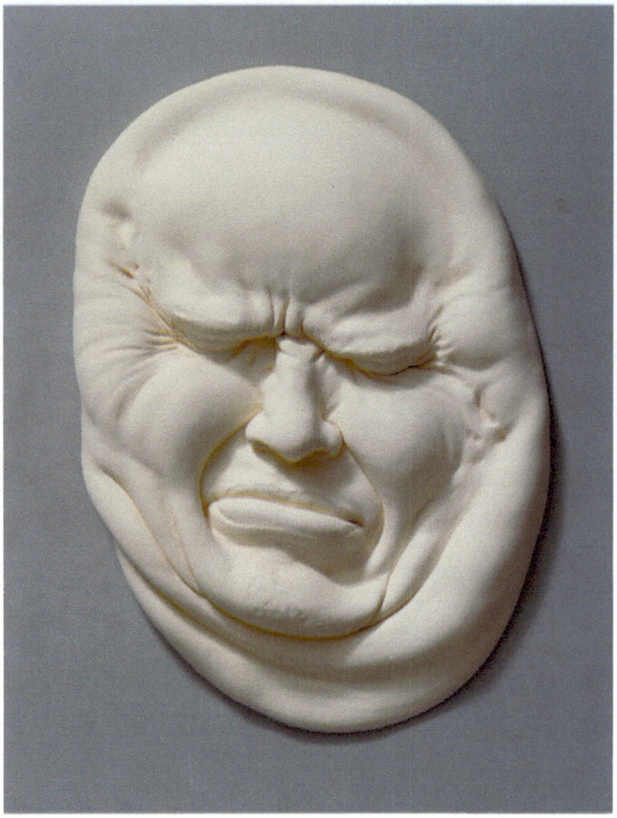

Against the Wall (Lucid Dream Series), 2016, porcelain, 30 x 22 x 4cm

Hang in There, (Lucid Dream Series), 2016, porelain, 39 x 12 x 10cm

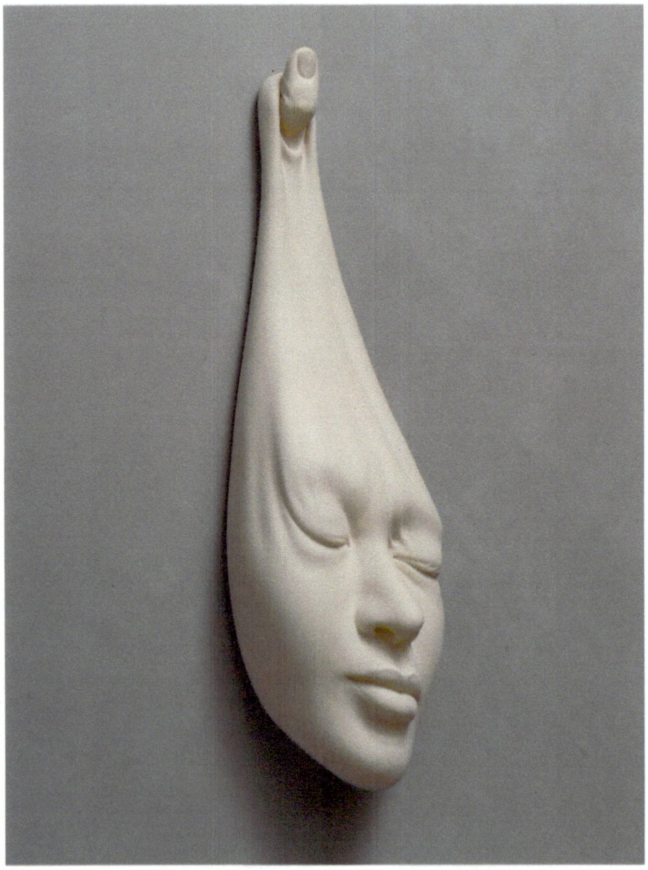

Shopping (Lucid Dream Series), 2016, porcelain, 37 x 21 x 11cm

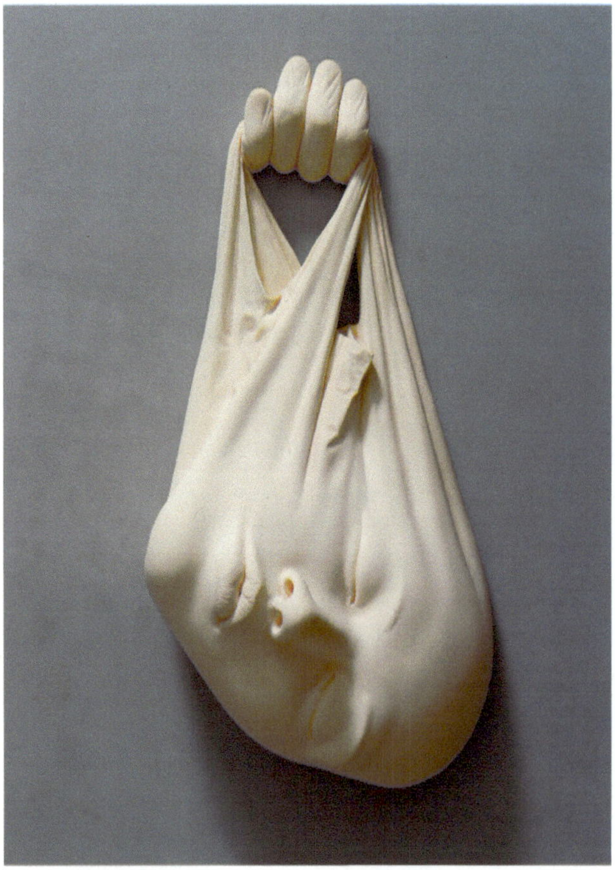

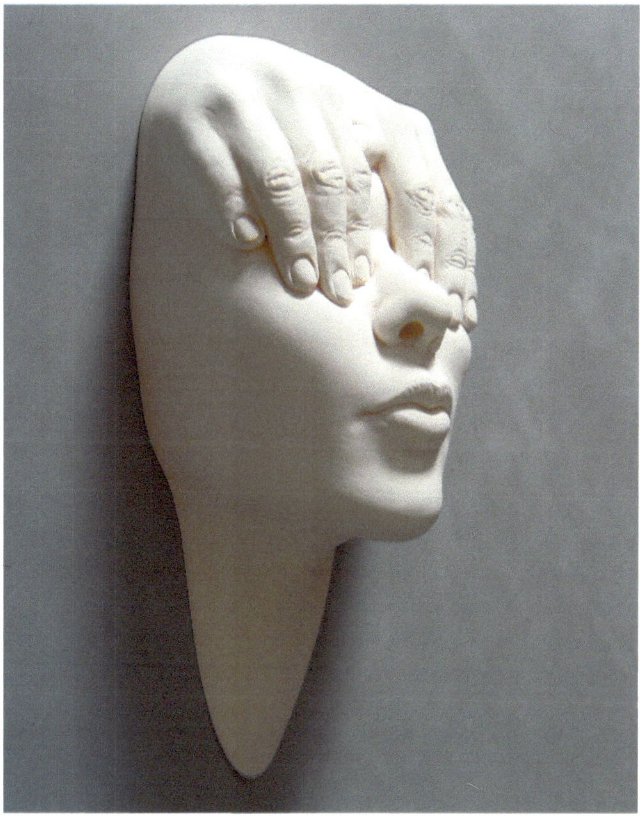
The Windows (Lucid Dream Series), 2016, porcelain, 30 x 14.5 x 11cm

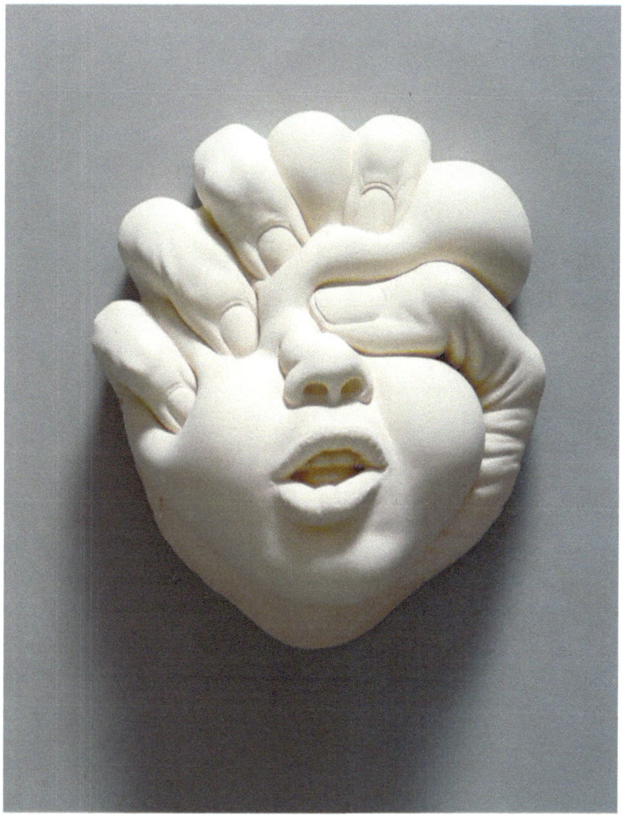
Shaping Love (Lucid Dream Series), 2016, porcelain, 24 x 20 x 10cm

Still in One Piece (Lucid Dream Series), 2016, porcelain, 40 x 28 x 10cm

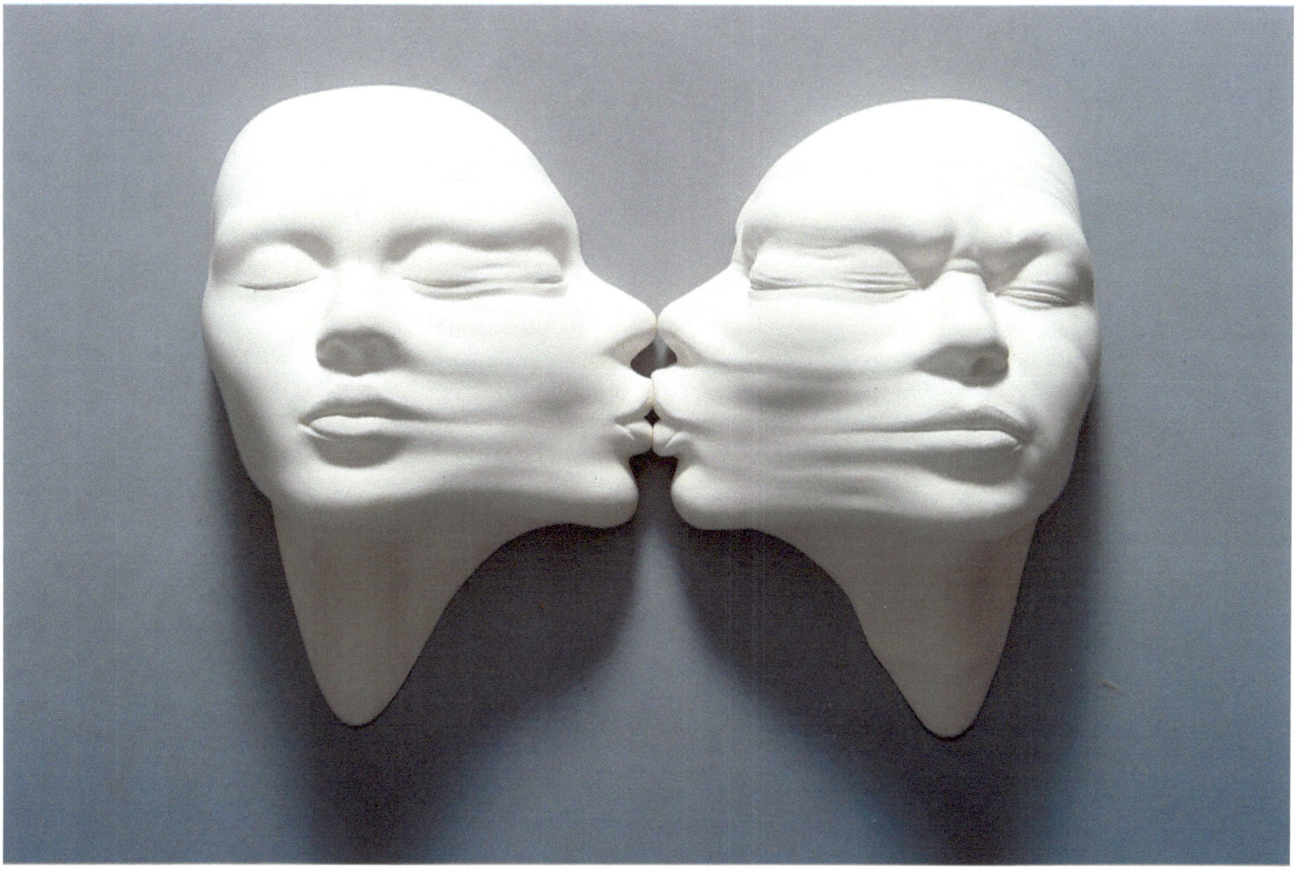

KAZUHIRO TSUJI

SCULPTURE - JAPAN

www.kazustudios.com

Kazuhiro Tsuji is a sculptor who is based out of Los Angeles. He worked for 25 years as a special effects makeup artist on Hollywood movies, and since 2012, he has worked exclusively on fine art sculpture. Specializing in sculpture with the use of resin, platinum silicone, and other unconventional materials, he is best known for crafting 3D portraits that are scaled to double life-size. A self-taught hyperrealist, he is a pioneer in the field of contemporary materials used to mimic life.

Kazuhiro first became enamoured with special effects makeup while he was a teenager, and he developed his skills through trial and error, basing his works off of the works that he saw in magazines. Dick Smith agreed to mentor him while he was still in high school, and upon graduation, he landed his first film gig. He then founded one of Japan's first special effects makeup companies, Makeup and Effects Unlimited, and collaborated with Akira Kurosawa on "Rhapsody".

Kazuhiro worked on "Men in Black" in 1996, and that led to a professional relationship with Rick Baker, who had sponsored him as a project supervisor and makeup artist. In 2007, Kazuhiro founded KTS Effects Inc., through which he has gained a reputation for limit-pushing portrait painting, photography, and sculpture. More recently, he has collaborated with contemporary artist Paul McCarthy, supervising some of McCarthy's latest projects to success.

Right: Portrait of Lincoln, 2012, human hair, platinum cured silicone, resin, wood, fabric, fiberglass resin, 231cm tall

Soft Construction of Dali, 2015, human hair, platinum cured silicone, resin, wood, fabric, fiberglass resin, composite bronze, 231cm tall

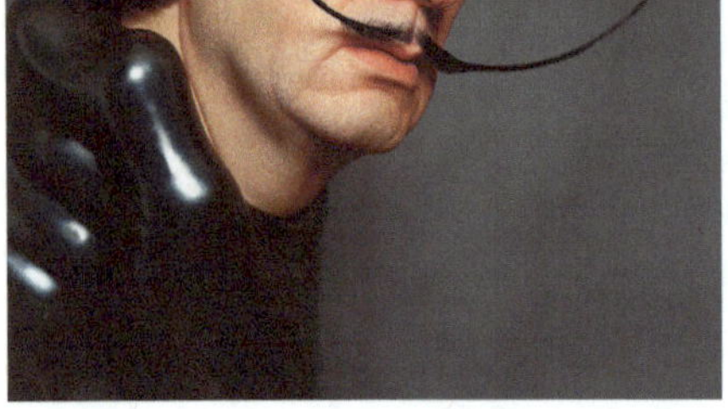

Portrait of Frida Kahlo, 2016, human hair, silicone, resin, wood, fabric, fiberglass resin, composite bronze, 224cm tall

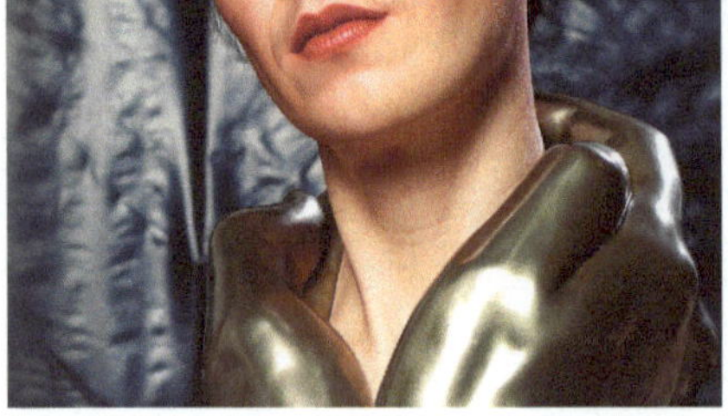

Two Periods of Andy Warhol, 2014, human hair, platinum cured silicone, resin, wood, fabric, fiberglass resin, chrome plating, 231cm tall

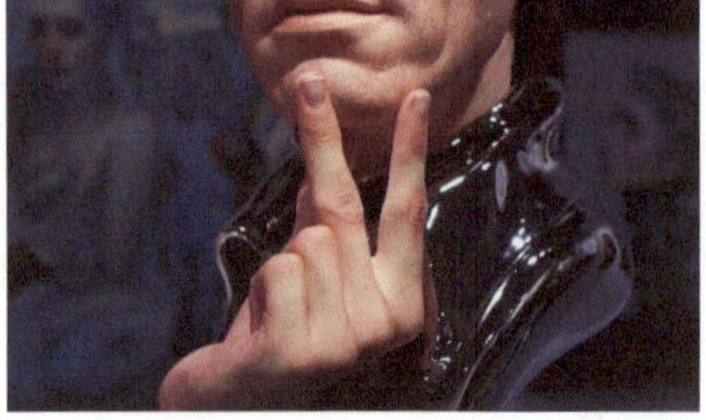

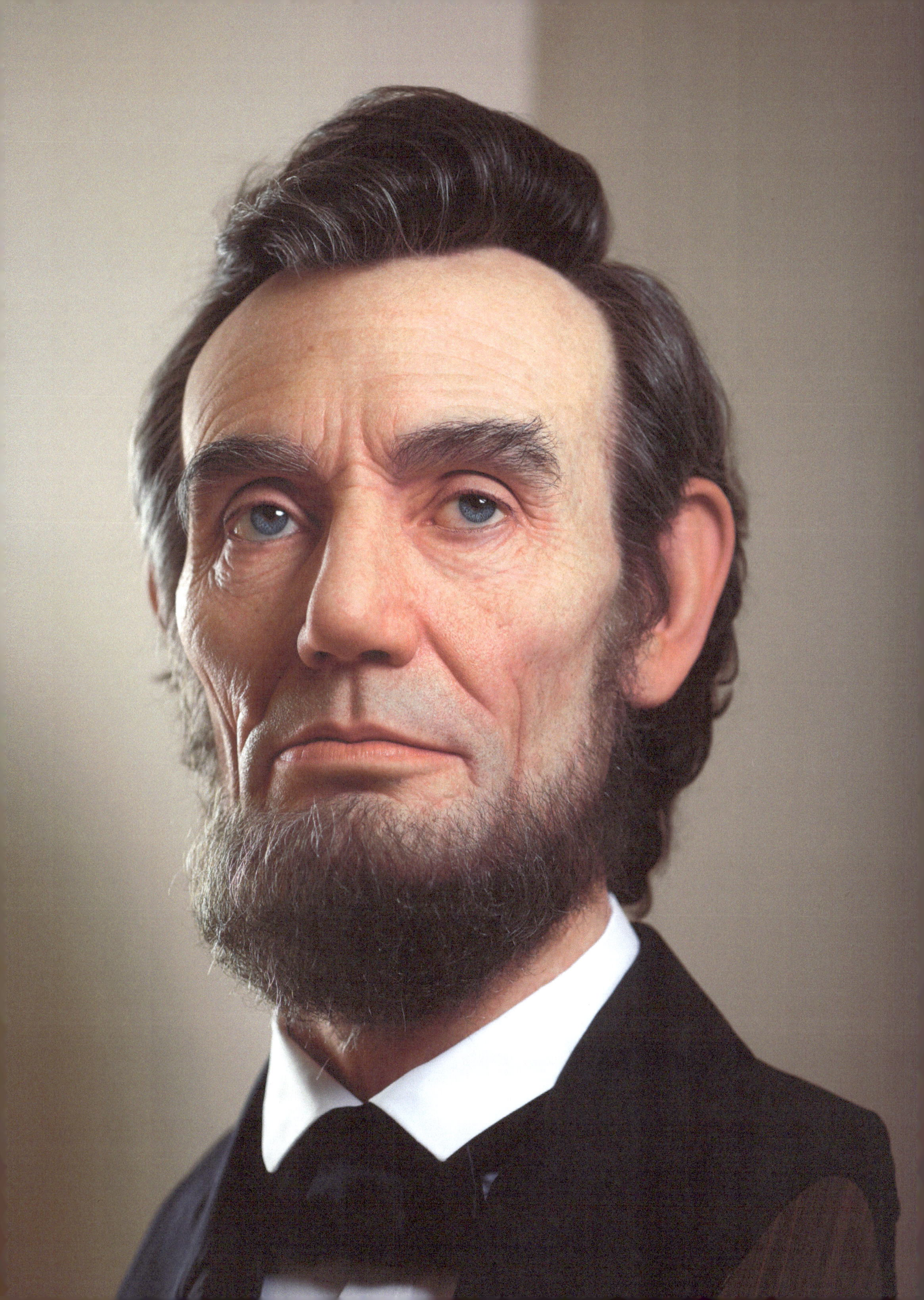

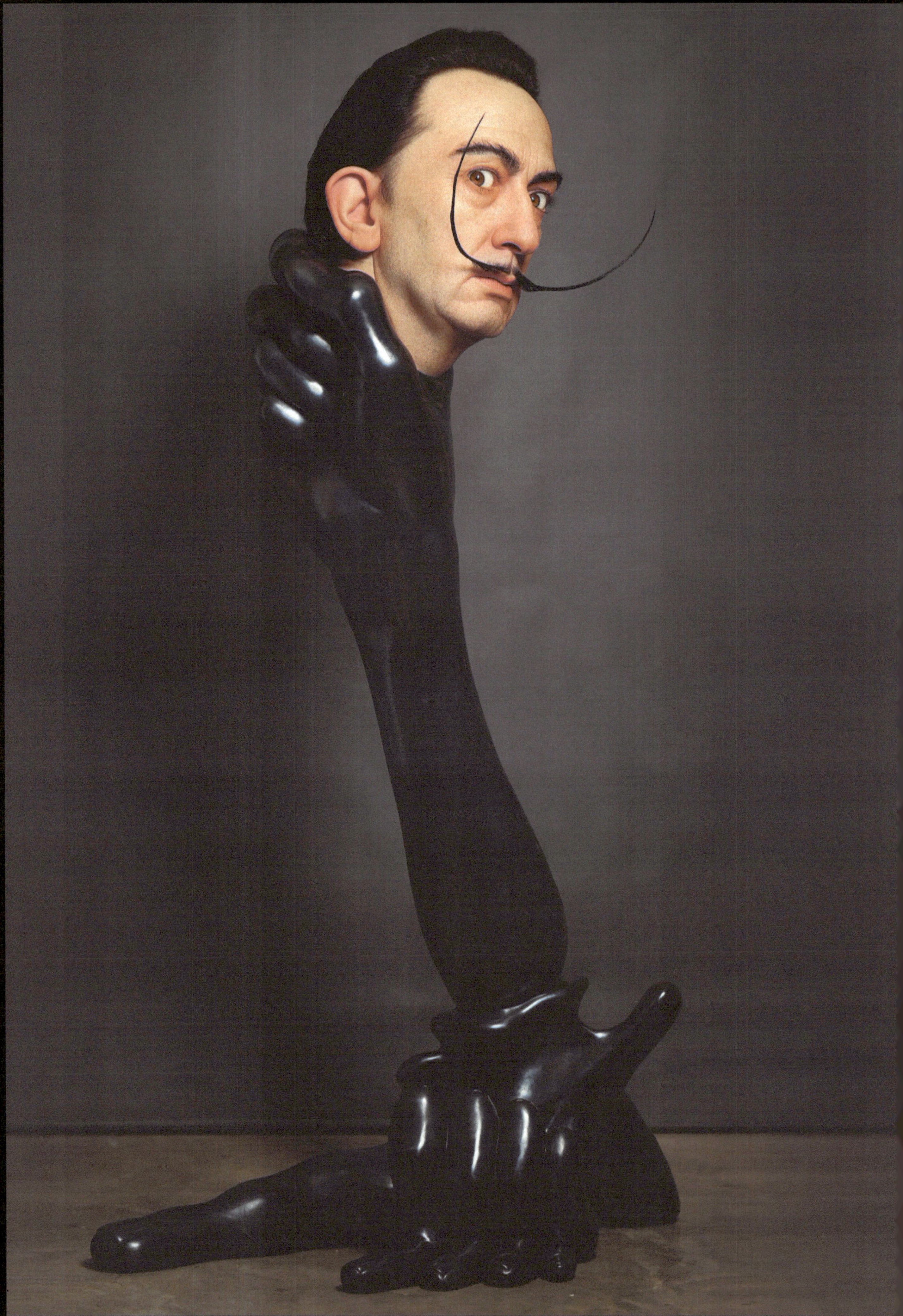

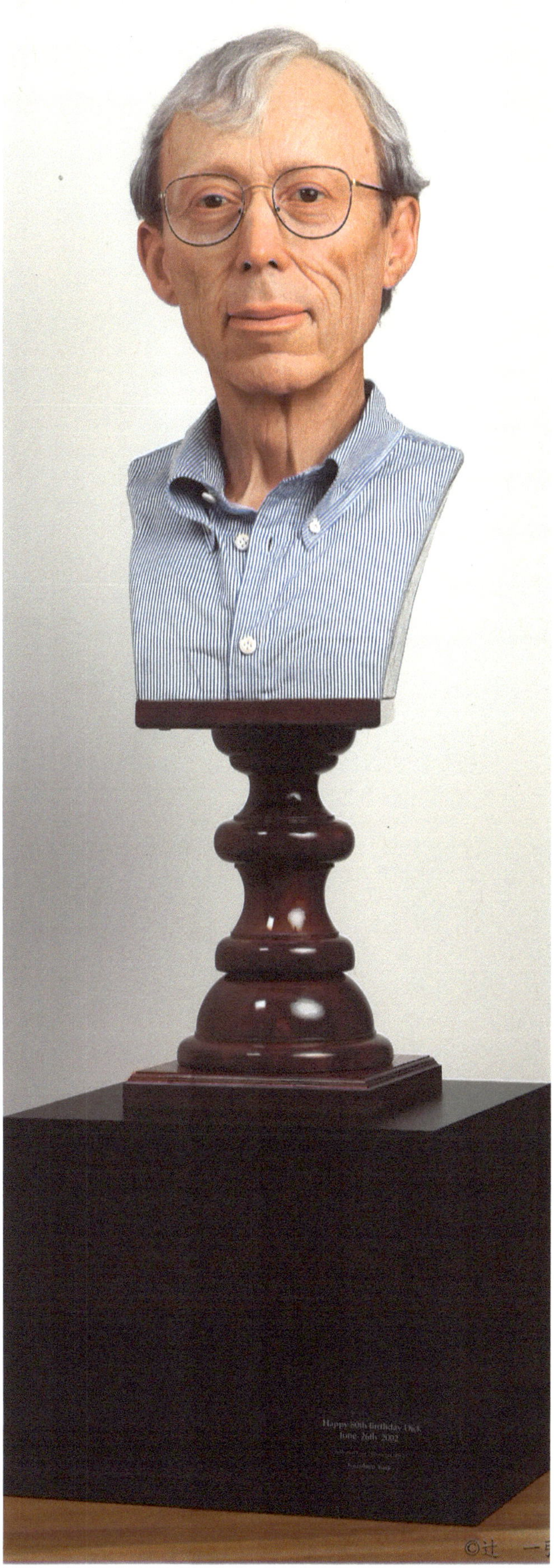

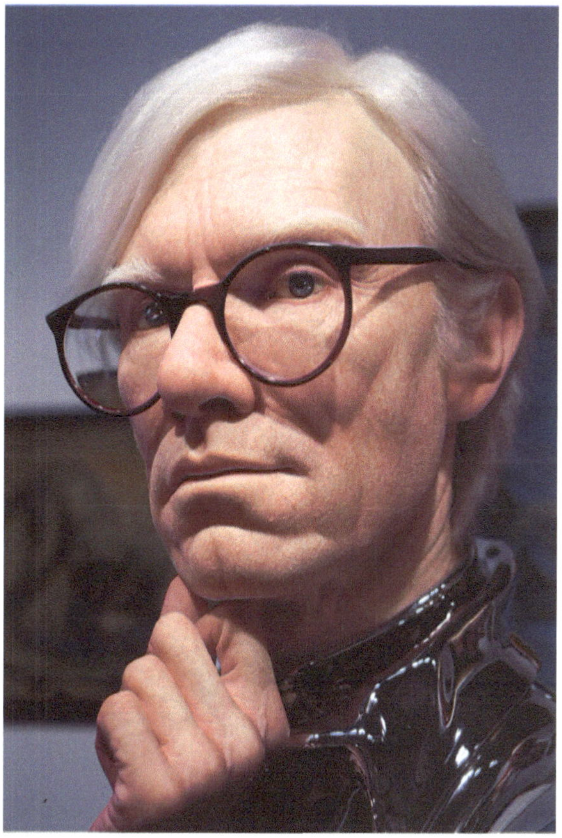

Top: Portrait of Andy Warhol - American Enlightment, 2013, 231cm tall
Left: Portrait of Dick Smith - A Moment from 1997
Far Left: Soft Construction of Dali, 2015, 231cm tall
Bottom: Portrait of Frida Kahlo, 2016, 224cm tall

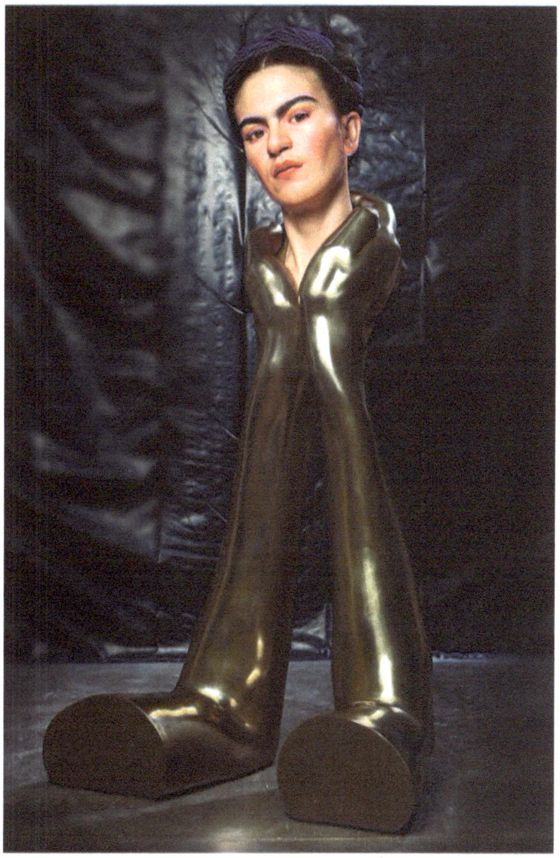

MAREK ZYGA
SCULPTURE - POLAND

www.marekzyga.pl

Marek Zyga is a Polish sculptor. Specializing in the human body and its many diverse gestures, he takes as his subject the individual, doing what he can to capture the variety of behaviours and reactions that the individual exhibits.

He is self-taught, and his style is distinctly his own even to the untrained eye. Rather than using sketches to plan his works, he makes models out of clay. In order to finalize his sculptures, he works with agobas and pigments and glazes them. Before he ever starts using his hands, however, he visualizes in his mind exactly what he wants to see in front of him.

Marek is held in high regard for his work in gypsum. He draws inspiration from classic sculptural forms, and his busts, torsos, and heads are imbued with symbolic and sensual meanings. Taking as his style a modified form of surrealism, he communicates the relationships between people by illustrating their similarities and differences in his sculptures.

Marek's work has been exhibited in Belgium, the Netherlands, and Denmark, among other places. His works speak to a world population that is itching to find meaning in the actions of the people around them, and when it comes to expression, no one is more insightful or descriptive than he is. He is like a human camera, capturing what he sees and then replicating it with greater precision than most other eyeballs can.

Right: Let's Waste Some Time

I Had to be You

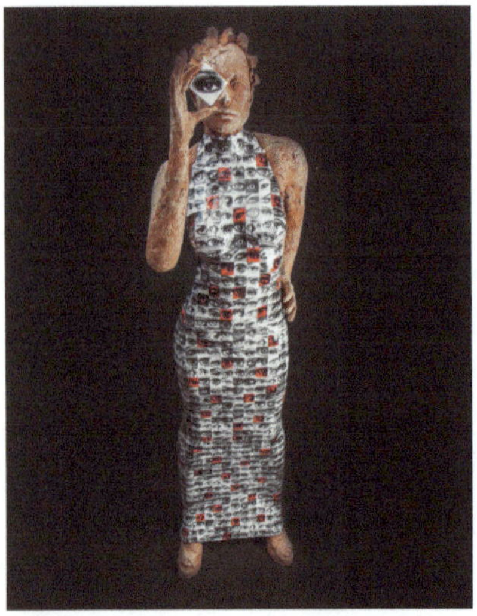

Young at Heart II

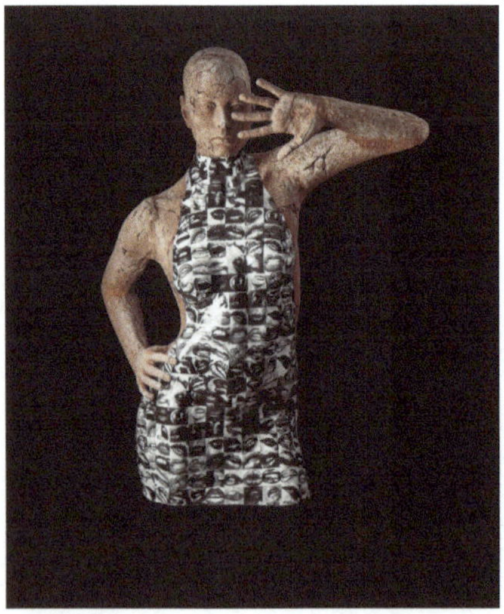

Call Me Irresponsible

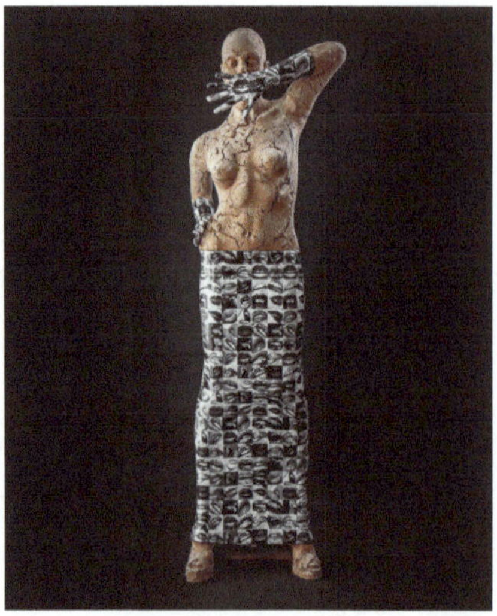

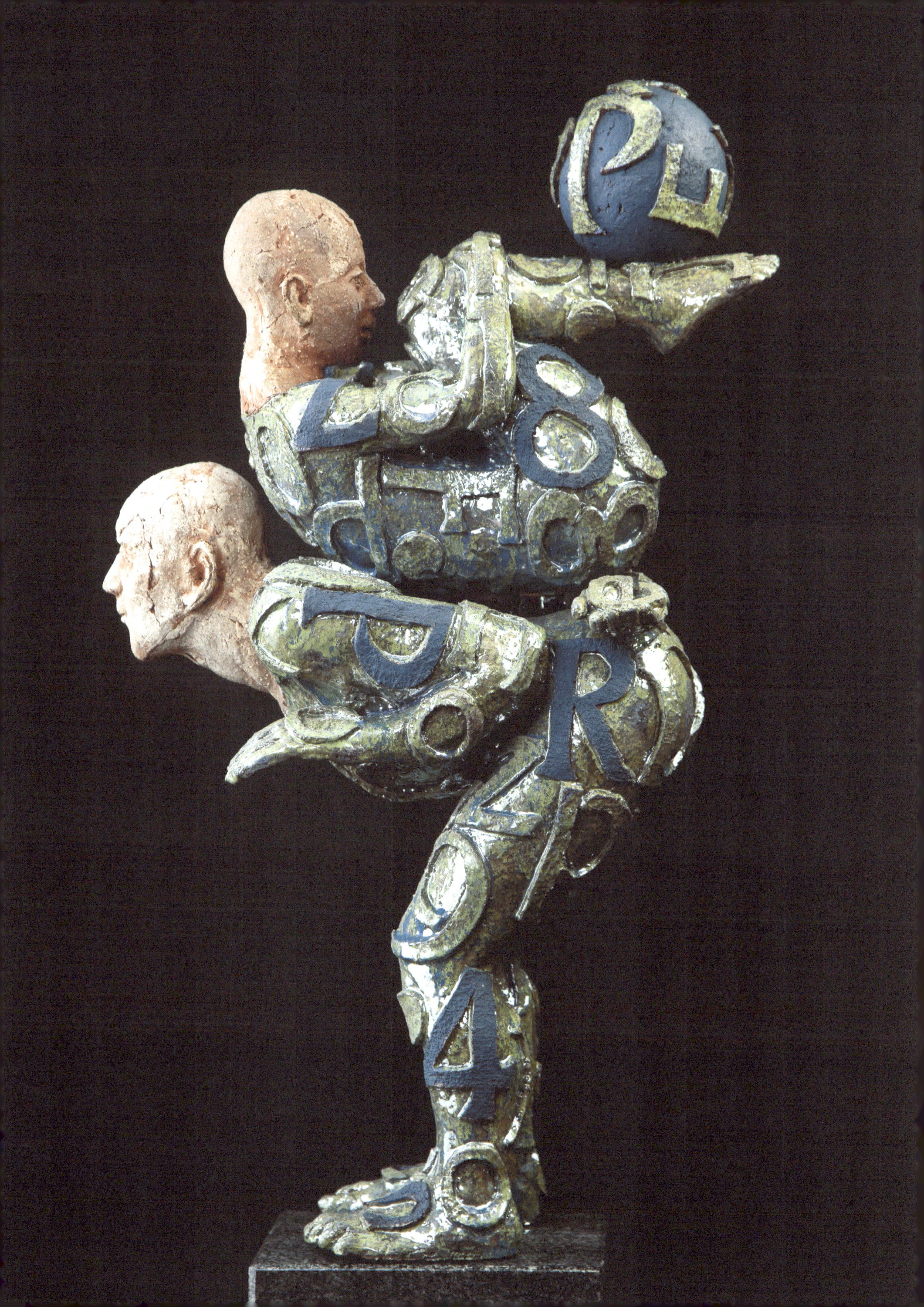

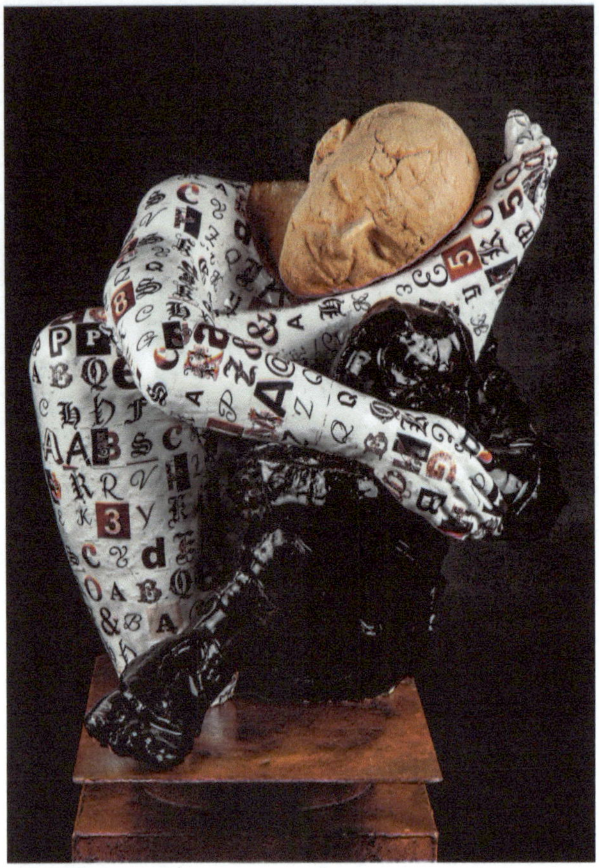

Talking Dreams

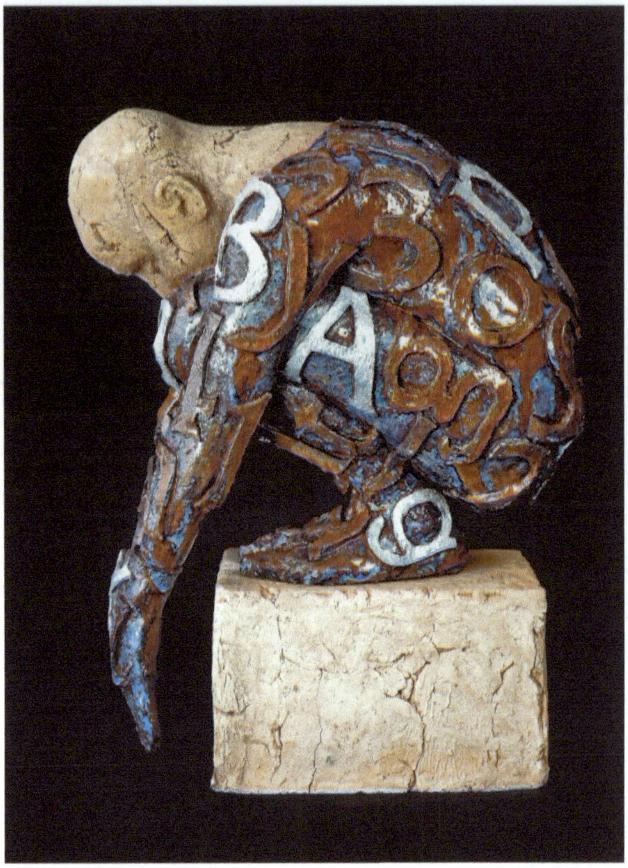

Jumper

You have Got a Friend

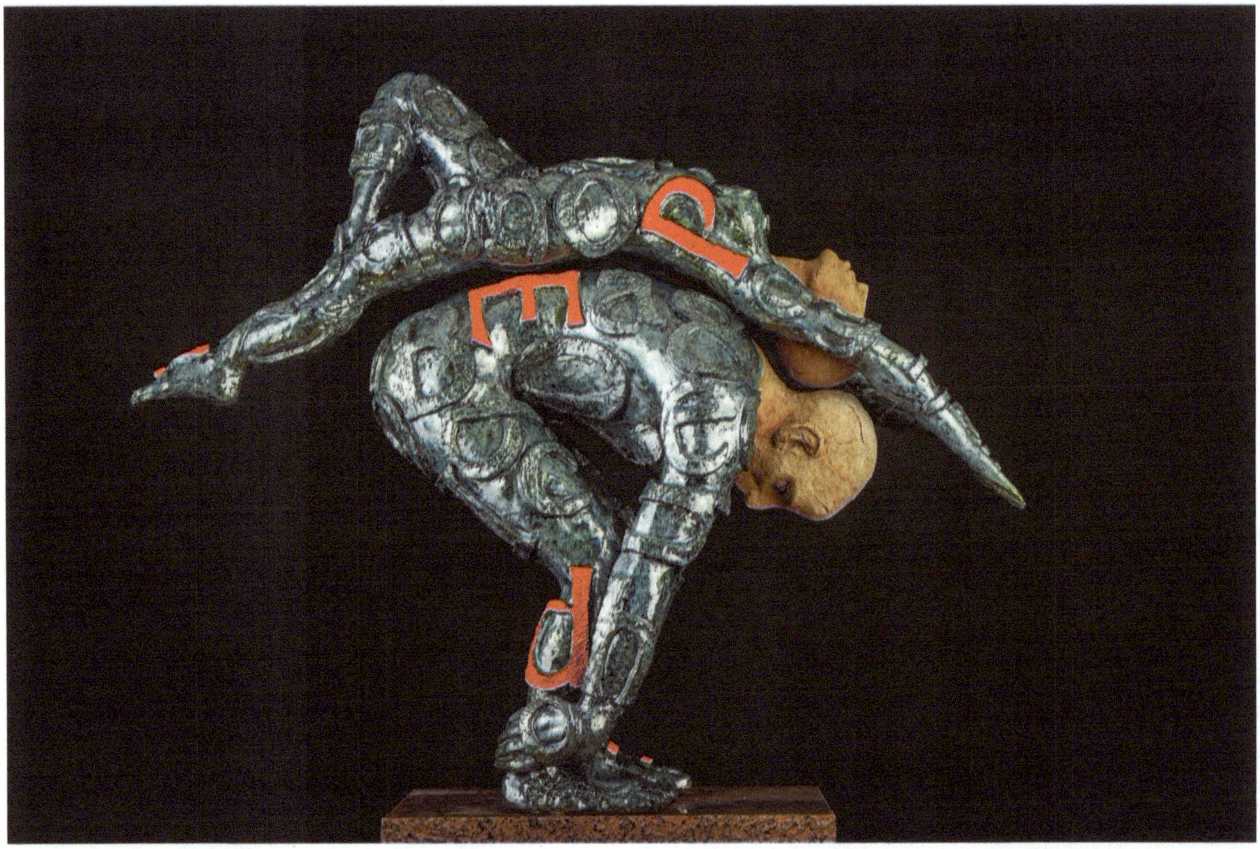

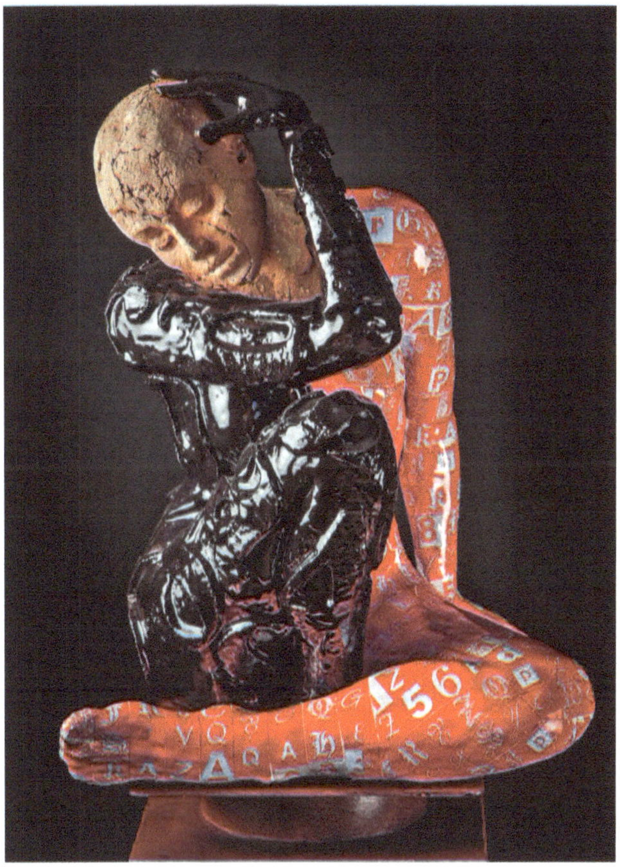

You're not Alone

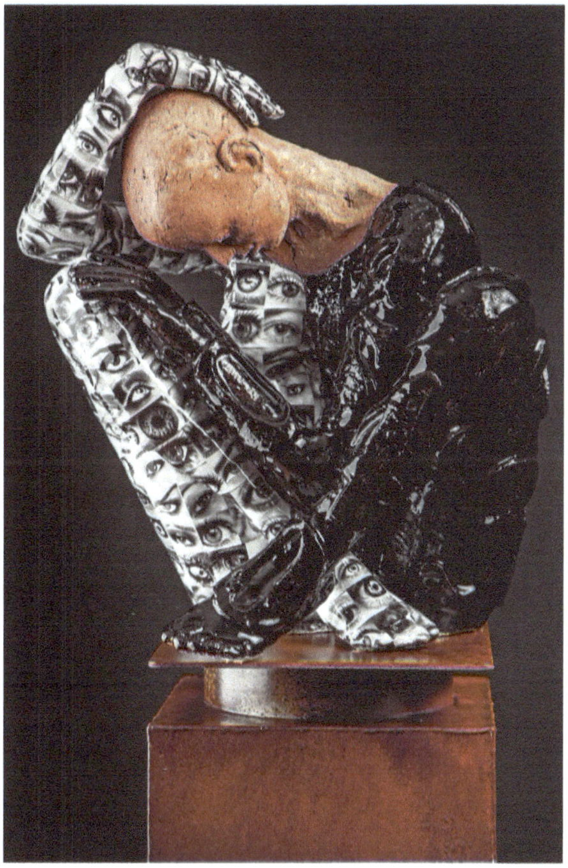

The Other Woman

All Good Friends

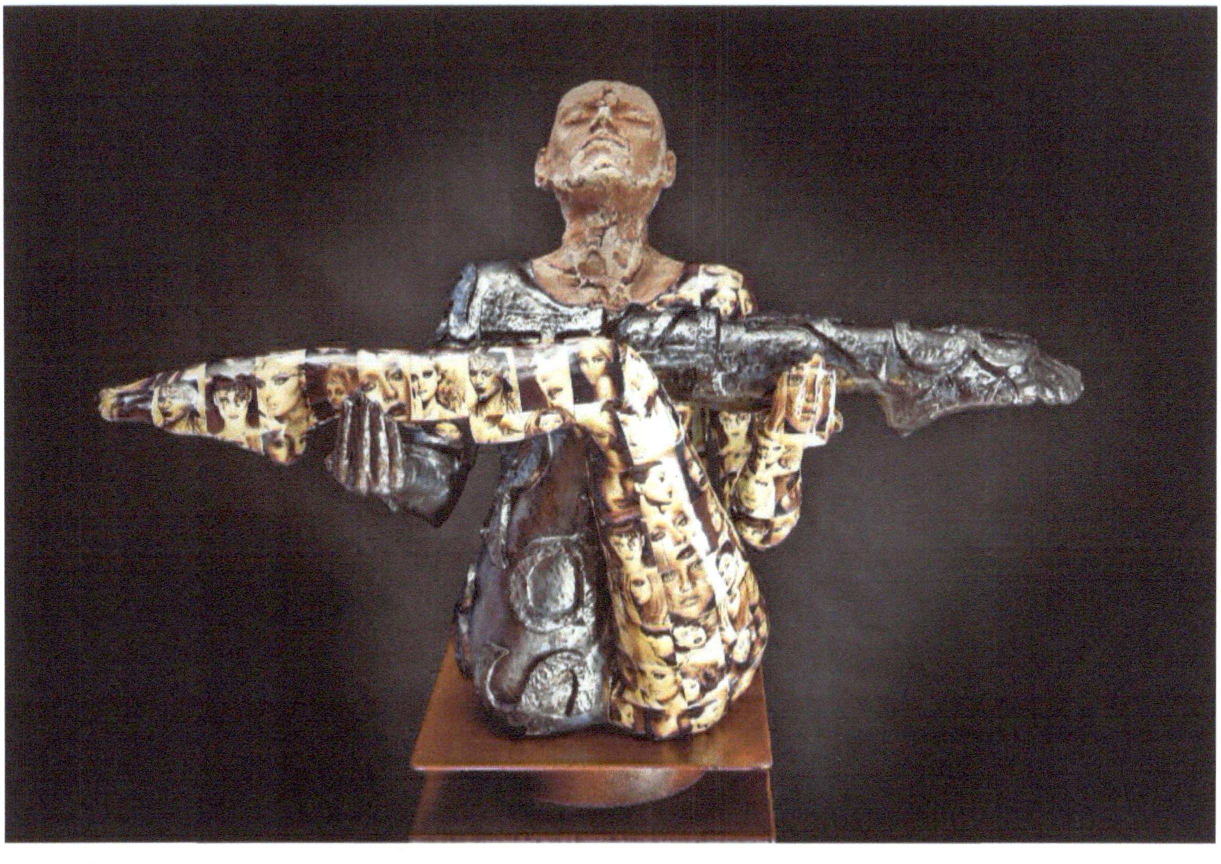

PAOLA GRIZI

SCULPTURE - ITALY

www.paolagrizi.com

Paola Grizi is an artist who is best known for her contemporary artwork.

She won the 3rd Biannual International Ceramics Contest of Acoli Piceno, and in 2014 and 2015 she was invited by the Chinese Changchun Municipality to represent Italy in the third and fourth China Changchun International Ceramics Symposiums. She also won the Special Public Award at the 35th CICA International Competition de L'Alcora in Spain and then went on to serve on the jury of the same contest in 2016. Additionally she was chosen by the Pontifical Gregorian University in collaboration with the Kunst-Station of Köln in Germany for a contemporary art project in the Church of Saint Peter, along with eleven other international artists.

Paola first became interested in art while she was still a child, mentored by her grandfather, who was a famous Italian painter and sculptor. She studied Classics in high school and earned her degree in Italian Literature with first-class honors. After that, she embarked on a career in journalism and editing, at the same time spending time on her art, working heavily with clay.

Particularly well-known around Italy, she has been featured at exhibits in Rome, Faenza, Venice, Florence, Milan, Pisa, and Ferrara, among other cities. She is respected as a sculptor and highly sought-after when it comes to projects both professional and personal.

Right: In-Fondo, 2015, terracotta with engobes, 38 x 29 x 22cm

Ris-Volto, 2015, patined terracotta, 32 x 28 x 20cm

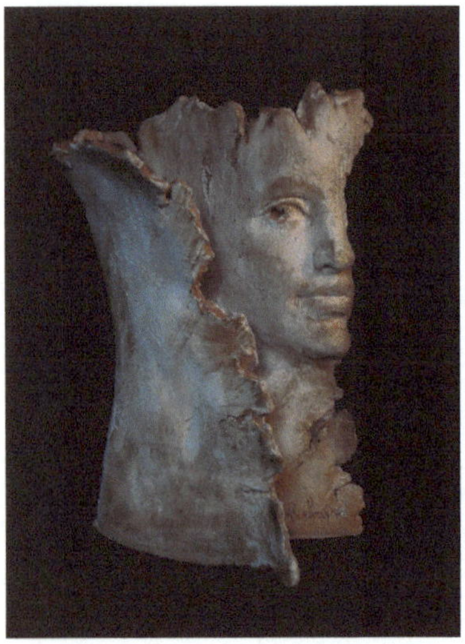

S-Composizione, 2015, patinated terracotta, 24 x 32 x 41cm

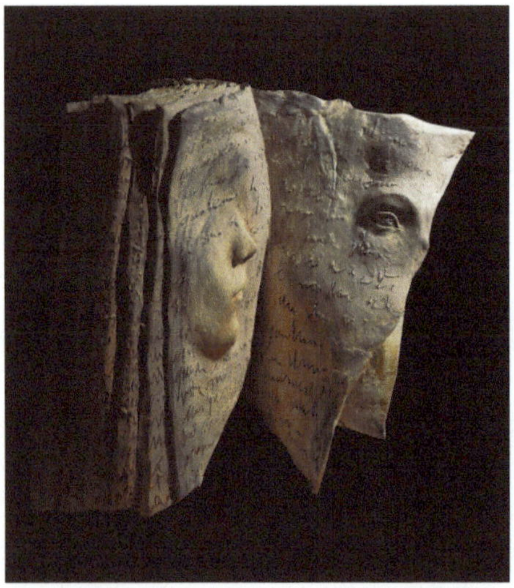

The Secret, 2014, patined white terracotta, 40 x 32 x 25cm

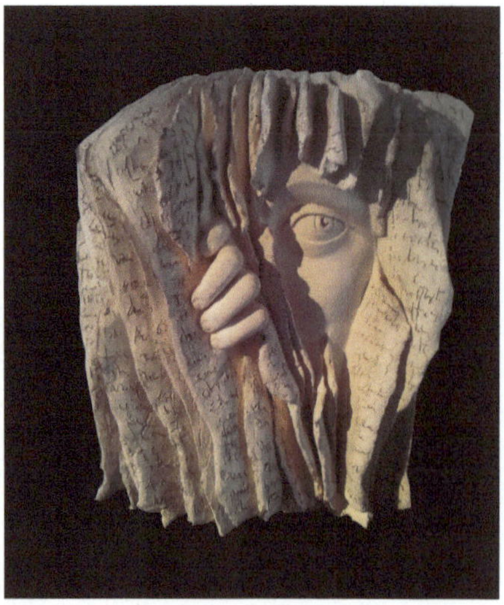

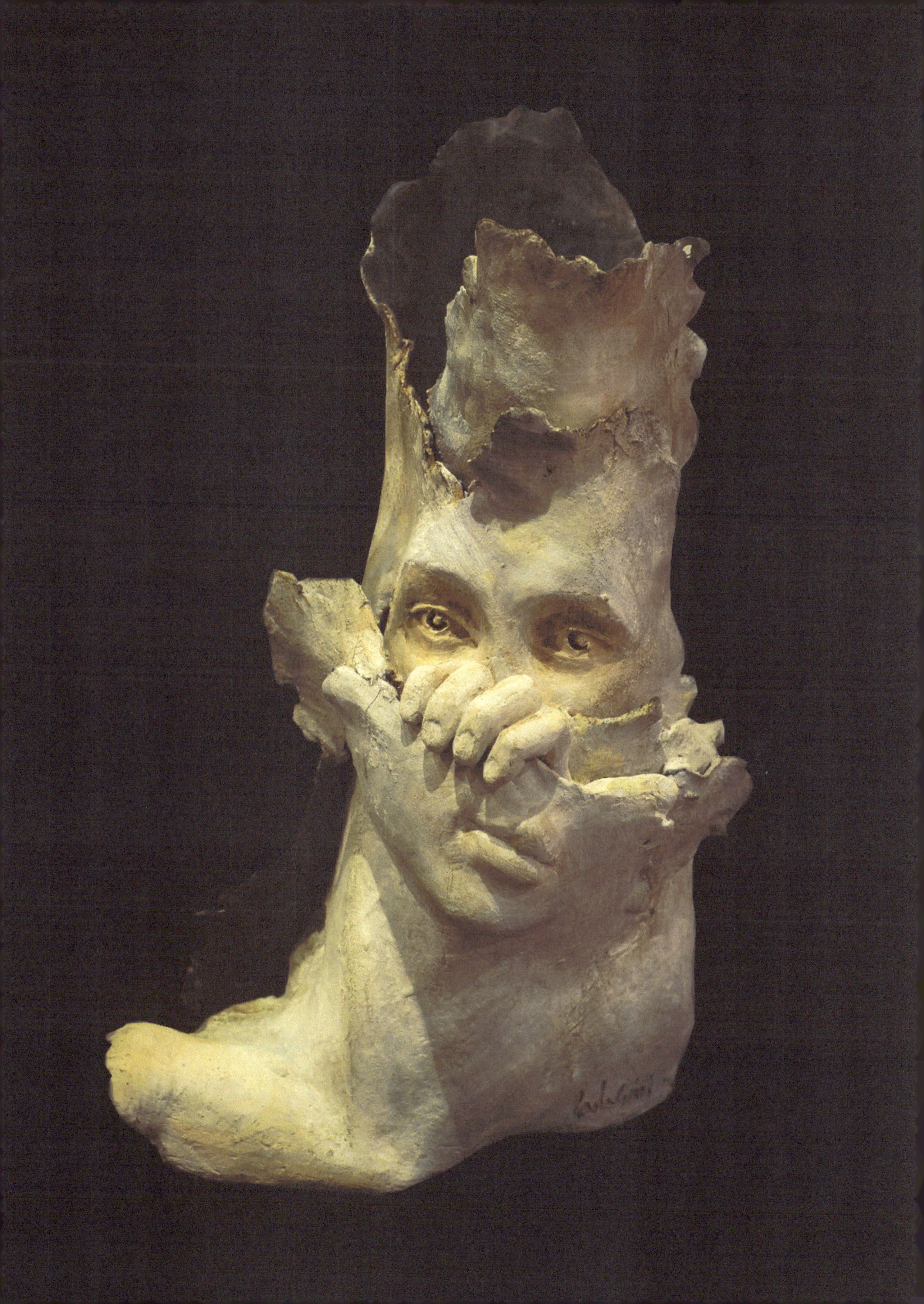

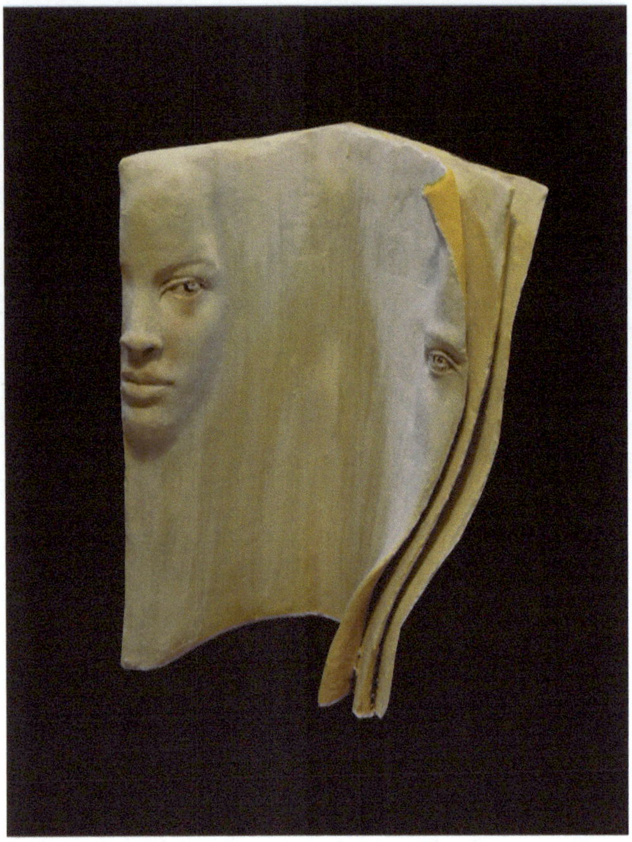

White Pages, 2015, terracotta with engobes, 27 x 36 x 19cm

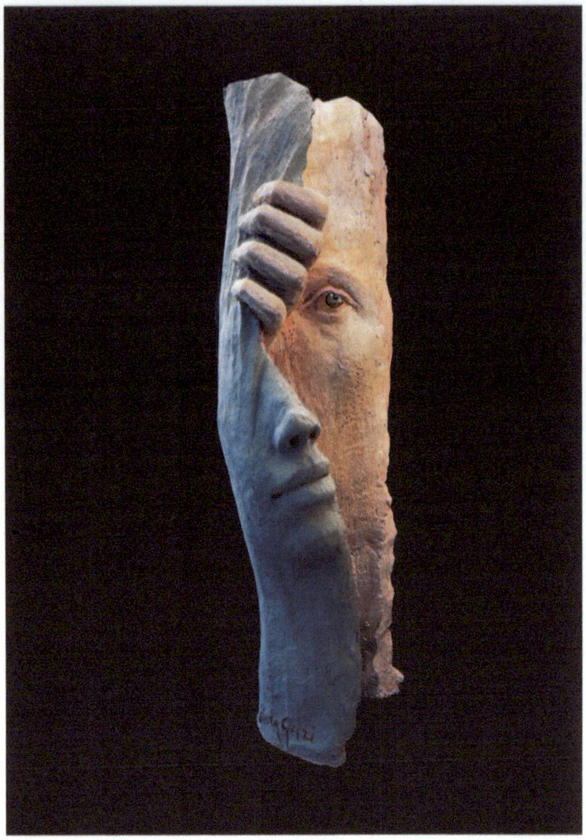

Curtain, 2015, terracotta with engobes, 41 x 15 x 12cm

Vital breath, 2015, patined terracotta, 31 x 40 x 20cm

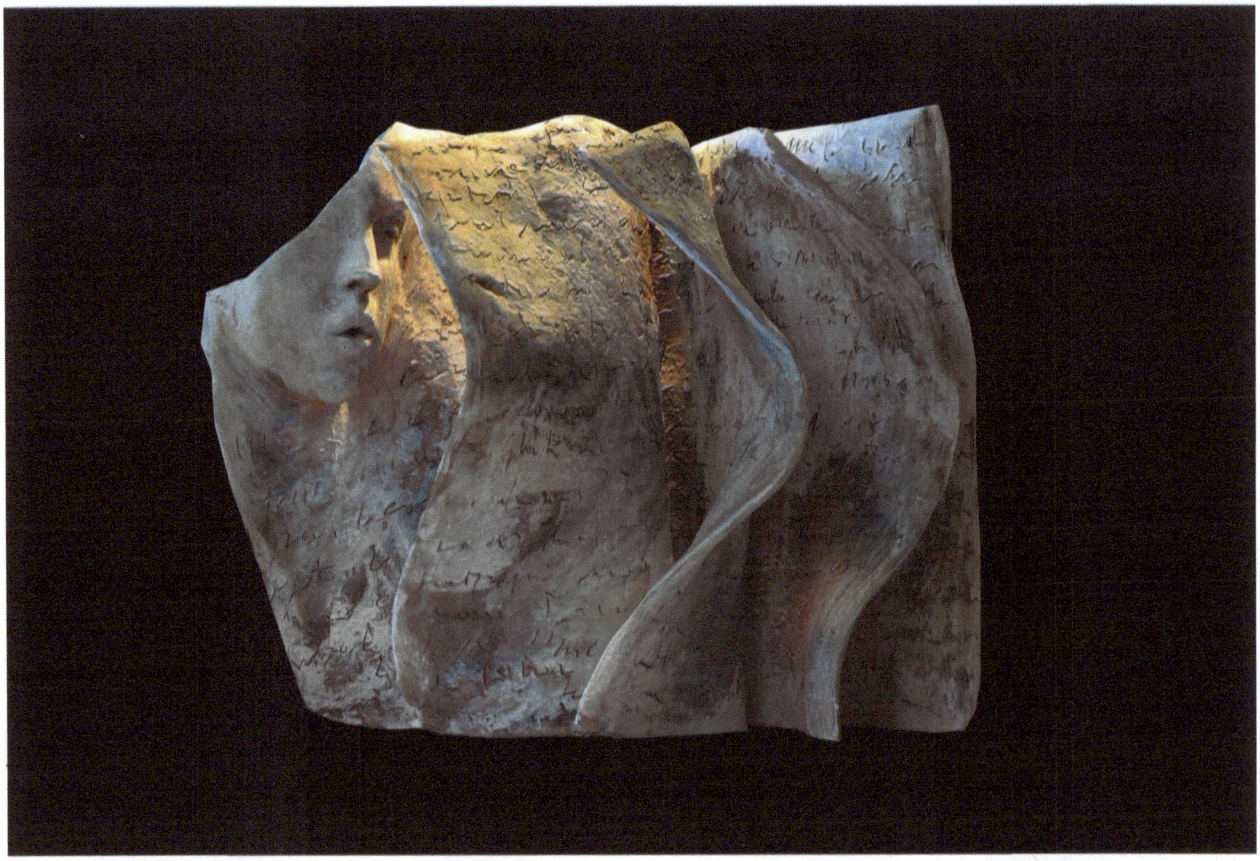

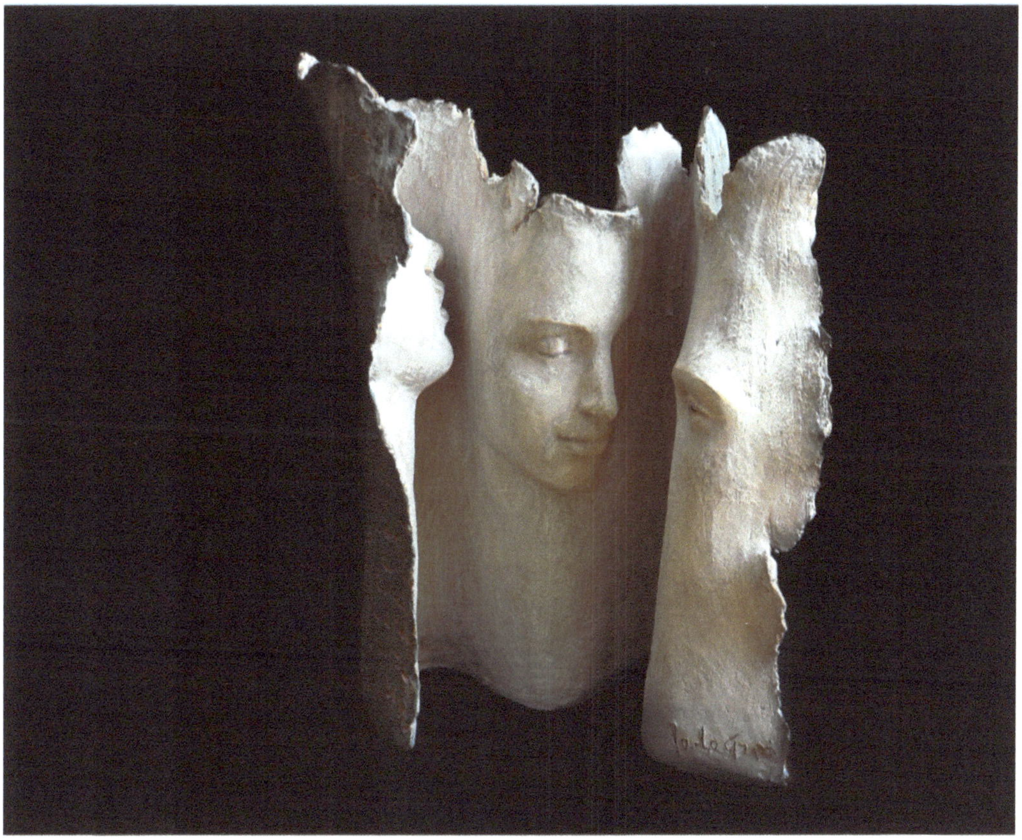

Ara Mara Amara, 2016, refractory terracotta with engobes, 40 x 29 x 21cm

Costellazione, 2016, terracotta with engobe, 28 x 25 x 15cm

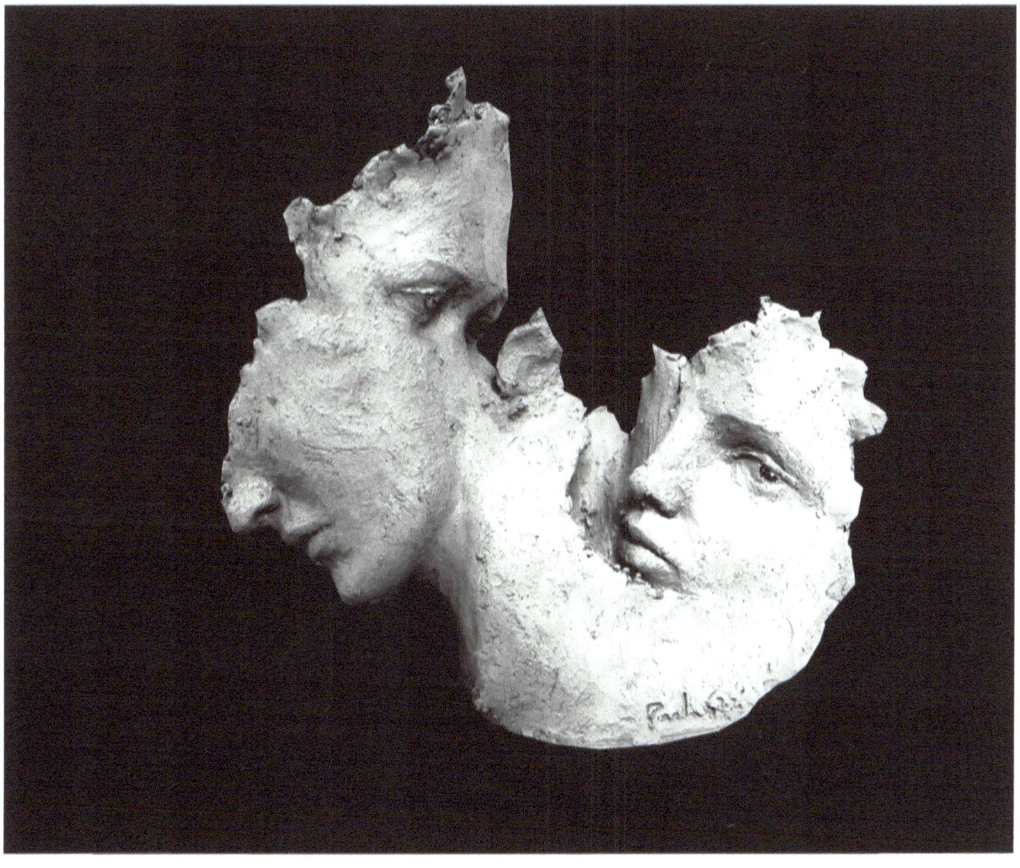

PATRICE PIT HUBERT

SCULPTURE - FRANCE

www.1661235.com

Patrice "Pit" Hubert is a French artist who is known around the world for his Kinetic Mecaniks, a series of sculptures that he started work on in 2003.

Making use of metalworks, lights, and motion, Kinetic Mecaniks is in a way reminiscent of insects, birds, and carnivorous plants that do not exist today but could potentially exist in some alternate, alien world. He adds a fourth dimension to his sculptures by also making use of motors and rotating parts. Cutting and bending metal and stainless steel into intricate shapes, he prefers to create works that are inspired by nature in some way, commenting on that choice by combining the organic with the mechanical.

Pit has a fiercely analytical mind, and he is fascinated by dates and other numbers. Bringing this fascination into his sculptures, he engraves a serial number into every one of his works. These serial numbers in a way connect every part of the Kinetic Mecaniks series. Most recently, in 2015, Pit launched the Naia Museum, a museum that is all about Fantasy and Visionary Art.

When you look at one of Pit's pieces, you get a glimpse of the place where the world that people have created merges with the world into which people were born. This glimpse can at times be unsettling, but it is also deeply illuminating, bringing into our line of sight a vision of what is possible.

Kinetic Mecanik 52, steel, motor, 180cm tall

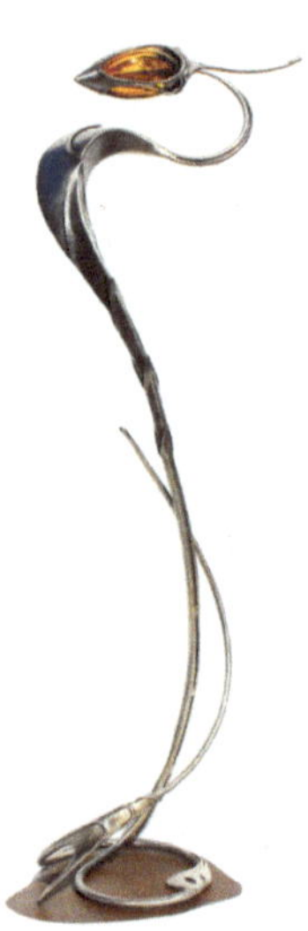

Kinetic Mecanik 49, steel, motor, 69cm tall

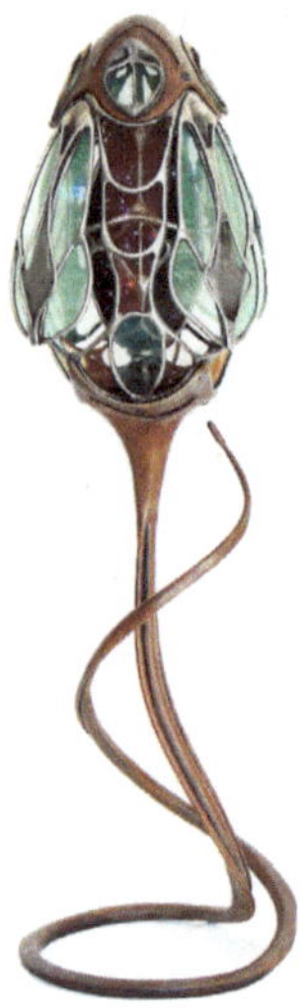

Kinetic Mecanik 53, steel, motor, 255cm tall

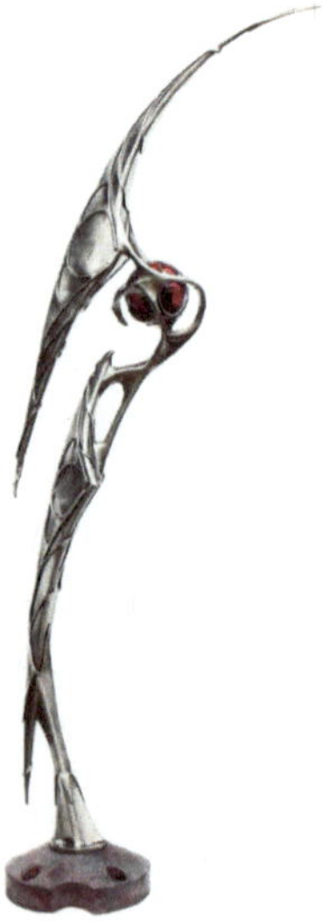

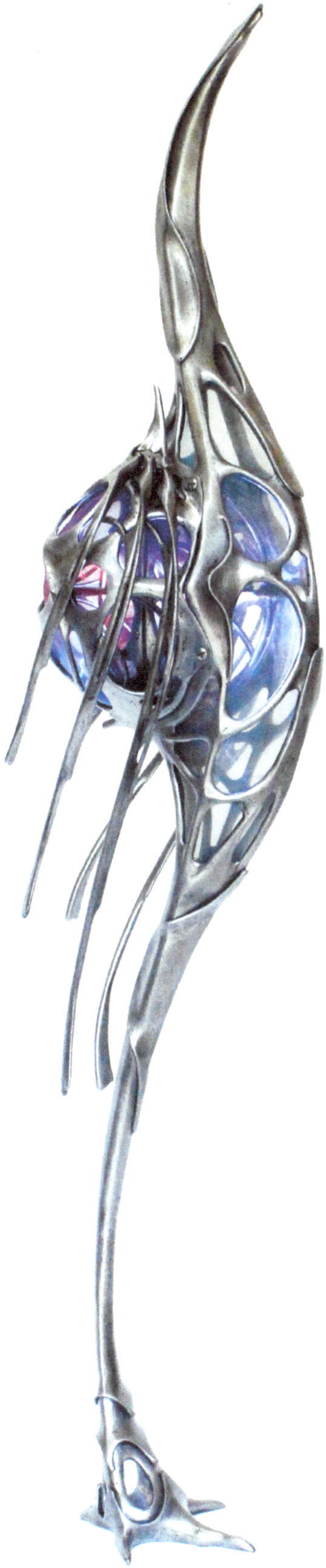

Kinetic Mecanik 56, 2014, steel, motor, 125cm tall

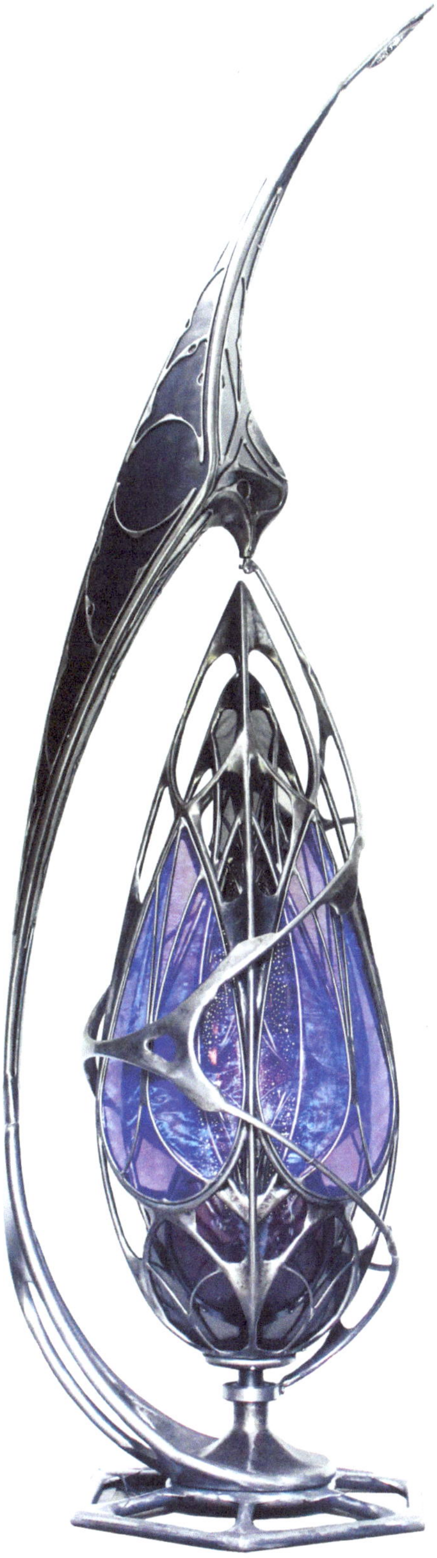

Kinetic Mecanik 54, steel, motor, 410cm tall

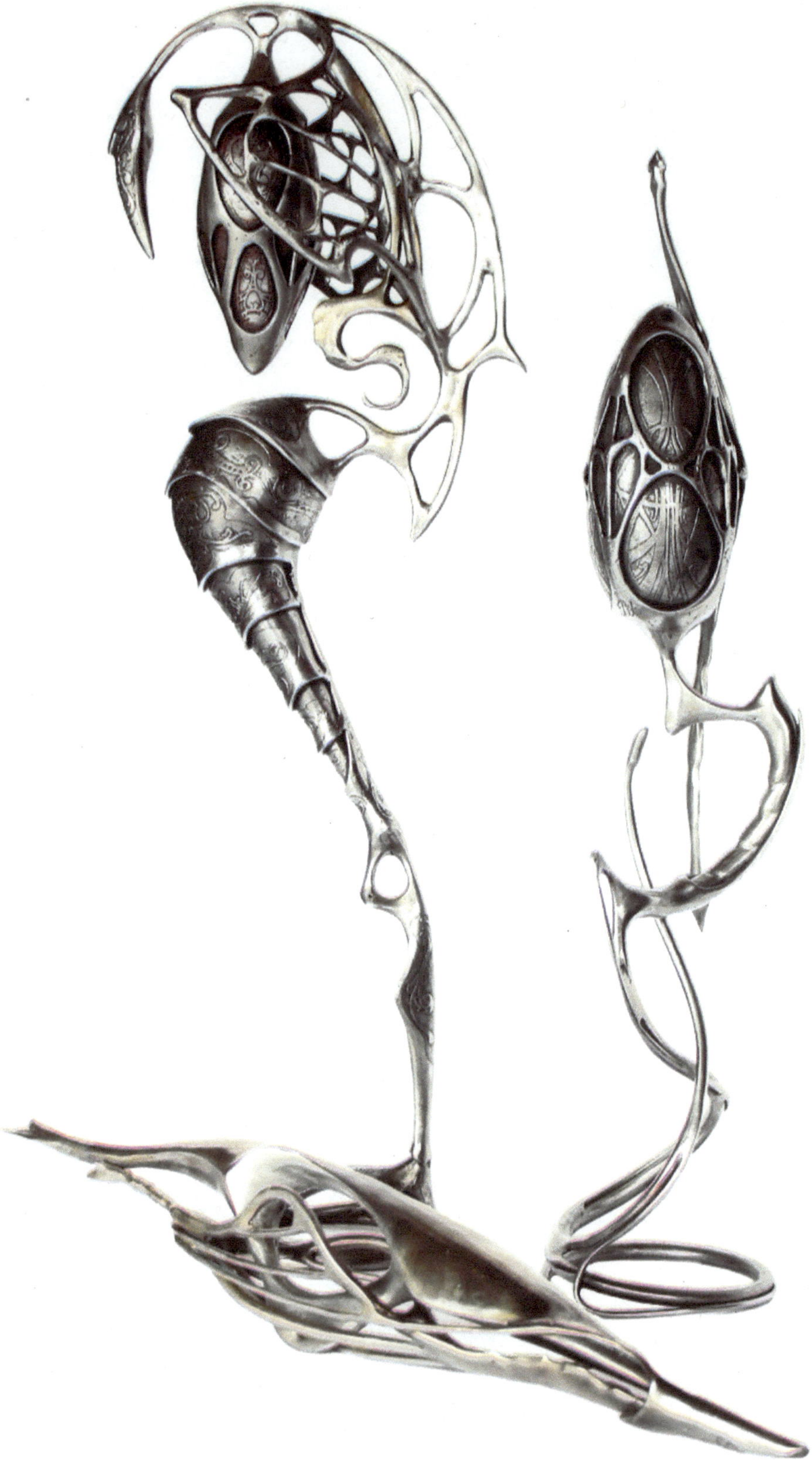

Clockwork Eggs & Fish, 2014, steel, motor, glass, 65cm

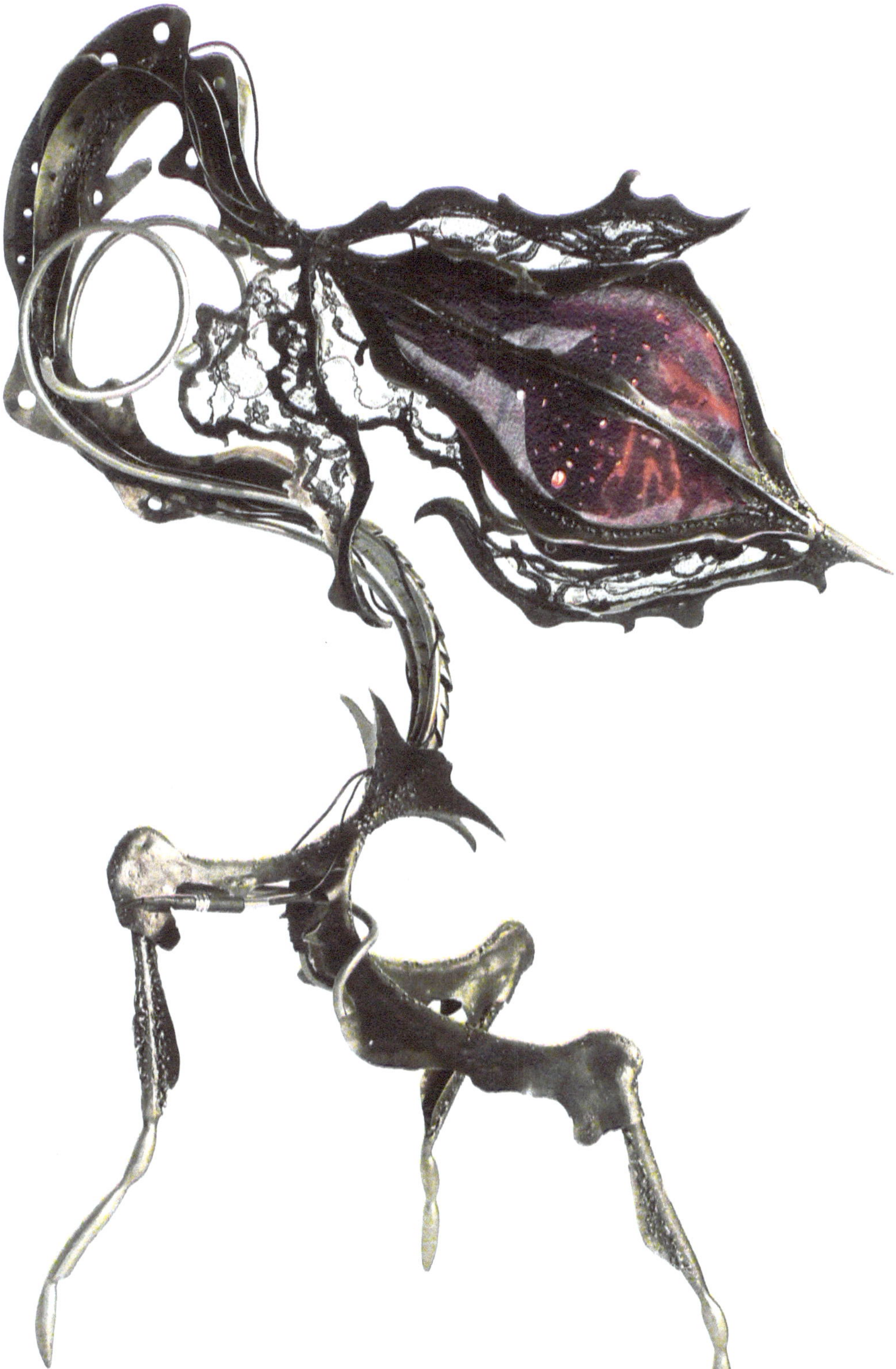

Kinetic Mecanik 23, 2009, steel, motor, glass, 65cm tall

SALAVAT FIDAI

SCULPTURE - RUSSIA

www.salavatfidai.com

Salavat Fidai is a Russian artist. He grew up in a small Ural Mountains village, and from a young age, his talent for art was fostered. His first love was for the visual arts, but because he worried about supporting himself financially, he decided to pursue a career as a lawyer. After studying law, he went on to work for trading companies over a twenty-year period. Successful in this role, he rose up into a senior position.

While he was living a comfortable lifestyle, he was never content in the corporate world. Eventually, he made the brave leap out on his own, taking up spiritual practices and spending more time reading and seeing the world with his family by his side, exploring and going on adventures in order to discover himself.

Salavat is today recognized widely for his sculptures, which he carves out of wood and chalk. In addition, he recently took up pencil graphite rods as a medium, a medium with which he had practiced when he was younger. Because graphite is so brittle, sculptures made with it crumble frequently, frustrating many artists who work with it. He draws influence from films, cartoons, animals, pop culture, comic books, other artworks, household items, and even architecture. Because his sculptures are so varied in their theme, he is sometimes seen as a cultural connoisseur, seeing the connections between forms that are traditionally considered high-brow and low-brow.

Right: Don't hear, don't see, don't speak,
2016, graphite pencil, 1.6 x 0.5cm

Lorde Voldemort,
2015, graphite pencil, 1.2 x 0.5cm

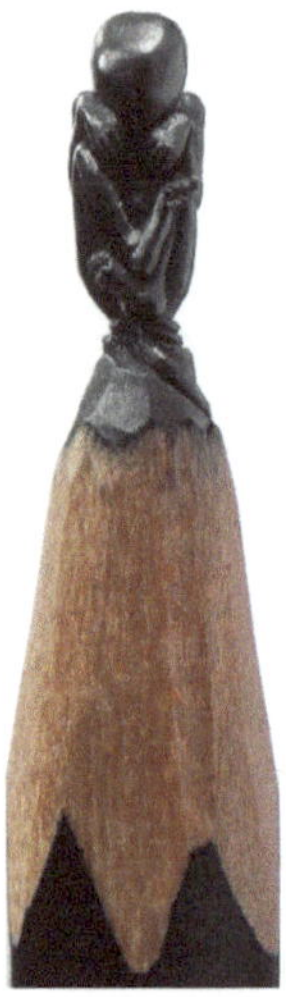

Horse, 2015, graphite pencil, 0.8 x 0.5cm

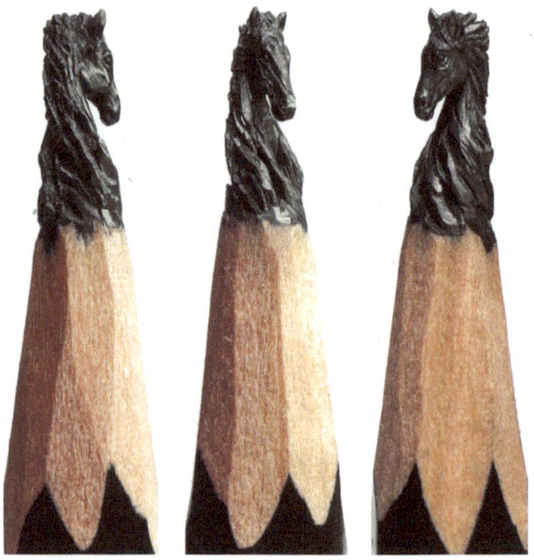

The Bremen Town Musicians, 2016,
graphite pencil, 1.2 x 0.6cm

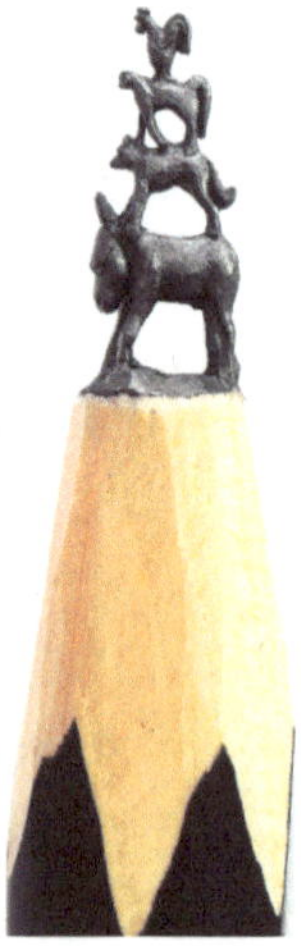

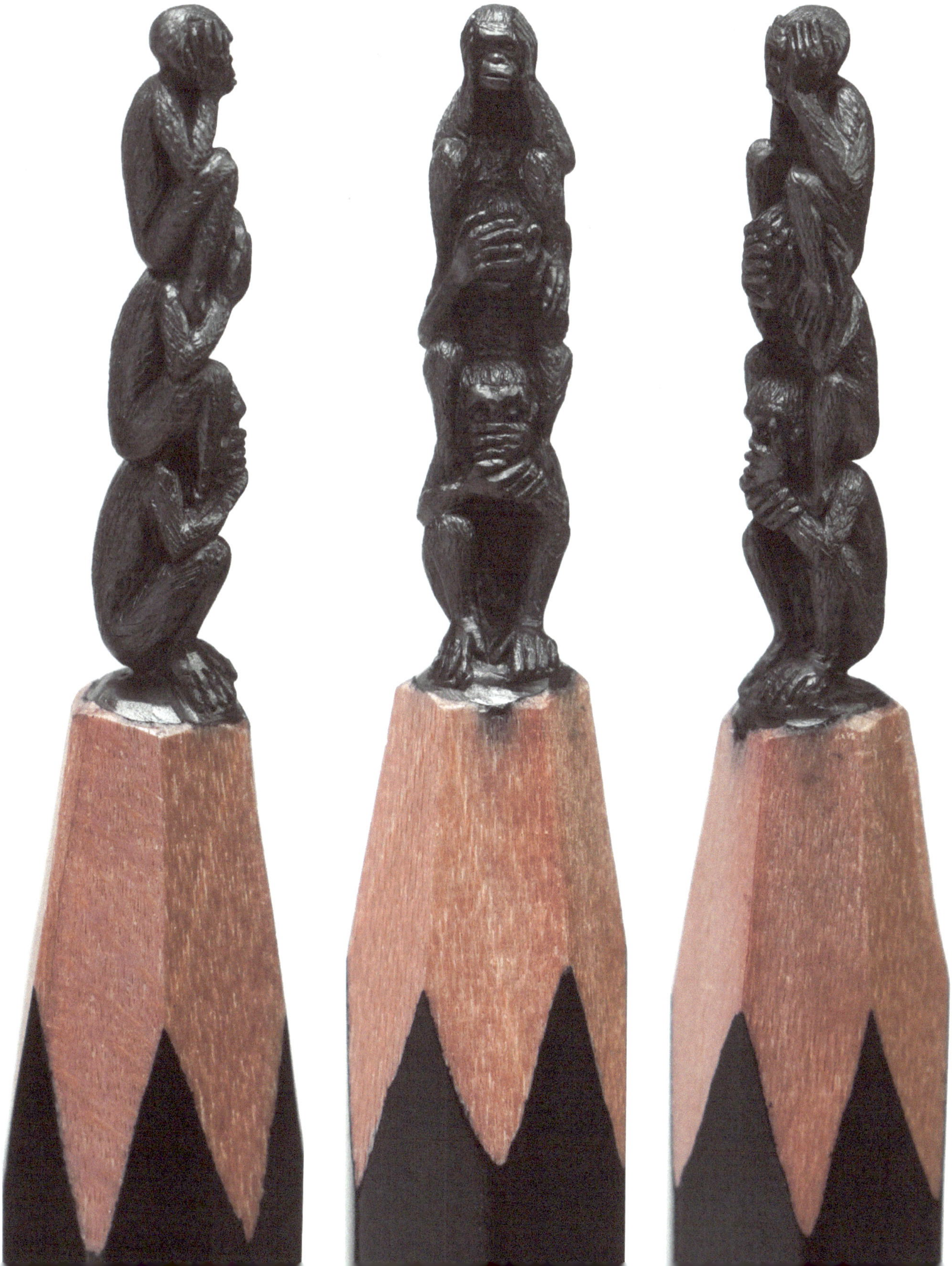

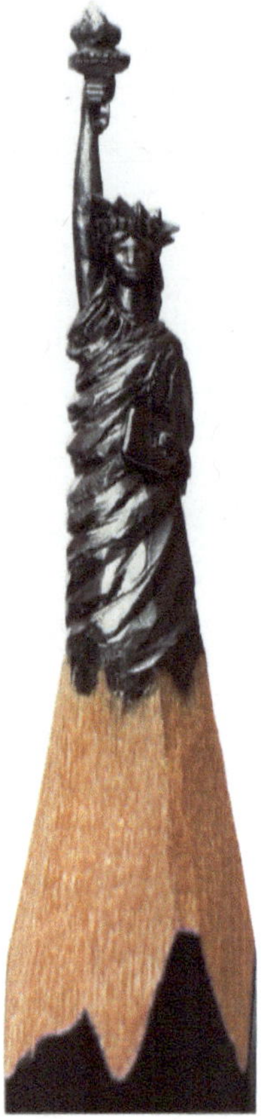

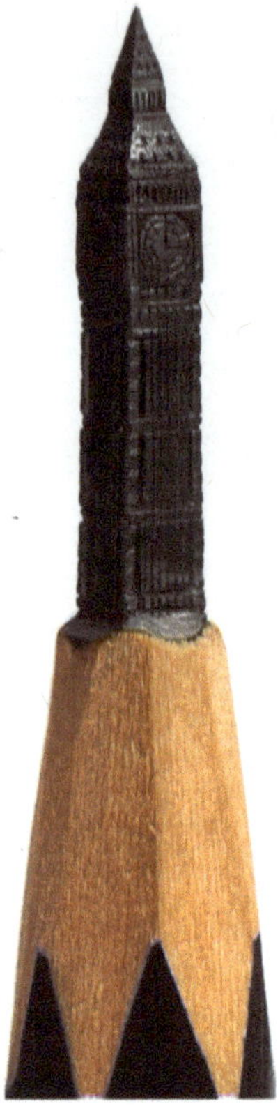

Statue of Liberty, 2015, graphite pencil, 1.6 x 0.5cm

Big Ben, 2015, graphite pencil, 1.5 x 0.5cm

Lock and Key, 2015, graphite pencil, 1.2 x 0.5cm

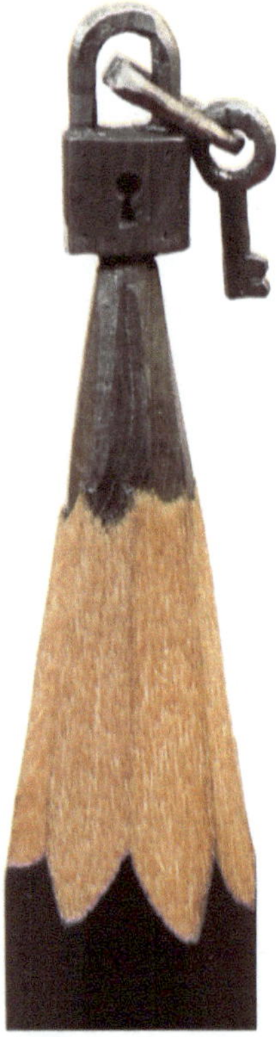

The Voice, 2016, graphite pencil, 1.2 x 0.6cm

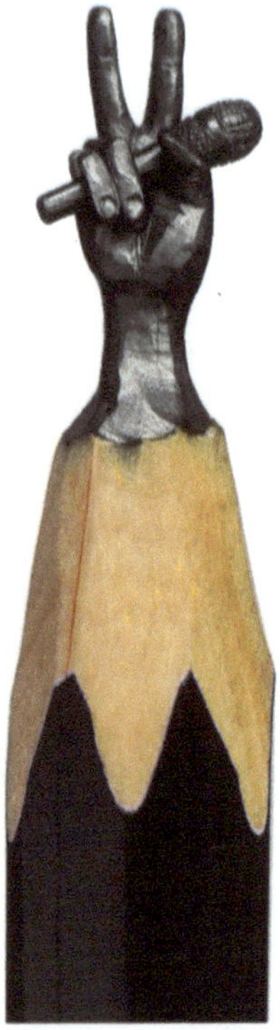

Heart, 2016, graphite pencil, 2 x 0.5cm

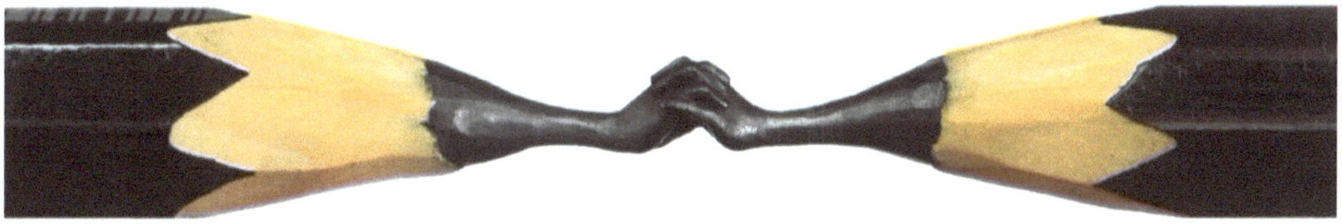

Holding Hands, 2016, graphite pencil, 2 x 0.5cm

Swamp Wallaby, 2016, graphite pencil, 1 x 0.5cm

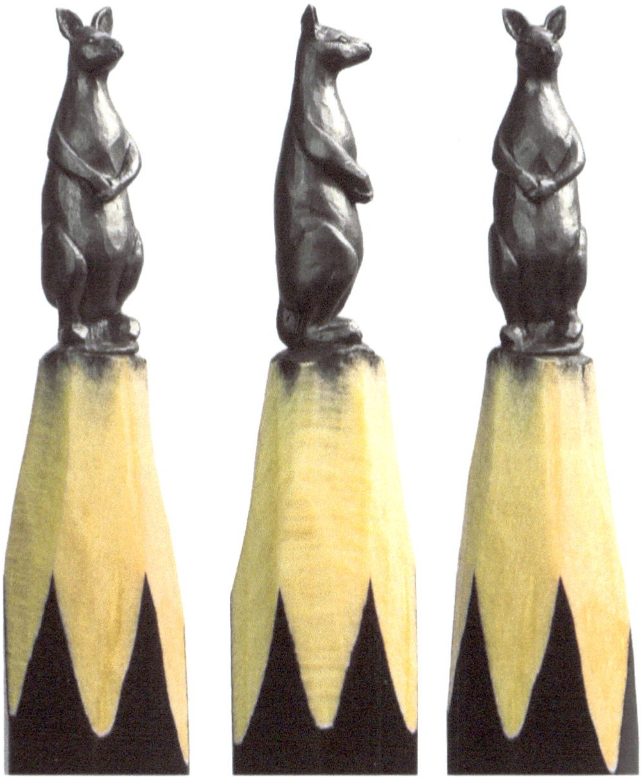

STANISLAW TRZEBINSKI

SCULPTURE - KENYA

www.stanislawtrzebinski.com

Stanislaw Trzebinski is a Kenyan artist who is now based out of Cape Town. He grew up in Nairobi, and even as a child, he knew that he needed to get away, that he needed to see the Rift Valley and the East African coast.

By high school, he showed prodigious talent, which was fostered by one of his teachers. He first worked in painting, collage, and photography before taking on welding and sculpting, and after graduation, he moved to New York and matriculated into Pratt, where his portfolio had in a sense preceded him. Working today out of a studio in Woodstock, he is recognized for his exploration of the symbiotic relationship between humans and the natural world.

Recently, Stanislaw started working on a series that is about the deep, personal bonds between life and the earth, focusing especially on marine life. The Coral Series is a vision underwater, one in which humanity could not be any more present. Seen by many as a prophet of our contemporary world, he is intent on revealing to people the mirror that they would see if only they would step outside of their constructed environments, the mirror that would show them their true face in the absence of all the accoutrements and all the niceties.

In Stanislaw's mind, there is only one world, yet that one world is being ignored wilfully by a species that prefers to see itself as separate from it.

Right: Aphrodite, 2016, bronze, 140 x 45 x 33cm

Faith's Portrait (side view), 2016, bronze, 59 x 23 x 74cm

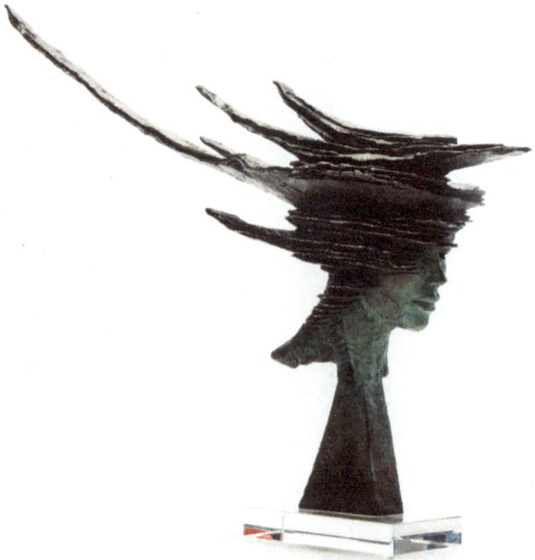

Faith's Portrait, 2016, bronze, 59 x 23 x 74cm

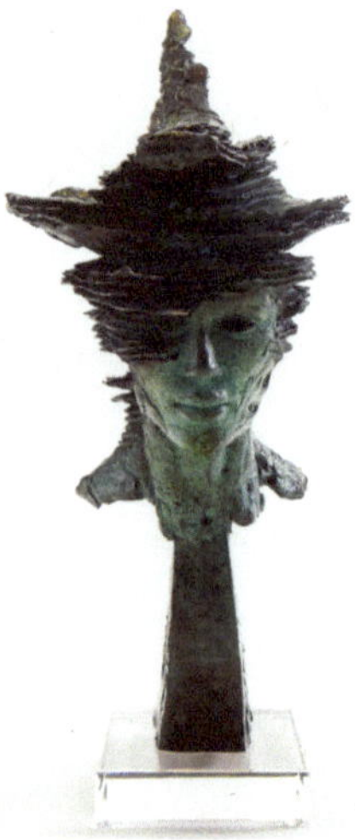

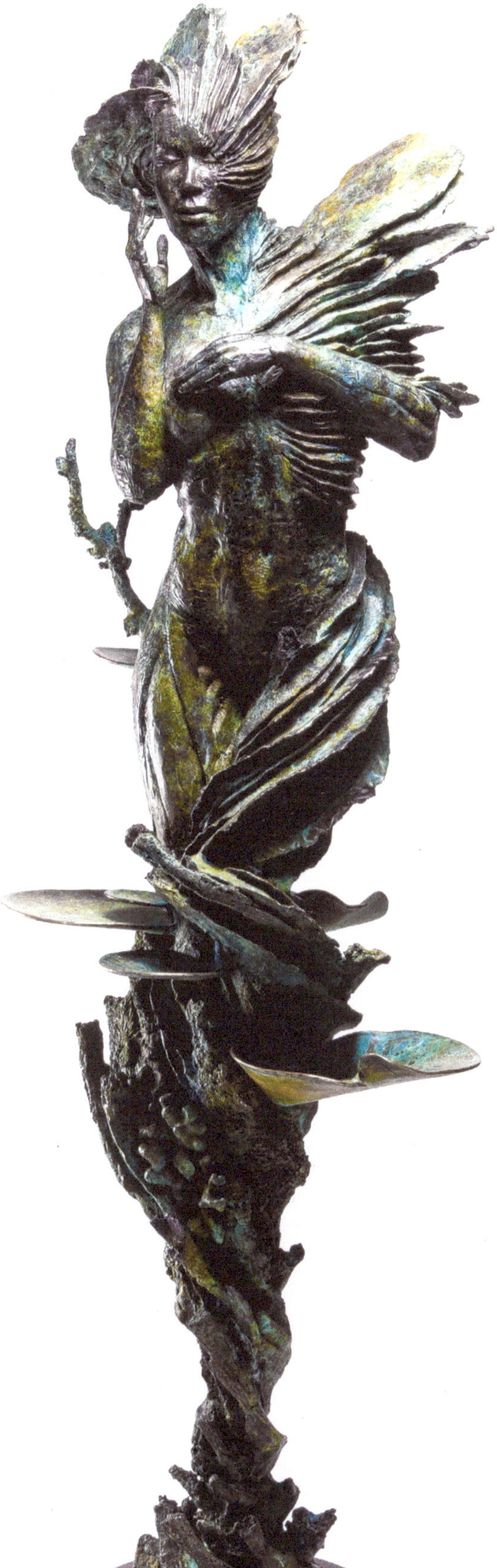

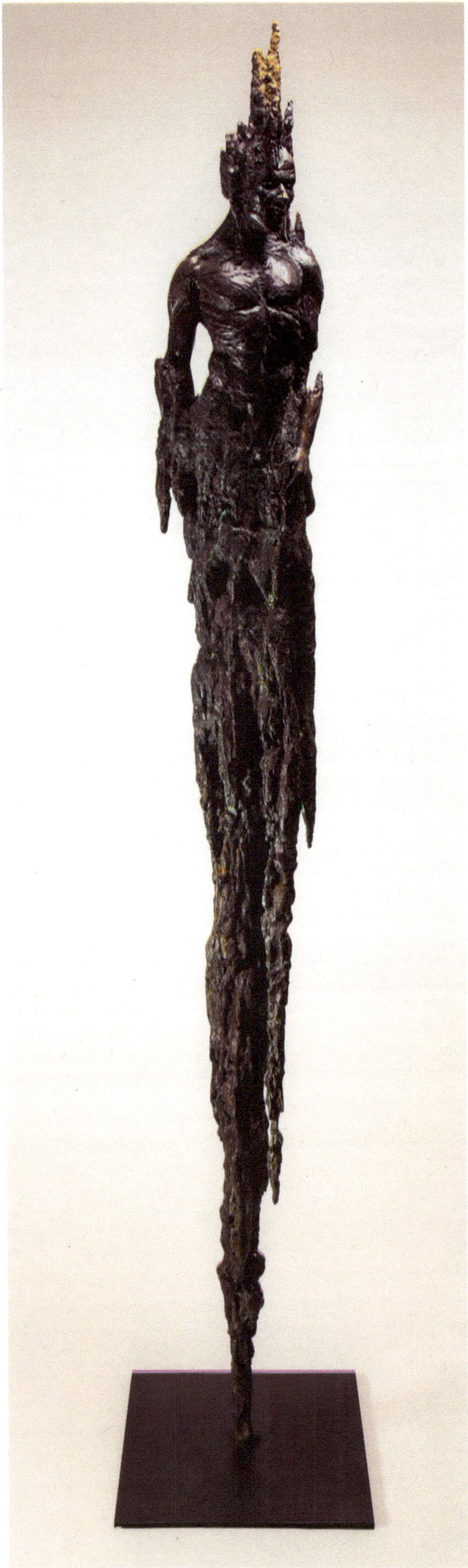

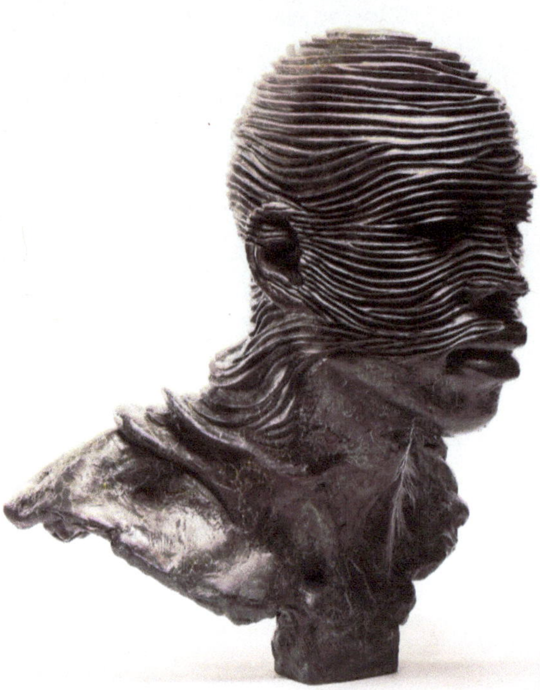

Large Layered Joseph, 2016, bronze, 103 x 45 x 60cm

Left: Stalactite Man, 2015, bronze,242 x 28 x 18cm

Encrusted, 2015, bronze, 78 x 49 x 27cm

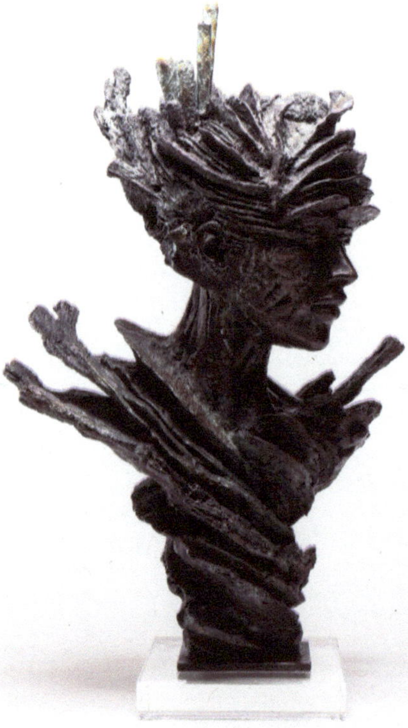

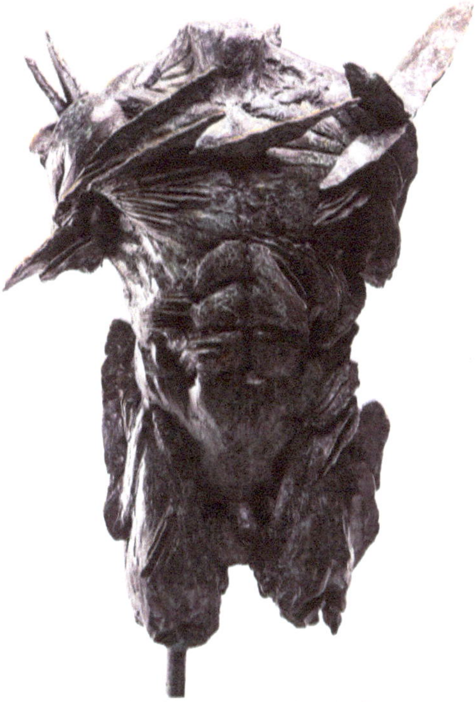

Male Torso - Coral Version, 2016, bronze, 63 x 43 x 25cm

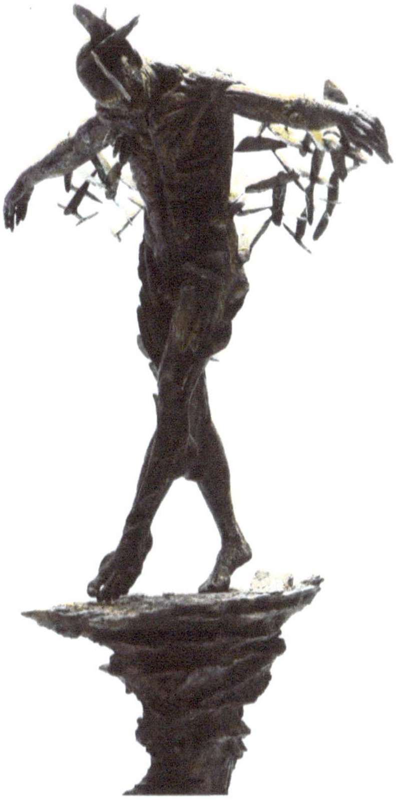

Ortus, 2016, bronze, 130 x 80 x 90cm

Vires, 2016, bronze, 56 x 70 x 30cm

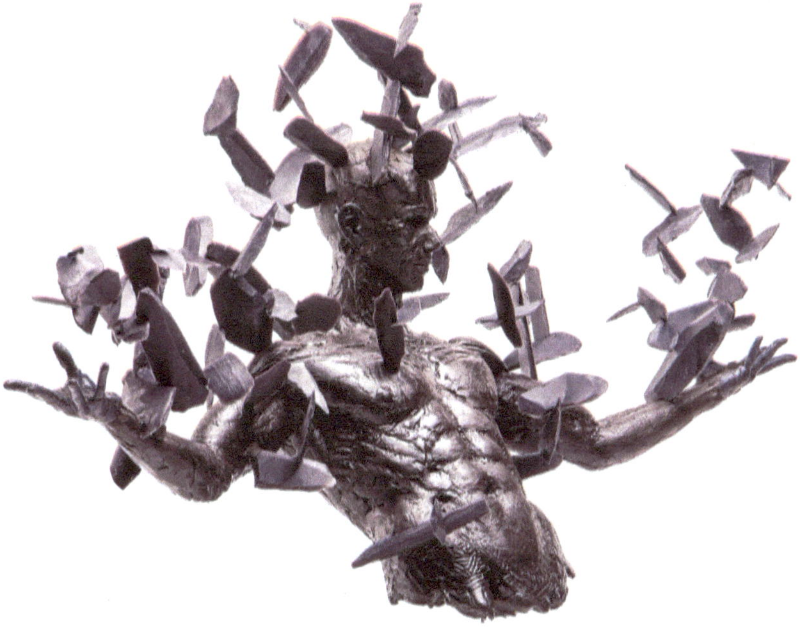

TOMAS VITANOVSKY

SCULPTURE - CZECH REPUBLIC

www.vitanovsky.com

Tomas Vitanovsky has always loved cars and motorbikes since his childhood. When his successful motorcycle stunt career ended due to injury, he spent a lot of time tuning and fixing bikes to earn a living.

While continuing to be surrounded by chains and ball bearings, he had a vision while throwing out some used engine parts from a motorbike and decided to weld them together. This became a pivotal moment in his life and bearings, gears, chains and outlets began to transform into animals, beetles, cars and bikes.

Over time his techniques has not only improved and become more complex, but he has discovered many new ways to bring the life-like quality that many of his recent works have been appreciated for. The high-wattage UGI welding technique he uses for his sculptures is difficult and dangerous, and this provides him with the adrenaline buzz that partly replaces the lost rush since retiring from motorcycle stunt riding.

Tomas has exhibited his artwork in Harley Davidsons in the UK as well as in Lamborghini showrooms. His sculptures have also be published in articles from all over te world. Overtime his work has gained more international recognition and is now being sold thoughout the United Kingdom, Europe and the United States of America.

Right: Dictator, motorcycle parts, 35cm tall

Man on Motorcycle, motorcycle parts, 45 x 25cm

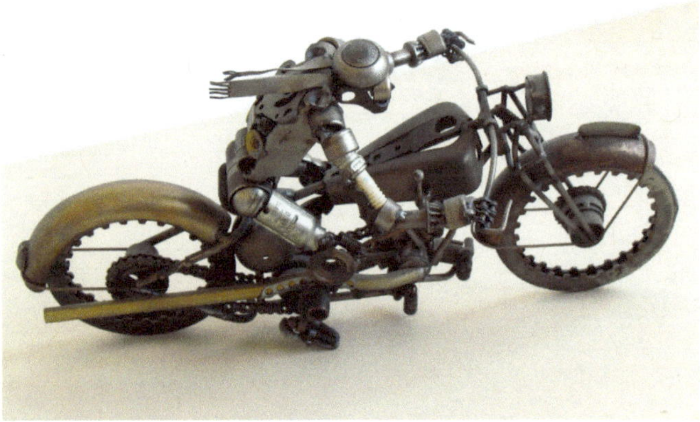

Running Beast , motorcycle parts, 45 x 30cm

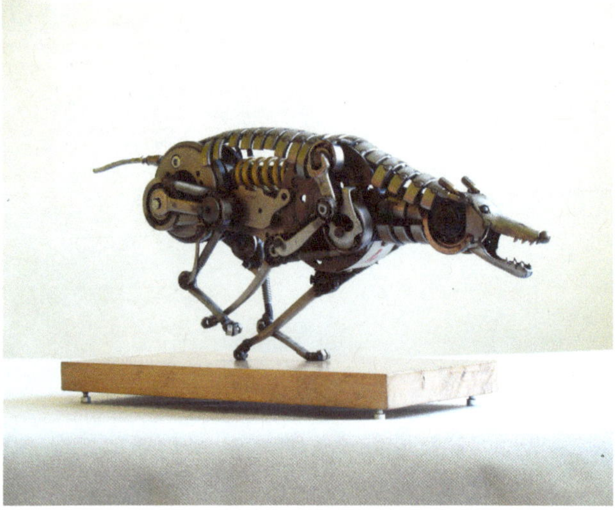

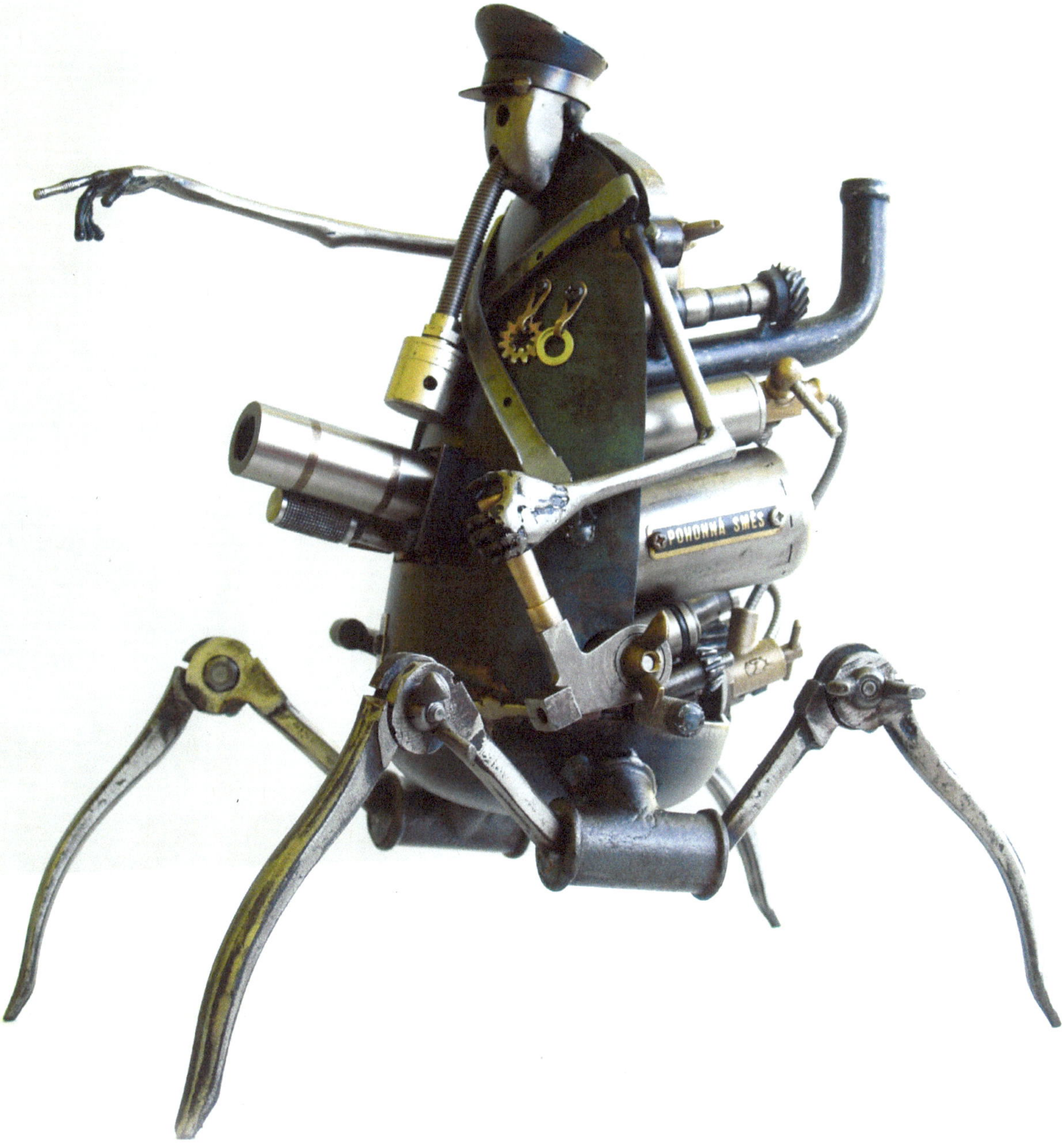
POHONNÁ SMĚS

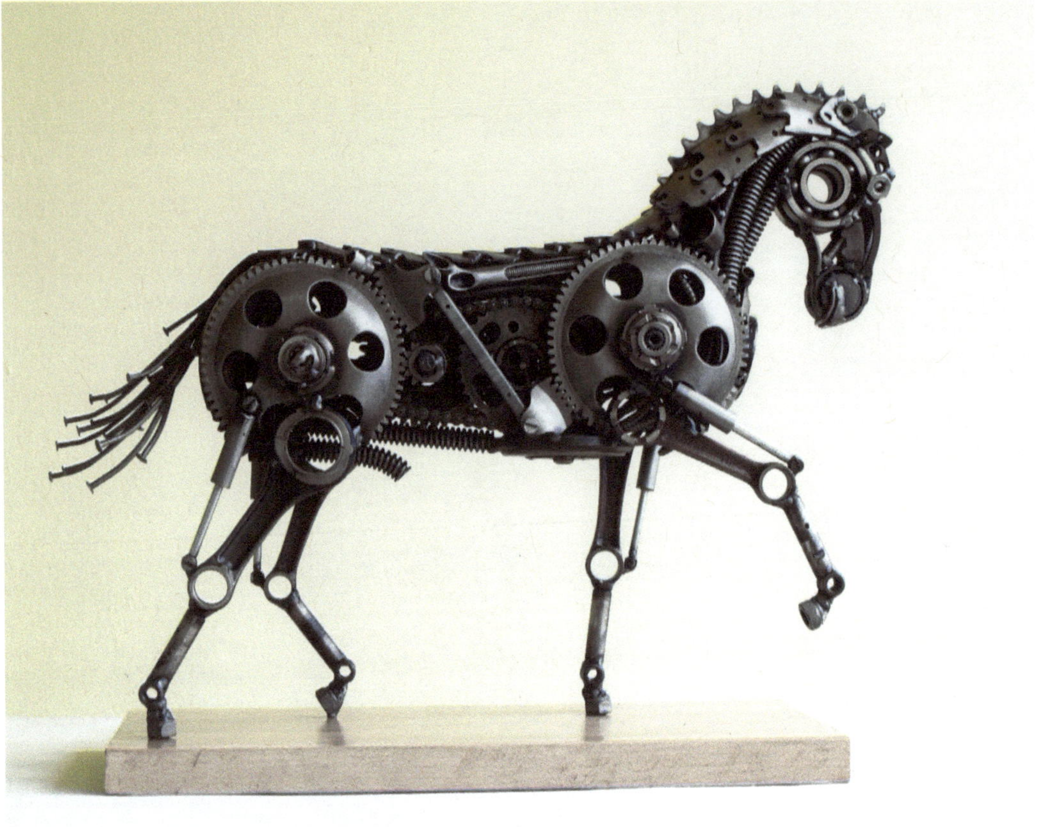

Horse , motorcycle parts, 50 x 45cm tall

Gorilla, motorcycle parts, 39 x 32cm tall

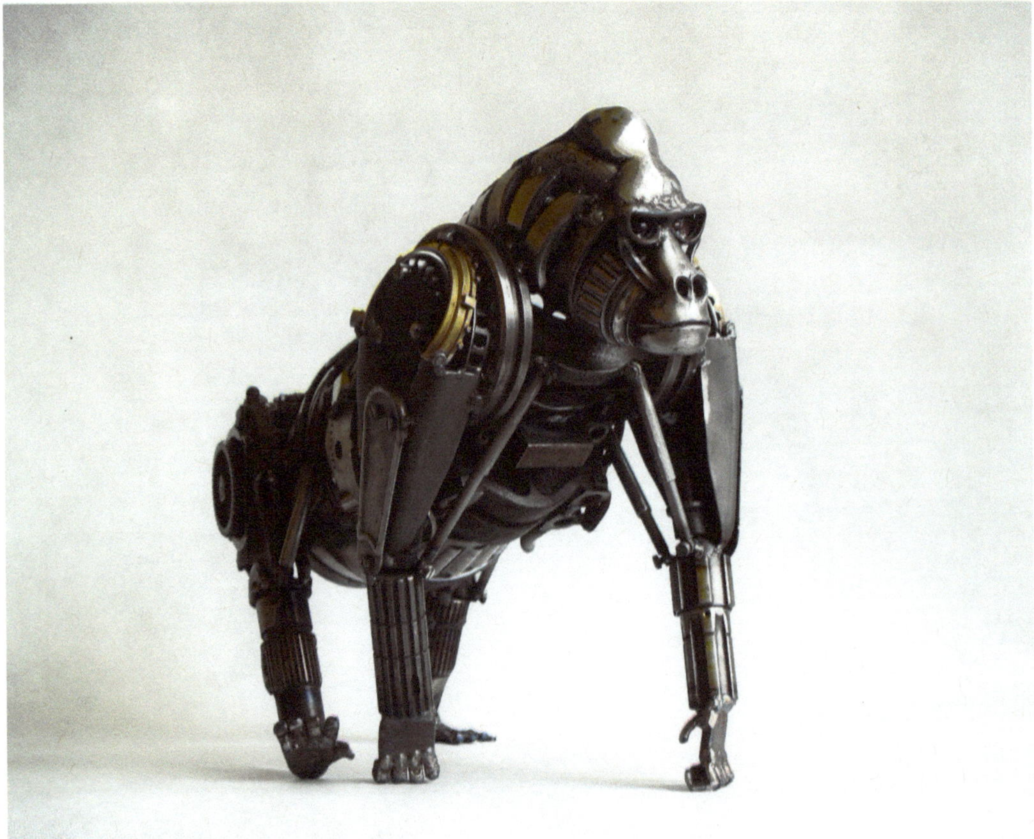

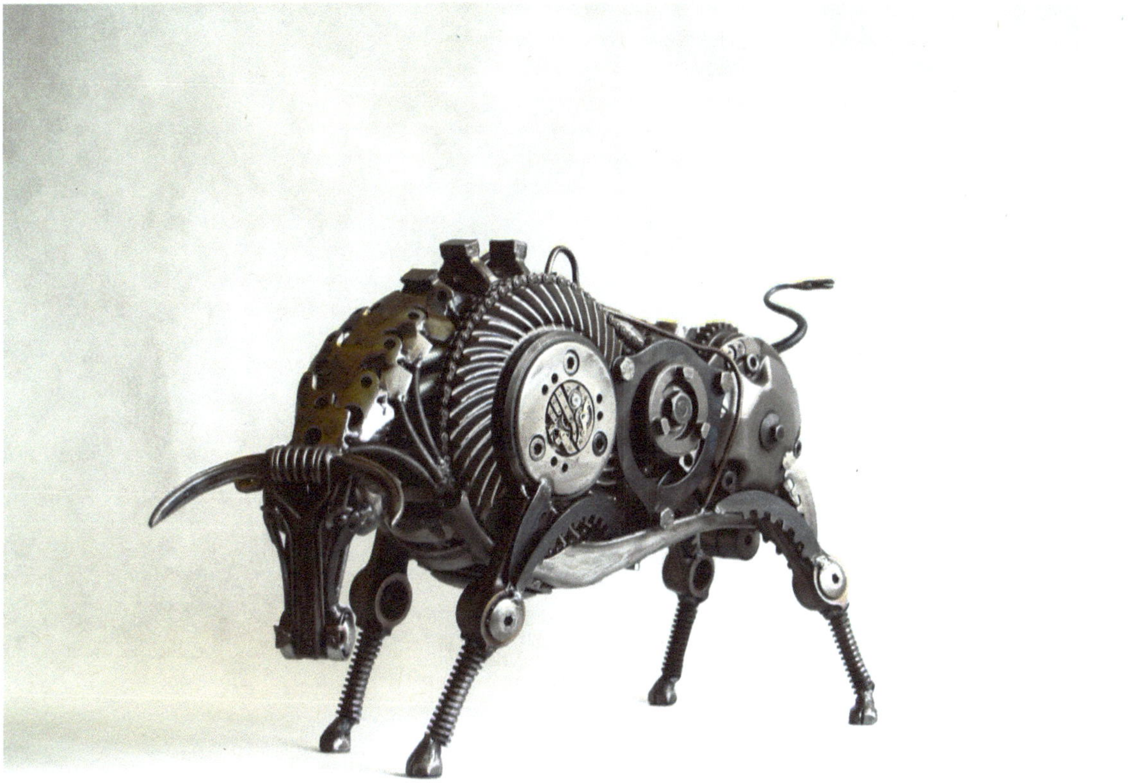

The Bull, motorcycle parts, 60 x 16 x 30cm

Man on Bicycle, motorcycle parts, 33cm tall

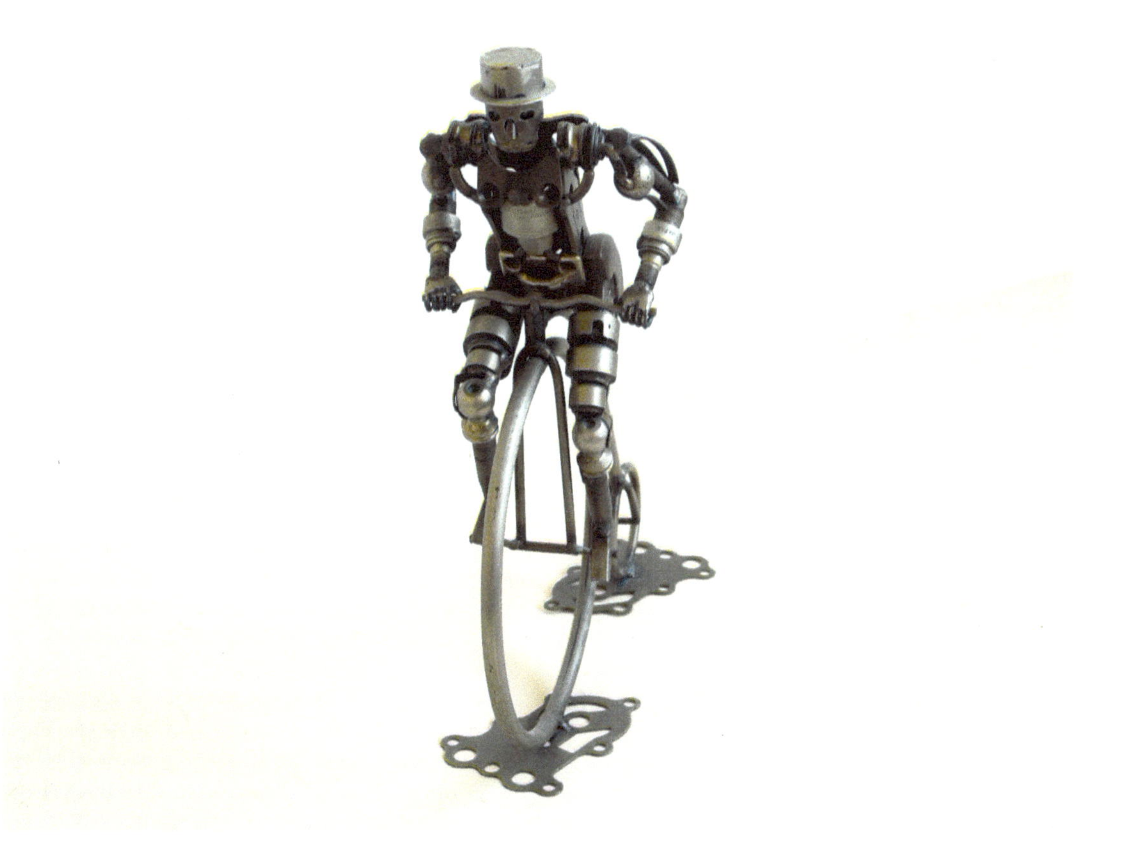

ANTERO GUERRA

DRAWING - PORTUGAL

www.anteroguerra.arteglobal.eu

Antero Guerra was born in 1957, in central Portugal. He was very young when he discovered that he had a strong vocation for visual arts. His first drawings date back to the time when he discovered paper and pencil, even before starting primary school.

In his youth, he immersed himself in photography, painting and experienced the amateur cinema. He took part in dozens of exhibitions of painting and photography, both collective and individual. Nevertheless, everything he produced was always imbued with a sense of experimentation and on-going self-learning.

During the 80's, he took up a professional career in video and graphic arts. At this time, he also collaborated with various activities linked to clubs, politics and journalism. Drawing and painting lay dormant practically during almost three decades, until 2010. He has received honourable mentions and awards for his Painting, Photography and Video.

As opposed to the minimalist or surrealist language of his youth, he decided upon a style of classical realism and portrait drawing out of a strong necessity for relearning, self-discipline and method training. He began to exhibit these new works in 2013 and at this time he portrayed more than thousand people from several towns. This new experience, painting more freely and secure, begins to rise a personal style for new projects on the horizon.

Right: Old Town, 2013, graphite on paper,
22 x 30cm

Charolinha Tomar, 2015, graphite on paper, 22 x 30cm

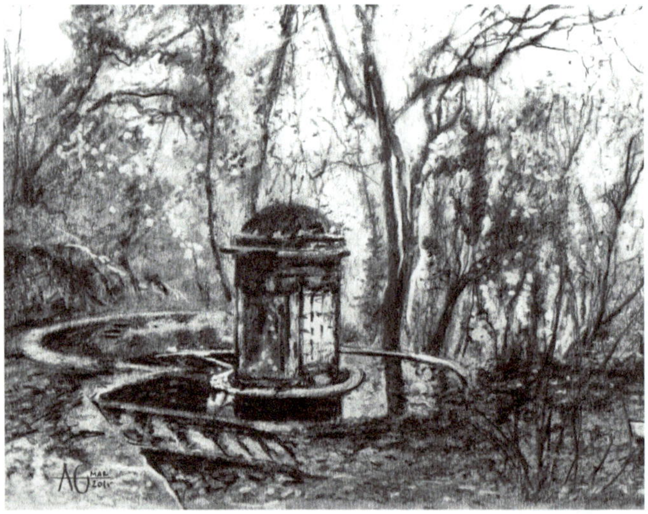

Memories, 2013, graphite on paper, 22 x 30cm

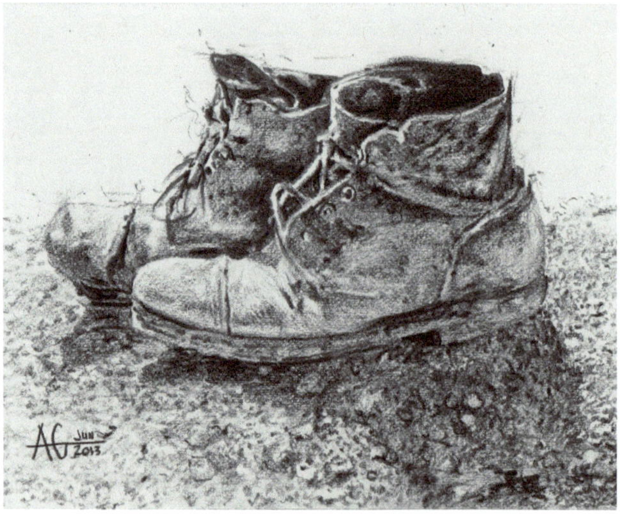

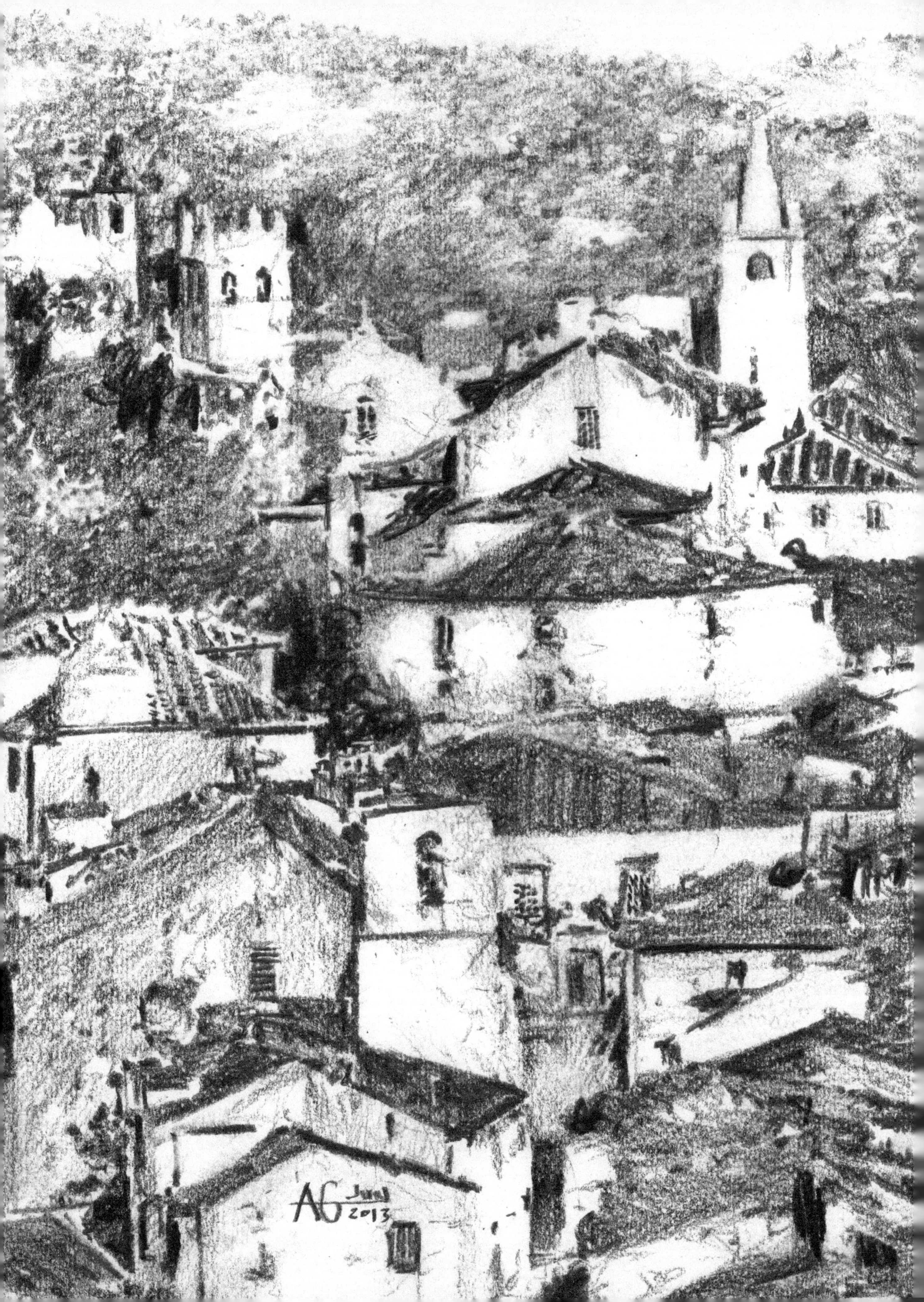
AG
Jun
2013

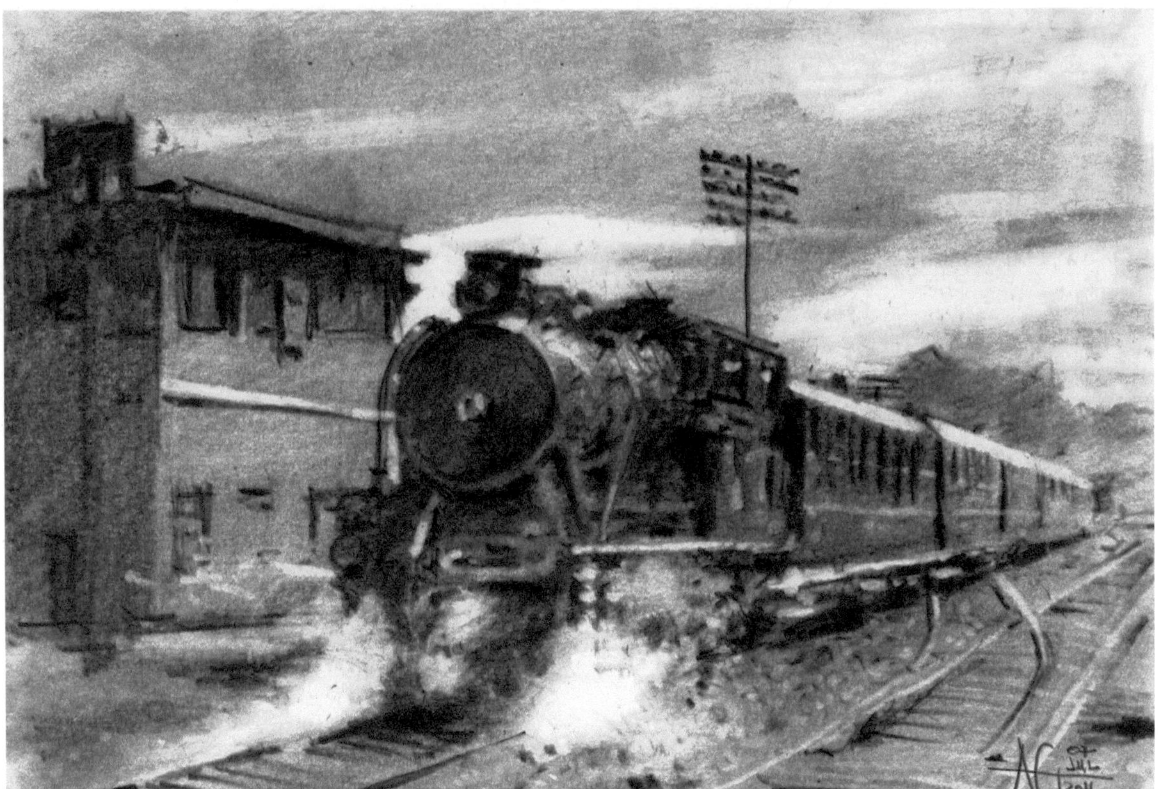

Presidential Train, 2015, graphite on paper, 29 x 21cm

Oviedo, 2015, graphite on paper, 30 x 22cm

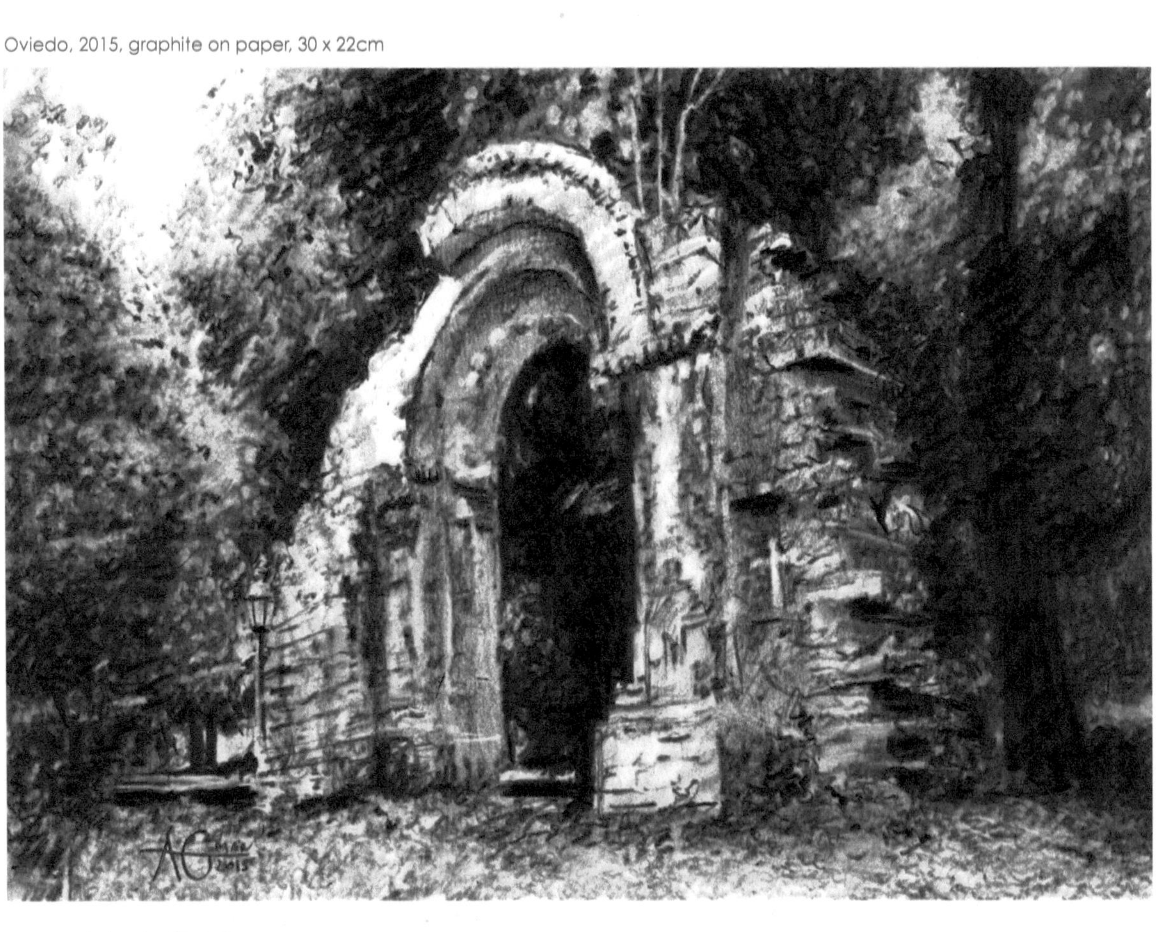

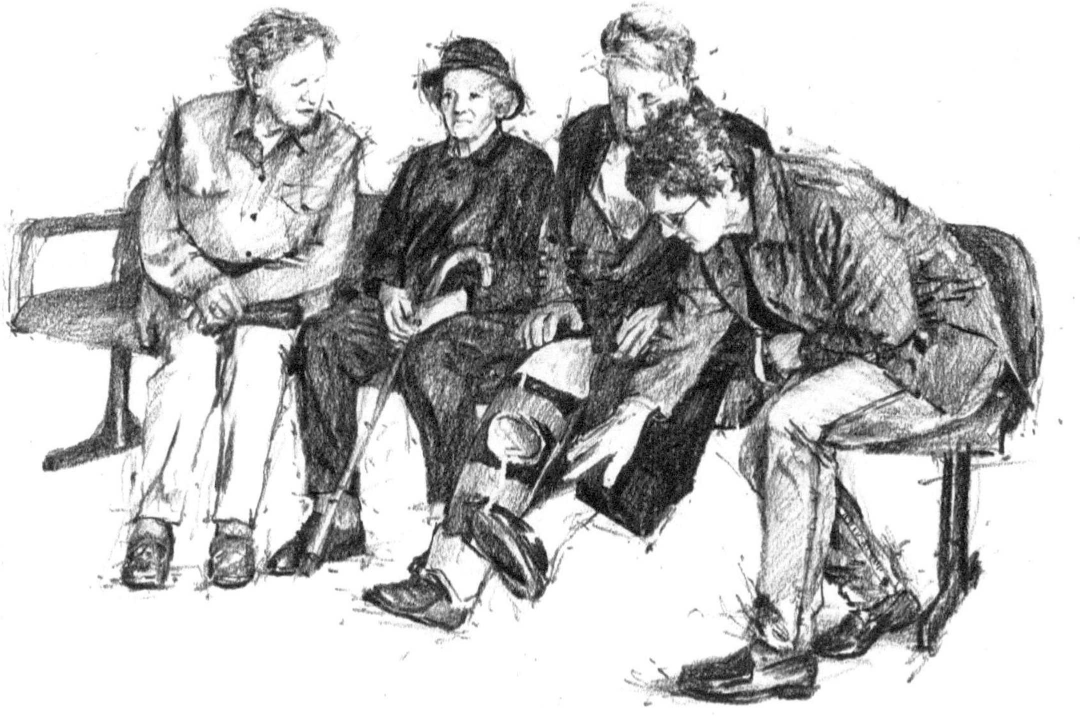

In the Hospital, graphite on paper, 28 x 20cm

Stares of Santo Antão Island, charcoal and graphite on paper, 60 x 42cm

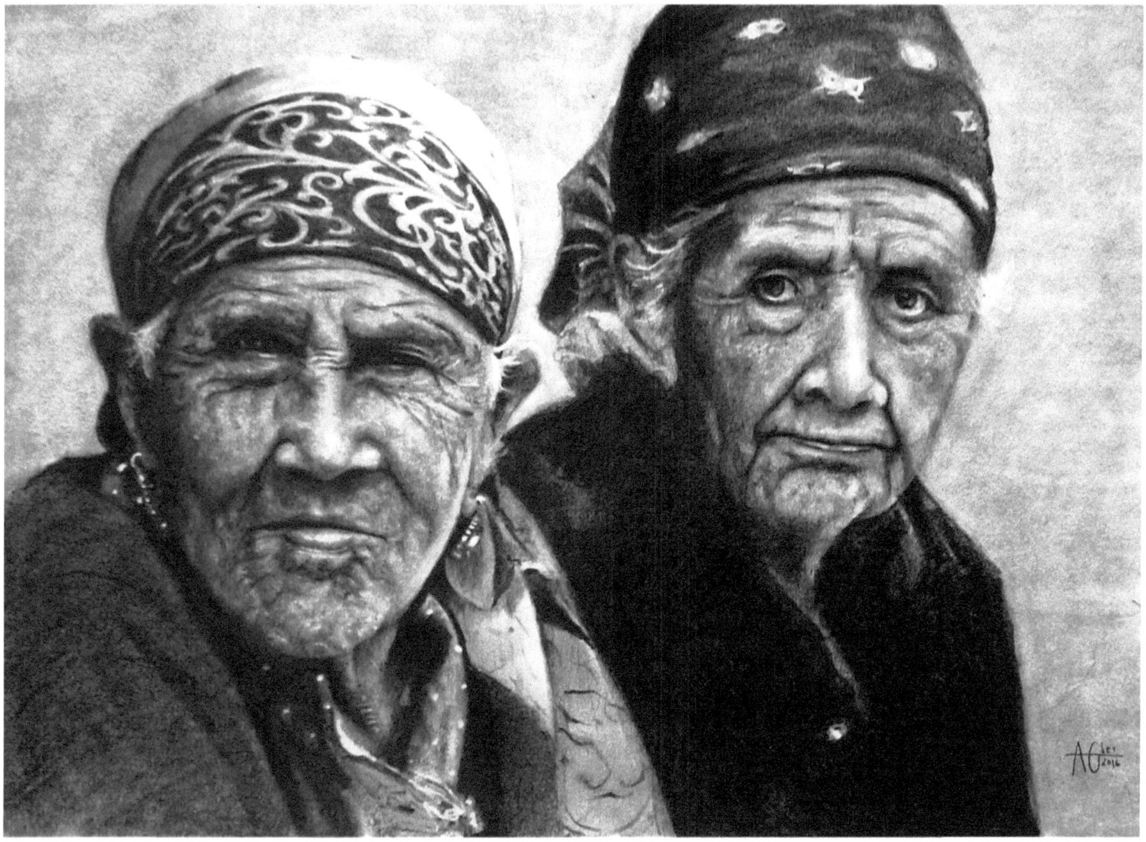

BERNARD DUMAINE

DRAWING - FRANCE

www.artgalaxie.com

Bernard Dumaine is a French artist whose work in the schools of photorealism and surrealism has earned him both critical and commercial success. He has designed backgrounds for television cartoons, and he has done extensive work with oil pants, acrylic paints, graphite pencil, digital painting, digital collage, and video.

Since earning his degree in Sculpture and Drawing at the Ecole des Beaux-Arts in Angers, France, in 1977, he has gone on to exhibit his work internationally, first gaining widespread attention in 2004. His series "Humble" was completed with pencils, using model sculptures created with clay.

Given the colours and the styles for which Bernard is known, there is a blunt, psychological aspect to his work. In his paintings, figures may seem to fall apart, to crack or break, but cohesion is unavoidable. There may be chaos in his works, very likely there is, but there is also a distinct sense of order. He does nothing haphazardly and absolutely nothing without purpose. Always eager to express himself and to see that his message cannot be misconstrued, he creates art with unshakable intention, clear about his own path and sure of himself as he sets out to work.

Bernard is respected also largely because of his bravery as a drawer. He will do what others will not, because he believes that by taking risks he is setting himself on a path towards growth.

Right: Humble 5, 2009, pencils on canson lavis studio, 40 x 50cm

Humble 10, 2010, pencils on canson lavis studio, 40 x 50cm

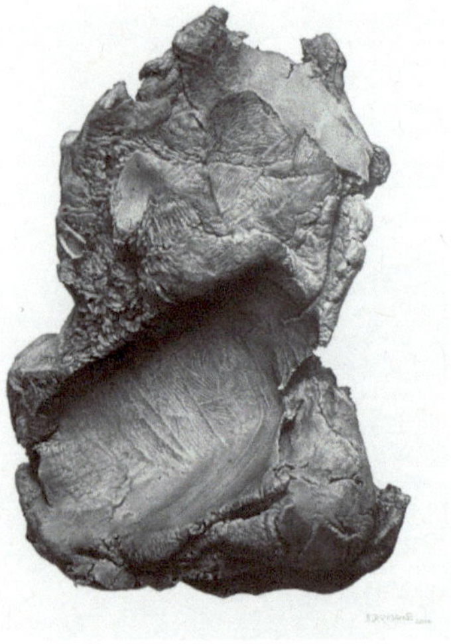

Humble 7, 2009, pencils on canson lavis studio, 40 x 50cm

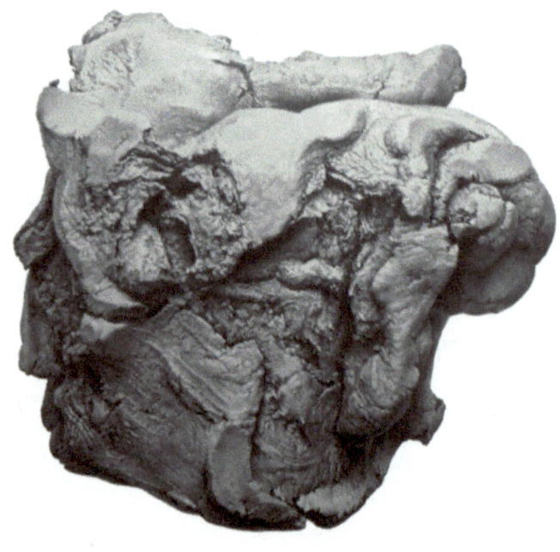

Humble 3, 2009, pencils on canson lavis studio, 40 x 50cm

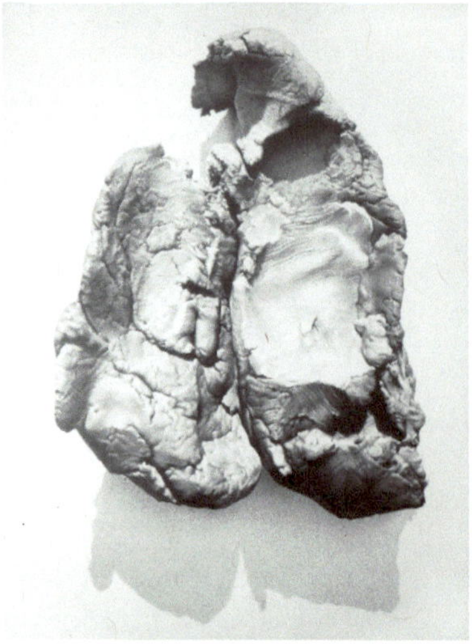

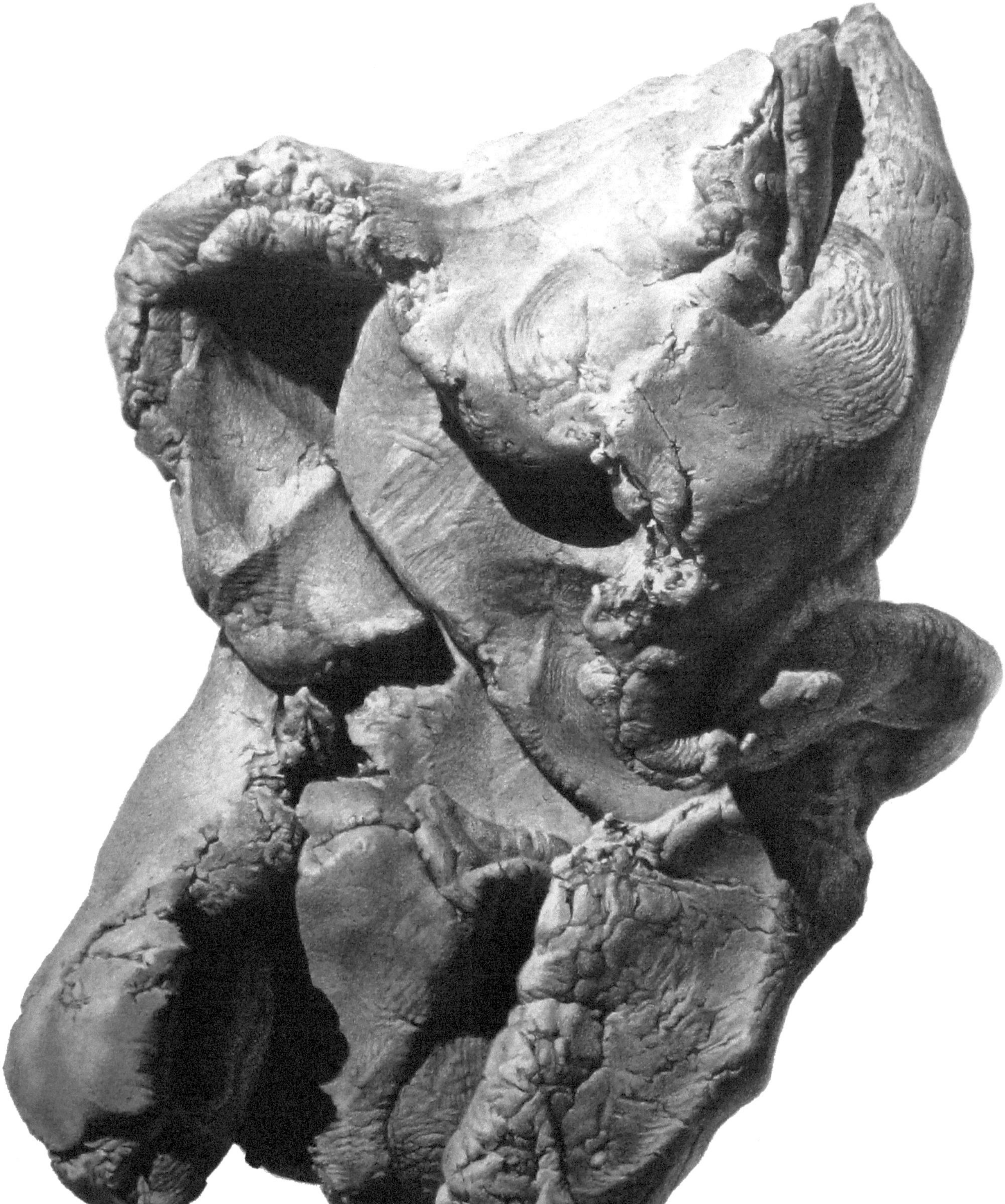

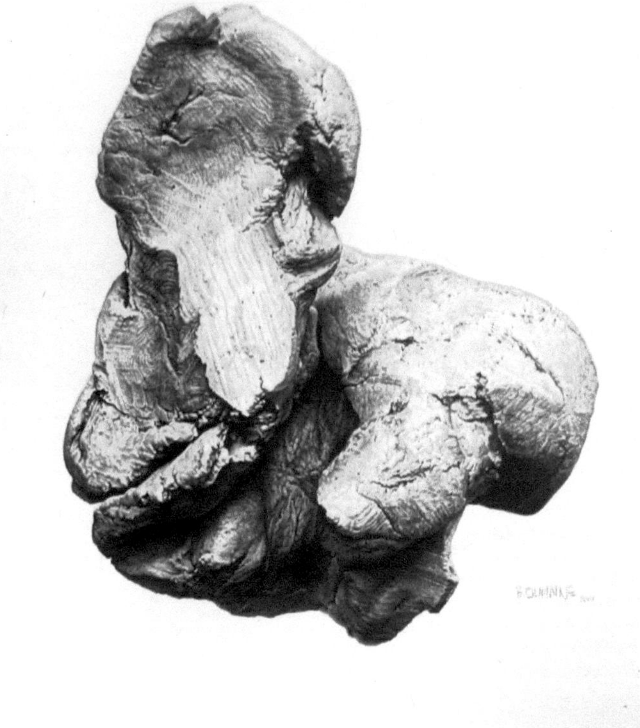

Humble 8, 2010, pencils on canson lavis studio, 40 x 50cm

Clay, 2011, pencils on canson lavis studio, 40 x 50cm

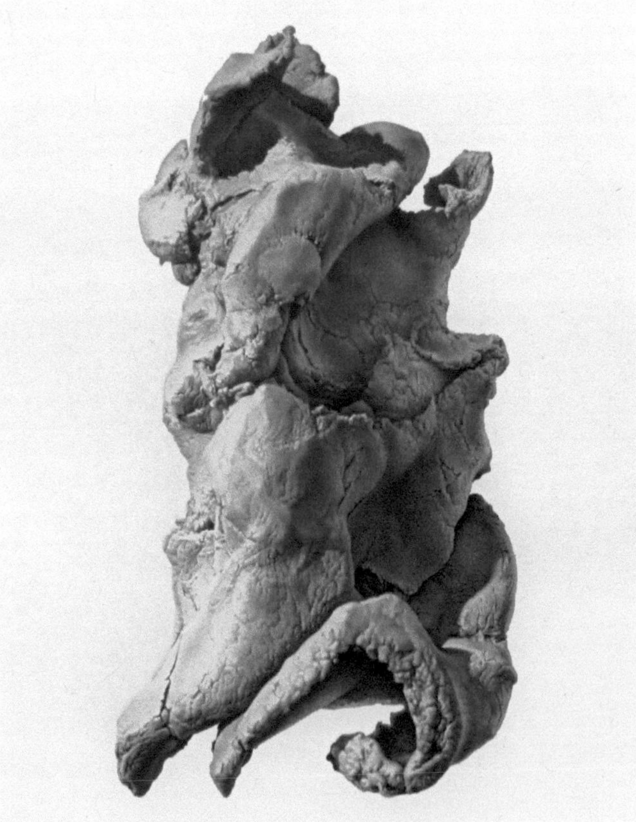

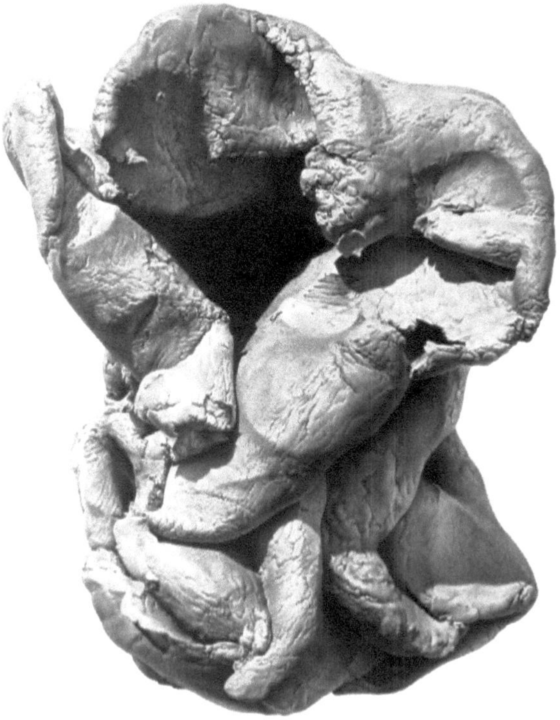

Humble 9, 2010, pencils on canson lavis studio, 40 x 50cm

Humble 2, 2009, pencils on canson lavis studio, 40 x 50cm

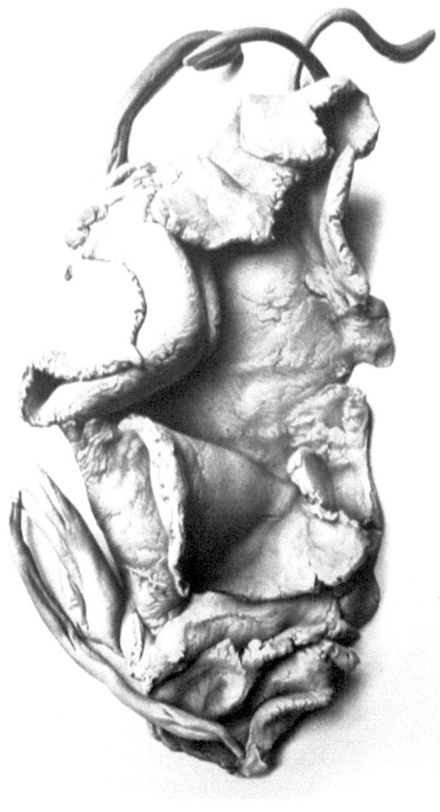

JONO DRY

DRAWING - SOUTH AFRICA

www.jonodryart.com

Jono Dry is a South African artist. Since making his professional debut in 2009, he has won a large following in the local art scene. Born in Pretoria and raised in Hermanus, he is South African through and through, a national treasure of sorts and someone who is now representing the country on the international stage and competing in larger and larger competitions. He taught himself how to draw, and his large works often take months to complete. Making extensive use of the golden ratio and the Fibonacci sequence, he does not hold back when it comes to incorporating details into his drawings.

A surrealist to begin with, Jono takes as his themes nature, people, and psychology. More recently, he has begun depicting horned nude figures, figures through which he expresses his own self-discoveries.

He believes in seeing ourselves fully, the dark parts and all, and by making himself vulnerable in his work, he hopes that he can encourage his audience to do the same and make themselves vulnerable in their everyday lives. Embracing the discomfiting and the disquieting, he is a seeker whose ambition is matched only by his skills, which he has sharpened over a lifetime of practice.

Jono reaches out and grabs people's attention with his work, but he does so in a way that is never needy. He expresses himself bluntly, and though his works may be shocking, he does not attempt to shock anyone. Forthrightness permeates his art.

Right: Life Spiral, 2016, pencil on paper, 56 x 76cm

Vulnerability, 2015, pencil on paper, 114 x 164cm

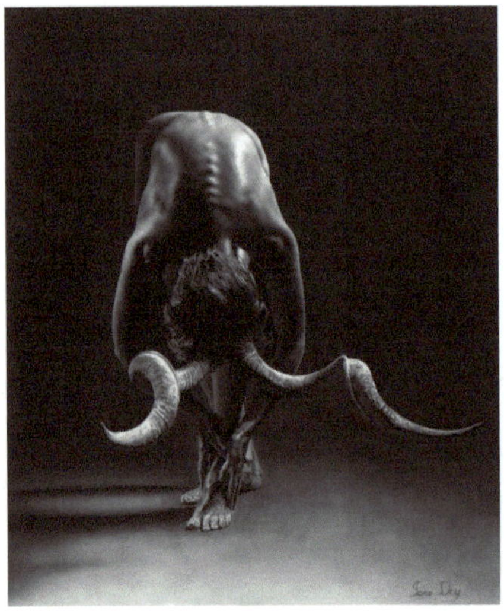

Pan, 2015, pencil on paper, 114 x 164cm

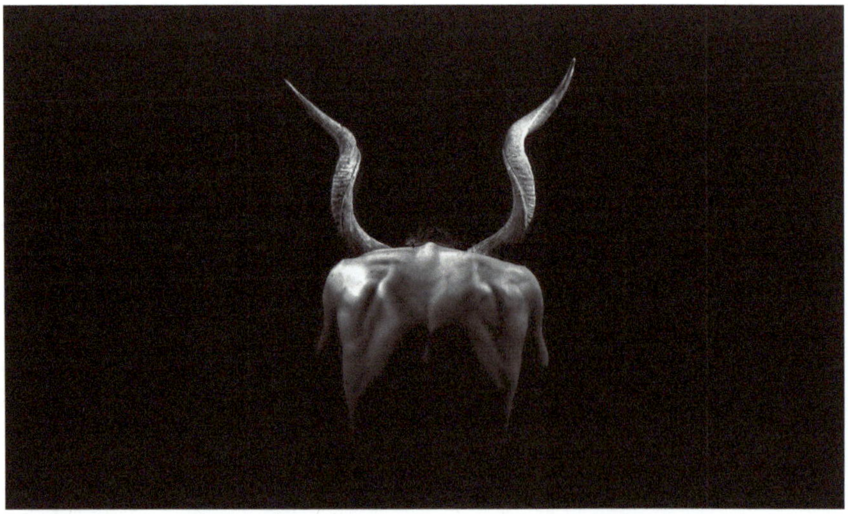

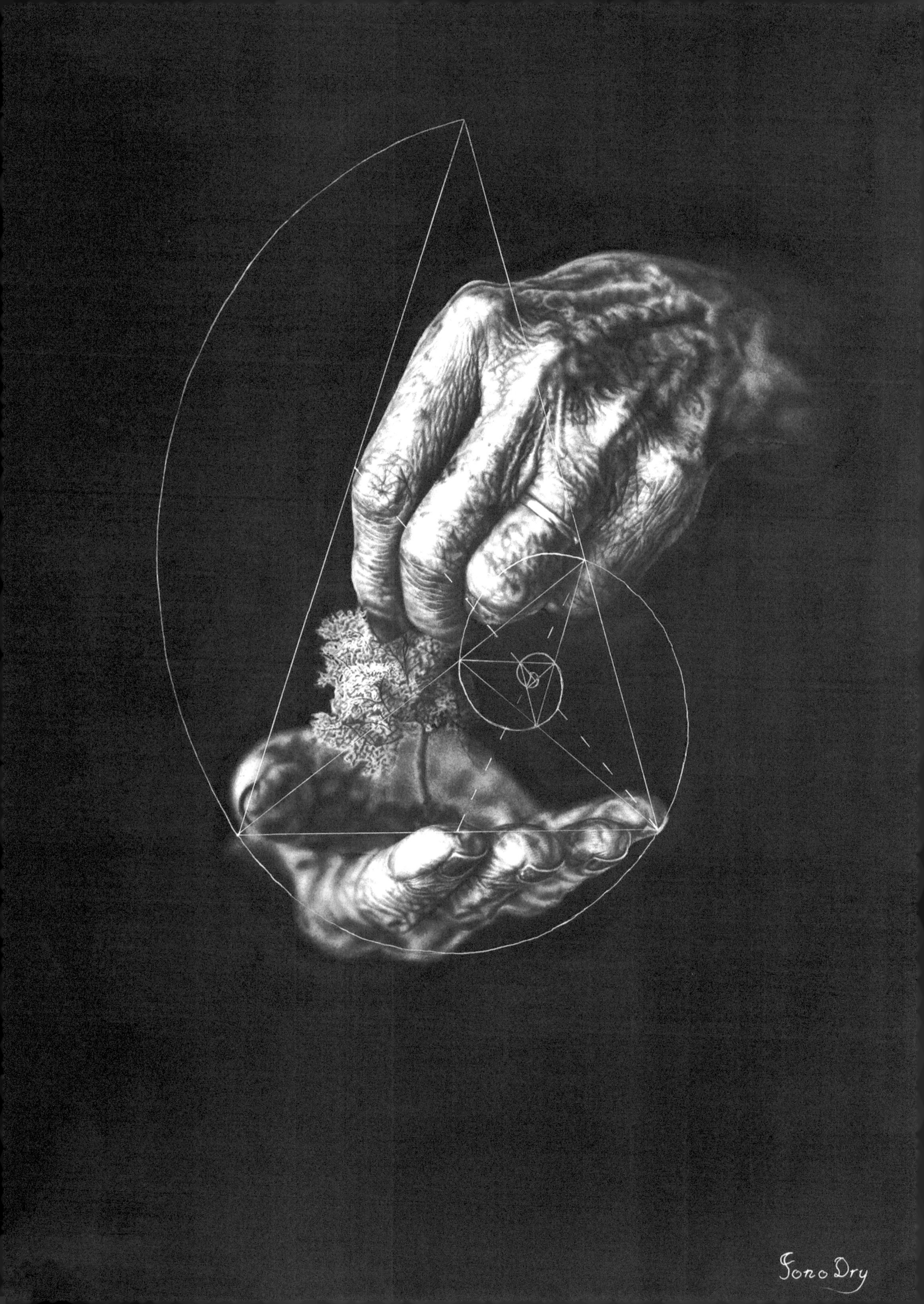

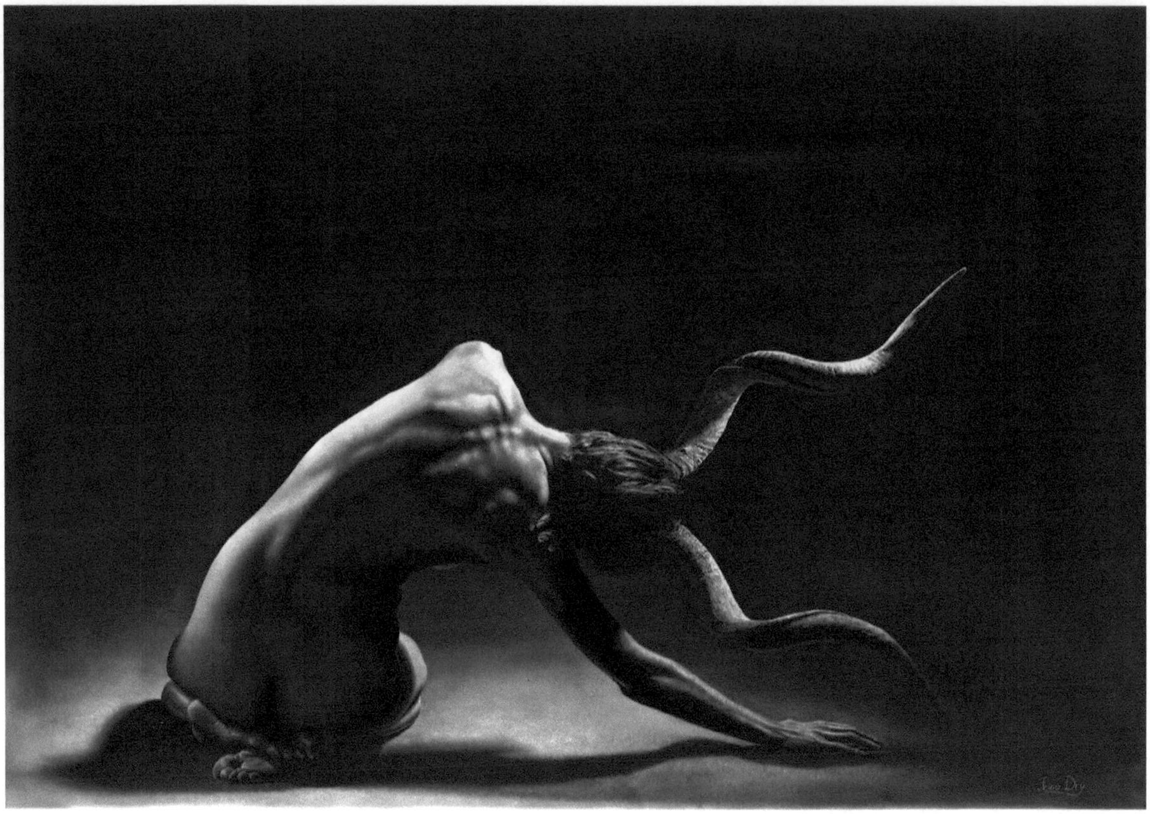

To be Tamed, 2015, pencil on paper, 114 x 164cm

Guardian, 2016, pencil on paper, 80 x 114cm

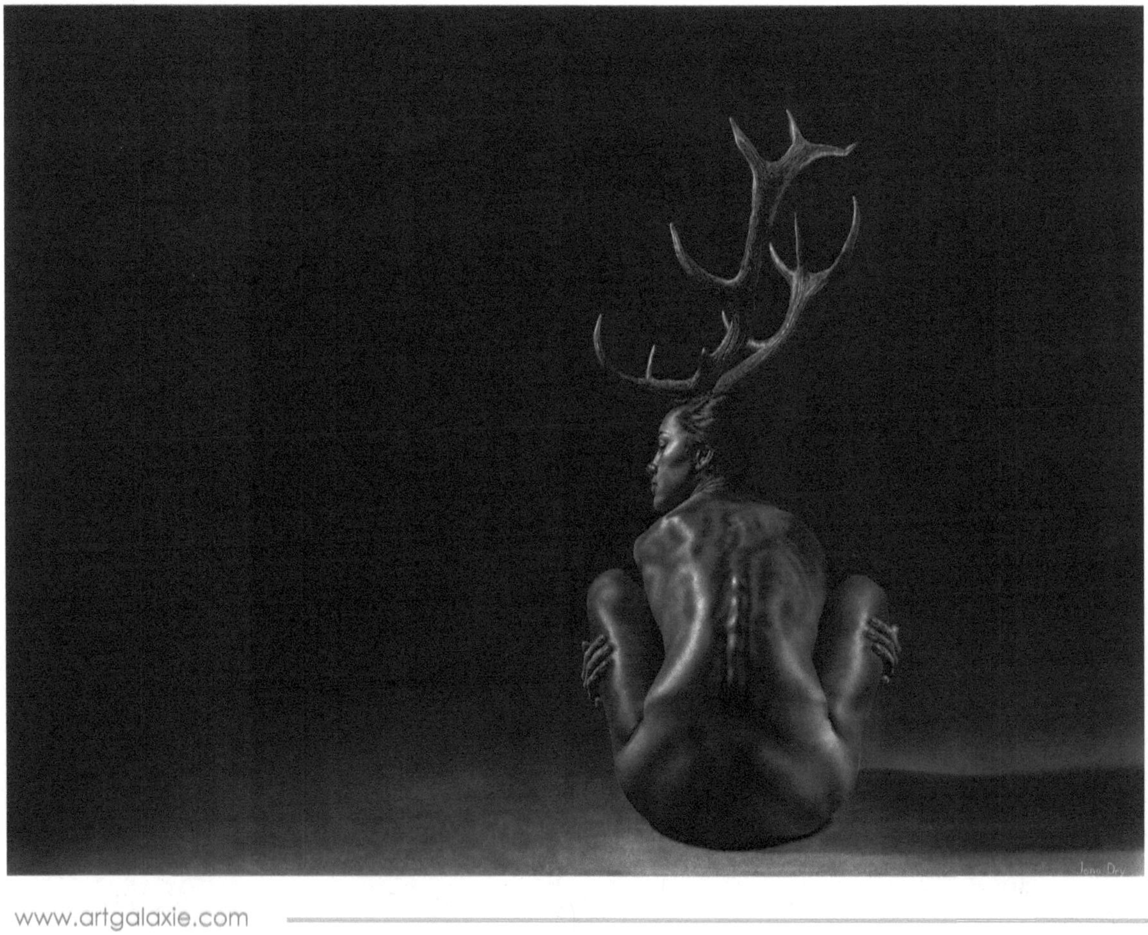

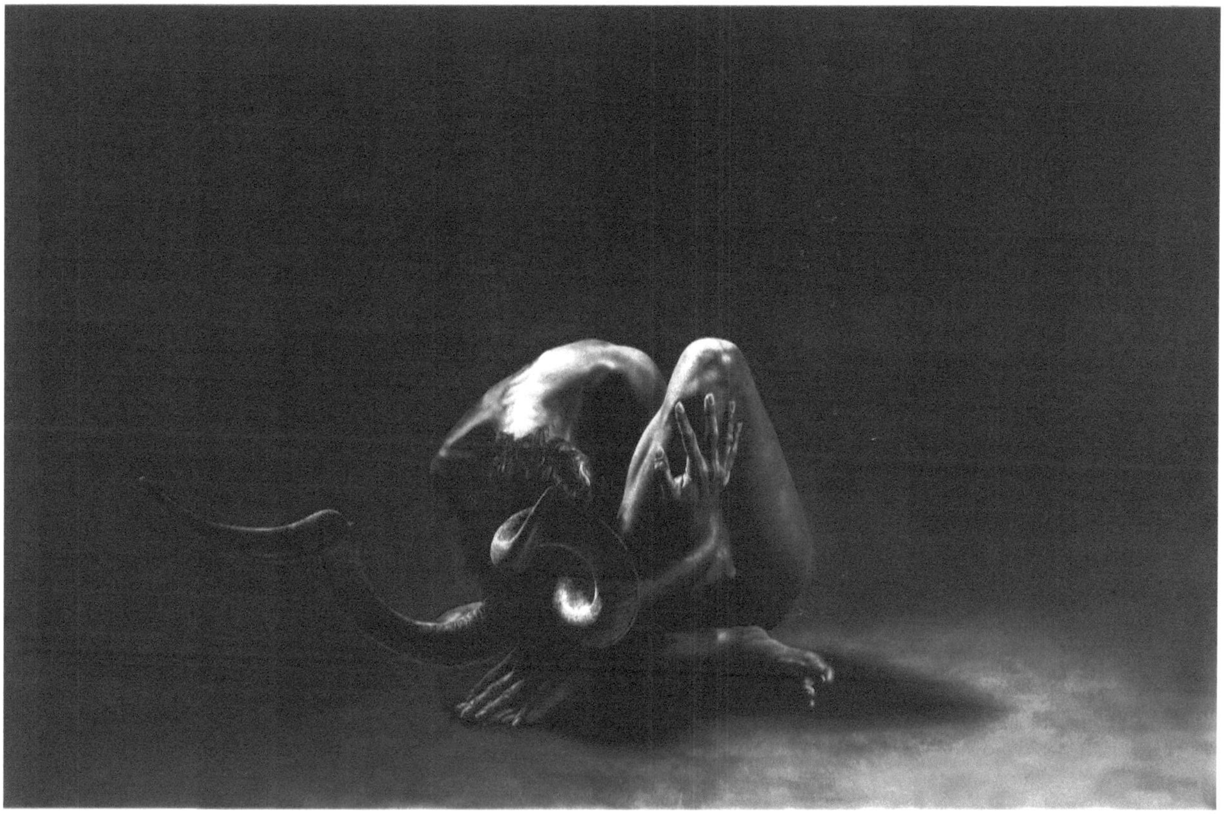

Bare, 2015, pencil on paper, 130 x 190cm

Reserve, 2015, pencil on paper, 114 x 164cm

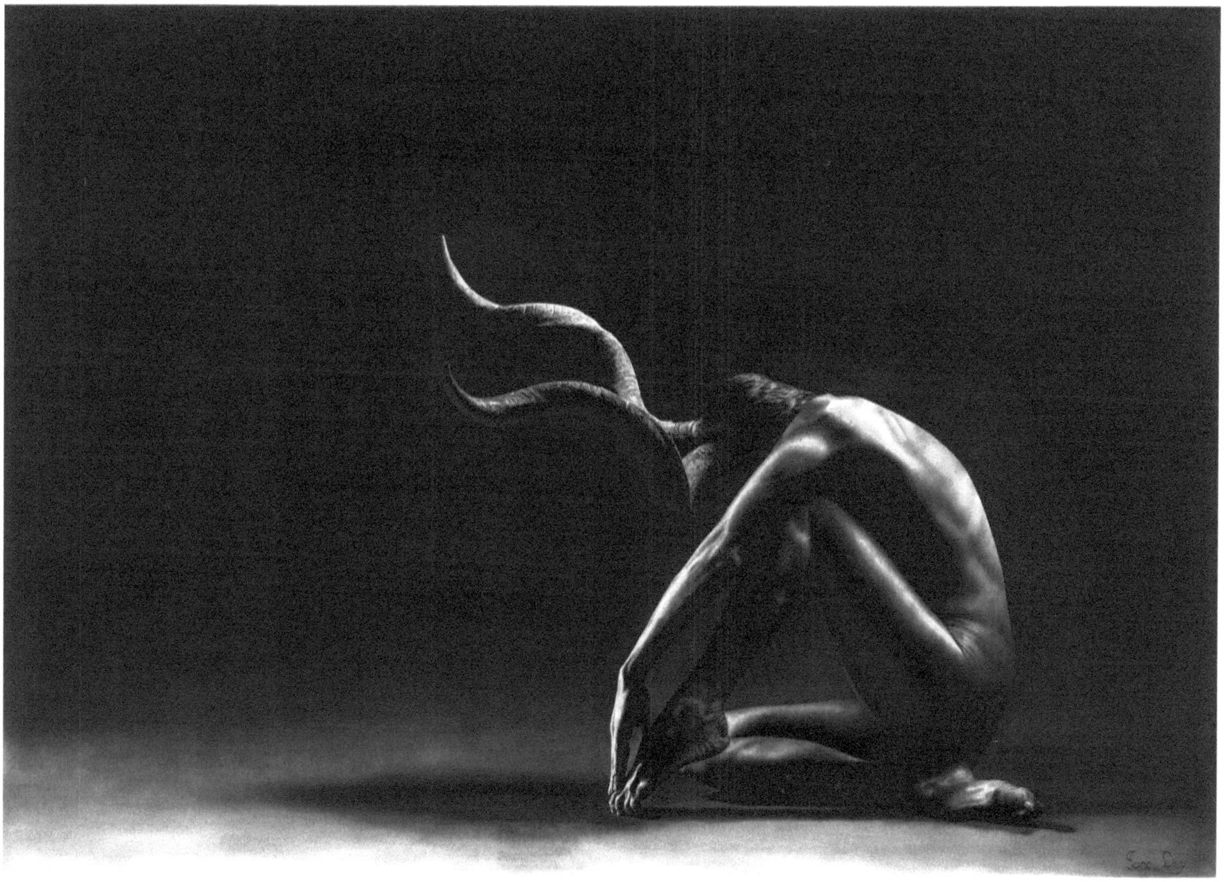

MARSHALL HARRIS

DRAWING - UNITED STATES OF AMERICA

www.marshallkharris.com

Whether the finished product is an elaborate drawing or a textured sculpture, Marshall Harris strives to make it remarkable — remarkable in the sense that the work creates a conversation between itself and the viewer, and then between viewers. It's meant to elicit remarks. The works are technically impressive in their execution and the subject matter, unusual in presentation. If you believe that you are looking at a photograph, and it is not, then Harris believes he has achieved his figurative intent. Yet it is through the contemplative nature of the work that Harris wants to engage the viewer. "I want to make you ask questions of the work, of its significance and its purpose. The work is drawn to inspire investigation," he says.

The chosen subject matter is compelling. These works contain texture and contrast, depth of field and breadth of history. Whether the work is a life-size nude figure study or an intricately decorated western saddle, it always contains historical data within itself that adds life and relevance to its existence. The works are sometimes daunting in size or starkly impactful, and are all meant to make you stop, look, look again closer and then ponder why this and that detail exist, where did they come from and under what circumstances. The scar on the skin or the cut in the leather link to a consequential incident, and the artist includes those life events in order to make a more profound picture. Harris adds, "I include them because they make the subjects believable."

His works are designed with intention. The contrast of mass and void, harsh diagonals or serpentine form are all elements constructed to grasp the attention.

Right: Paper-Boy - Edward H. Bolin Saddlery,
Circa 1947, 2015, graphite on Mylar, 137 x 152cm

Detail, Saddle Silver Paper-Boy, 2015, graphite on Mylar

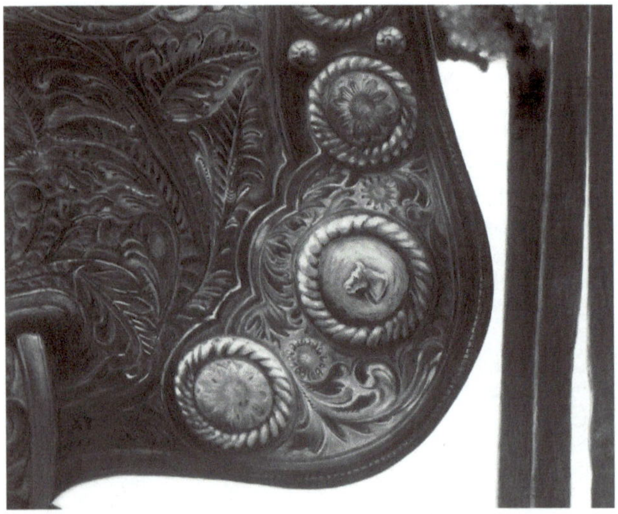

Detail, Saddle Horn and Gullet, Paper-Boy, 2015, graphite on Mylar

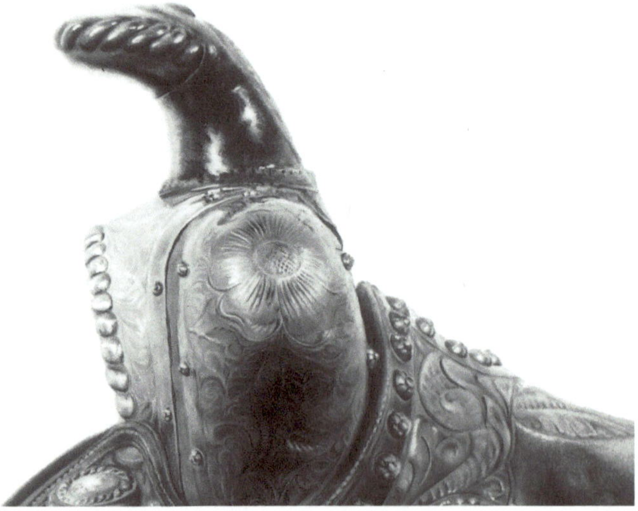

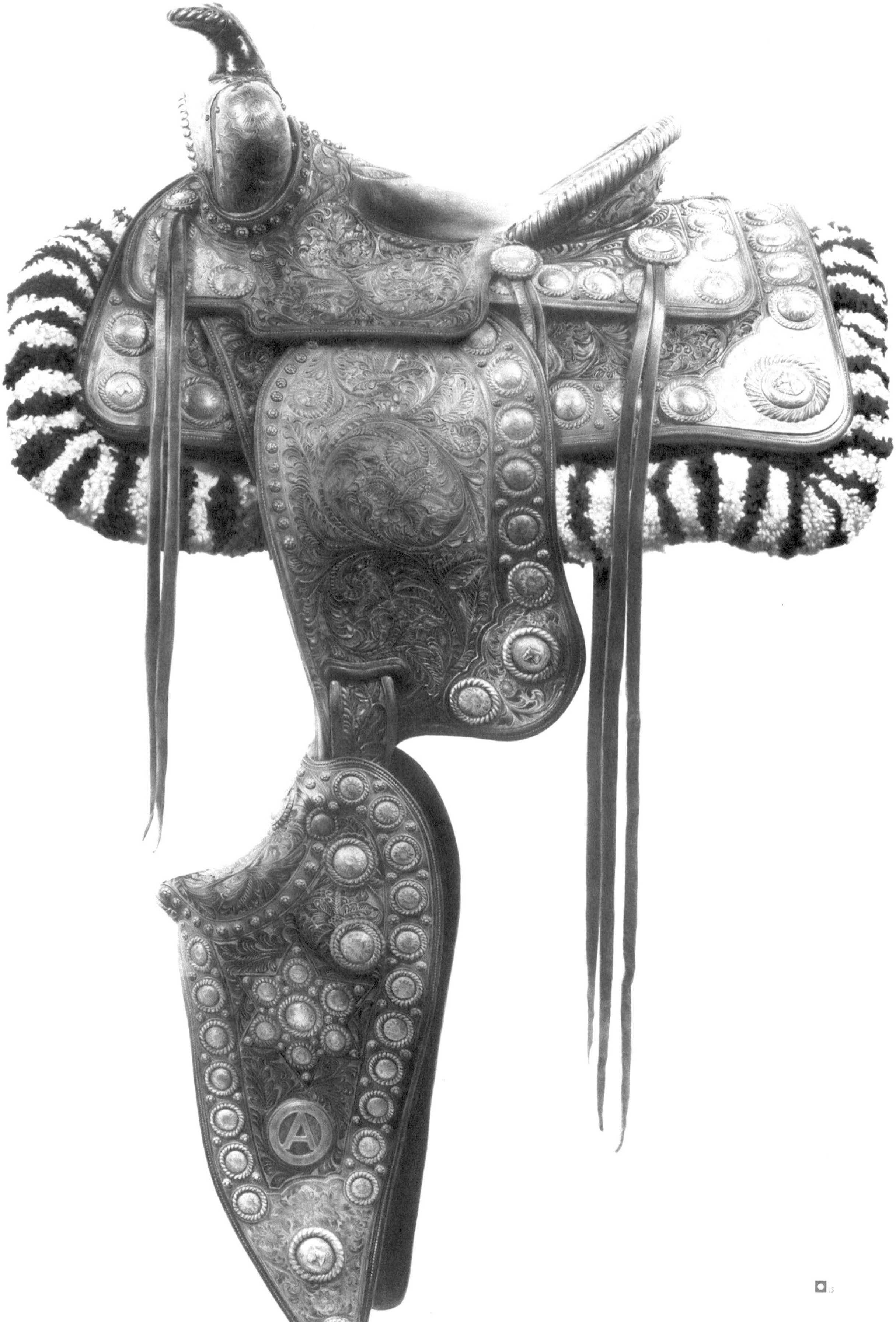

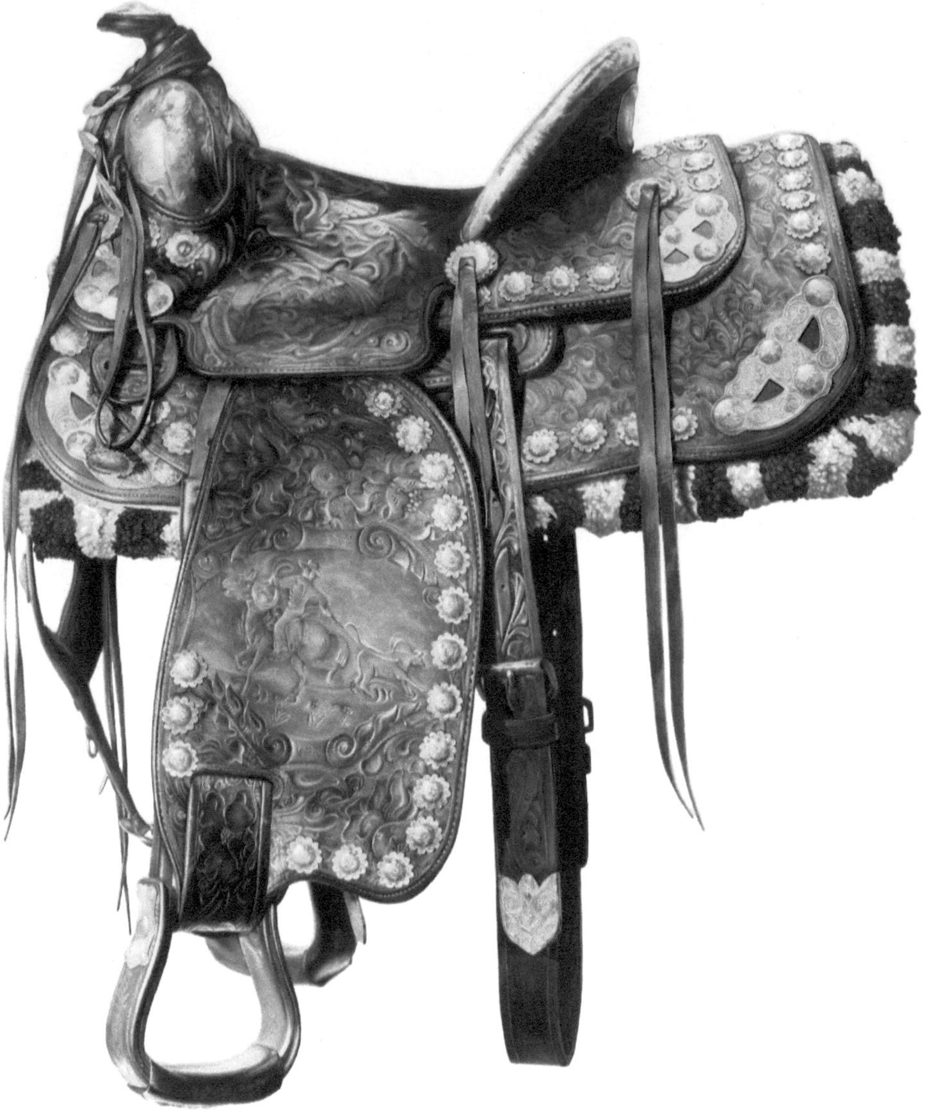

Round Up - B. F. Smith and Sons Saddlery, Circa 1942, 2011, graphite on Mylar, 137 x 145cm

Detail, Saddle Skirt, Round Up, 2011, graphite on Mylar

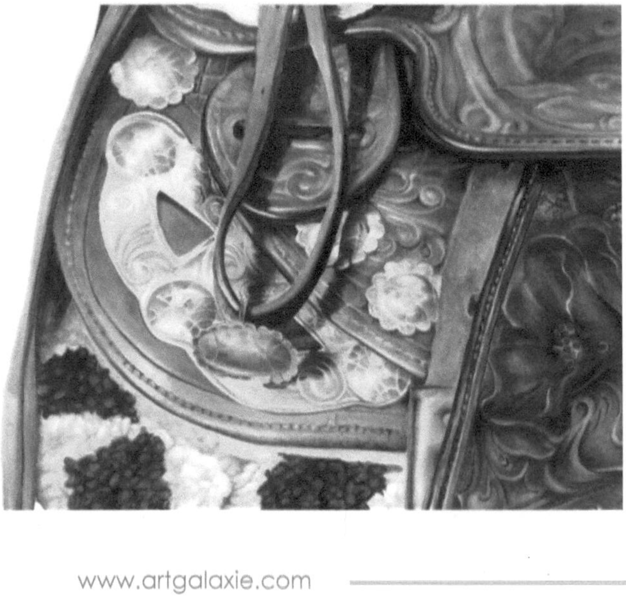

Detail, Saddle Silver on Skirt, Round Up, 2011, graphite on Mylar

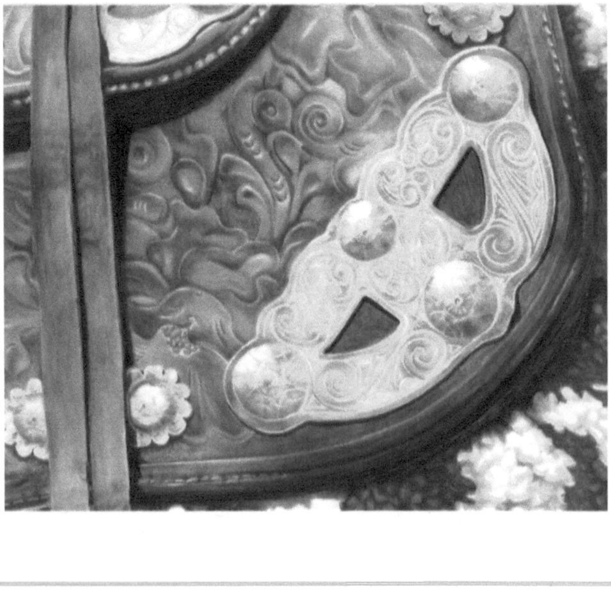

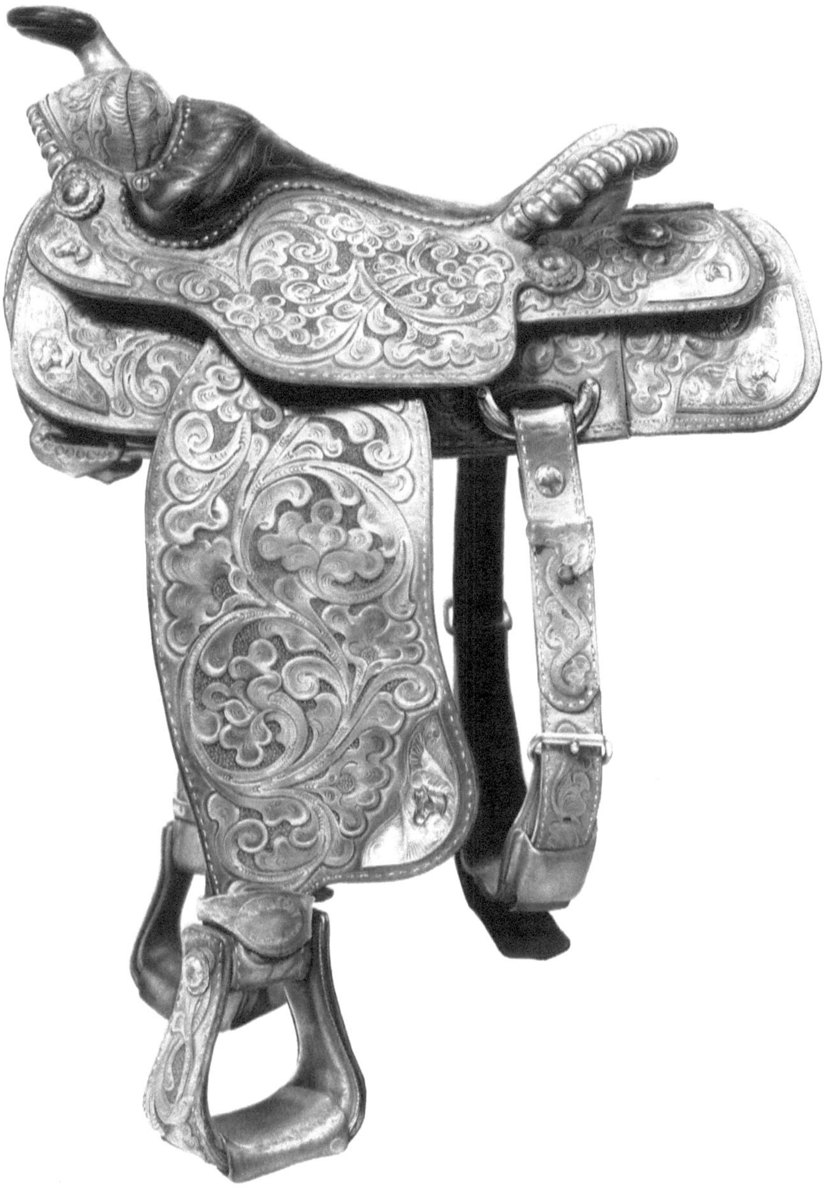

M.L. Leddy Saddlery, Circa 1920, 2011, graphite on Mylar, 137 x 152cm

Detail, Saddle Horn, Fancy Frills - M.L. Leddy, 2011, graphite on Mylar

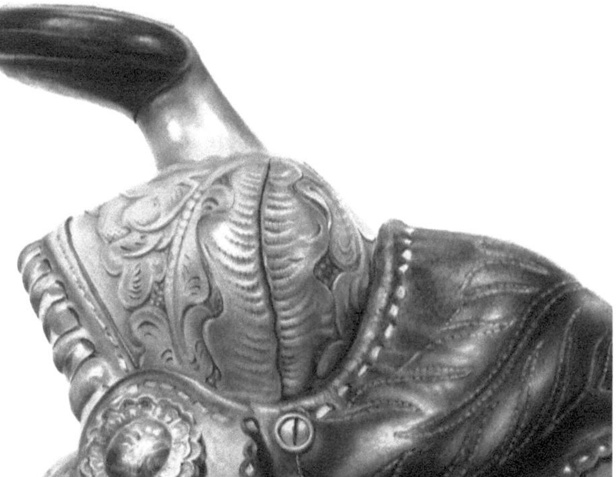

Detail, Saddle Cantle, Fancy Frills - M.L. Leddy, 2011, graphite on Mylar

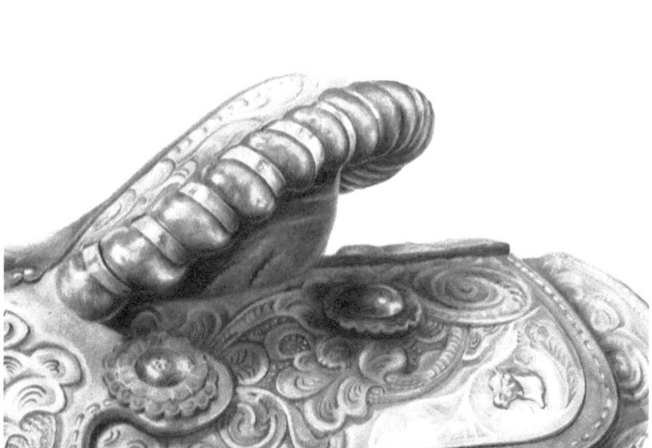

NATHALIE PICOULET

DRAWING - FRANCE

www.picoulet.com

French painter, Nathalie Picoulet, specializes in pastels. Between 1987 and 1991, she served on the faculty of Arts of Amiens, and after that, she moved on to the faculty of the Higher School of Art and Design of Amiens. Since her entrance into the world of pastels, she has been doing portraits, landscapes, and seascapes. Eventually, she discovered the subject that has brought her the greatest fame and acclaim: the female nude.

Recognized as beautiful, delicate, and sublime, Nathalie's female nudes in pastel are unique in their perspective. While female nude paintings have in the past been a subject primarily painted by men, Nathalie takes them as her subject unapologetically and with a purpose. She seeks to represent the female nude positively and honestly. In 2005, she was named Master Pastelliste by the Society of Pastellistes of France, who also had exhibited her work in Paris in 2004.

Fearless in her search for truth via pastel, Nathalie wants the world to recognize that the female nude is a subject the depth of which is comparable to even the loftiest of subjects. She does not flinch in the face of difficult decisions, moving forward like someone who knows where she is going, confident in her abilities and in the solidity of what she is attempting to communicate. Her distinction in pastels is just as much a credit to her bravery as an artist as it is to her technical ability.

Right: Présent Bleu (This Blue), 2016, pastel on cardboard, 105 x 67cm

Le Lys Blanc (The White Lily), 2015, pastel on cardboard, 34 x 25cm

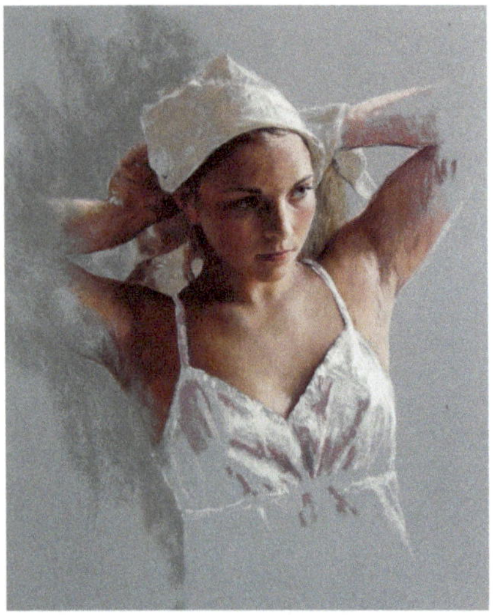

Le Foulard Noué (The Knotted Scarf), 2016, pastel on cardboard, 32 x 26cm

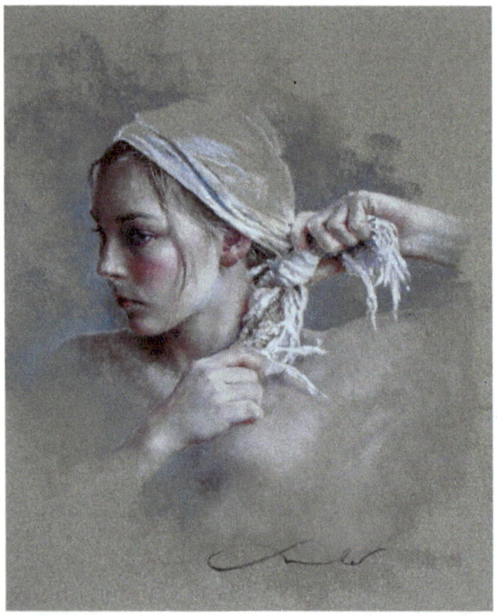

L'ourlet Doré (The Golden Hem), 2014, pastel on cardboard, 40 x 32cm

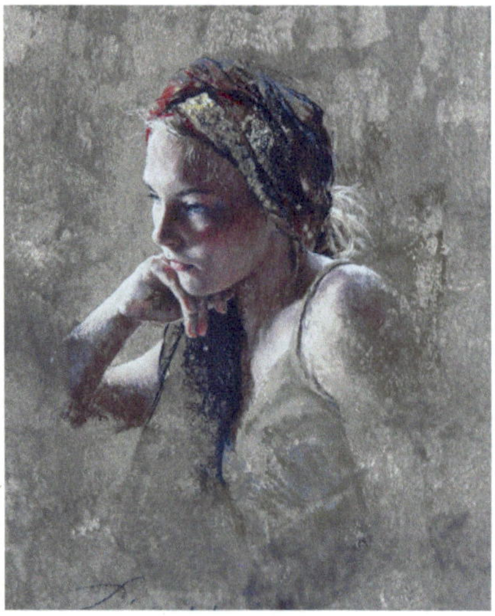

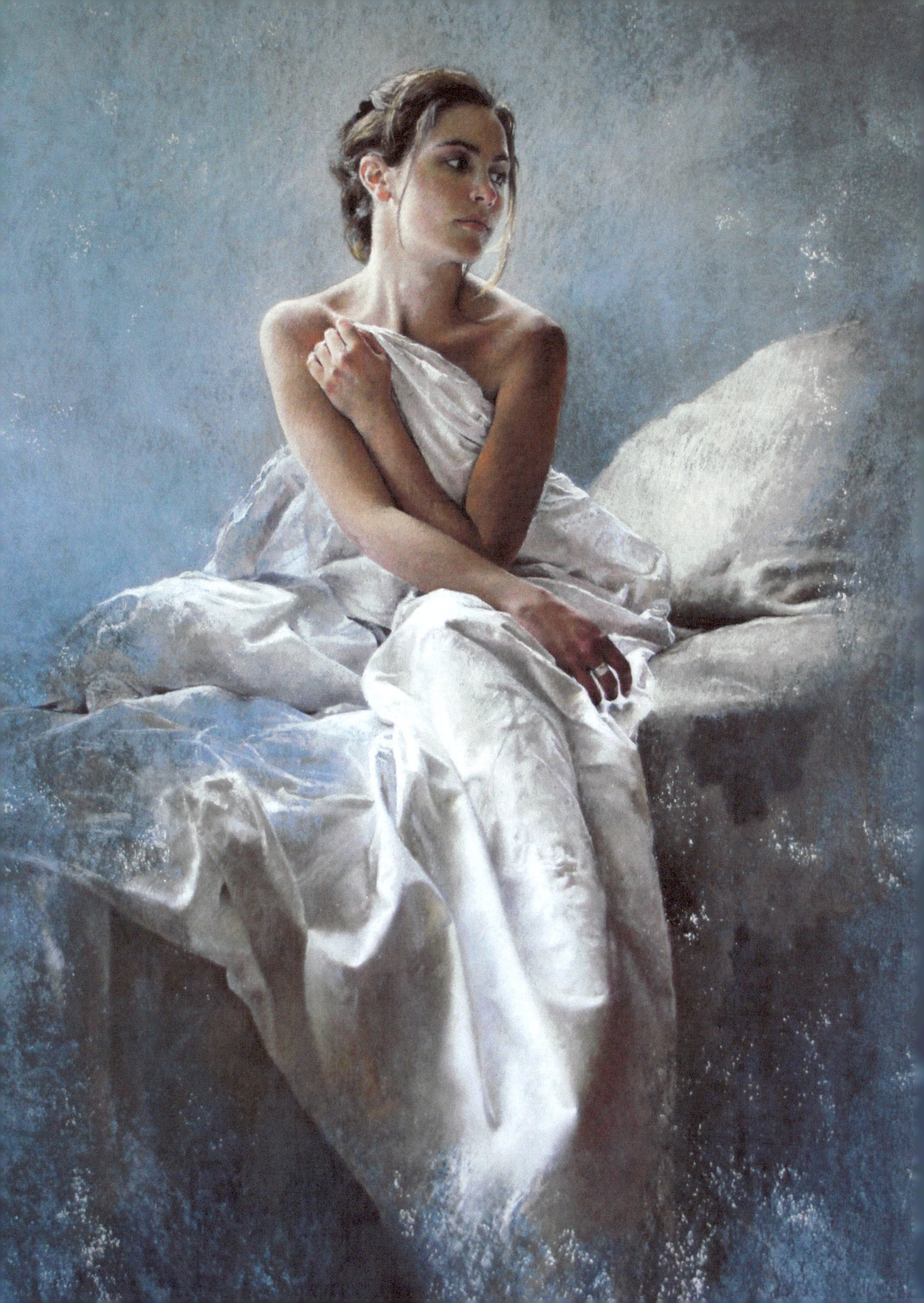

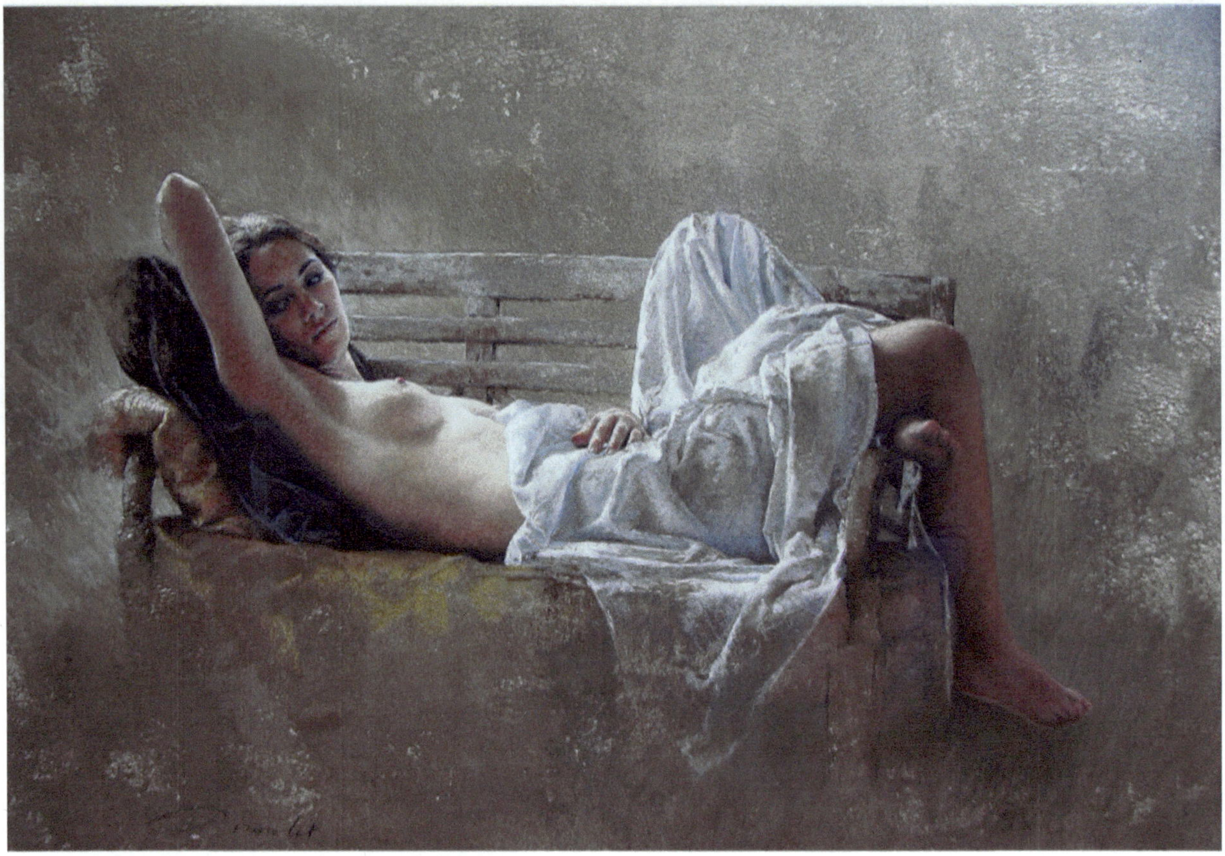

Le Banc (The Bench), 2014, pastel on cardboard, 58 x 75cm

Ne rien faire (Doing Nothing), 2016, pastel on cardboard, 54 x 68cm

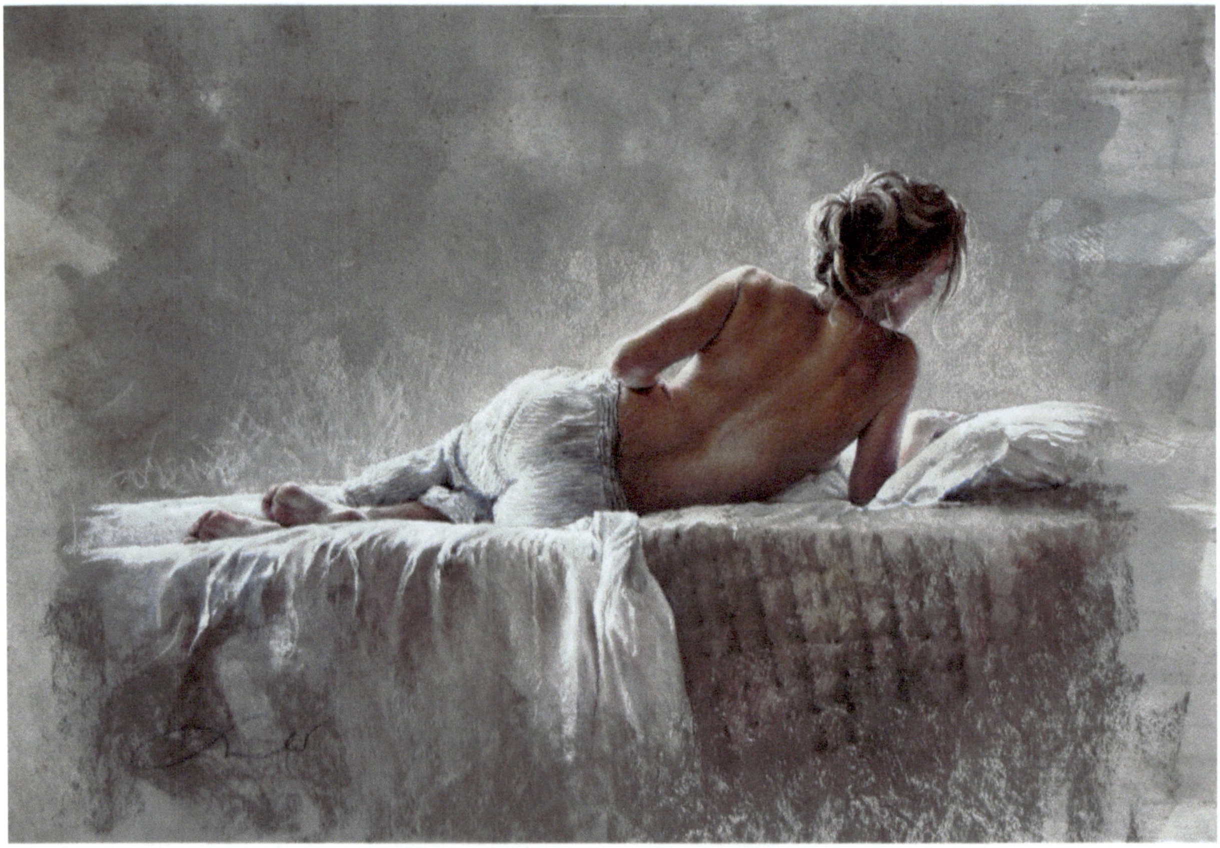

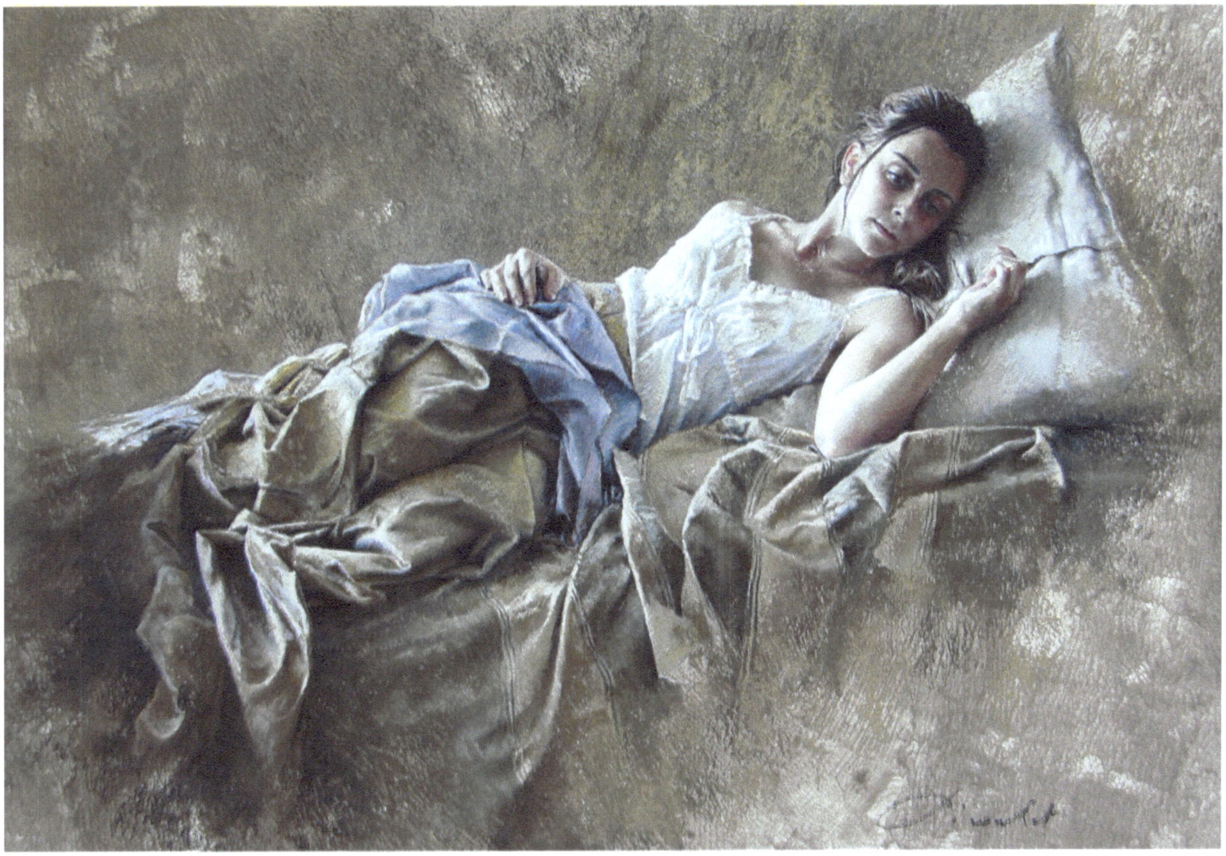

La Source (The Source), 2015, pastel on cardboard, 61 x 80cm

Jardin de Chine (China Garden), 2016, pastel on cardboard, 53 x 74cm

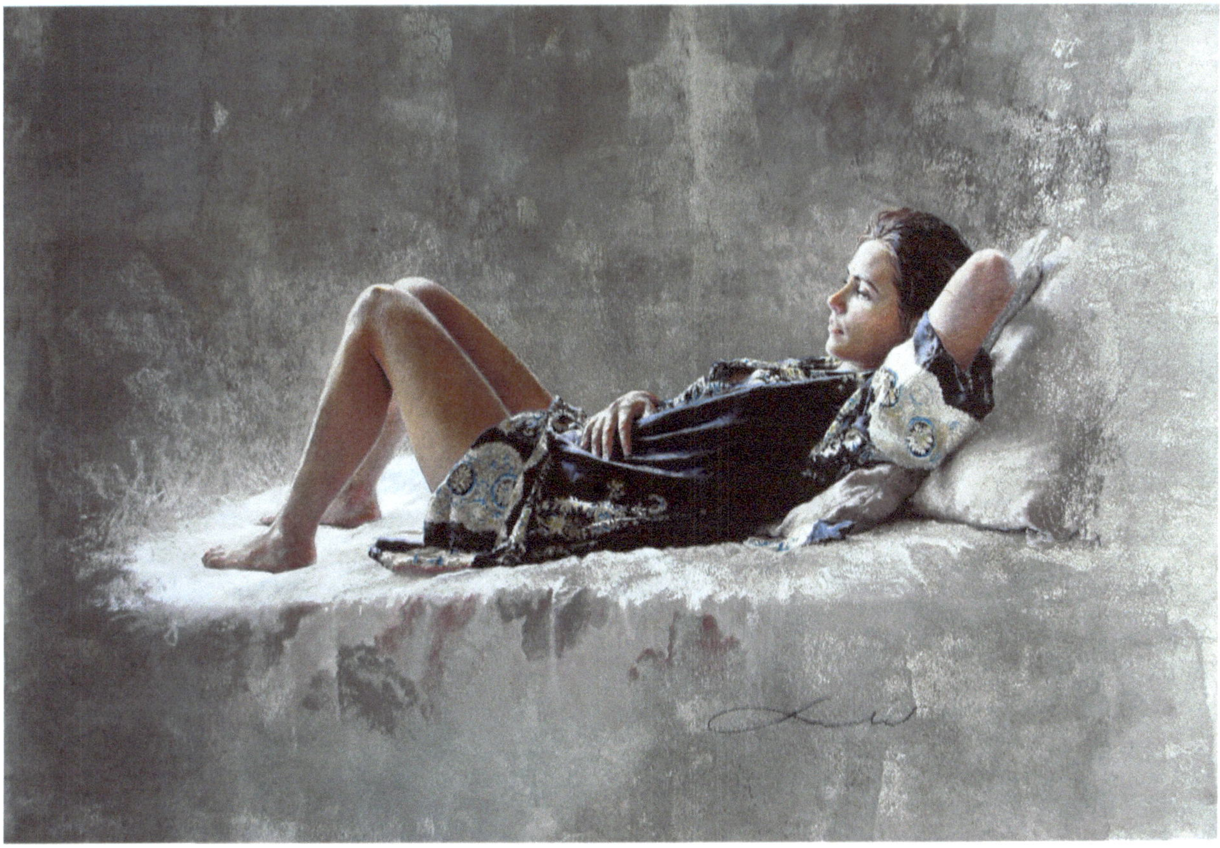

RAMON BRUIN

DRAWING - THE NETHERLANDS

www.ramon-bruin.com

Ramon Bruin is an artist whose optical illusionism style has brought him fame and recognition worldwide. Merging the fields of drawing and photography, he produces images that are distorted, creating a striking, vibrant effect in his works. He plays with varying perspectives in his art, forcing his audience to imagine what others may be thinking and seeing when they are looking at presumably the same object.

His experience with airbrushing is also evident, as his shapes – though strong in nature – are not without a gentle touch. Talented in such additional media as oil paint, water paint, acrylic paint, paint pens, charcoal, and graphite, he is an artist who never stops asking questions of himself.

Based out of The Netherlands, Ramon was born in 1981. In addition to his career in art, he is an entrepreneur and businessman, owning and operating JJK Airbrush Company, a company known for producing custom airbrush art on different surfaces. He keeps himself remarkably busy, often running several projects simultaneously. His mind is one that perhaps functions best with multiple tasks, a trait that is evident in his multi-layered, complex works of three-dimensional art. Calculated in the way he approaches his work, he is so effective at what he does because he clearly understands so firmly what it is that he intends.

Ramon is a thinker and an artist on equal planes, someone who sees what he wants the world to see and then makes sure that he is not being misunderstood.

Right: To the Clouds, ink on paper, photographed from an angle

Taped Clouds, pencil on paper photographed from an angle

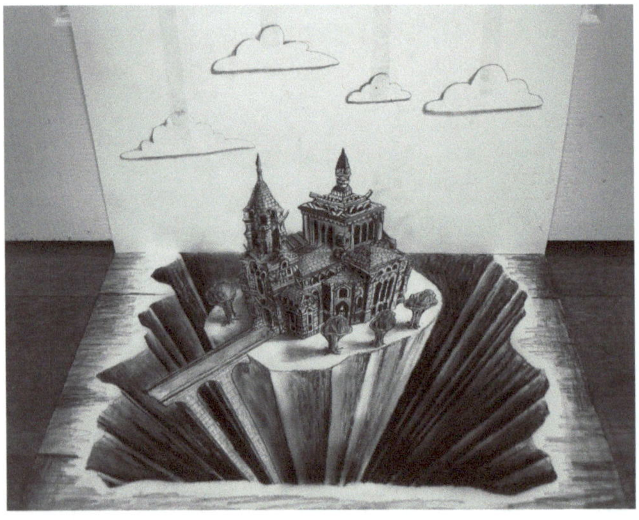

Sugar Skull, coloured pencil on paper photographed from an angle

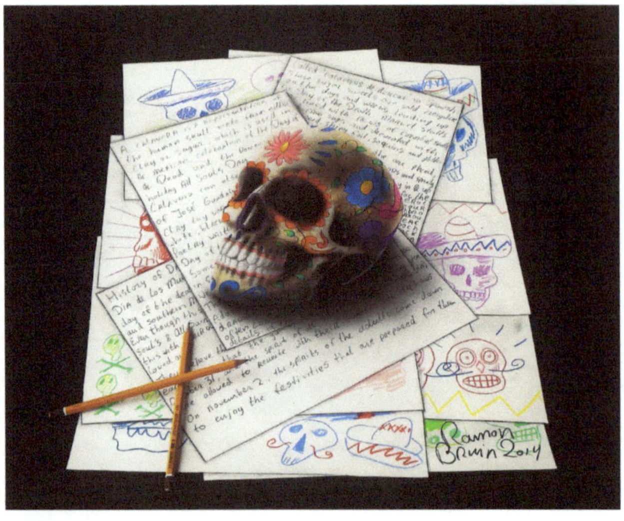

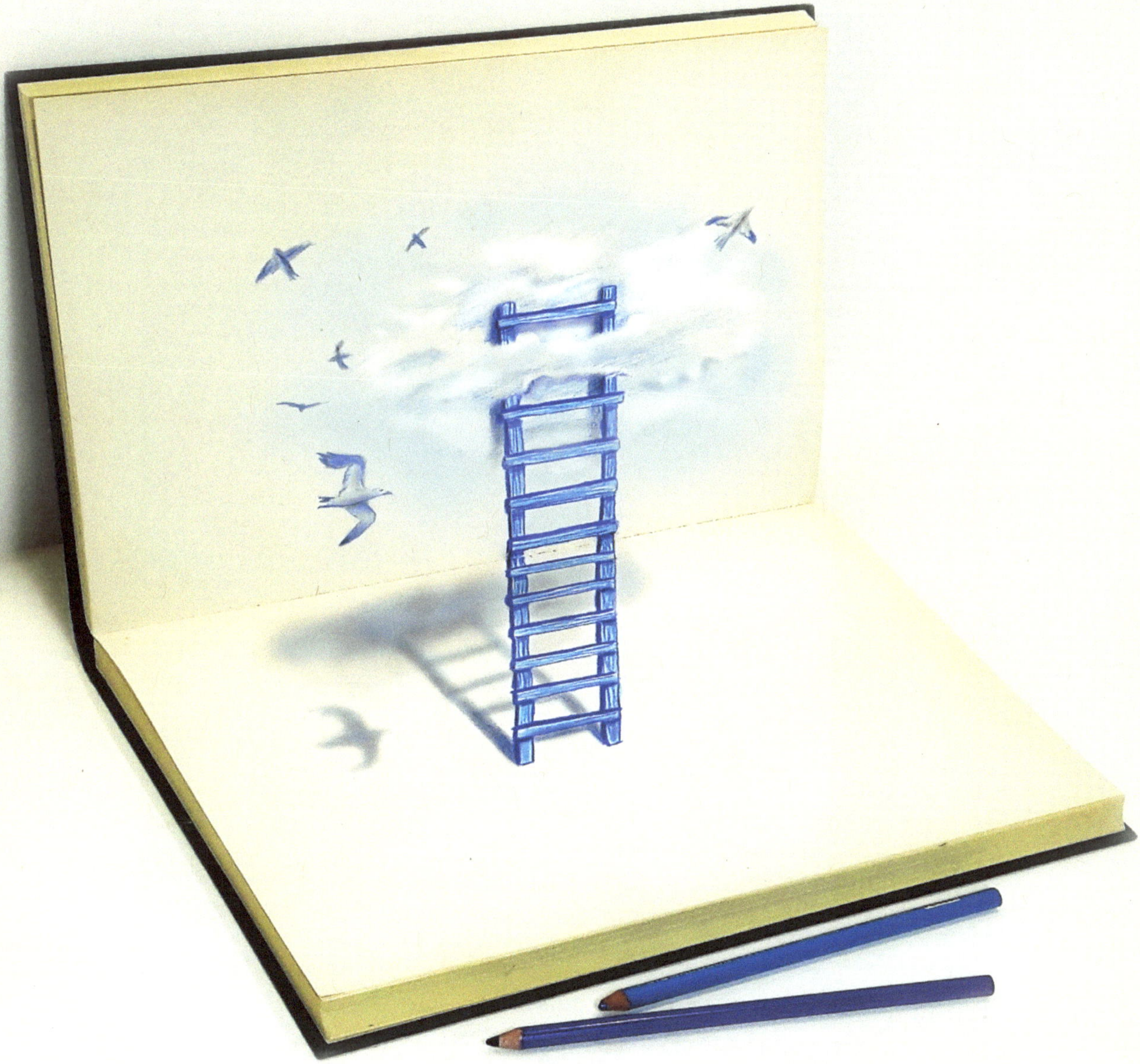

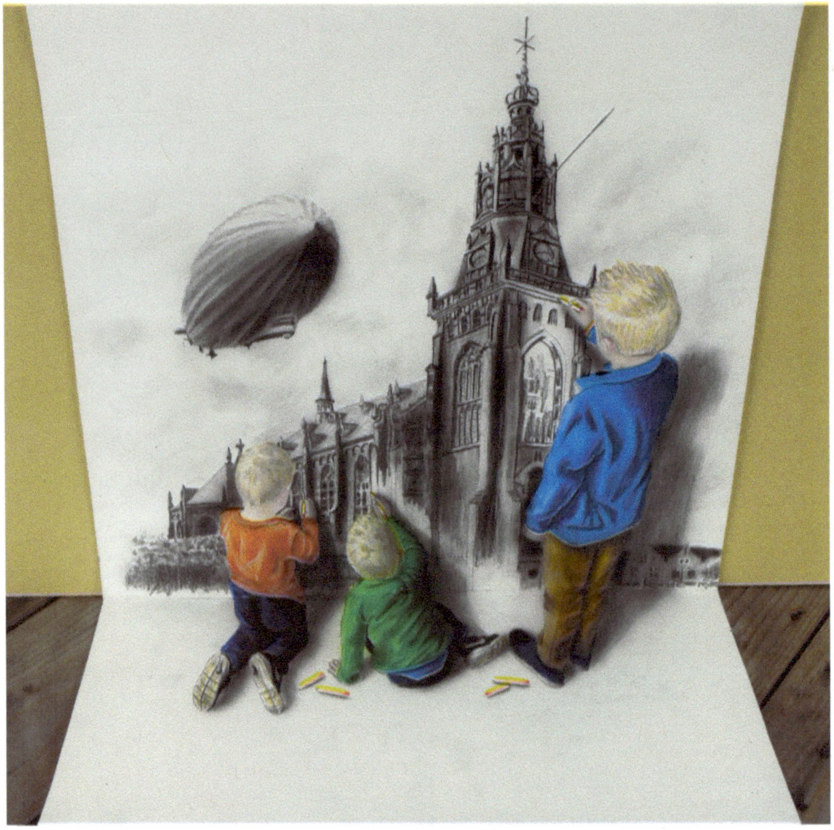

The Architects, coloured pencil on paper photographed from an angle

Keep Fishin', pencil on paper photographed from an angle

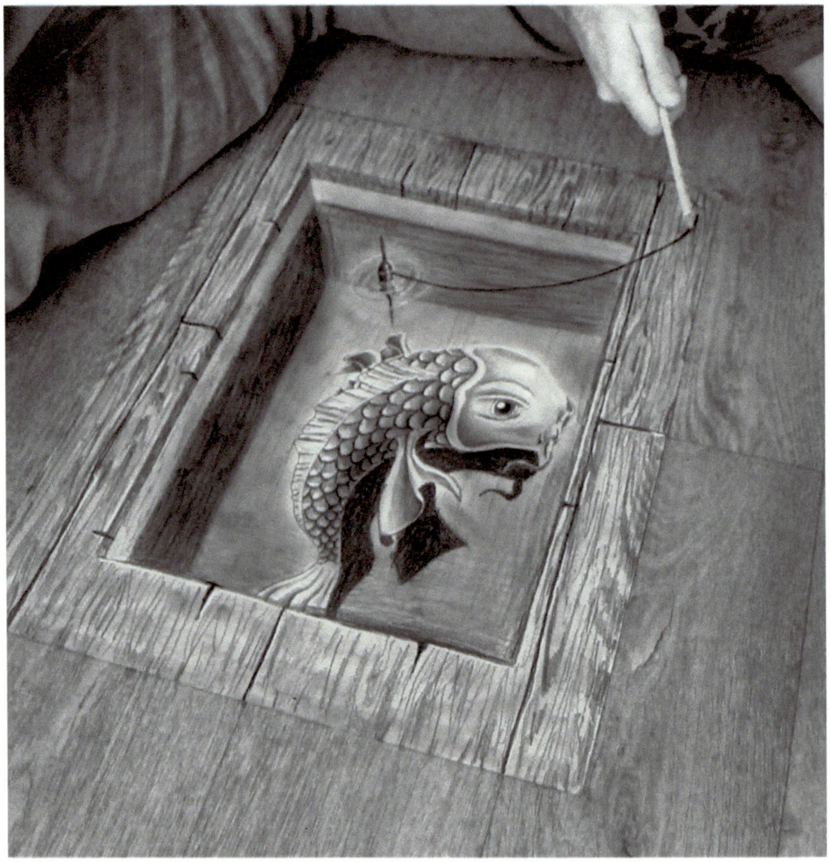

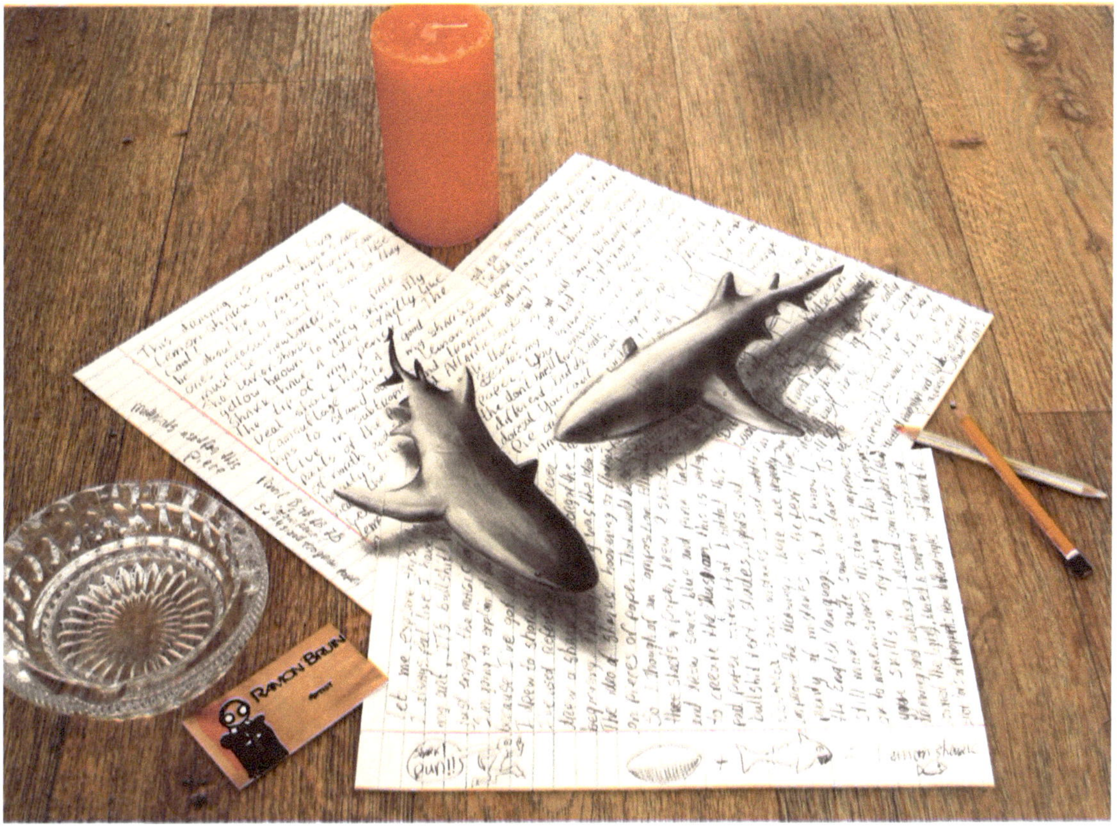

Book of Sharks, pencil on paper photographed from an angle

Shark Infested Furniture, pencil on paper photographed from an angle

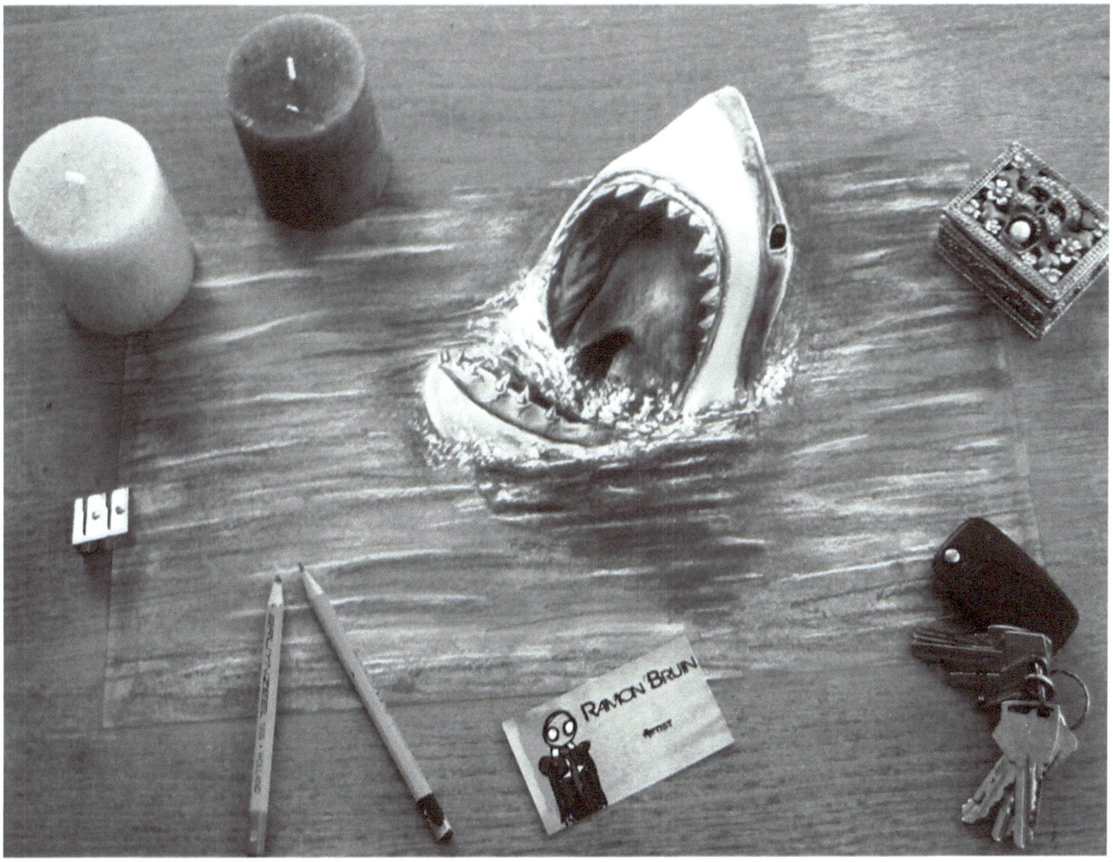

REMO

DRAWING - ARGENTINA

www.artgalaxie.com

Esteban "Remo" Molina is an Argentinian artist who has accrued more than twenty years of professional experience. Born in the Mar del Plata section of Buenos Aires, he taught himself how to draw at an early age, and once he reached a certain skill level, he moved around as a member from one art collective to another.

Simultaneously, he put on solo exhibitions of his work, and he was featured in large publications both national and international. An artist of varied interests and abilities, he has done extensive work on films and in the theatre as well. There is in his work the ever-present concept of dasein (Being-There), in which discovery of the physical world is paramount and what is above becomes apparent in our own natural world.

Currently based out of the San Telmo section of Buenos Aires, Remo works very long hours, constantly honing his message and practicing his technique. Every time he sets out to create a new work, he sees an opportunity to express high and lofty ideals, focusing on such large themes as the divine and mankind's destiny. He is unforgiving of the world, perhaps, but even more so, he is unforgiving of himself, castigating himself for excuses in an effort to become the most effective artist that he can be.

Remo is an artist whose depths can only be comprehended as far as they can be felt in the presence of his work.

Right: God Scatological, ink on canvas, 180 x 140cm

Madonna with Child - Refugees - Vigilate, ink on canvas, 120 x 190cm

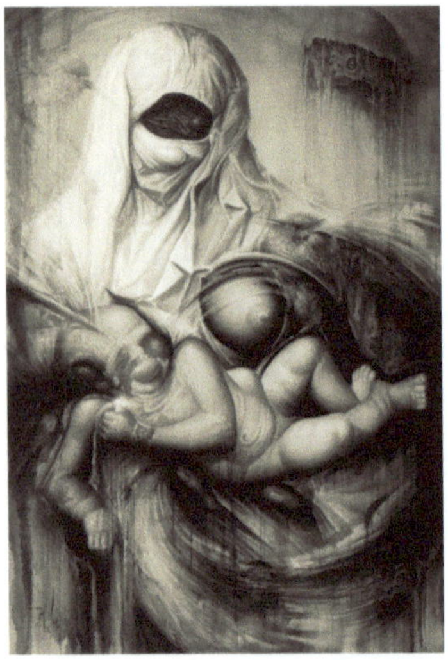

Transgenic Mother, ink on canvas, 35 x 60cm

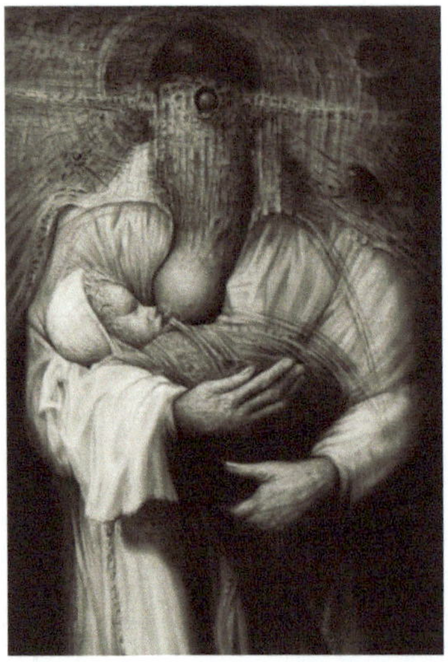

The Feast. ink on canvas, 110 x 75cm

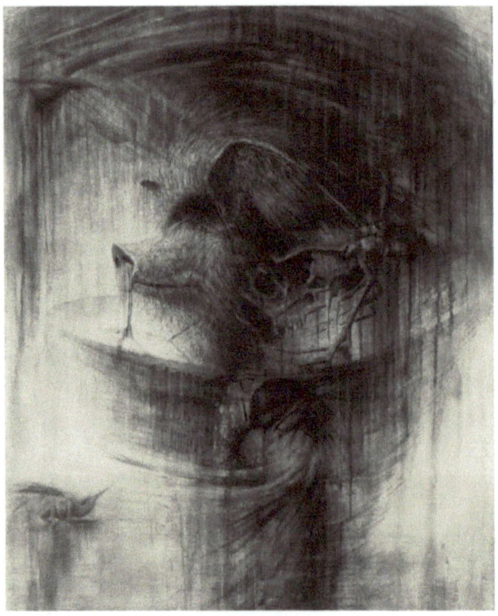

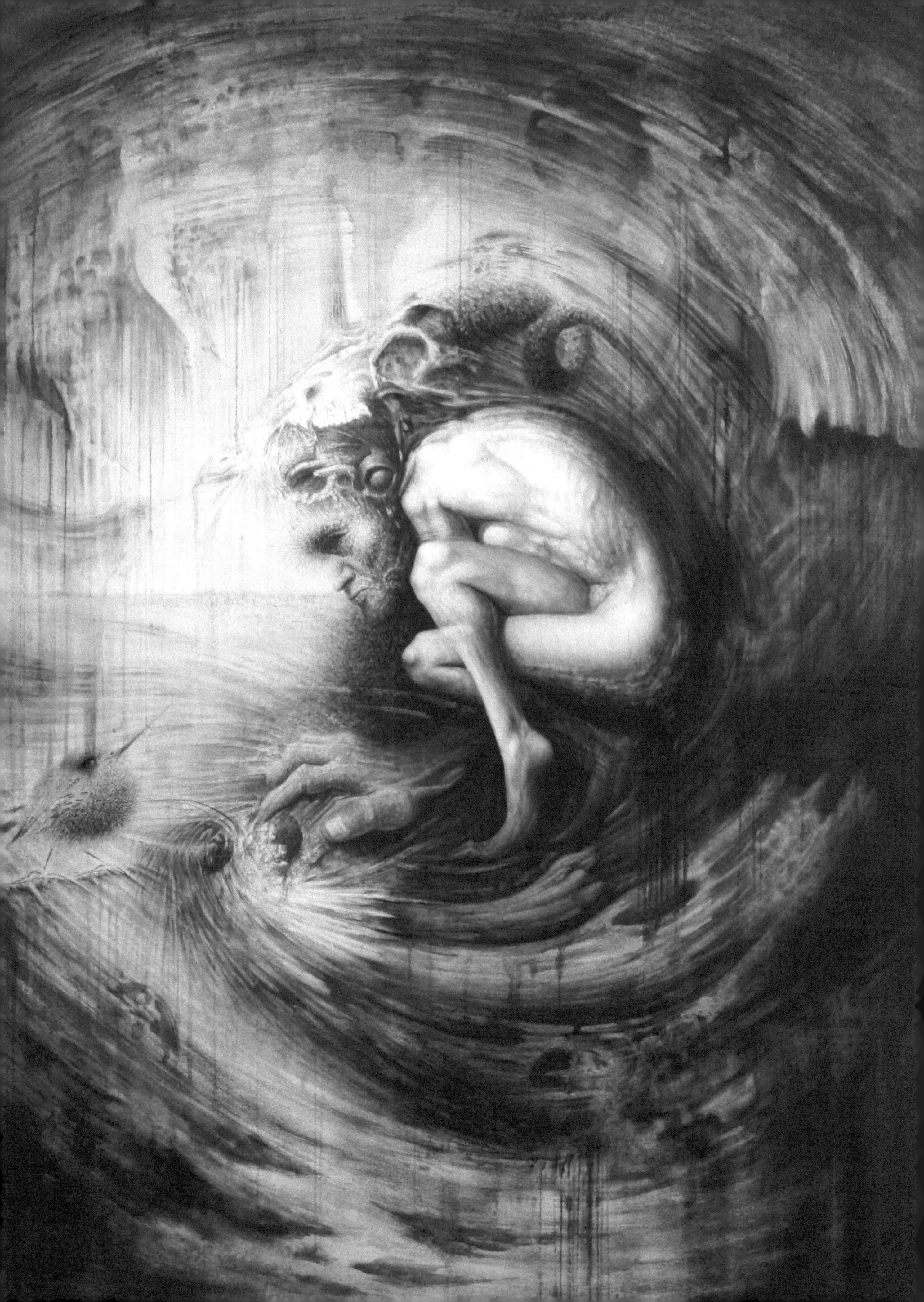

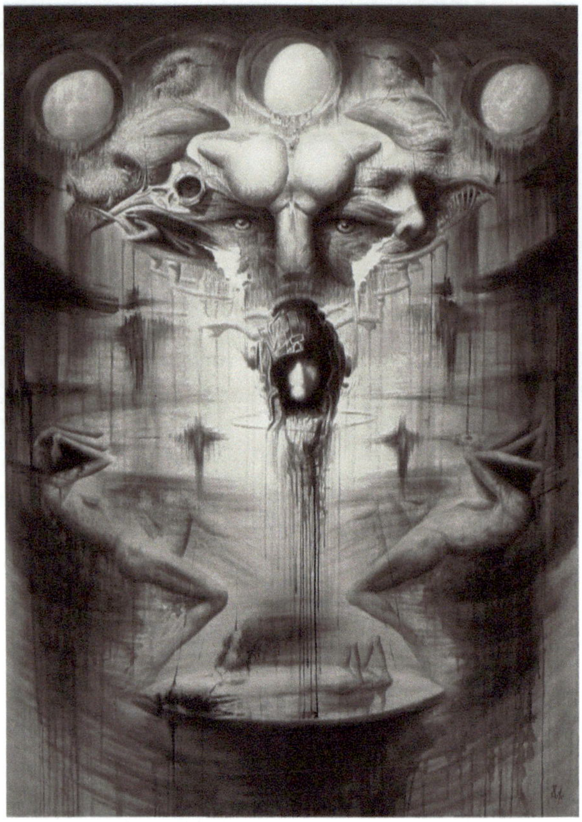

Panopticom, ink on canvas, 130 x 180cm

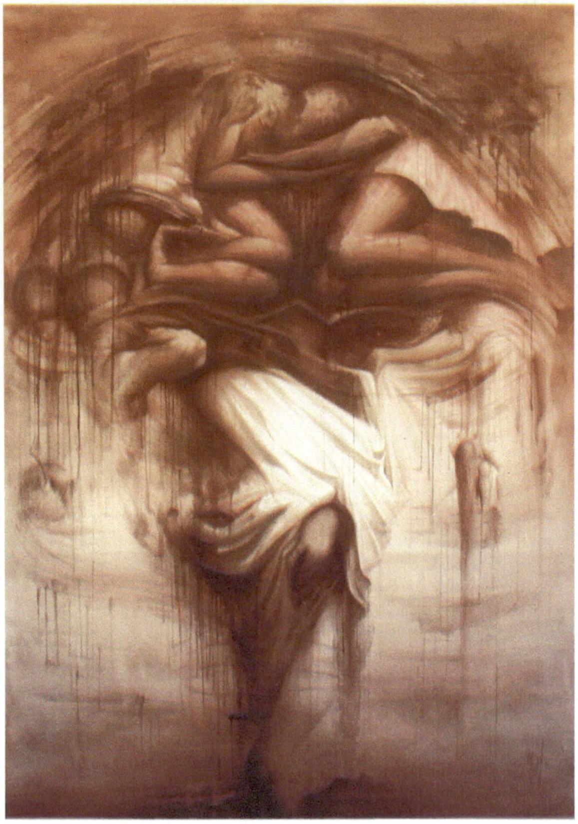

Dream Rain, sepia, ink on canvas, 130 x 180cm

The Triumph of Silenus, ink on canvas, 105 x 75cm

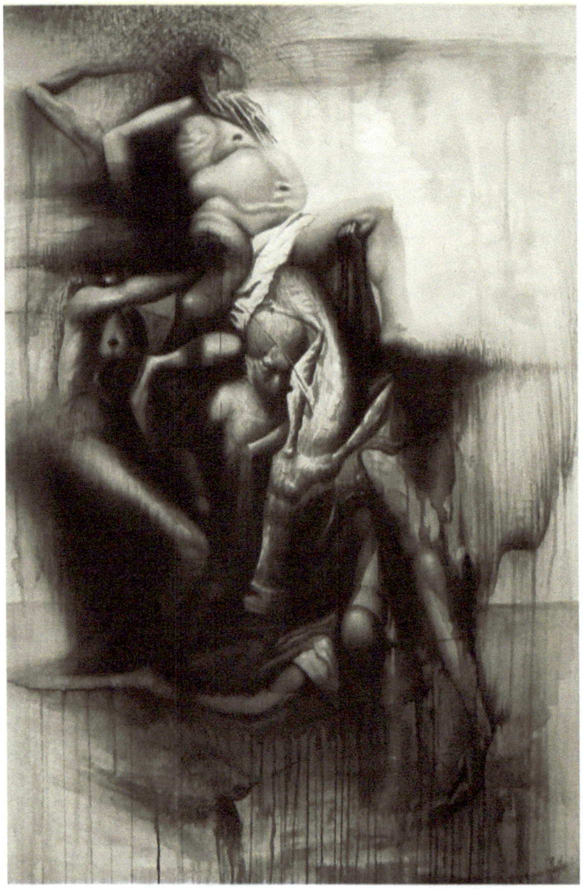

The Myth, blue ink on canvas, 120 x 190cm

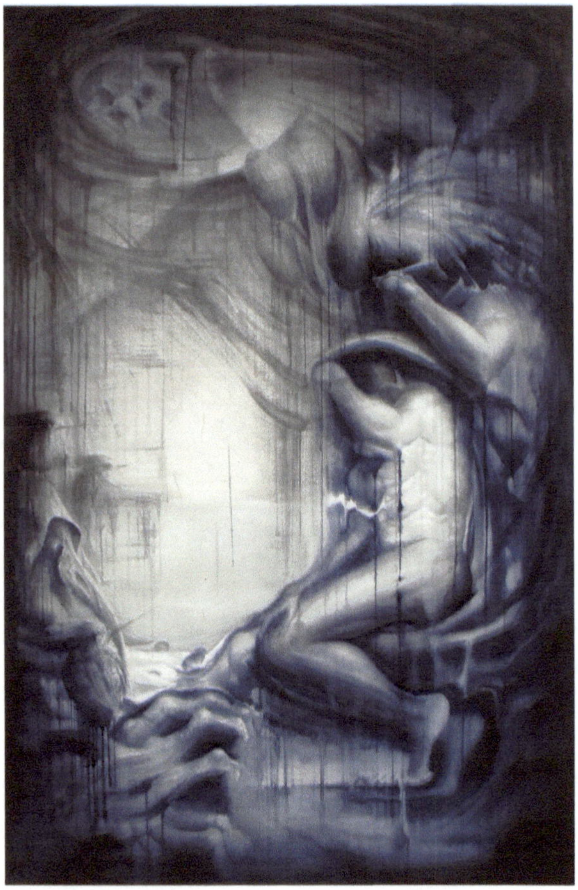

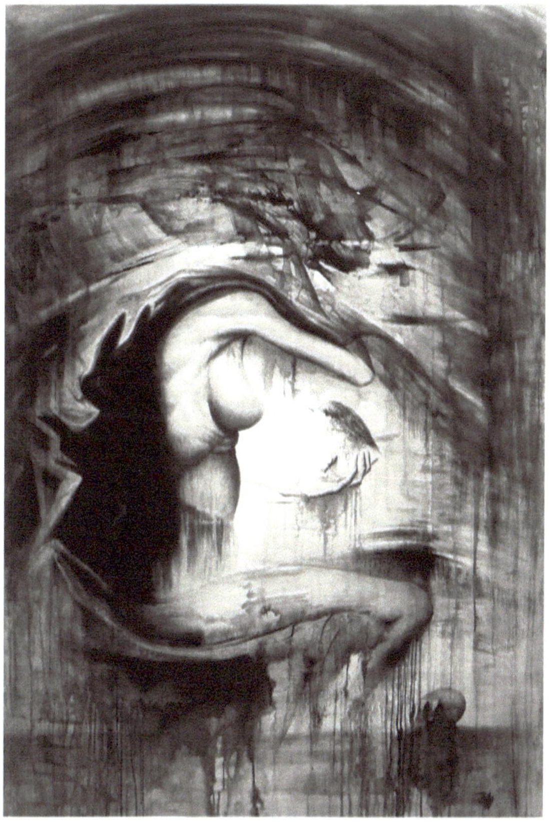

Pajarito (Birdie), ink on canvas, 120 x 190cm

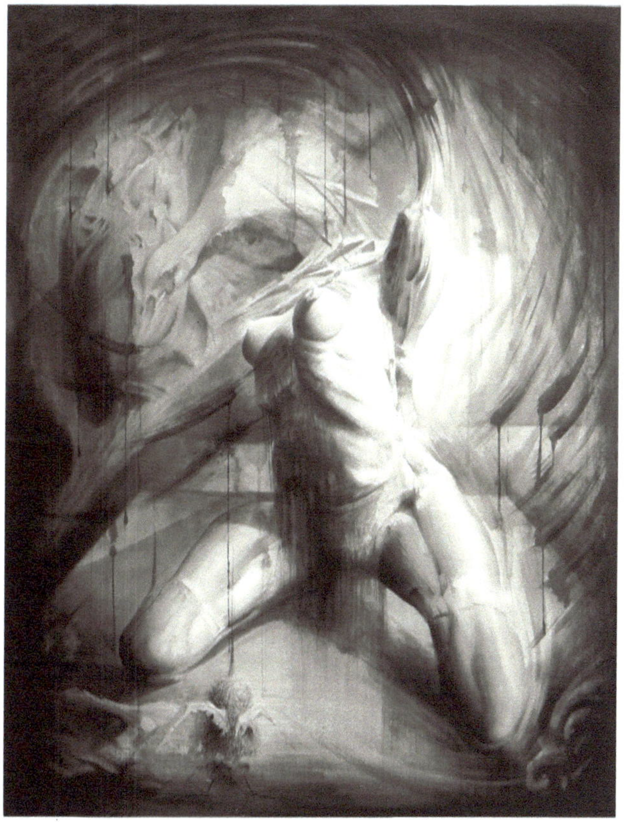

Flagelated Mother Earth, ink on canvas, 120 x 170cm

The Rabbit is no Longer White, it is now a Bird and no one is following him anymore (About Alice in Wonderland, 135 x 95cm

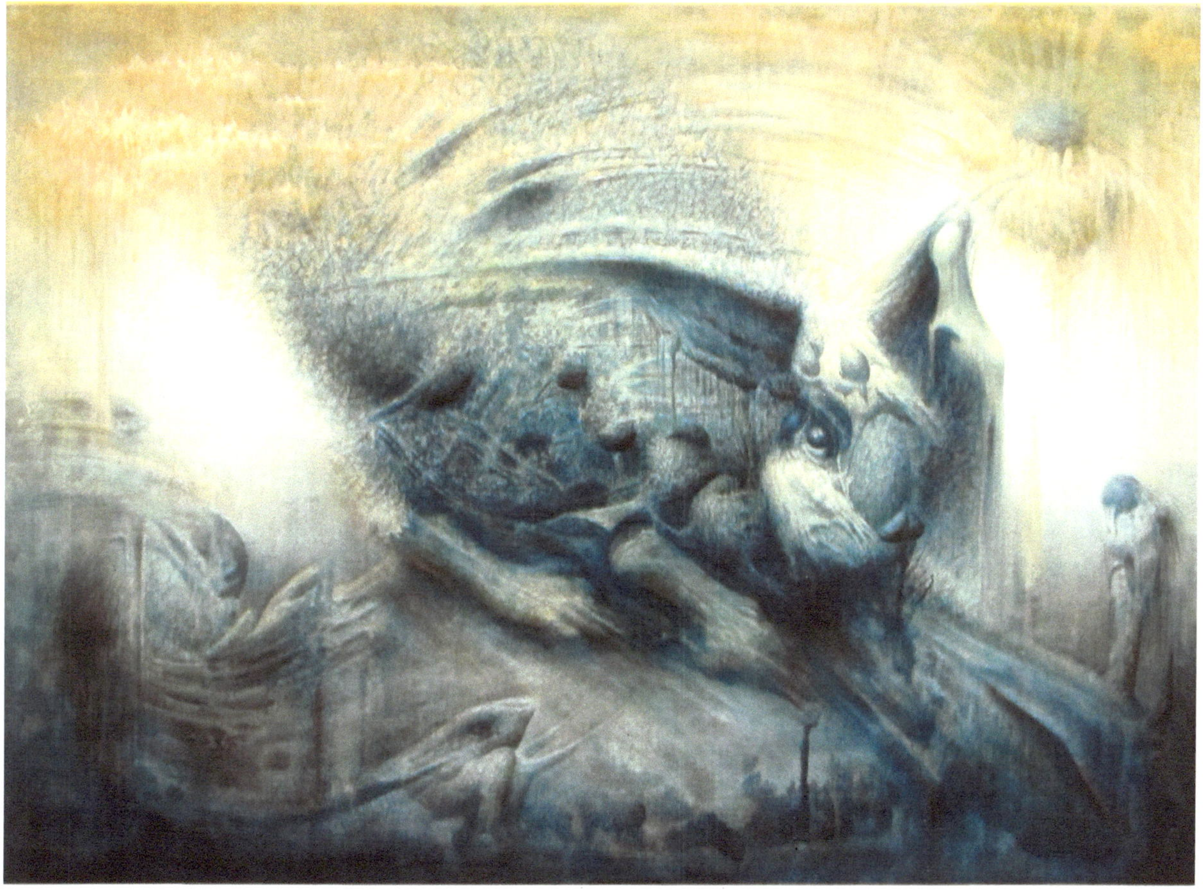

ZHAO NA

DRAWING - CHINA

www.artgalaxie.com

Zhao Na was born in Liaoning, China. Her passion lies in drawing, which she has been fond of since childhood, illustration and mural painting. She received her BA degree from the College of Art and Design and later her masters from The Mural Department of Central Academy of Fine Arts, both in Beijing.

Her portfolio reveals a versatile artist equally adept at colourful surrealist explorations as well as more traditional approaches. Her work has been used in several design pieces such as Romago watches and designer jewellery brands.

Zhao Na's artwork is connected to the notions of nature, peace and love. Influenced by earth and space, she delicately transforms floral motives into her own surreal, psychedelic scenes, rebelling against the remorseless actions of society and the continual destruction of the environment. Her compositions are descrived to hold an intense visual energy.

She has participated in several Solo and Group exhibitions in China, Singapore and Hong Kong. She has also received awards of excellence for her outstanding creativeness and imagination.

Her artworks have been published in several articles around the globe.

Right: 2 Come With Me, 2011, coloured pencil on paper, 150 x 80cm

Mini Forest, 2015, acrylic ink on canvas, 80 x 120cm

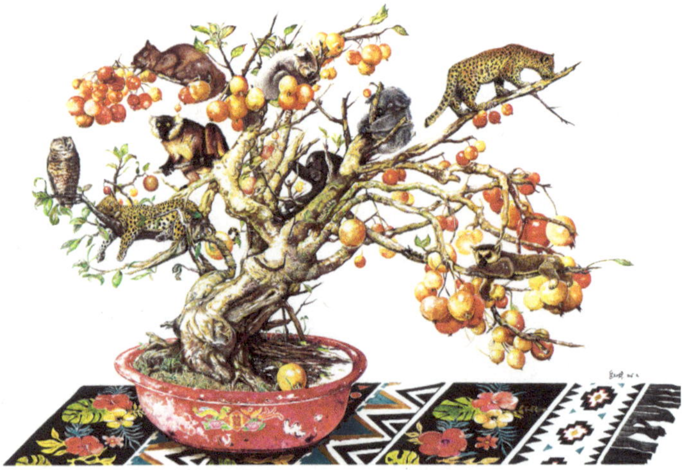

Autumn Drunk, 2016, acrylic ink on canvas, 120 x 90cm

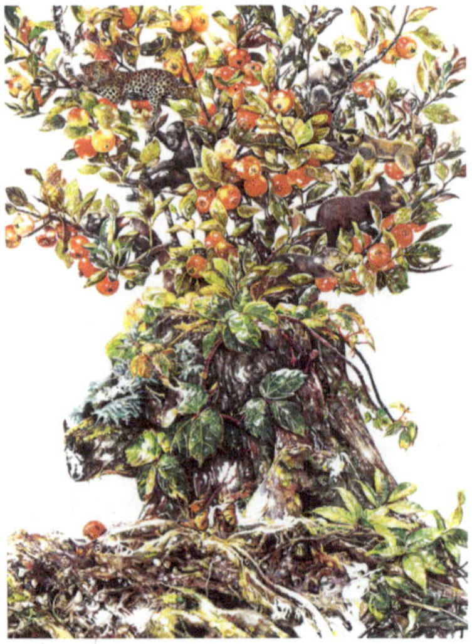

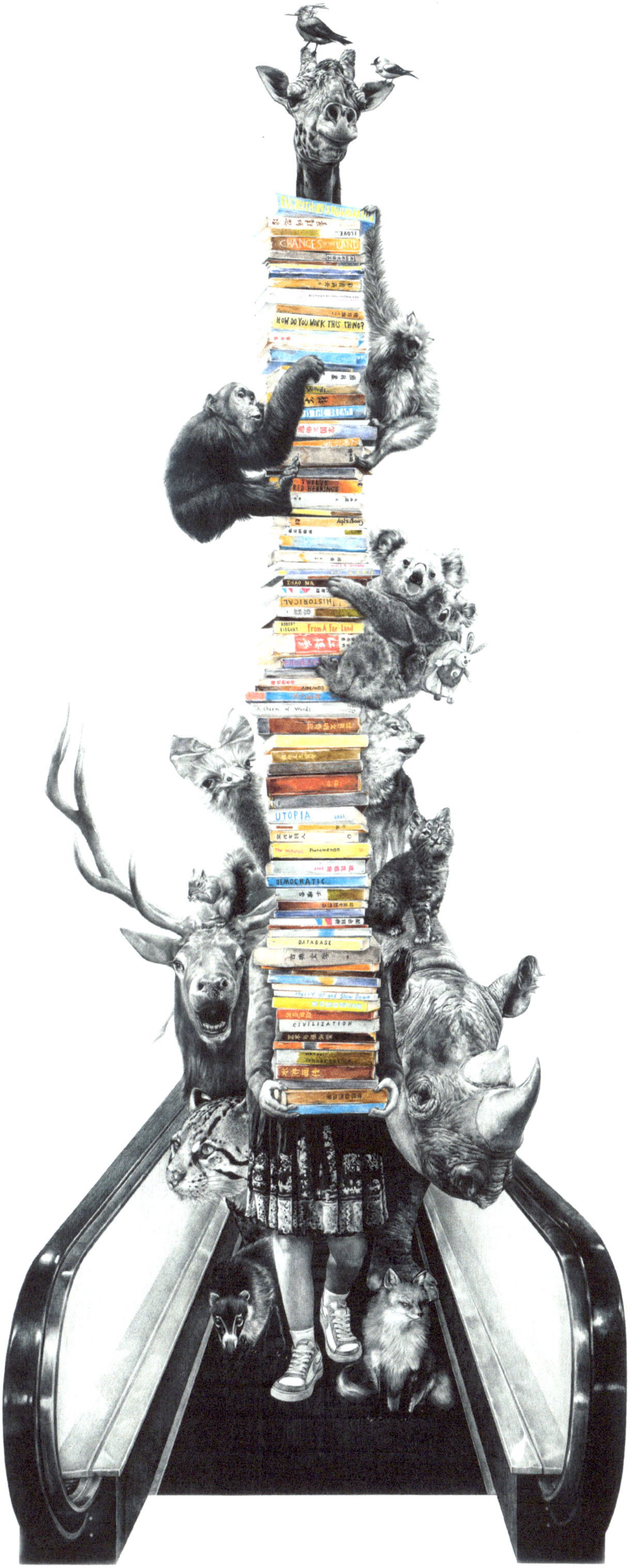
CHANGES of the LAND
HOW DO YOU WORK THIS THING?
HISTORICAL
UTOPIA
DEMOCRATIC
DATABASE
CIVILIZATION

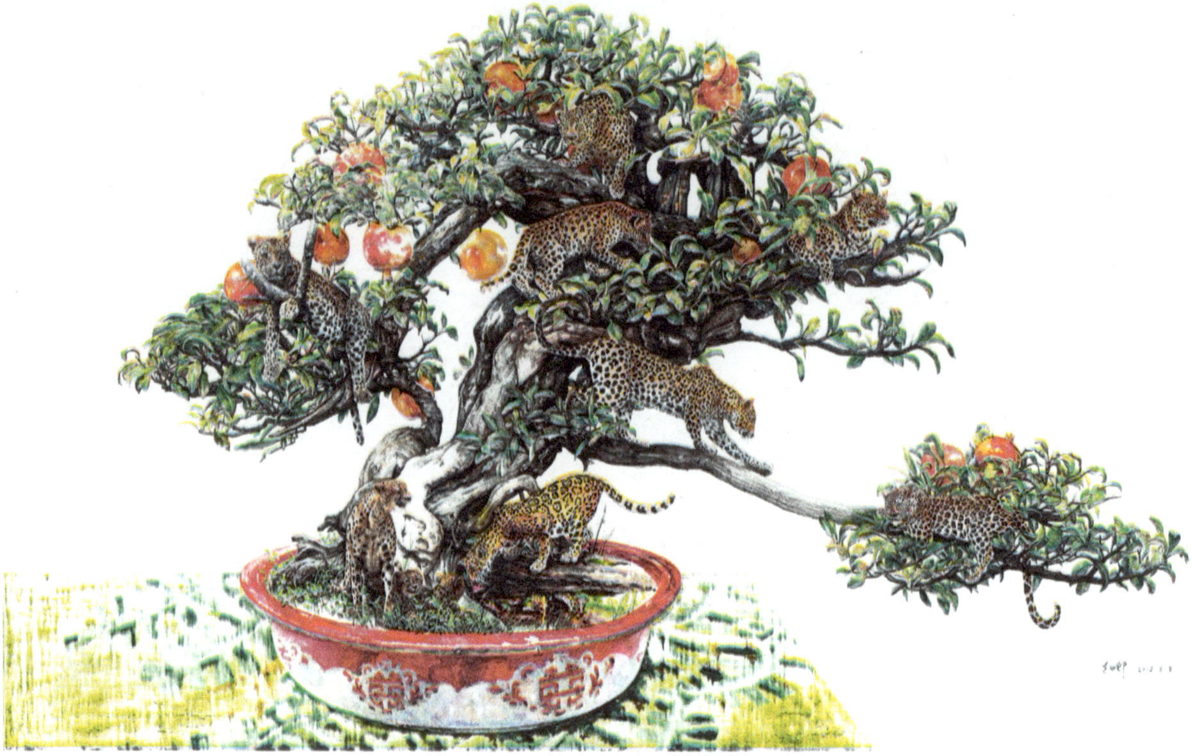

Wedding Banquet, 2015, acrylic ink on canvas, 70 x 120cm

Spring Fragrance, 2016, acrylic ink on canvas, 120 x 90cm

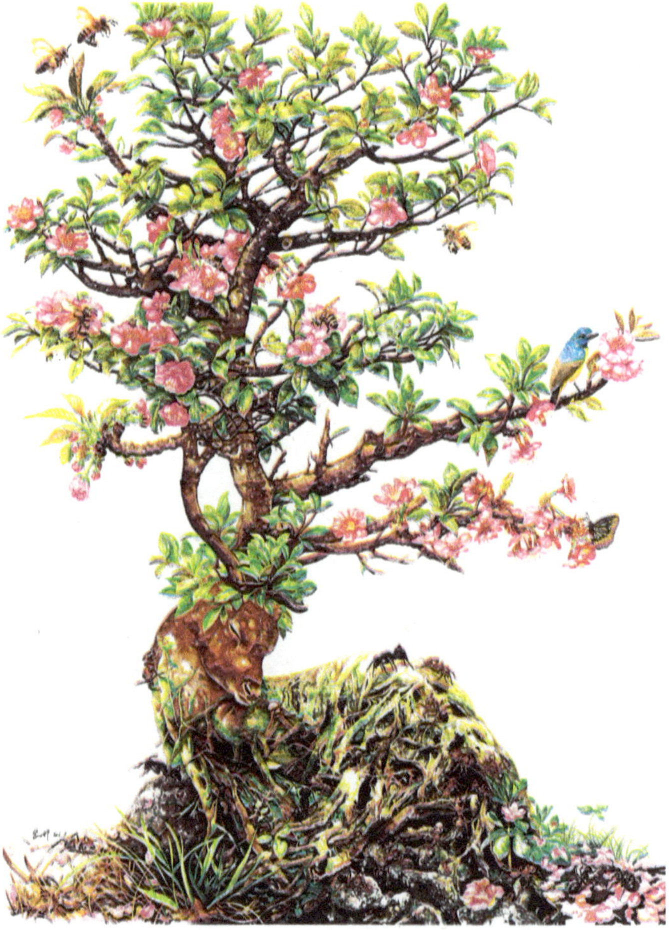

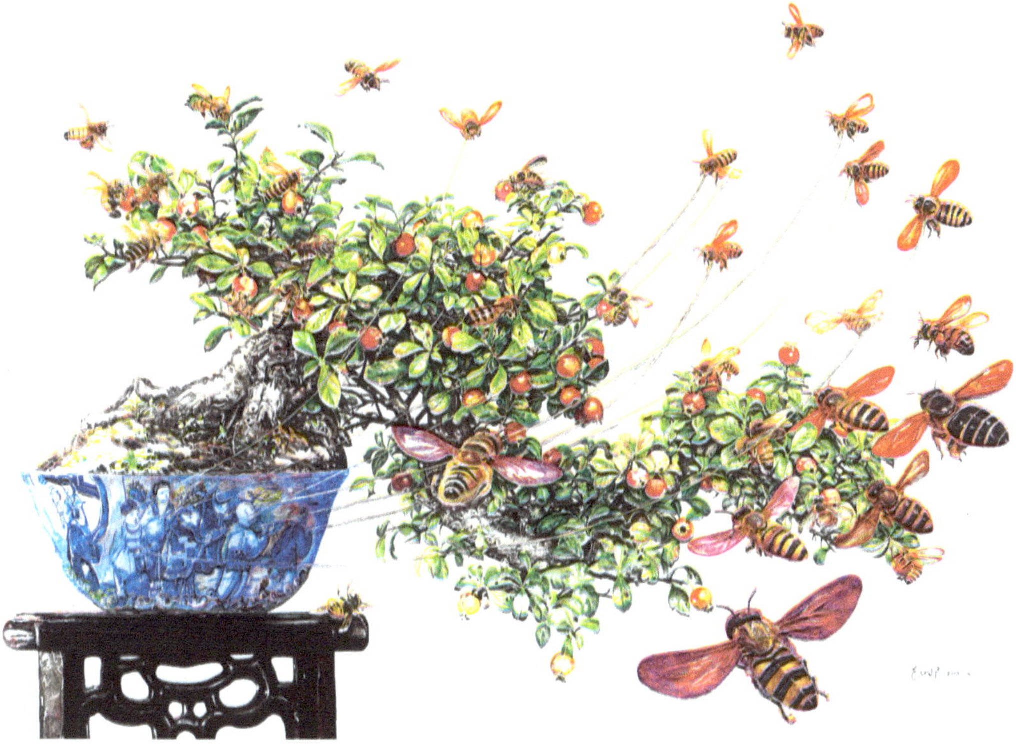

Flying the Bees Kite, 2015, acrylic ink on canvas, 80 x 120cm

Winter Hidden, 2016, acrylic ink on canvas, 120 x 90cm

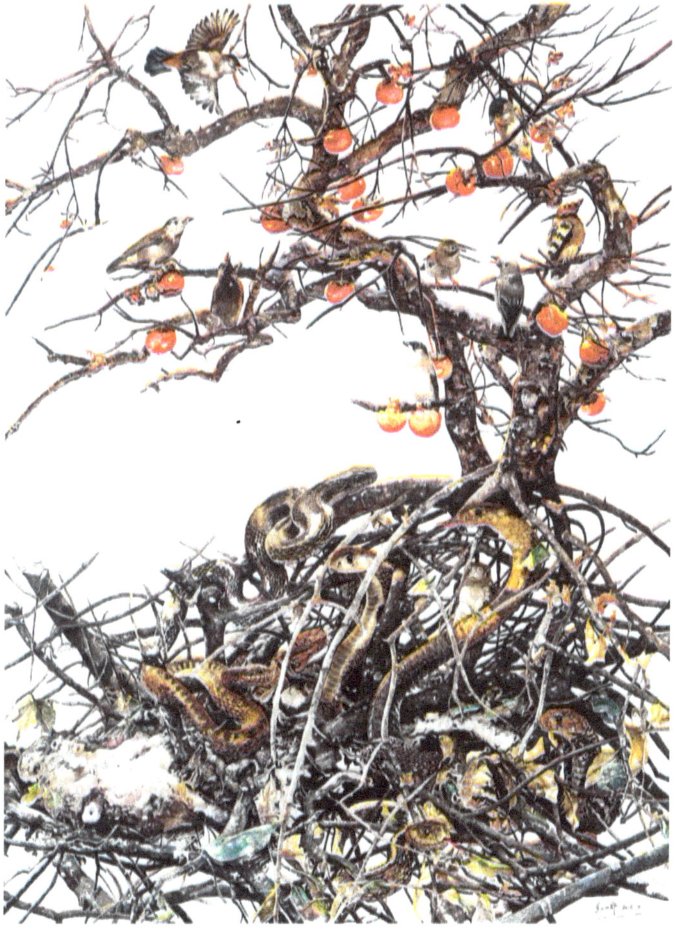

BOJAN JEVTIC

DIGITAL ART - SERBIA

www.artgalaxie.com

Bojan Jevtic is a Serbian visual artist. Born in Belgrade, he has had a long, illustrious career. His art has been featured on book covers and CD covers and inside such publications as Mercury, which is the official magazine of the Department of Business Studies Uppsala University in Sweden, and Saatchi Art's Fall 2016 catalogue.

He is also highly sought after by public collection curators and private art collectors all around the globe, known especially for his complex portraits of women in a variety of settings. Although there are elements of reality in his work, there is also the sense that what he is illustrating is not exactly of this world either, or if it is, then it is of this world in a way not usually perceived. He sees in women intrigue and excitement, and it is those things that he tries to put down onto canvas.

Wholly originally in his insights, Bojan bases his works on digital photos, making extensive use of textures, computer effects, and digital painting tools. Outside of Saatchi Art, he also has been featured on Artfido, Artfinder, Shadowness, and Onlyunique.

When you look at Bojan's work, you are looking at a vision of a vision. Something has been seen here, mirrored, and then its mirror has been seen in sequence. In doses magical and unsettling, his art is a true product of the time in which we live.

Right: Classy, digital media

Natural Girl, digital media

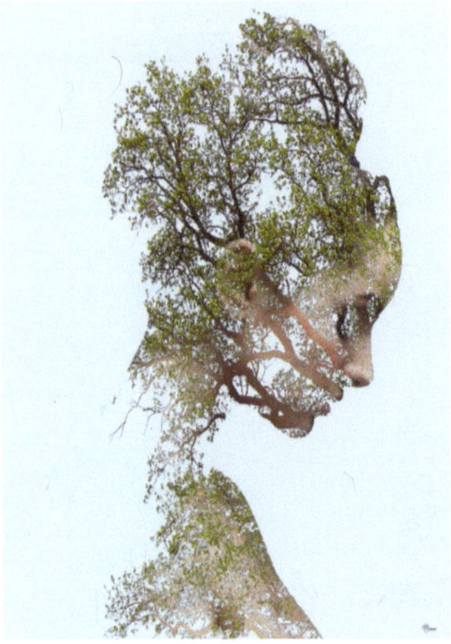

Autumn is Here, digital media

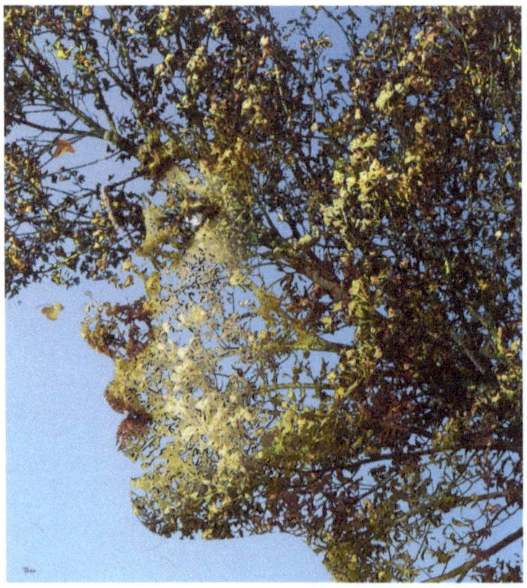

Kiss, digital media

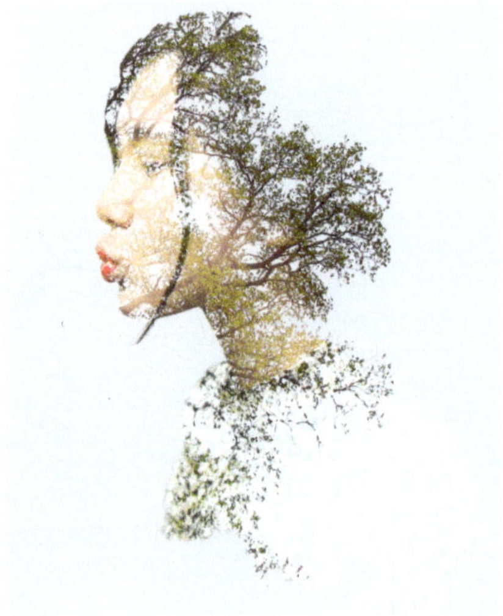

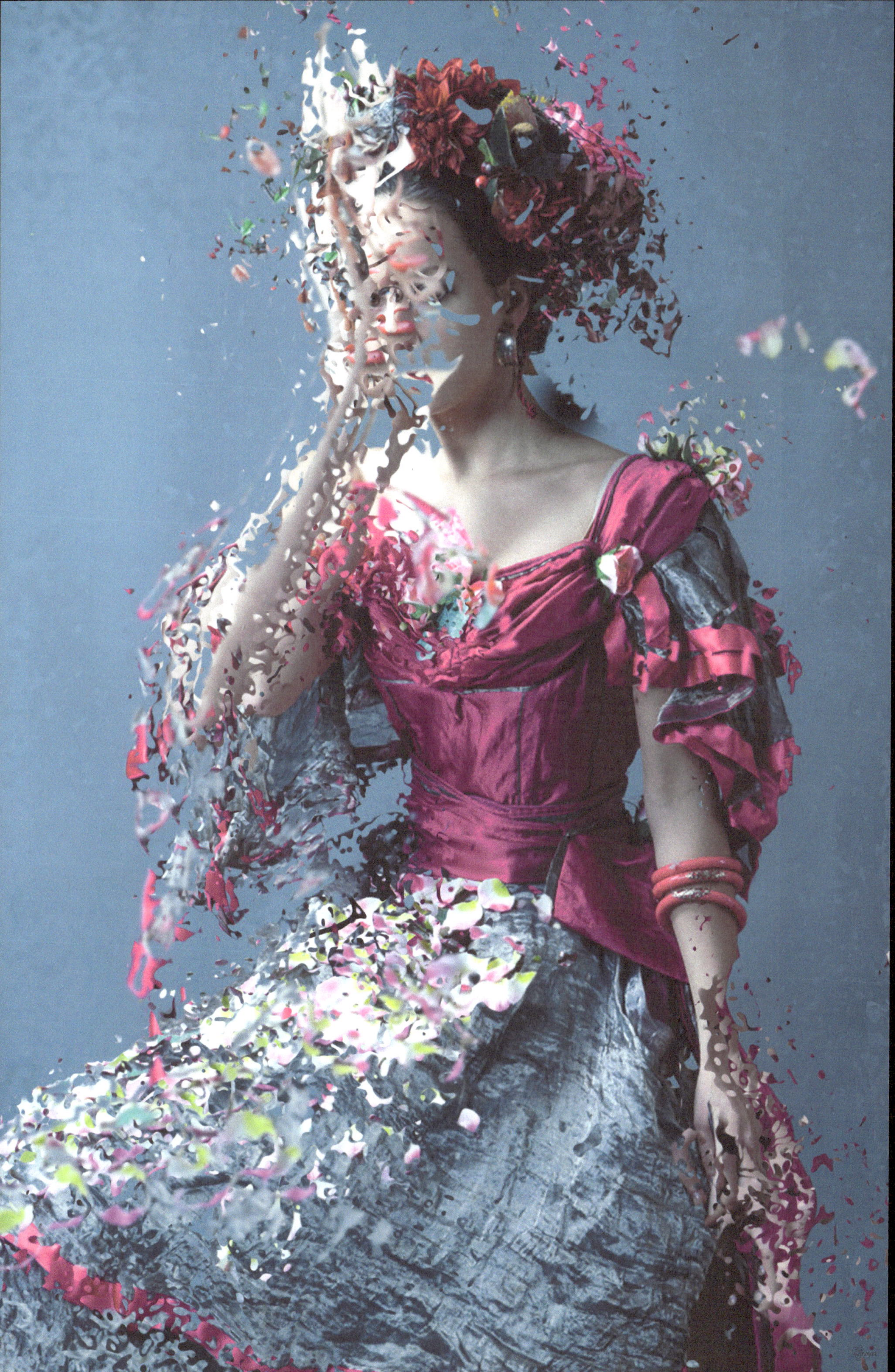

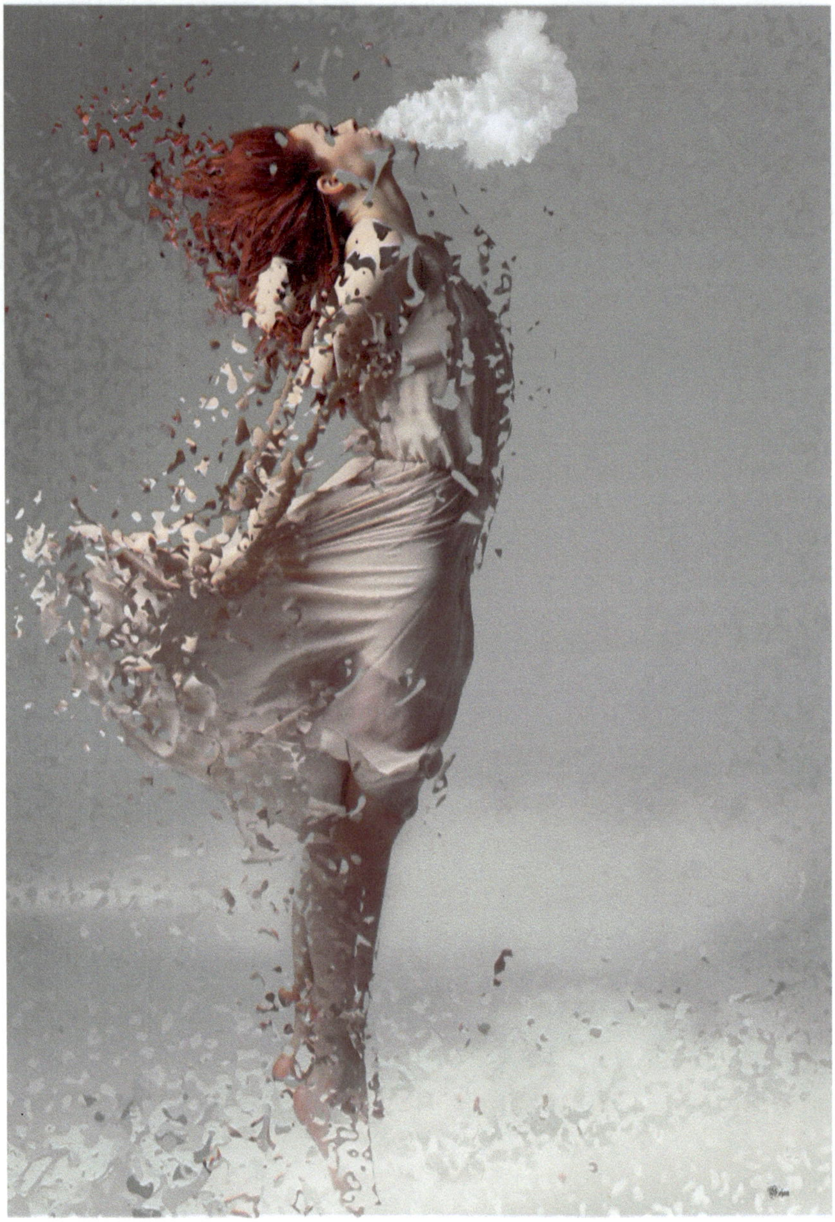

First Breath, digital media

Feel Me, digital media

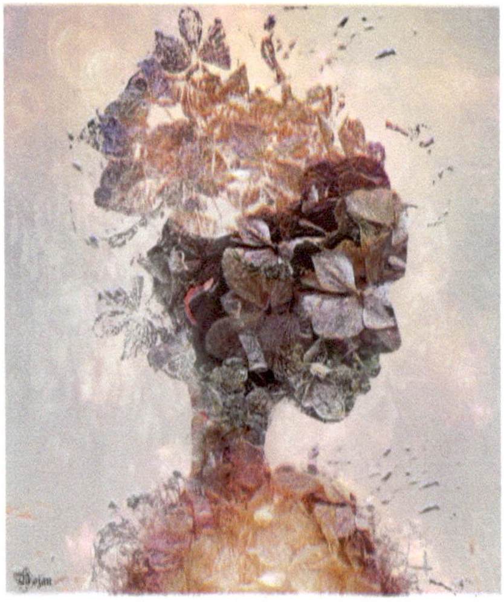

From Serbia with Love, digital media

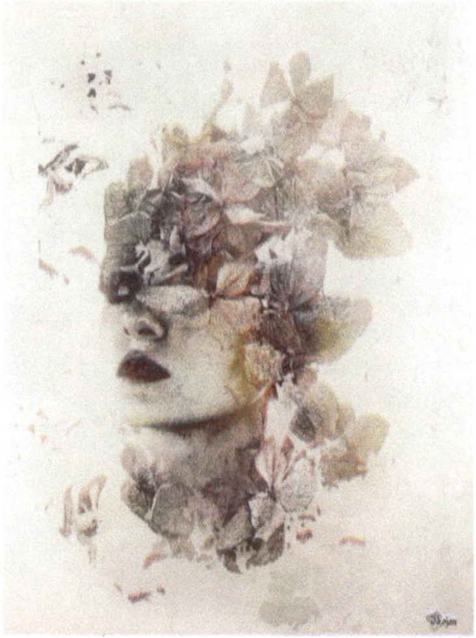

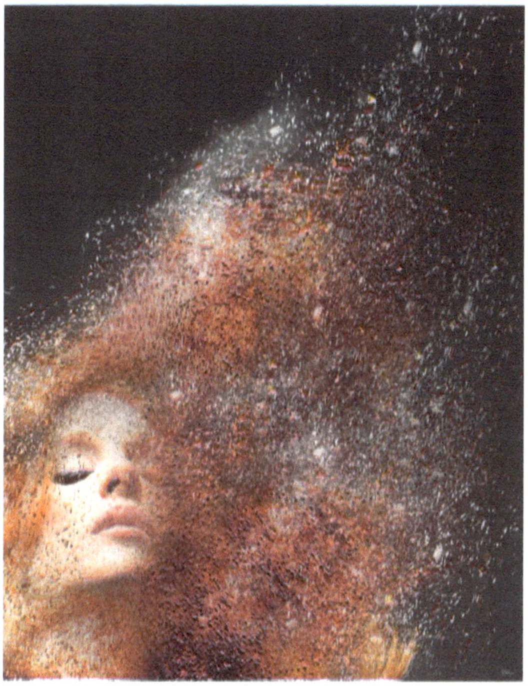
Don't Disturb, digital media

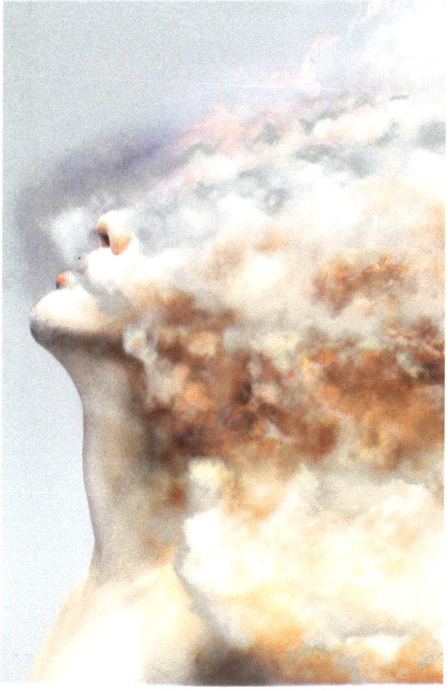
Thinking too much, digital media

The Fire in Me, digital media

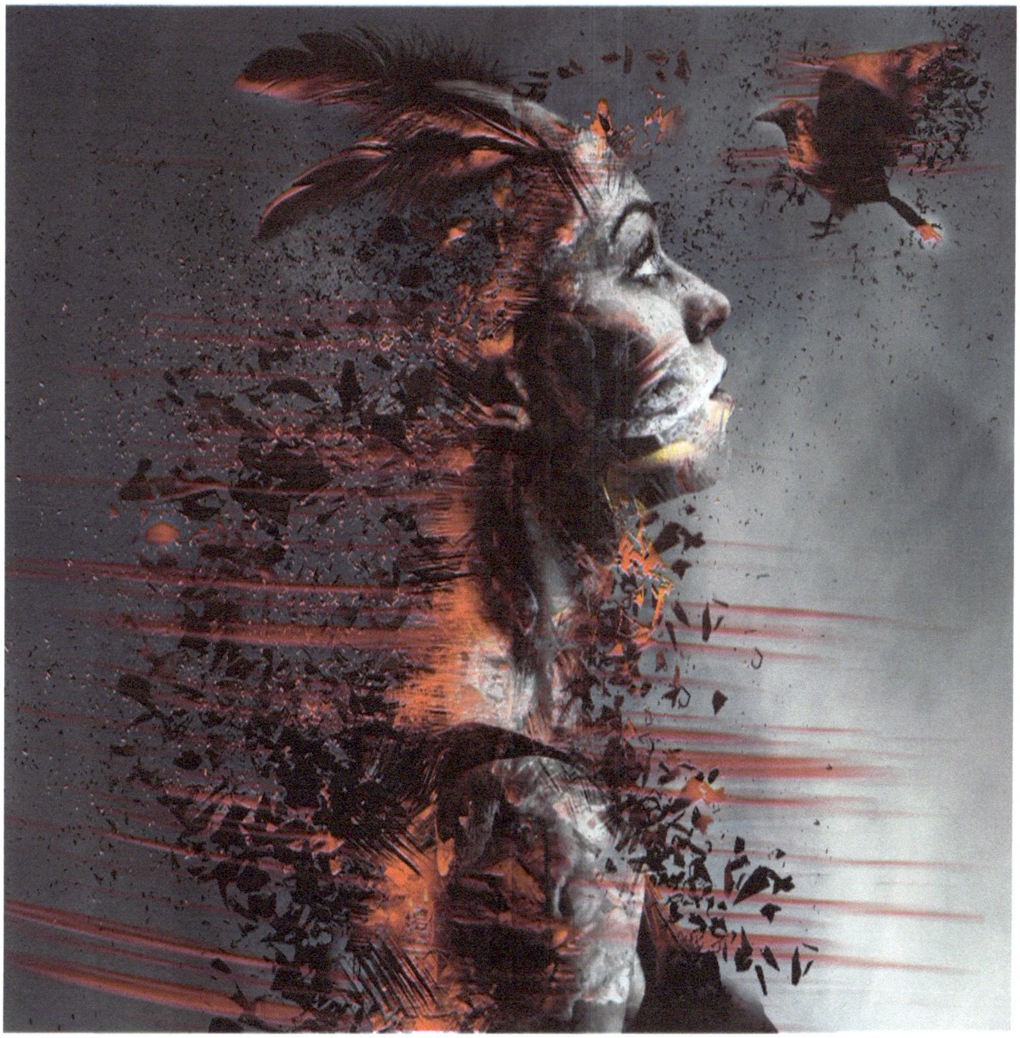

CATRIN WELZ-STEIN

DIGITAL ART - GERMANY

www.artgalaxie.com

Catrin Welz-Stein is a German artist who is known for her work in the field of surrealism. A digital artist, she often takes as her themes mysticism and dream worlds, drawing particular inspiration from old photographs and other remnants of antiquated culture, adding a familiar foreignness to her illustrations.

Standing before an image that she has crafted, her vibrant imagination is on stark display, and it is known for awakening in her audience imaginations of their own. She is inviting you on a journey, a journey unlike any you have ever experienced, a journey in which the normal becomes the strange and the strange becomes the normal.

Although it is clear upon further examination that Catrin's works are digital, they could be mistaken for oil paintings that have been put together one layer after another. Educated in graphic design and for several years after her graduation employed as a graphic designer, she has developed her technical abilities to a point of high precision. Her style is distinctly her own, and the stories that she tells in her works are uniquely exciting.

Catrin Welz-Stein is a dreamer who is asking the world to see into her imagination. From collages to paintings on canvas, she has worked in such a broad mix of media that her style is in no way confined to the medium in which she now works most frequently.

Right: Ennui, 2014, digital on canvas, 50 x 61cm

Liberty, 2014, digital on canvas, 40 x 61cm

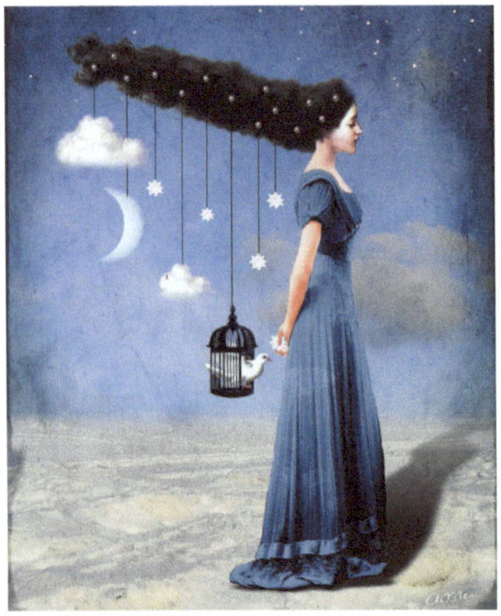

New Beginnings, 2015, digital on canvas, 50 x 61cm

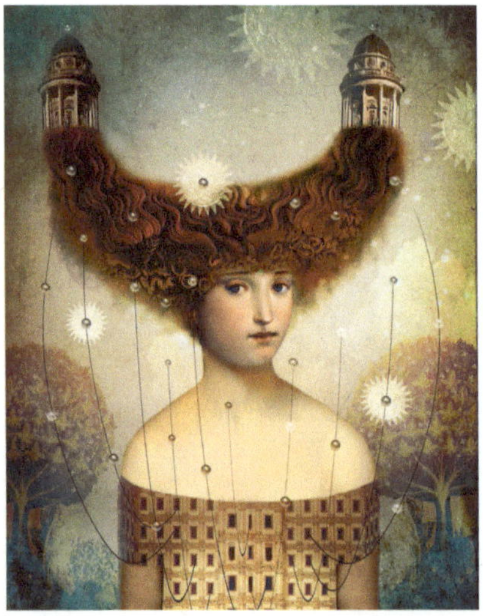

Plant me a Tree, 2012, digital on canvas, 50 x 61cm

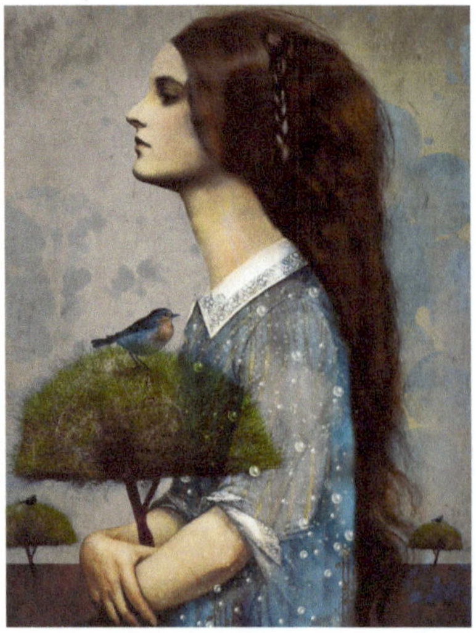

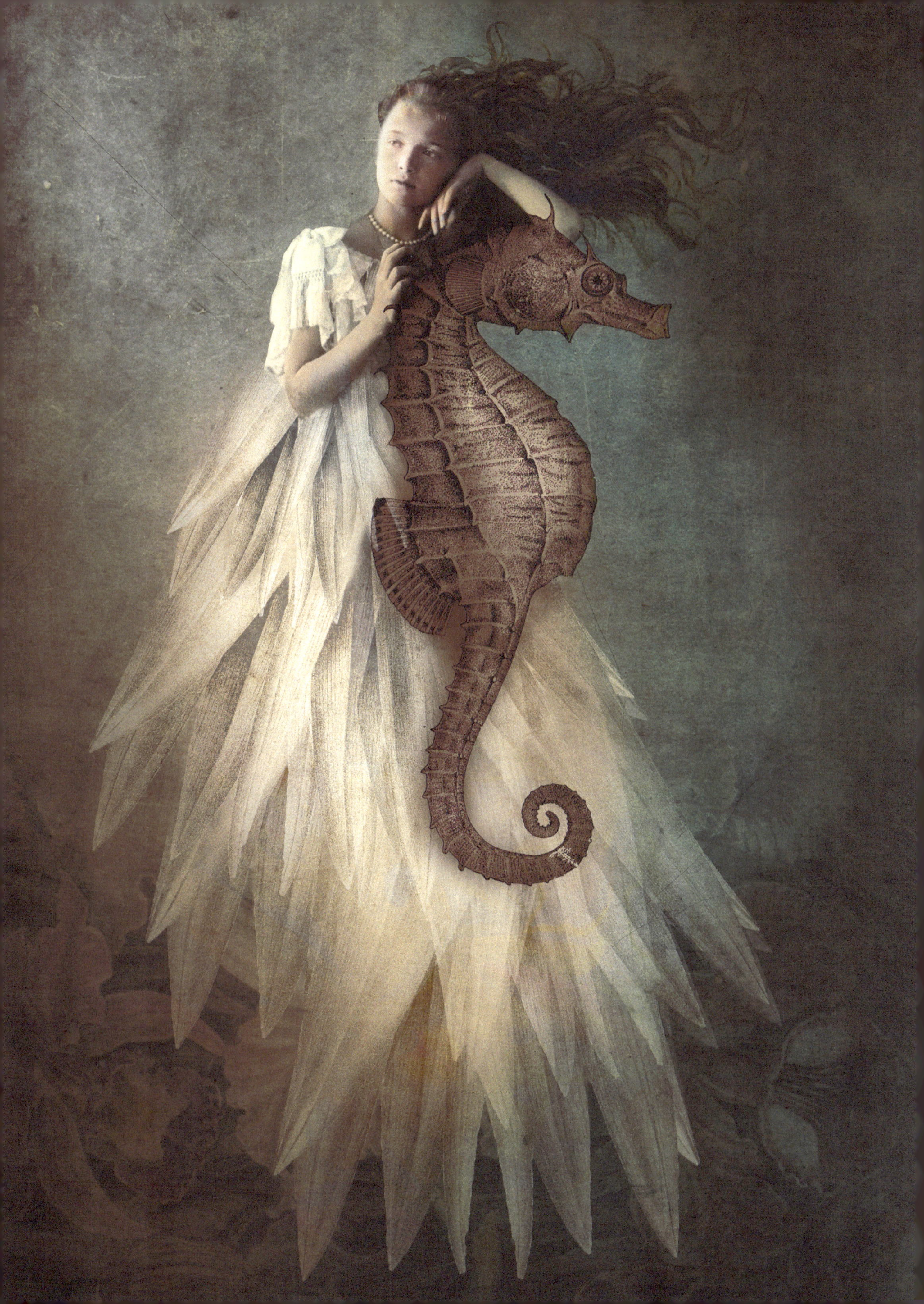

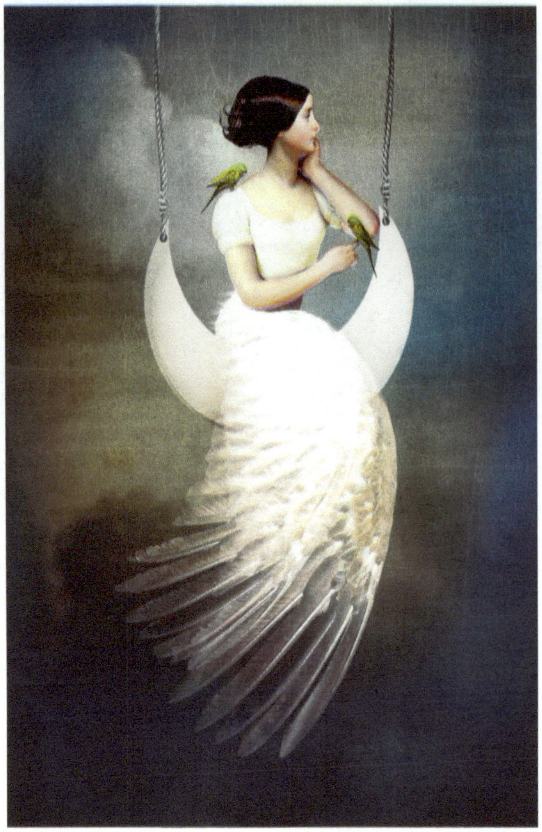

To the Moon and Back, 2015, digital on canvas, 50 x 61cm

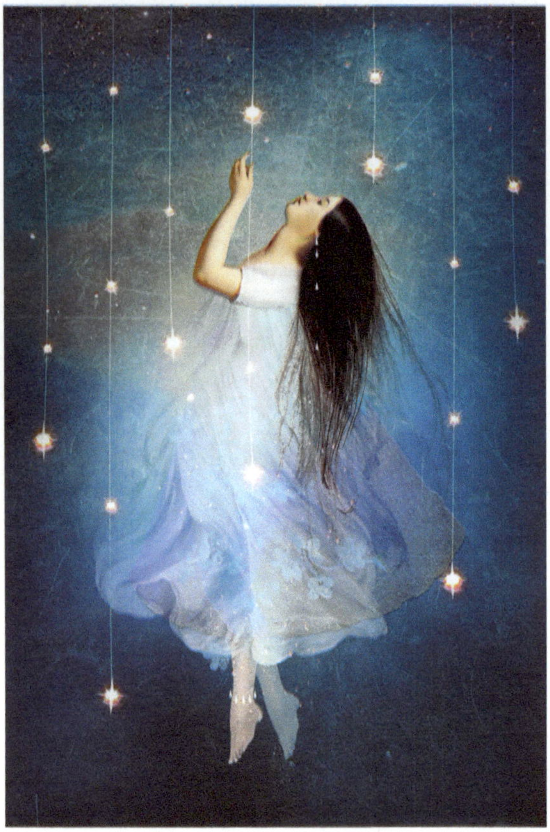

Star Sailor, 2015, digital on canvas, 61 x 40cm

Homeward Bound, 2009, digital on canvas, 76 61cm

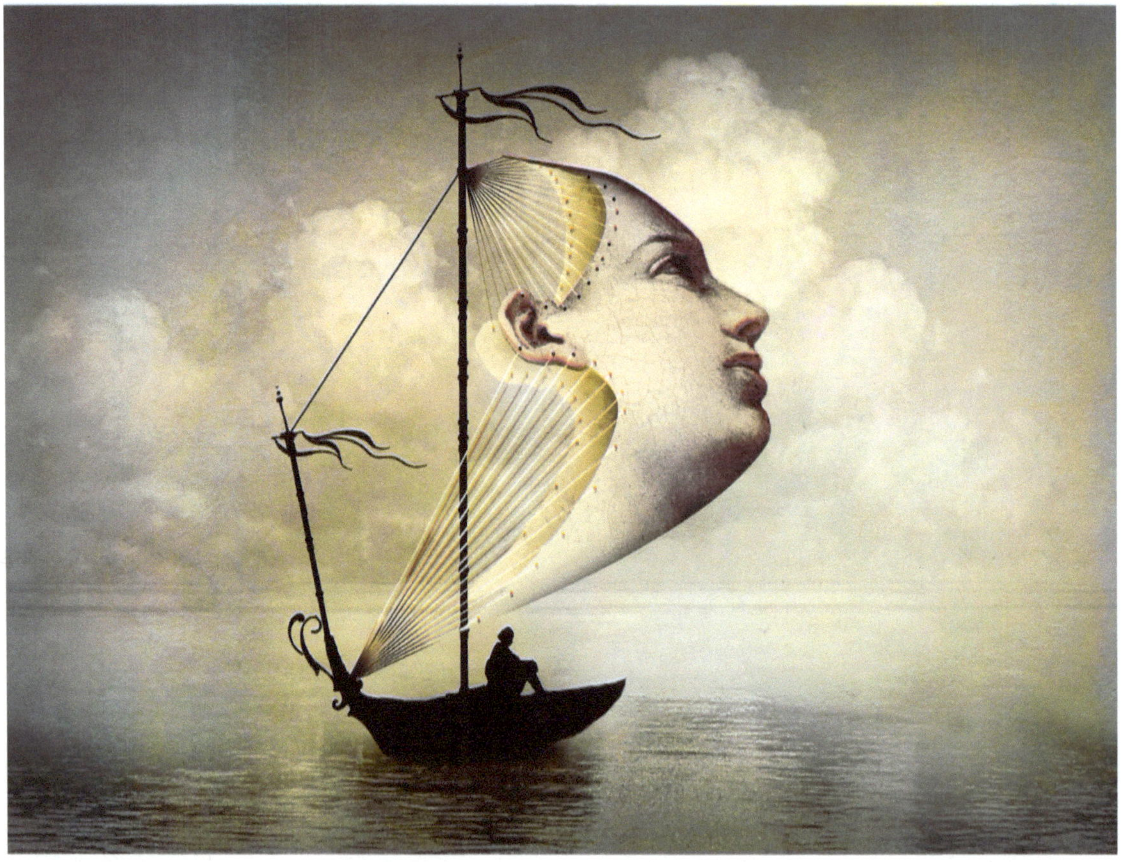

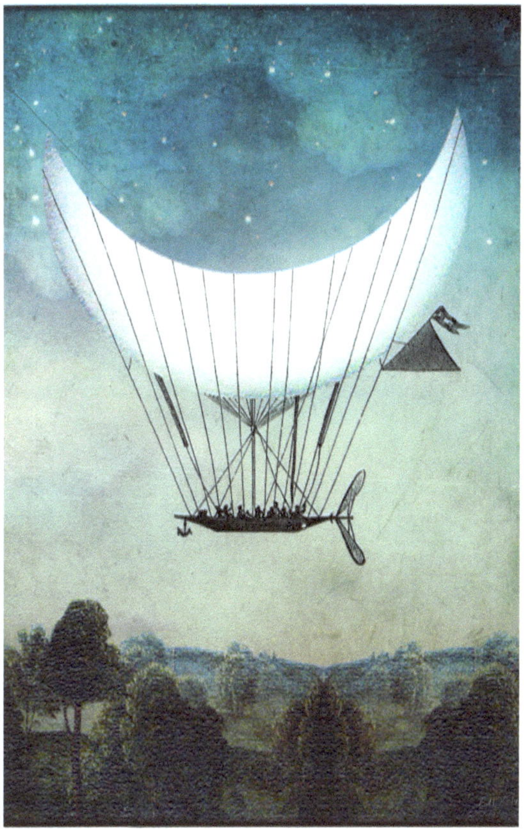

The Moon Ship, 2013, digital on canvas, 40 x 61cm

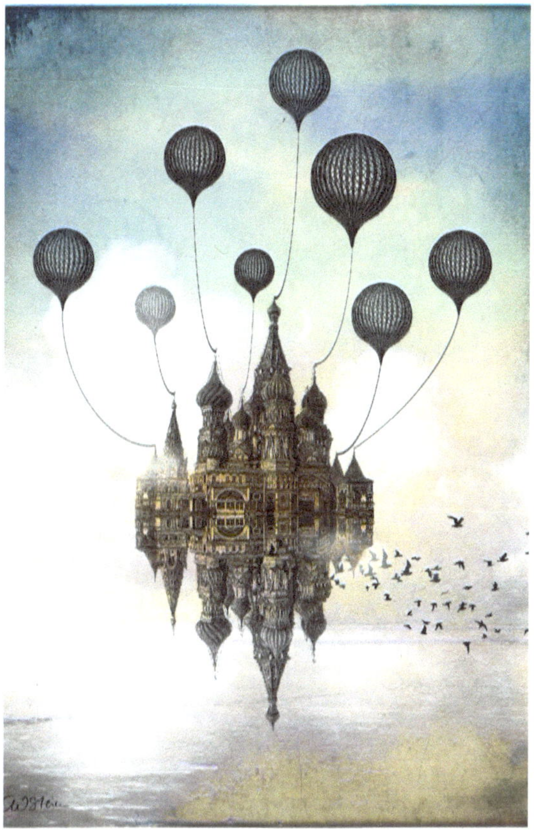

Journey to the East, 2011, digital on canvas, 60 x 70cm

Thats my Way, 2015, digital on canvas, 61 x 40cm

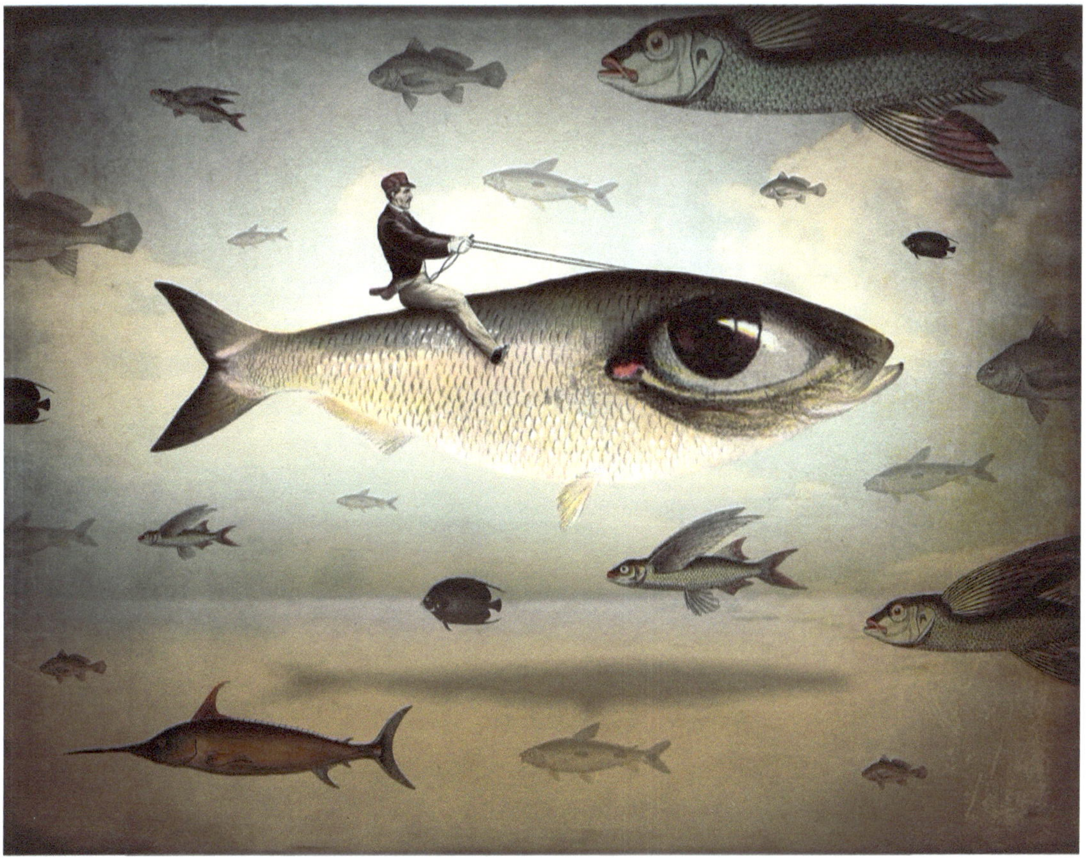

ENZZO BARRENA

DIGITAL ART - PERU

www.enzzobarrena.wix.com

Enzzo Barrena is a Peruvian digital artist. He got his start in the field as a graphic designer, training with such programs as Photoshop and Illustrator and honing his skills over a period of several years.

He draws inspiration from his dreams and from his life aspirations: he will sit down, imagine something that he wants, ponder that desire, and then get to work from there. Although he has worked analytically in the past, he is a visionary at heart, working from an energetically creative place inside himself. He prefers to work with digital media because it is the way that he feels he can express himself most fully, making use of all the luxury that the modern world has to offer.

In Enzzo's art, there are no questions that are out of bounds. Why are we here? Who are we? What is the difference between right and wrong? These are the types of challenging topics that he regularly takes on. Beyond the complexity, however, there is a recognition of beauty in all its wonderful and dazzling simplicity. He sees the sparkle in everything, finding the light side in all darkness and never judging anyone, accepting the human condition with all its variety.

Enzzo captializes wisely on the richness that can be found where oneness and multiplicity meet. He is deeply aware of the quirks of digital art and takes advantage of them any way that he can.

Right: Alter Mechanism,digital media

Fragmenta, digital media

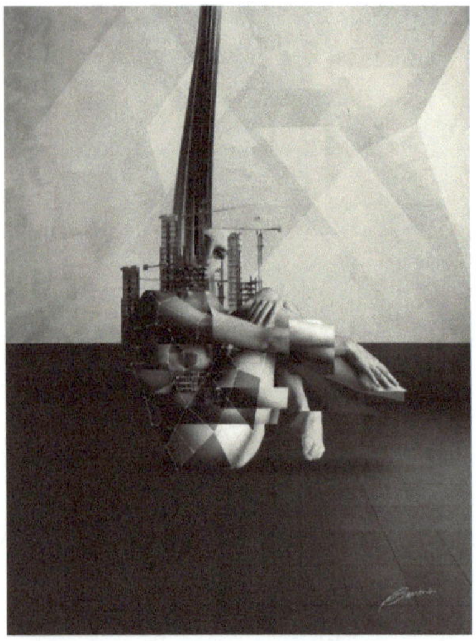

The Waiting, digital media

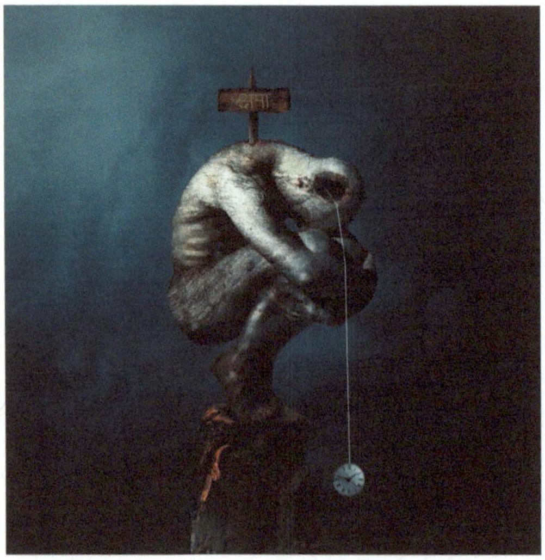

Automatrizz, digital media

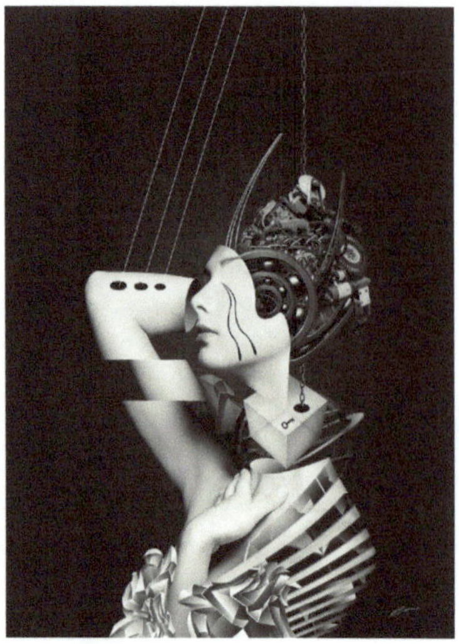

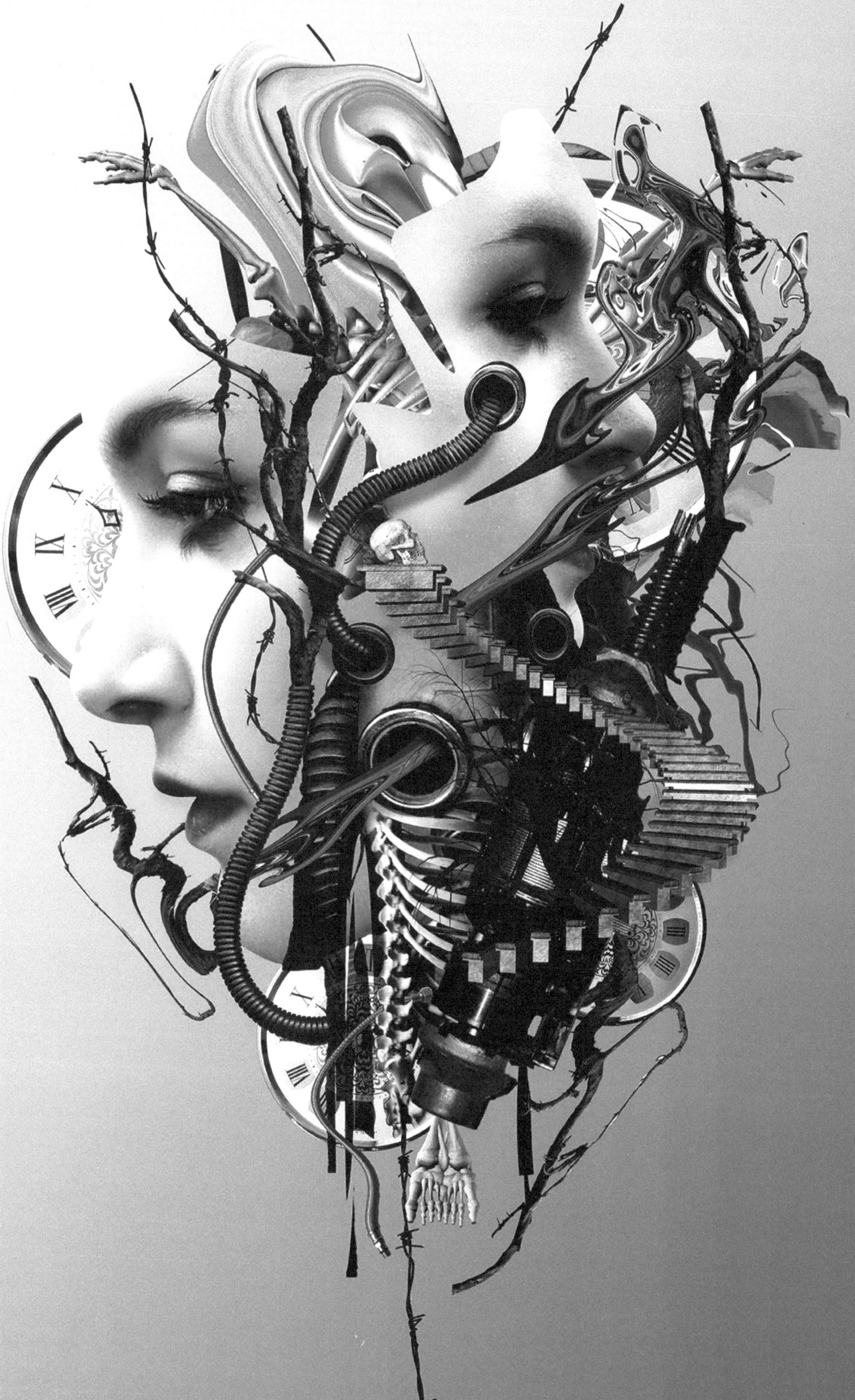

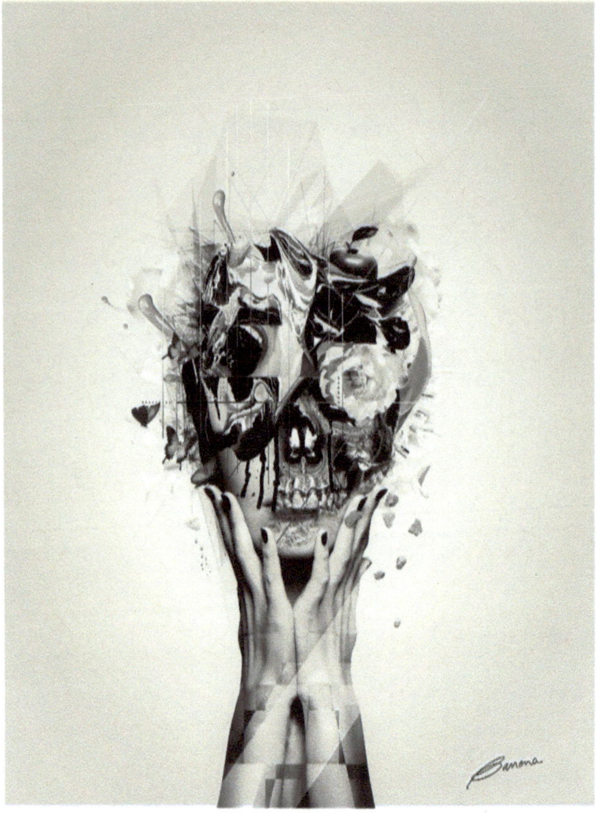

Evas Depiction, digital media

Skin Bonsai, digital media

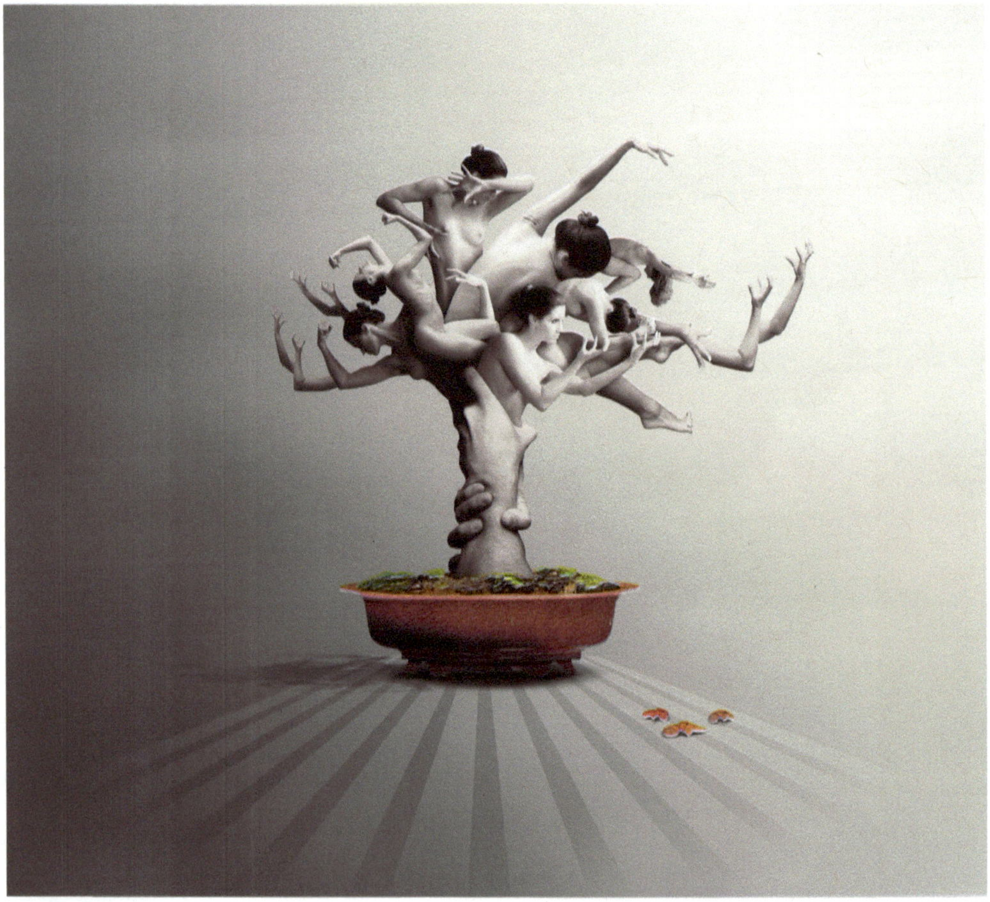

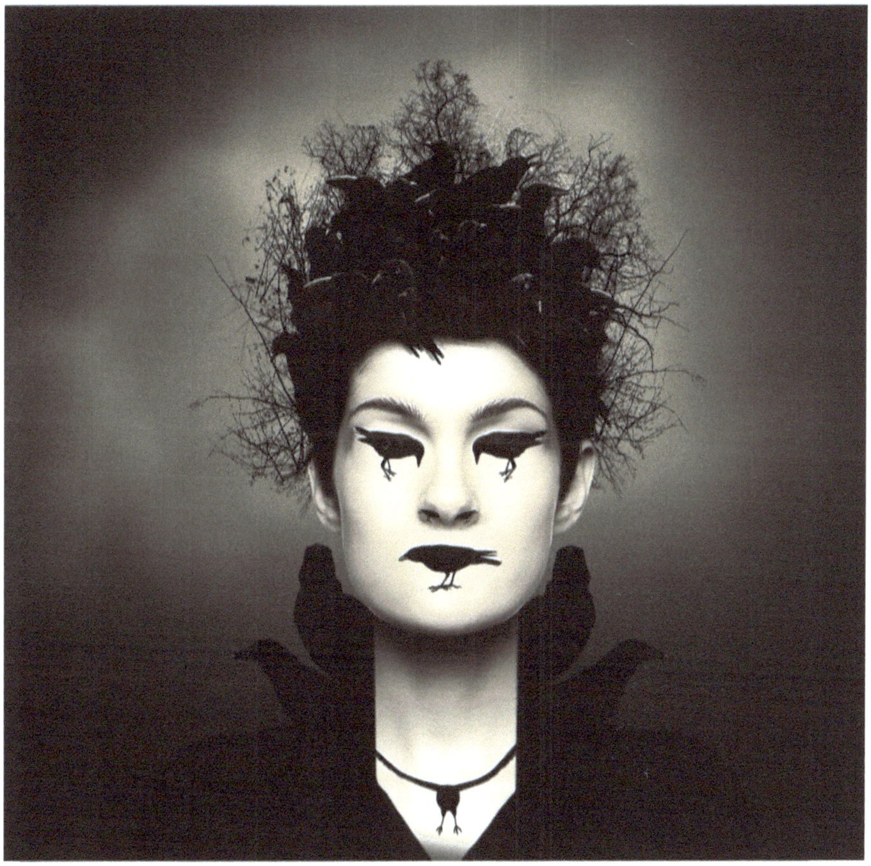

Crowned, digital media

El Trinar del Silencio (The Chirping of Silence), digital media

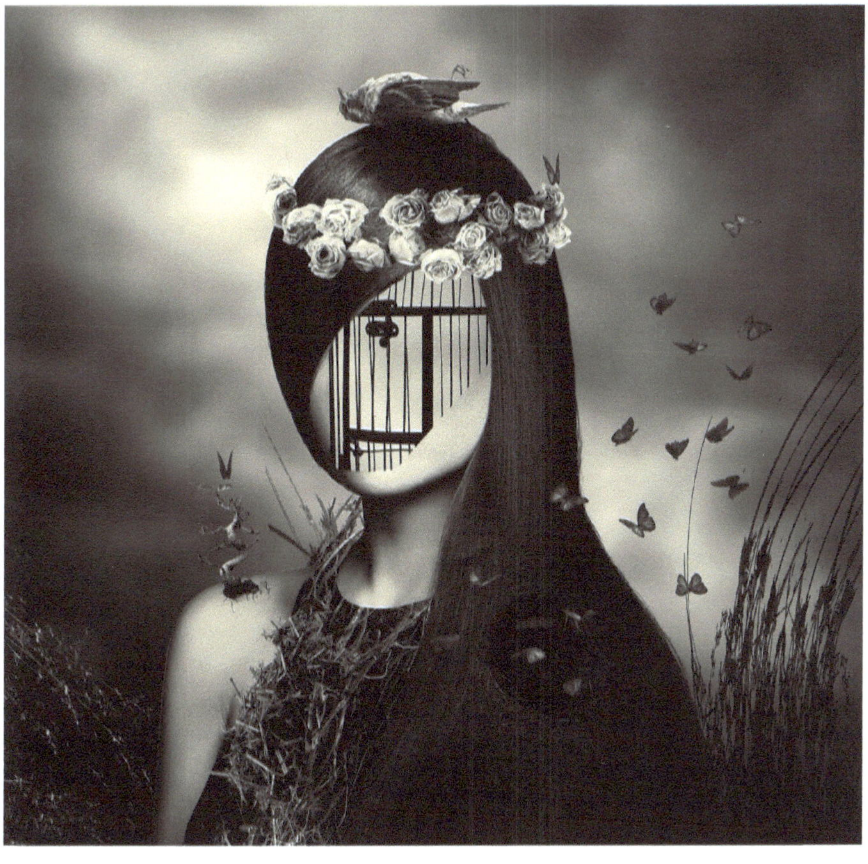

JANE LONG

DIGITAL ART - AUSTRALIA

www.janelong.fotomerchant.com

Jane Long, photographer and digital artist from Brisbane, Australia. Known for the novel ways in which she captures and also manipulates photos, she produces work that is mainly surreal, work that is reminiscent of our reality and yet incorporates large elements of fantasy as well.

She taught herself how to use Photoshop in the mid-90s, and ever since then, she has been using it day in and day out both for her own projects and to earn a living. It was much more recent that she began taking photographs of her own, and it was even more recent than that that she shifted into fine art.

Jane's Self-Preservation series, her debut in the world of fine art, fetched her widespread praise. Eventually, a group of images from this series were shortlisted for the Macquarie Photography Prize, while one image, "Cured," was a semi-finalist for the Moran Photographic Prize.

This series she followed up with Dancing with Costica, which was ever better-received, featuring on such websites as ABC News US, Daily Mail, SLR Lounge, PetaPixel, Bored Panda, and BuzzFeed. Later, that same series was presented at the Romanian Embassy in Australia and later at the Romanian Photo Festival and the Ballarat International Foto Biennale, both in 2015.

Jane's star continues to rise the more she works, and she has made a strong name for herself in a very short period of time.

Worth my Salt, 2014, 308 gsm photo rag, 50 x 50cm

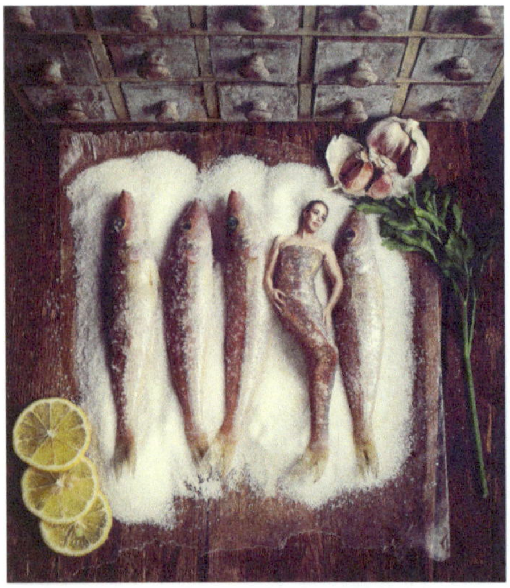

Pickled, 2014, 308 gsm photo rag, 50 x 50cm

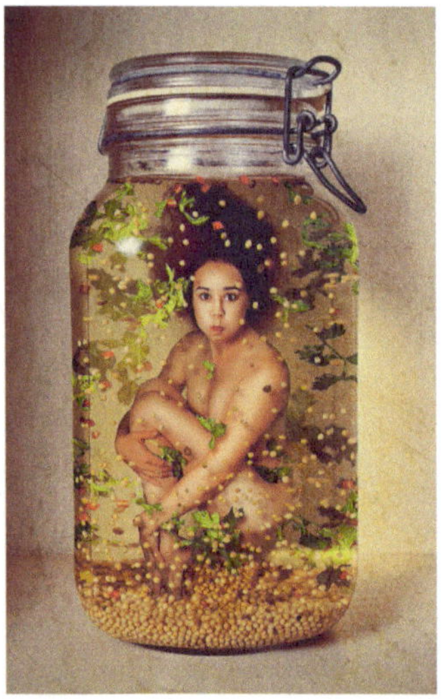

Cured, 2014, 308 gsm photo rag, 50 x 50cm

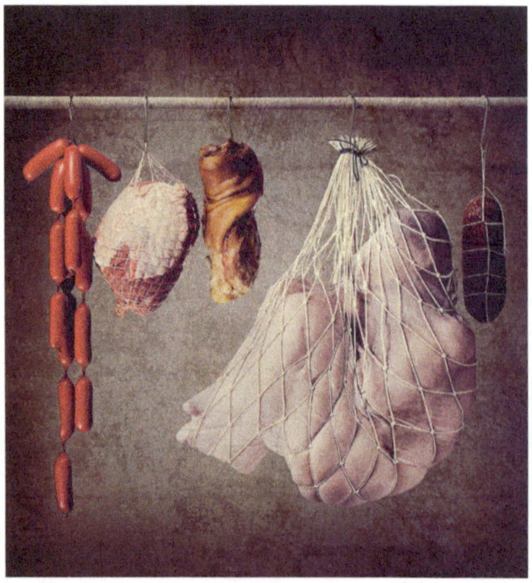

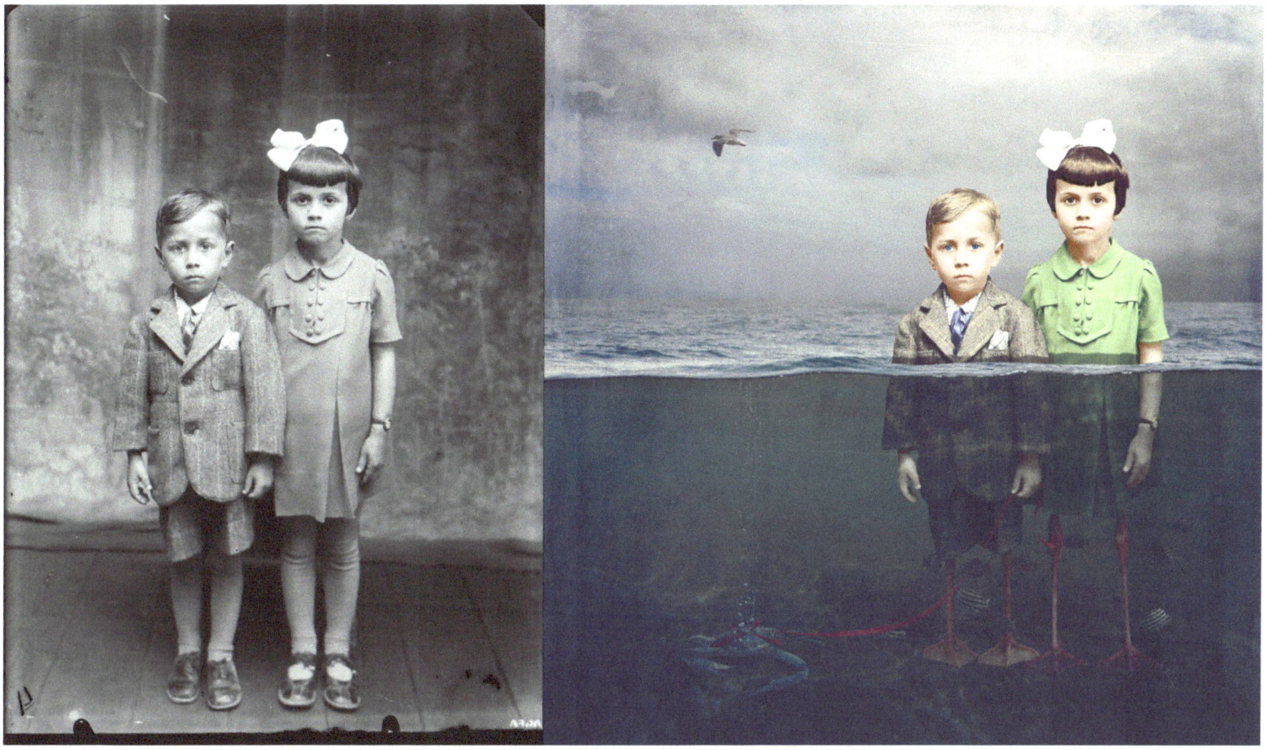

Underneath, 2014, 308 gsm photo rag, 40 x 40cm. Original image from the Costica Ascinte Archive

All Hands on Deck, 2014, 308 gsm photo rag, 40 x 40 cm. Original image from the Costica Ascinte Archive

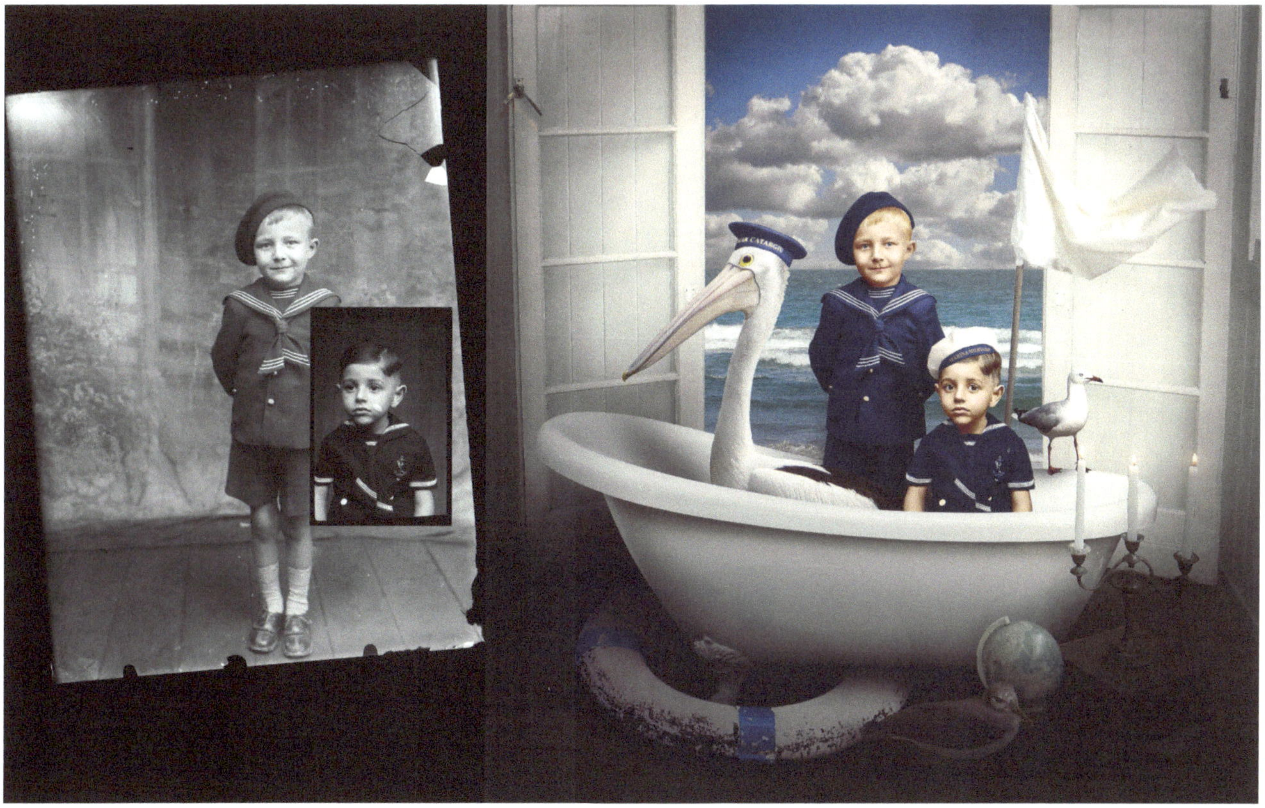

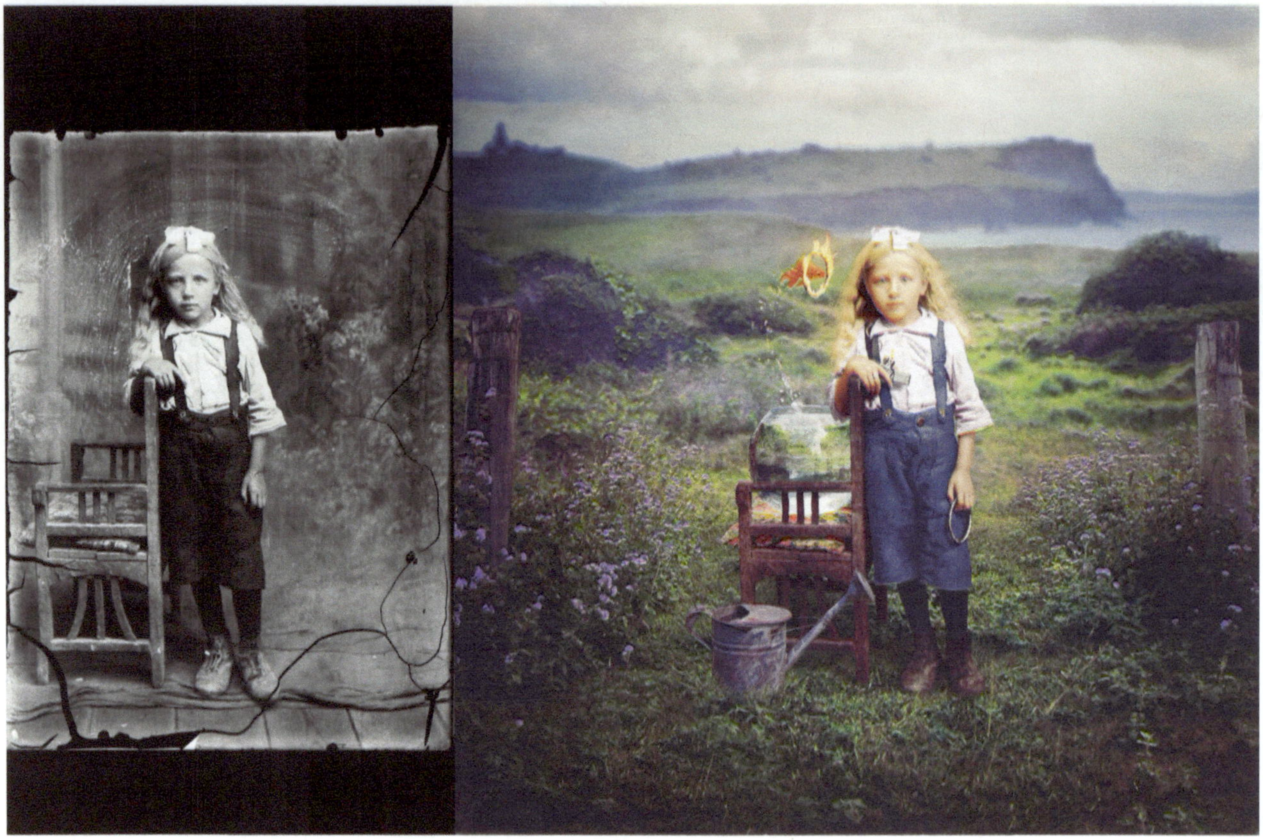

Innocence, 2014, 308 gsm photo rag, 40 x 40cm. Original image from the Costica Ascinte Archive

Corvo, 2014, 308 gsm photo rag, 40 x 40cm. Original image from the Costica Ascinte Archive

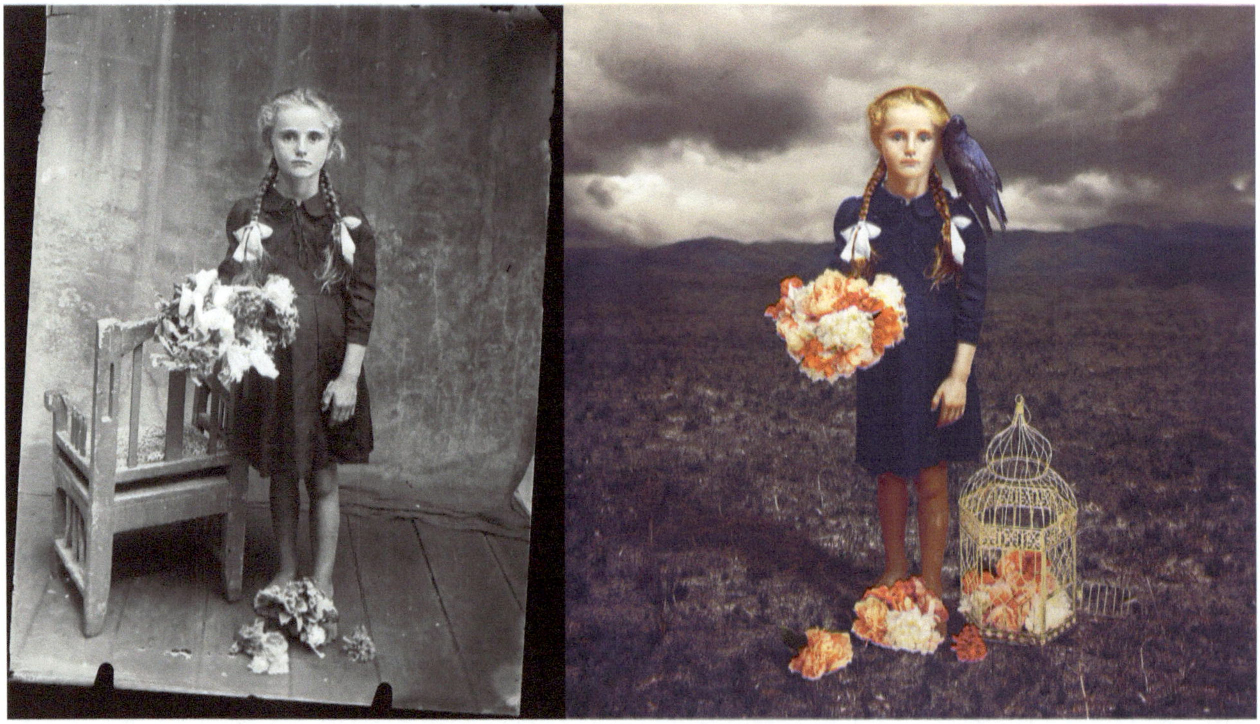

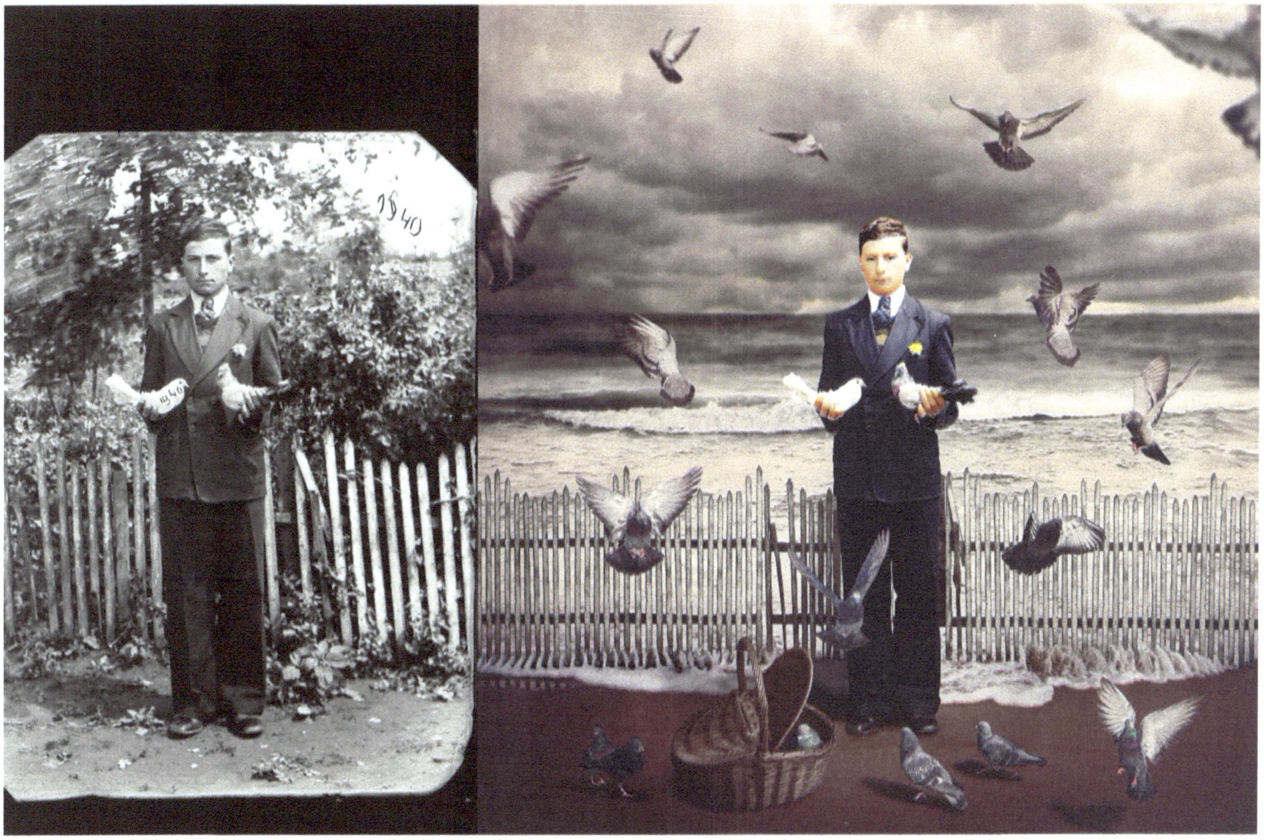

Flock, 2014, 308 gsm photo rag, 40 x 40cm. Original image from the Costica Ascinte Archive

Sweetheart, 2014, 308 gsm photo rag, 40 x 40cm. Original image from the Costica Ascinte Archive

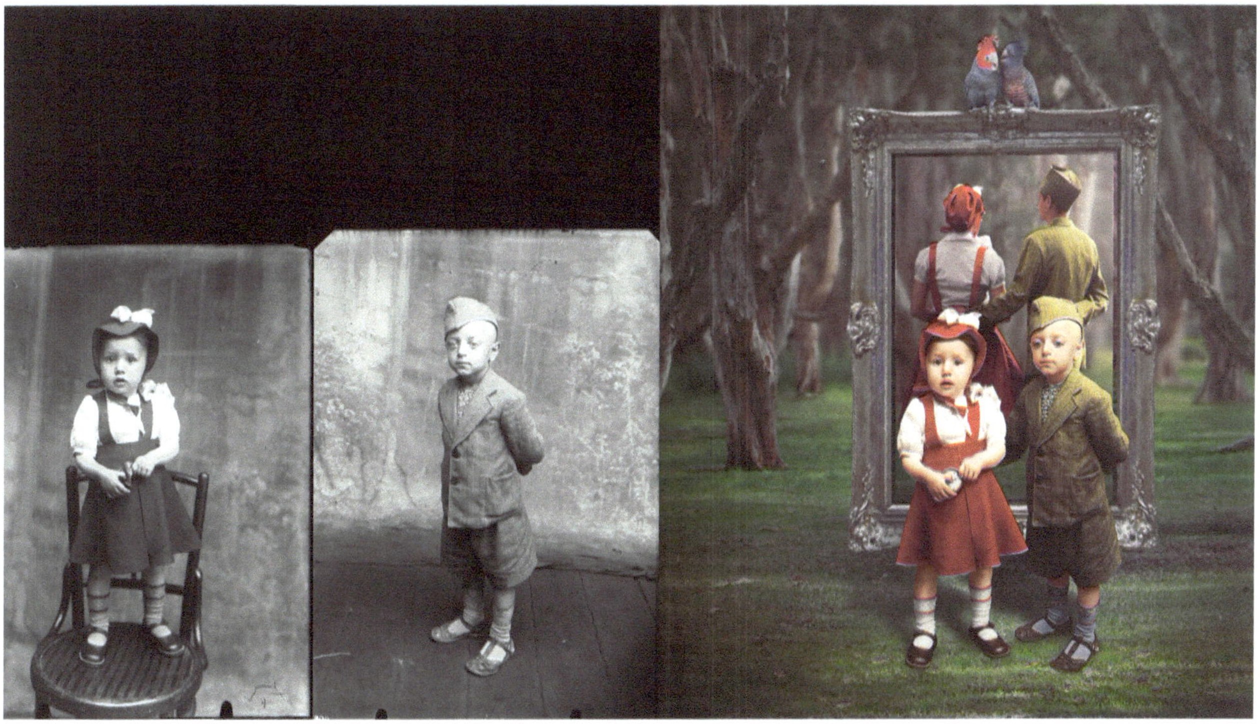

KAZUHIKO NAKAMURA

DIGITAL ART - JAPAN

www.mechanicalmirage.com

Kazuhiko Nakamura is a digital artist who has been creating 3D artworks since he first taught himself the medium in 1996.

Primarily known for his works in the surrealist and cyberpunk traditions, he has gained major momentum in the field of digital art over the last decade, exhibiting Carnivora: The Dark Art of Automobiles in 2008. His work Brain Towe was featured on the cover of the book Steampunk: The Art of Victorian Futurism in 2012, and he published the Steampunk 2014 Calendar in 2013. More recently, he published the educational book How to Draw Steampunk.

Although Kazuhiko's style and themes are in a sense conventional, in the way that he recalls the past, he is on further examination a revolutionary figure in the field of steampunk, and he has made an indelible mark on the style. To look at one of his works is to be transported into an alternate history, one that is distinctly his own, a history in which he alone is writing the narrative, borrowing pieces from our world, pieces from his progenitors, pieces from his own imagination.

Kazuhiko is fiercely creative, and that attribute is readily apparent in his work. He is not someone who produces anything lazily, always throwing himself headfirst into his pieces, eager to express something new amidst the parts of his art that reference the days of old and to be an original.

Right: Mechanical Silence, 2014, digital media

Glasshead, 2000, digital media

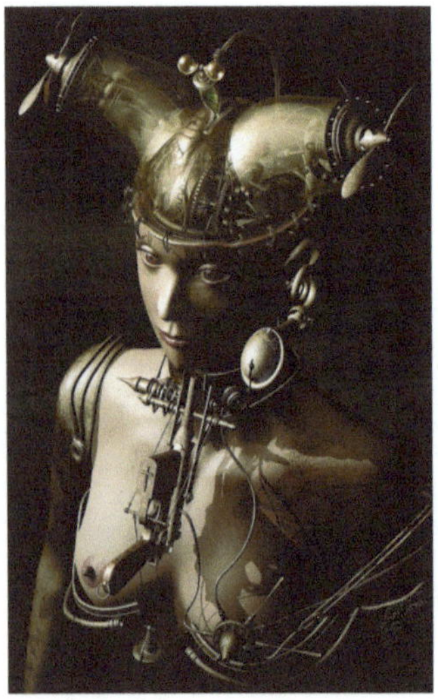

Head + Dead, 1997, digital media

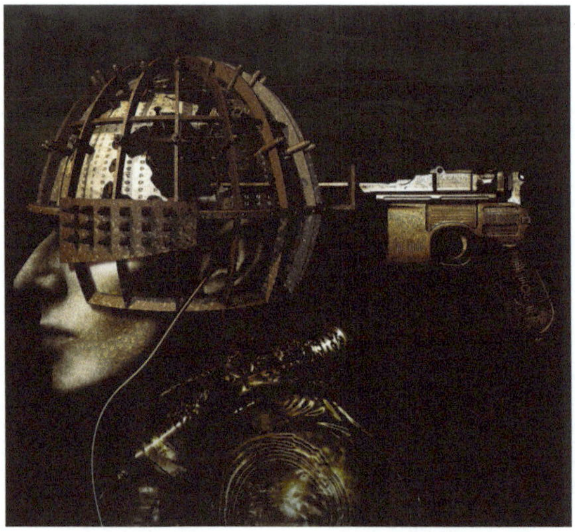

The Tower of Beetle, 1999, digital media

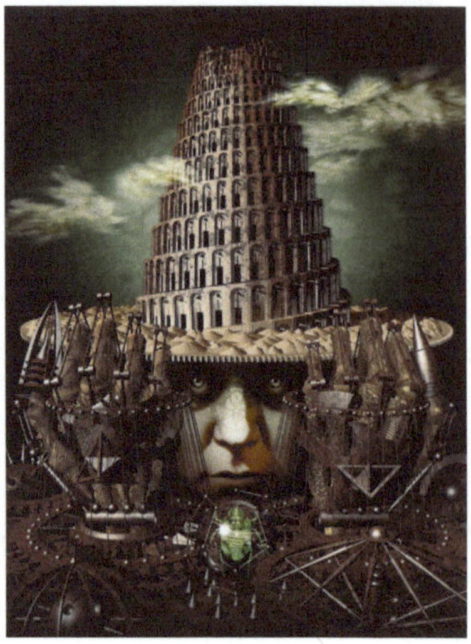

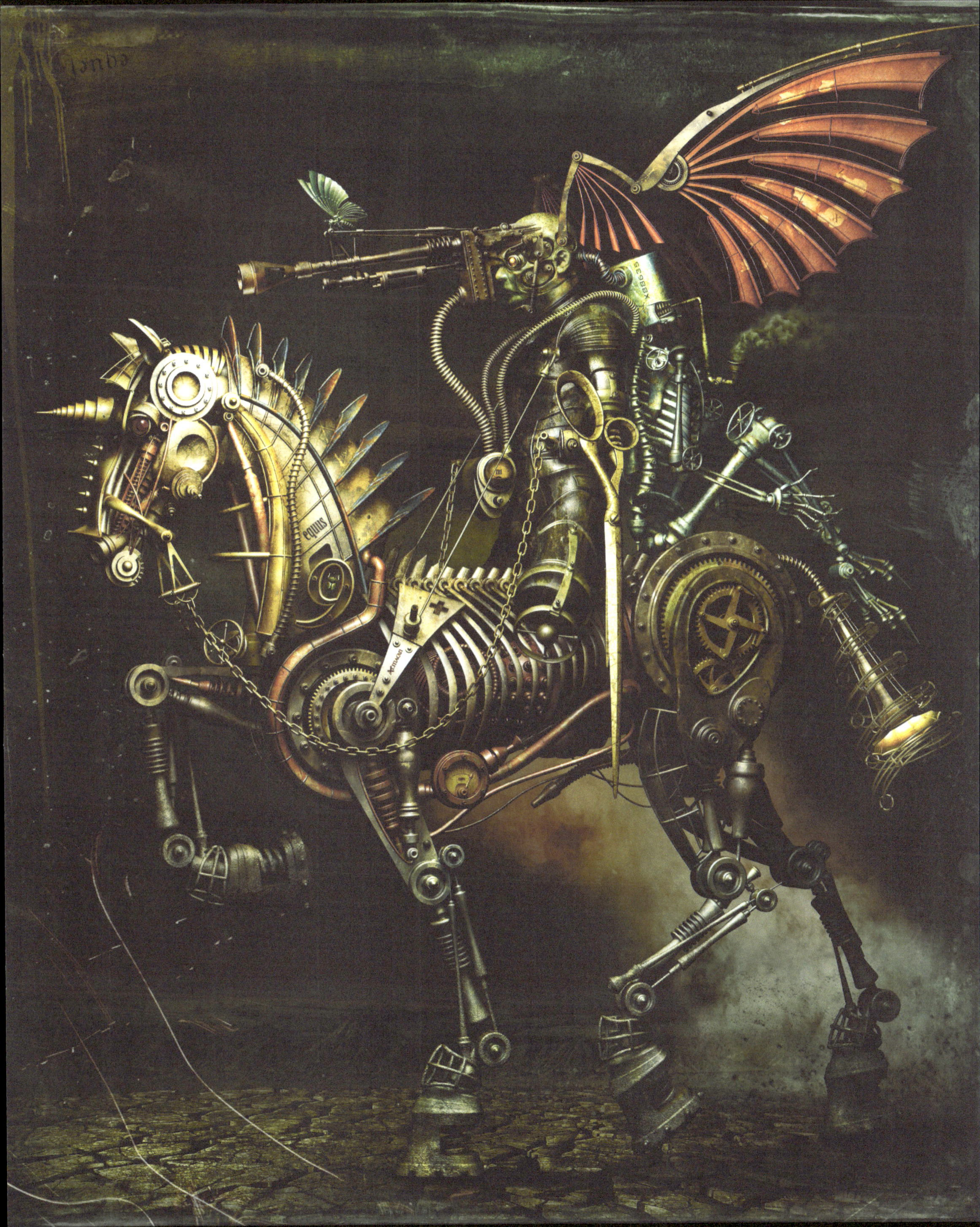
equus

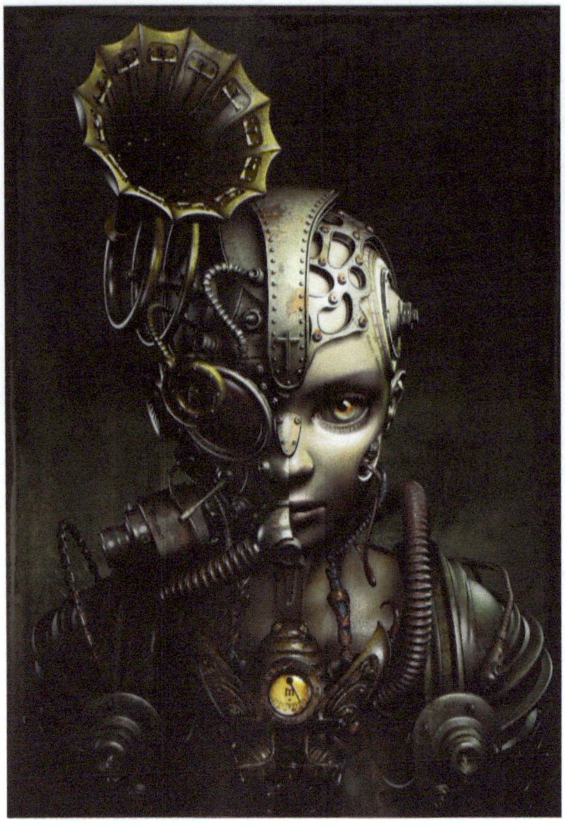

Jeanne D, 2015 digital media

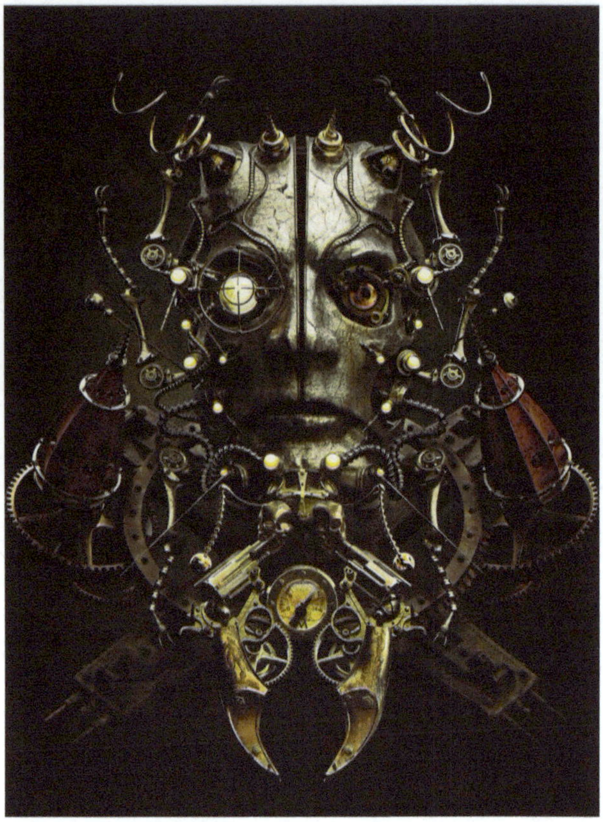

Mechamorphose, 2016, digital media

Atoma, 2011, ditigal media

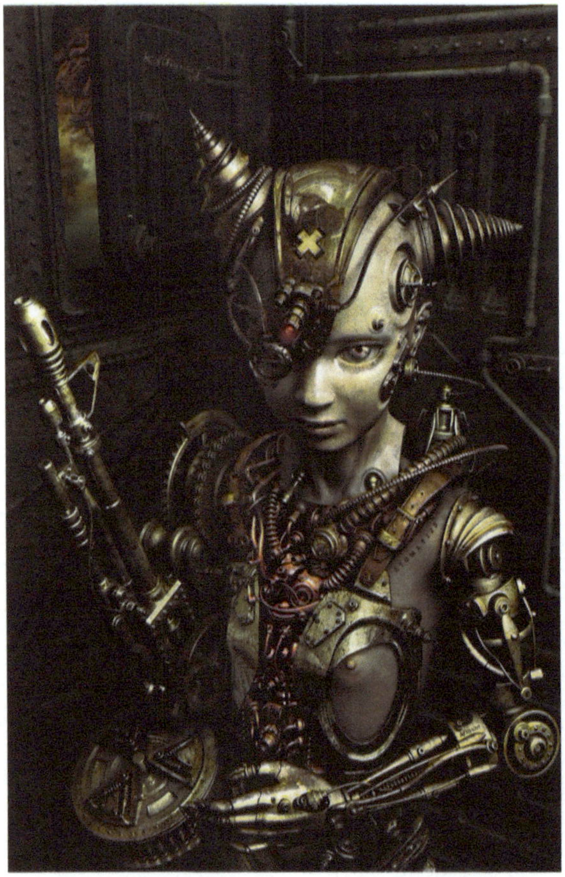

The End of Flight Zone, 2000, digital media

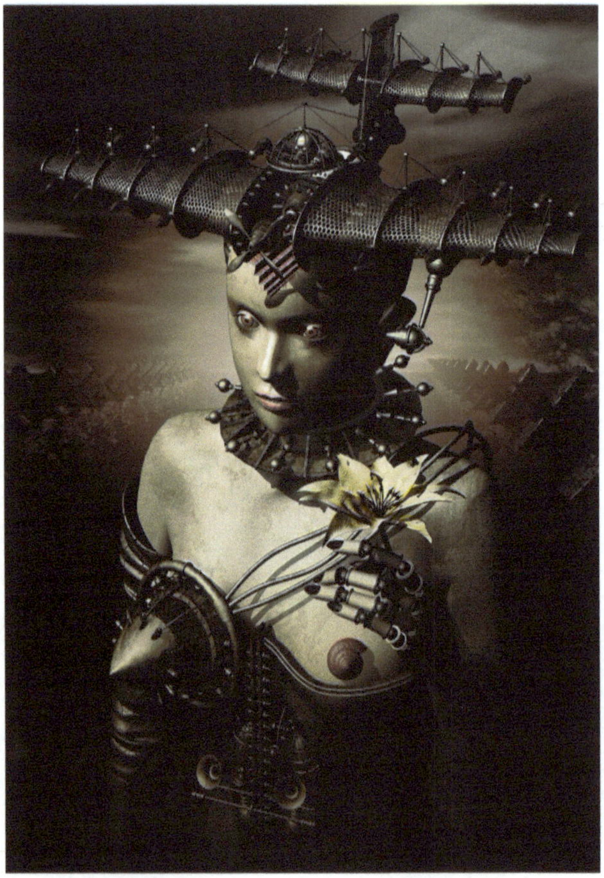

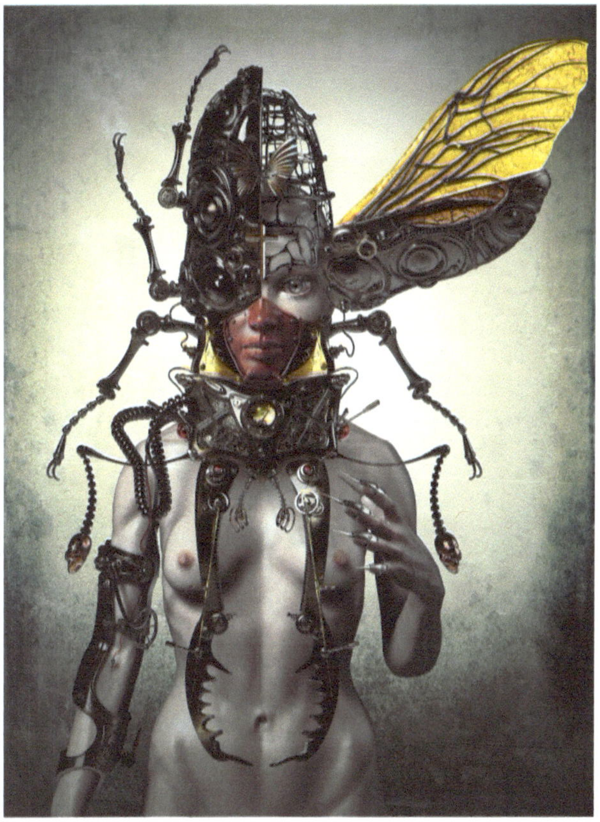

Venus, 2016, digital media

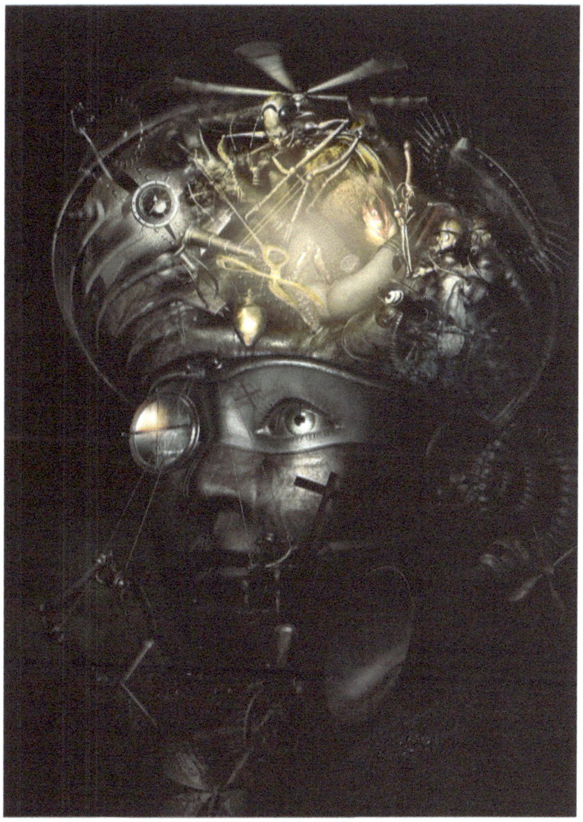

Monorogue, 2003, digital media

Requiem for Industry, 2007 digital media

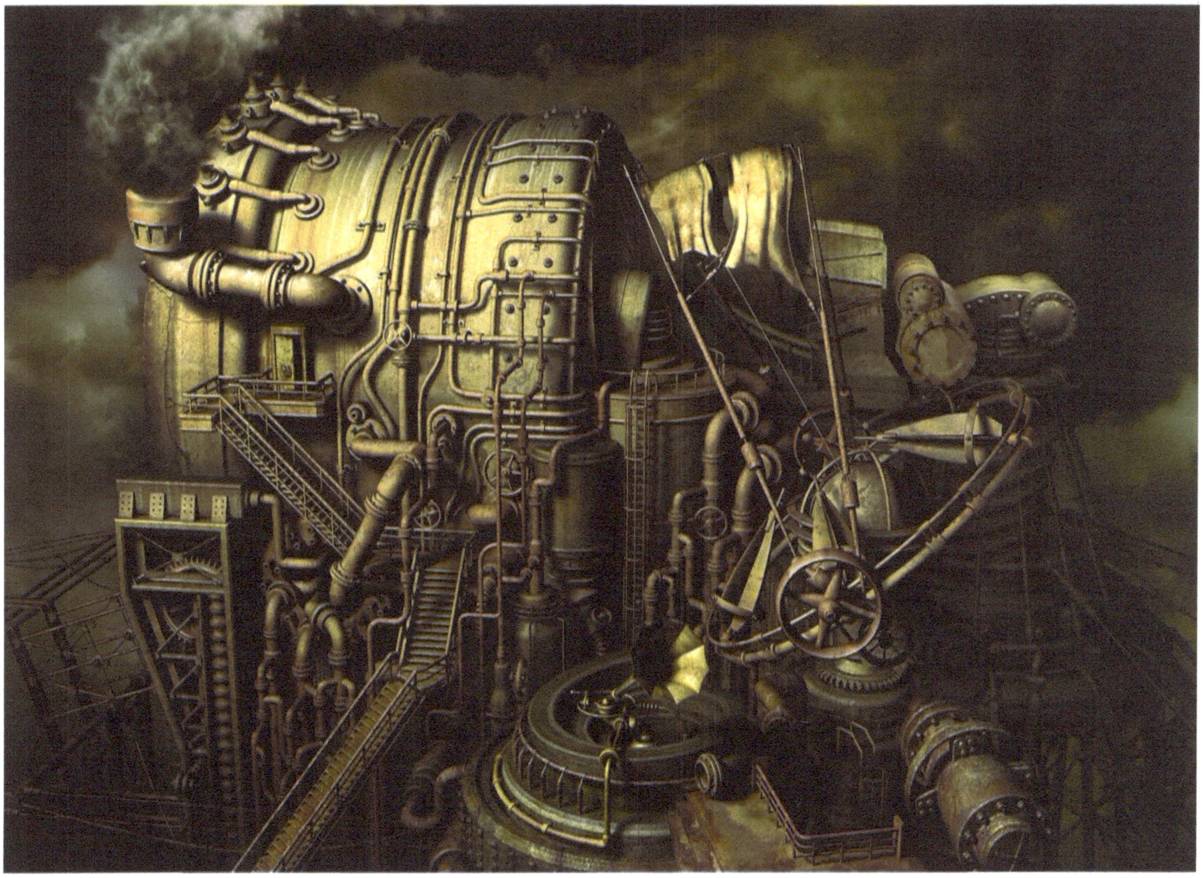

MAI ANH TRAN

DIGITAL ART - FRANCE

www.artgalaxie.com

Mai Anh Tran is a French-Vietnamese artist. She was a prodigy of sorts, displaying brilliance as a child in painting, sculpting, photography, and video editing. She drifted, however, toward digital art, studying Digital Matte Painting at world-famous Parisian Art & Design School. Today, she is based out of Montreal, where she works in the movie industry. Her matte paintings have been featured in such major motion pictures as Tomorrowland, Deadpool, Star Trek, Pirates of the Caribbean, and Warcraft, in addition to Game of Thrones and other big-name TV series.

A huge fan of fantasy and science fiction growing up, Mai Anh is living her dream today, exhibiting her own matte paintings depicting dystopian skylines and fantastic landscapes. Her watercolor paintings have also won her praise, and the works that she had done based on her Asian origins are especially acclaimed.

Born in 1990, Mai Anh is an astoundingly accomplished artist, both commercially and critically for her age, and she shows immense promise going forward. Someone whose work seems always to be improving, she possesses a remarkable mind and an impressive intuition when it comes to color and composition. Her works speaks to a wide audience, which has been a major factor in her early success in Hollywood. Refined and yet never even approaching sanitary, her matte paintings are the way that fine art and commercial art meet under ideal circumstances.

Scent of the Rising Steel, 2013/2014, digital media

Right: Sunset Castle, 2014, digital media

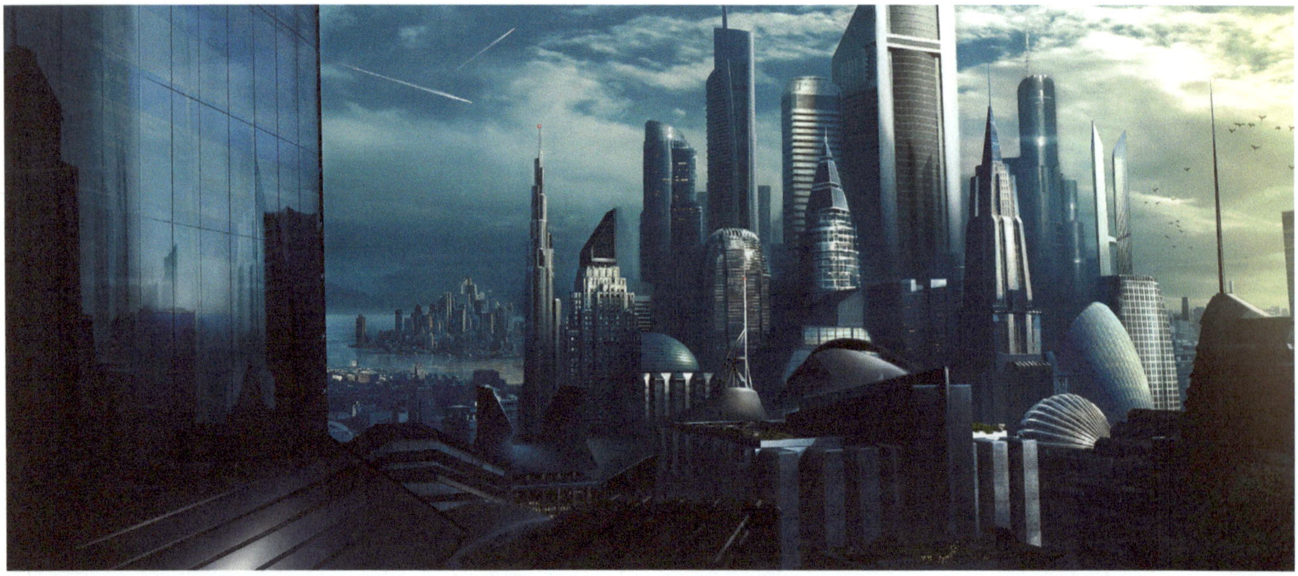

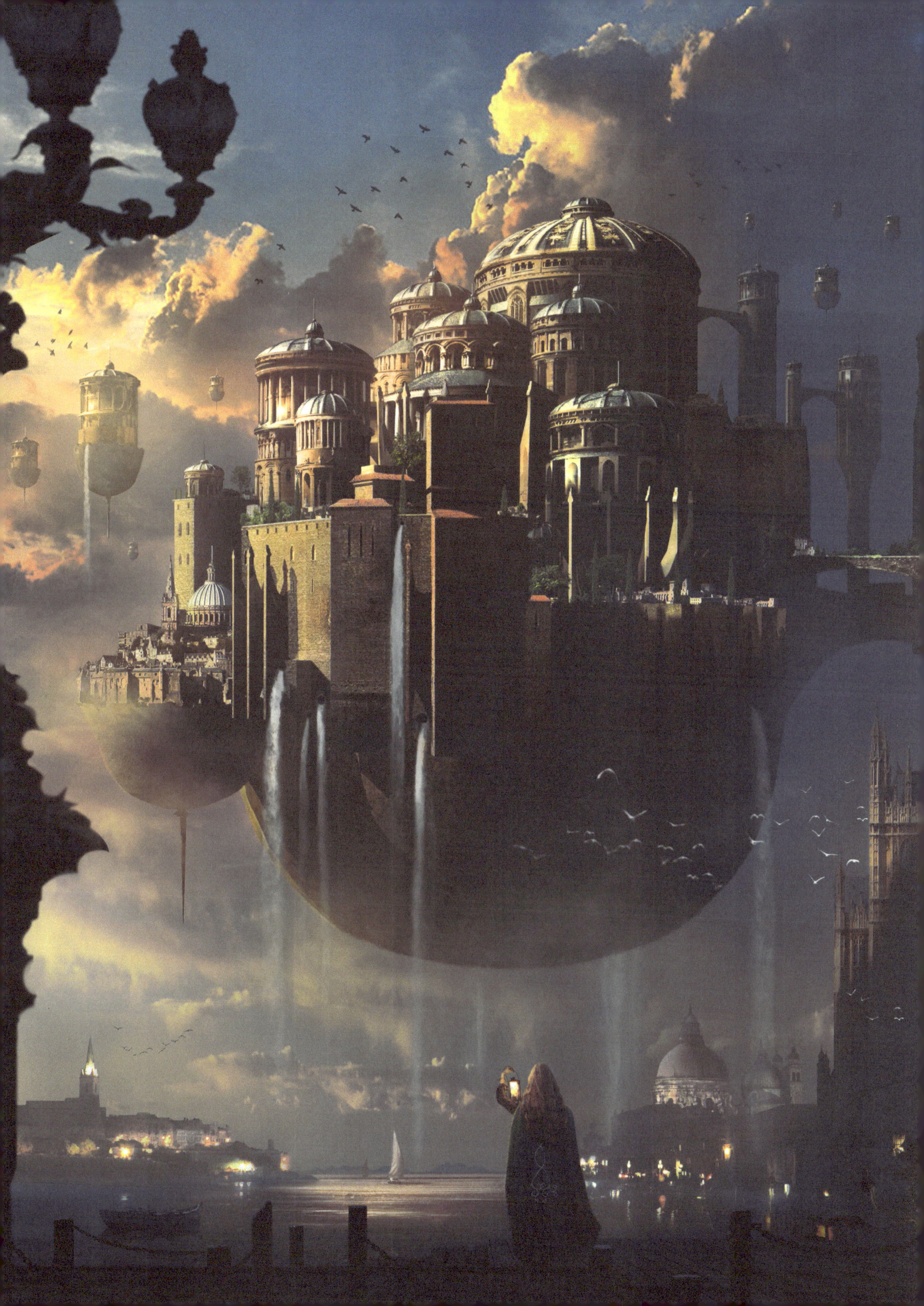

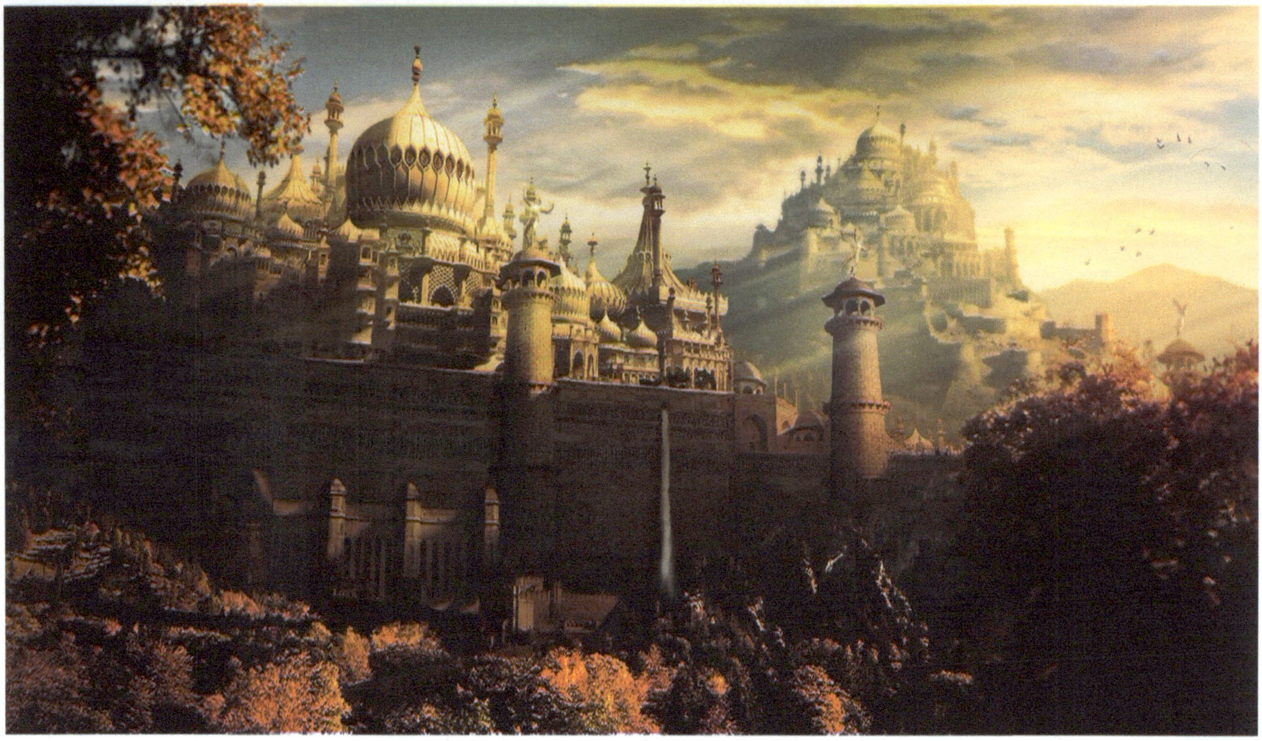

Ancient Walled Kingdom, 2014, digital media

Waterfall Kingdom, 2015, digital media

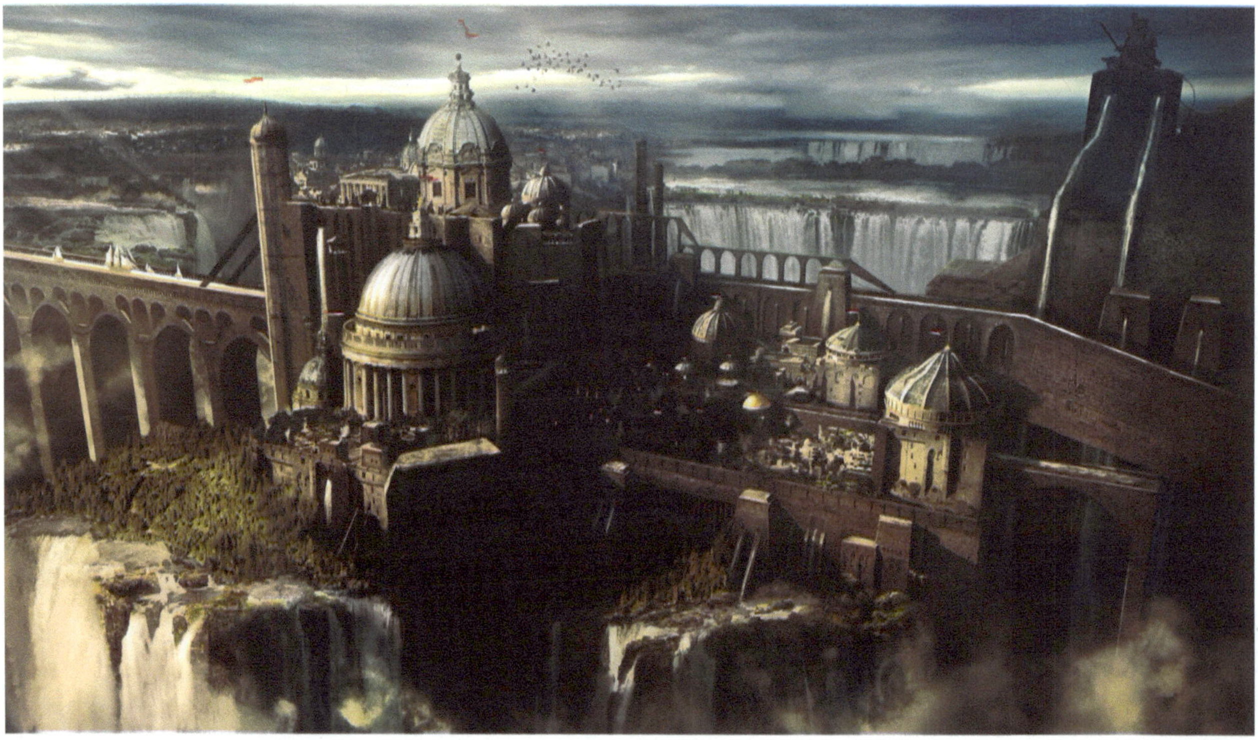

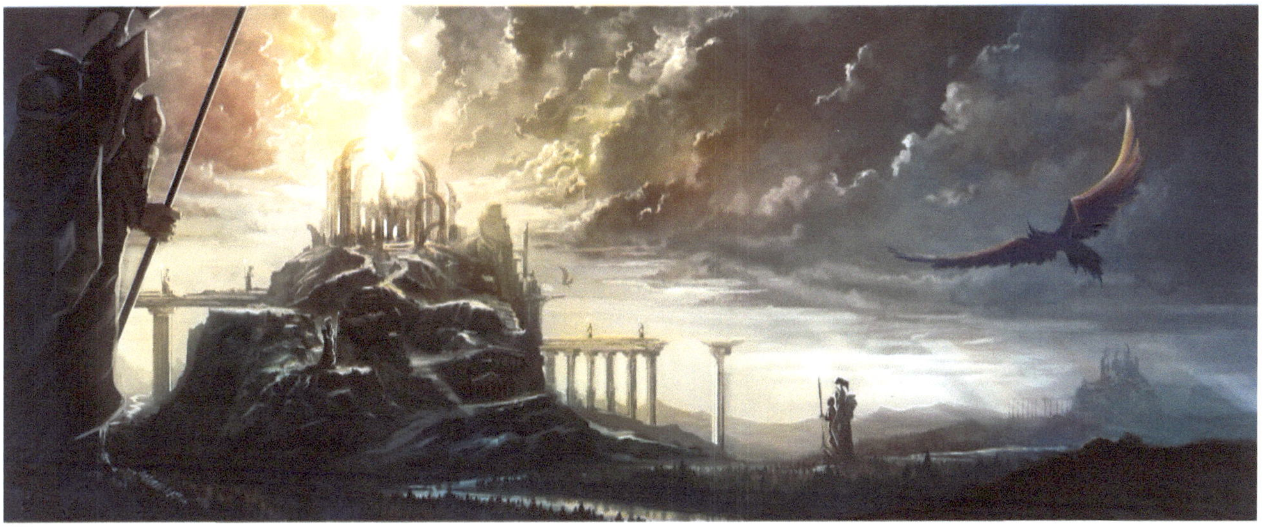

The Howling Rift, 2015, digital media

The Howling Abyss, Freljord, 2015, digital media

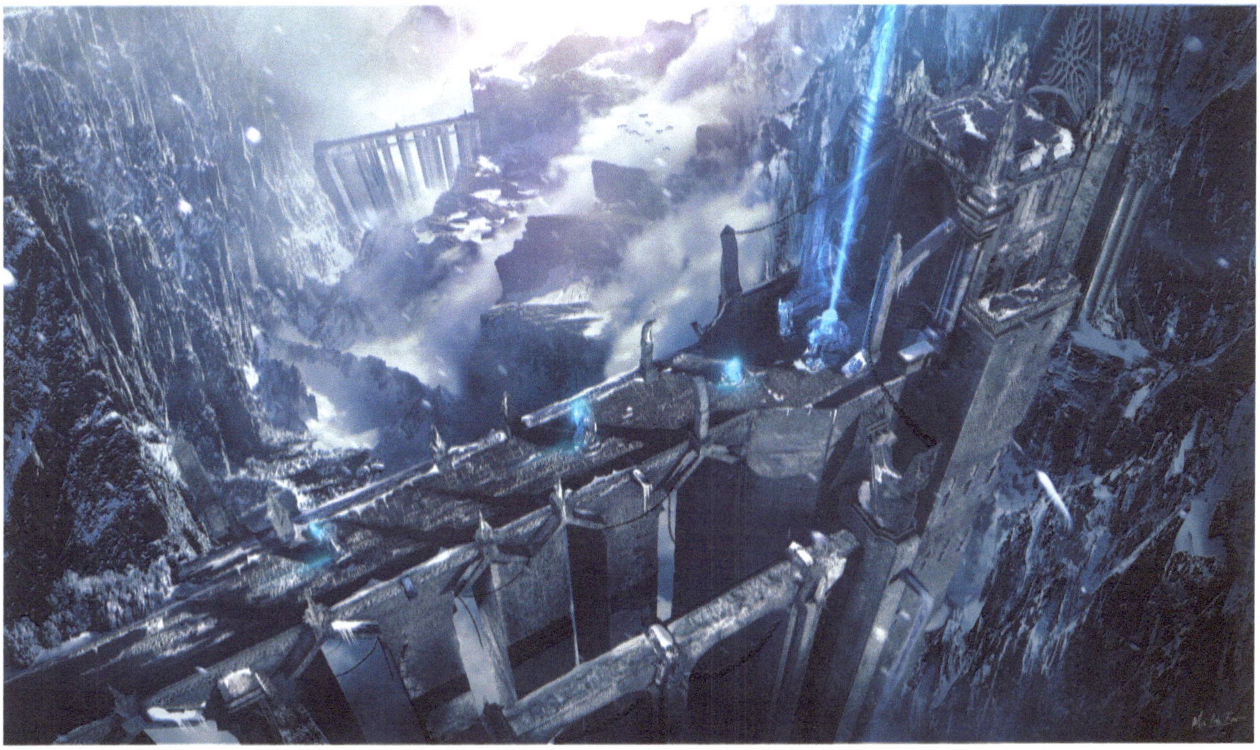

SARAH DEREMER

DIGITAL ART - UNITED STATES OF AMERICA

www.sarahderemer.com

Sarah DeRemer is an artist who has never been ashamed to be herself completely. She expresses the side of herself that many people try to hide away, baring all for the world to see. Her strange works, including "Animal Food", which portrays a mixture of animals, fruits, and vegetables, has made a wild stir since its debut.

At the heart of her works, however, as much as they may be based on everyday things, is a surrealist edge. She causes revulsion, sure, but she causes joy as well. Her work is in one instance unbearably frightening and in another stupendously heartening.

It is in this clash of emotion that Sarah most efficiently effects discussion from her audience. She will put something strange alongside something normal, telling us to look at it, telling us to feel it, telling us to think about what it would mean if it were right in front of us, if it were a part of our lives, a part of ourselves, a part of the world that we inhabit. Her art is like a playful nightmare, and she seems to be just as content provoking nightmares as she is sweet dreams.

Sarah was born in Los Angeles. She grew up attracted to art, and by the time she set out to make some of her own, she had already taken in a vast library of the masters who had come before her.

Penguimelon (Animal Food), 2014, digital media

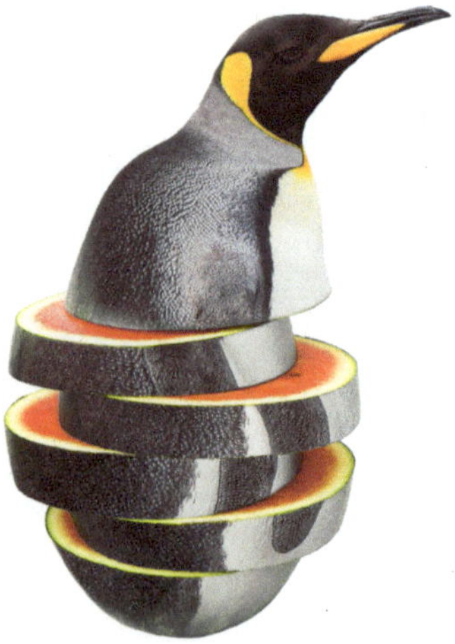

Hippotato (Animal Food), 2014, digital media

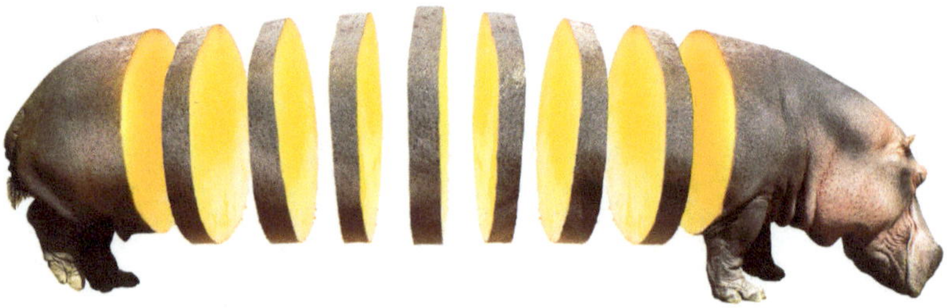

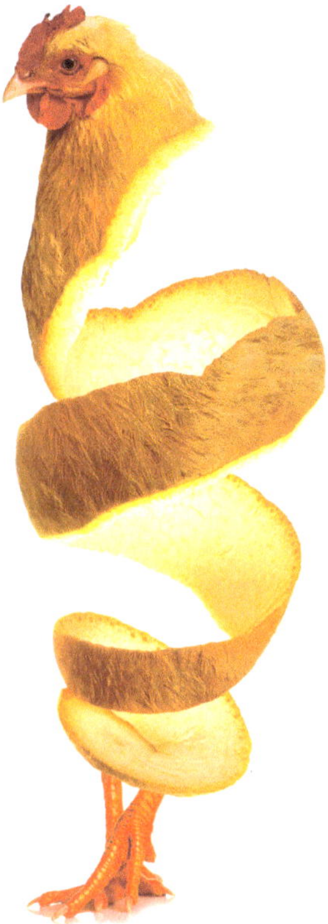

Orange Chicken (Animal Food), 2014, digital media

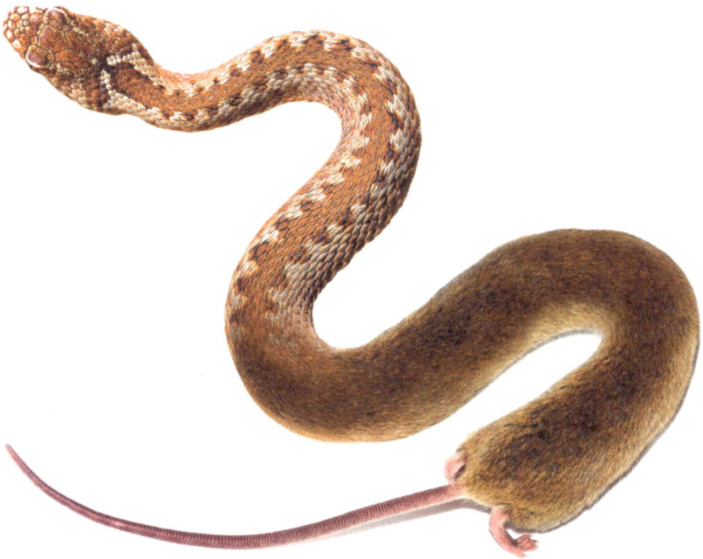

Snake Mouse (You are what you eat), 2015, digital media

Kiwi (Animal Food), 2014, digital media

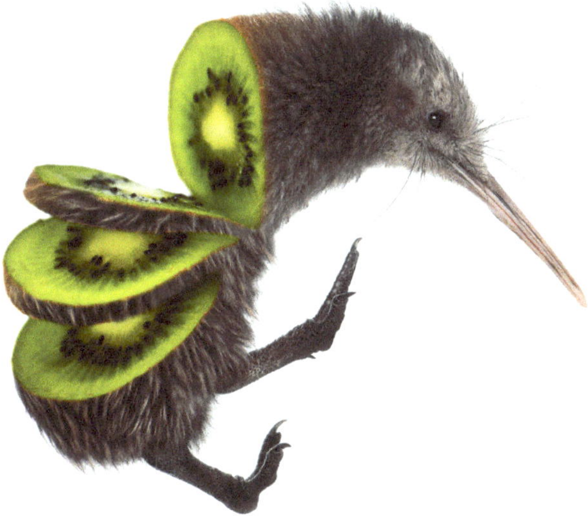

Frovacado (Animal Food), 2014, digital media

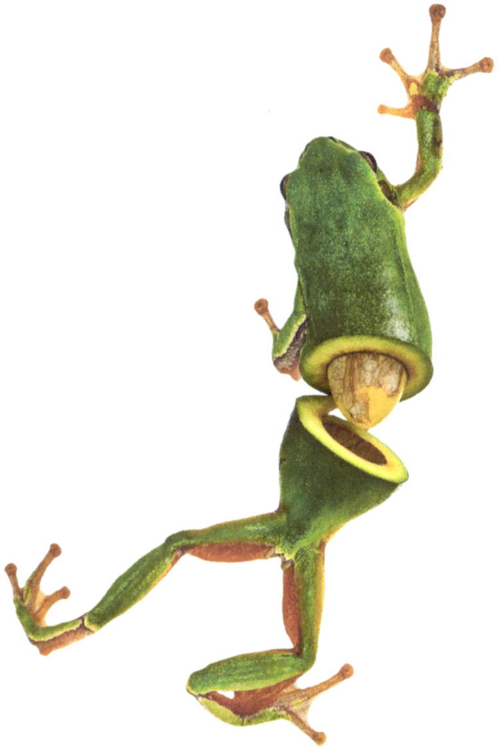

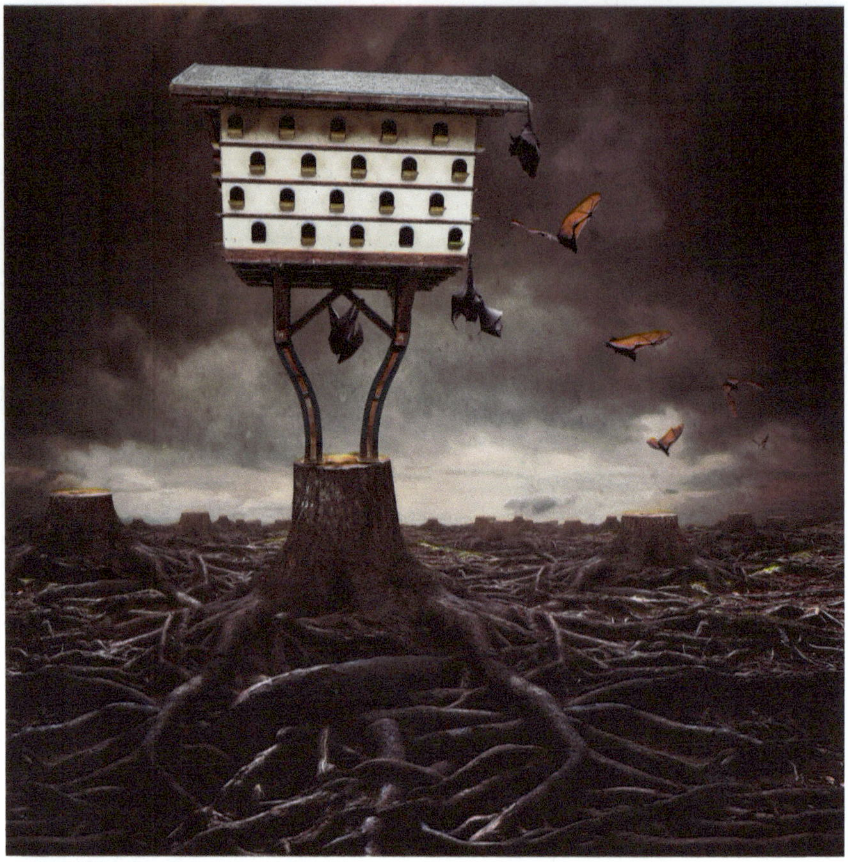

The Bat House, 2015, digital media

Aflame, 2015, digital media

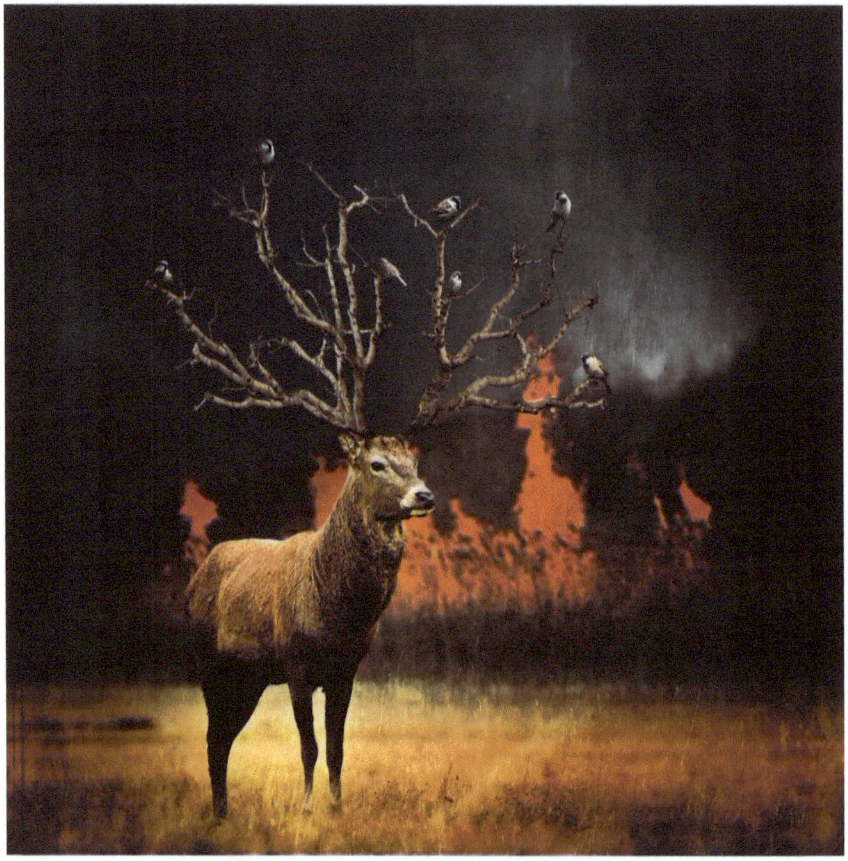

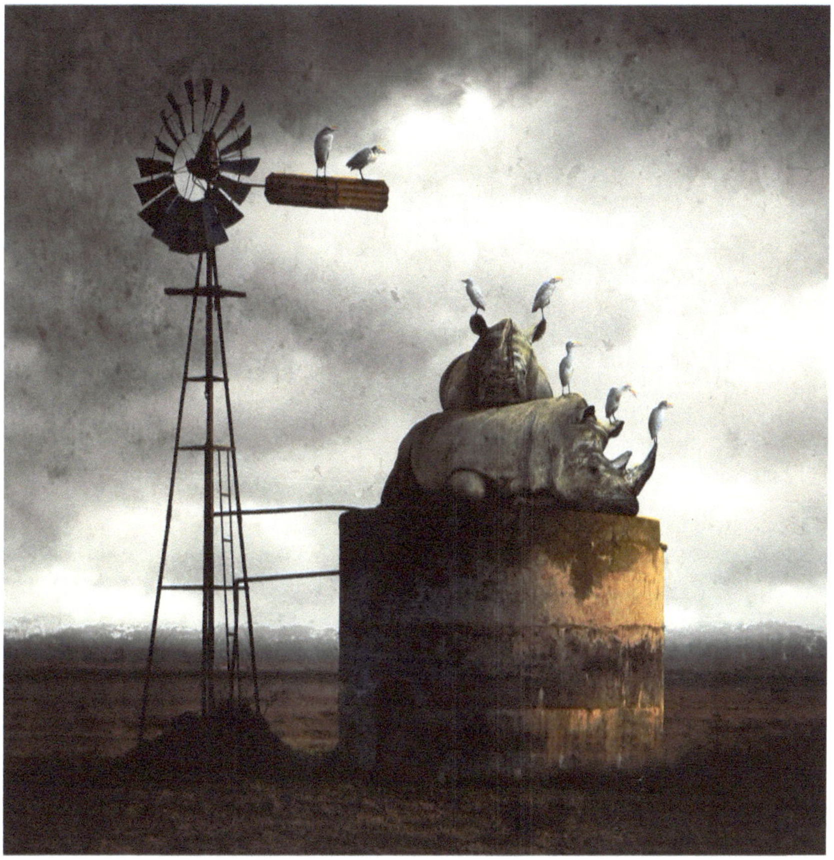
The Protectors, 2015, digital media

Find your Way, 2015, digital media
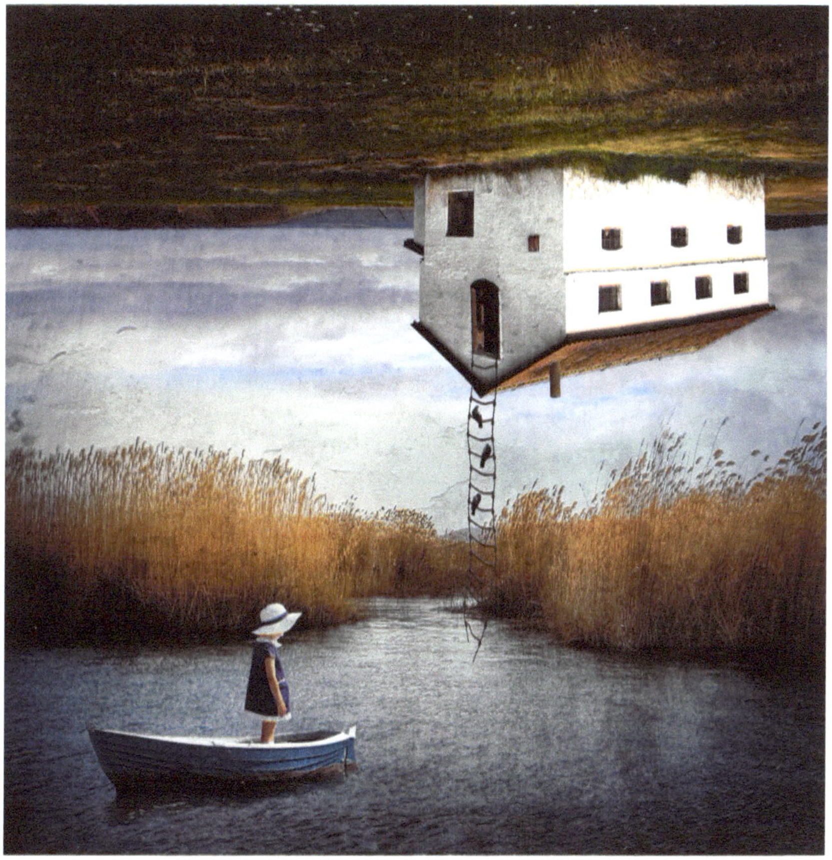

THOMAS DODD

DIGITAL ART - UNITED STATES OF AMERICA

www.thomasdodd.com

Thomas Dodd is an artist who has won a reputation for combining photography with classical art. He often takes for his themes mythology and religion, sometimes satirically and sometimes in the form of a homage. Working in digital art, he takes photographs that he later modifies using advanced software.

Based out of Atlanta, he has exhibited his work all around the world in Germany, Romania, Argentina, and Mexico, and in the United States in New York City, Orlando, Miami, San Antonio, Seattle, and Paris.

Featured on book covers and CD covers, Thomas's work is easily recognized. Many of his works could pass for Late Renaissance pieces, and he has produced art that is unsettling, surreal, dark, and vibrant, sometimes all in a single scene.

In addition to creating his own art, Thomas also teaches other people how to make art of their own. He runs a number of workshops every year about photo-editing and self-marketing. A community-minded individual, he does what he does because he enjoys seeing other artists succeed. Having experienced his own fair share of success, he is more than happy to give a leg up to others and to do what he can to alleviate their struggles. To meet him is to know friendliness and also to know artistic magnificence, and to know him well is to experience both of these wonderful traits in supreme abundance.

Right: Hope, digital media

The Cycle, digital media

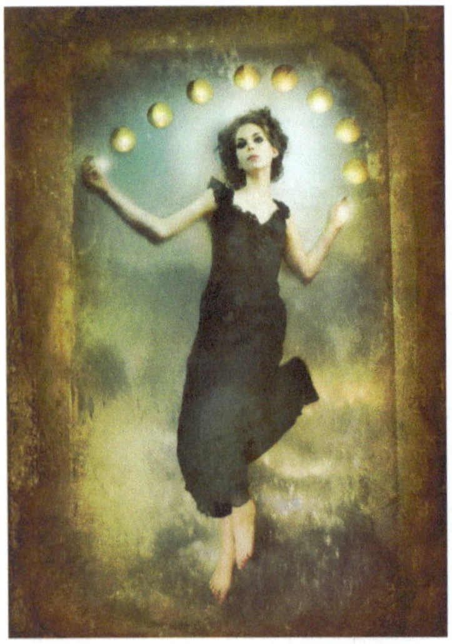

Woodshedding, digital media

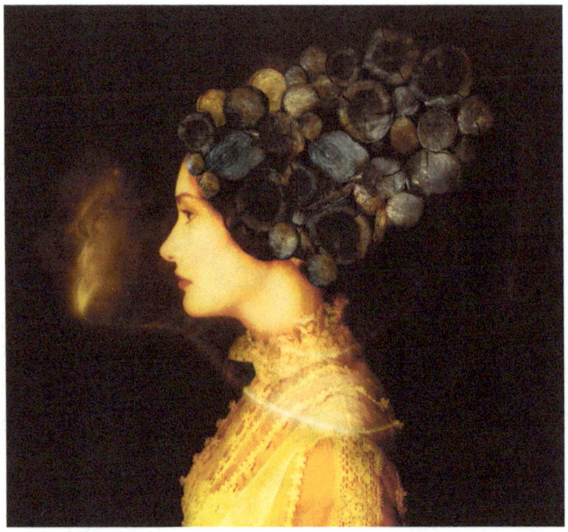

Dandelion, digital media

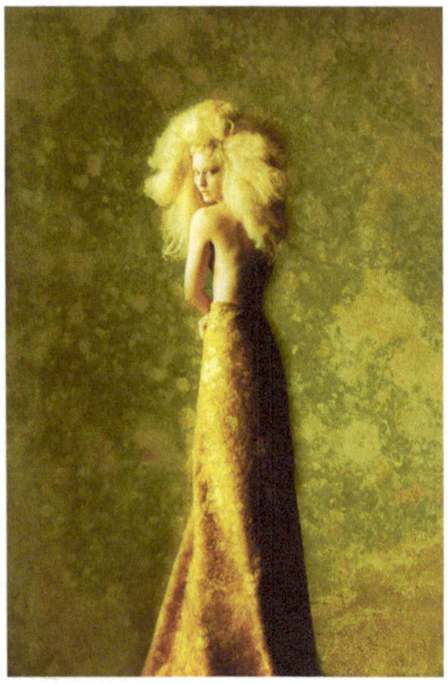

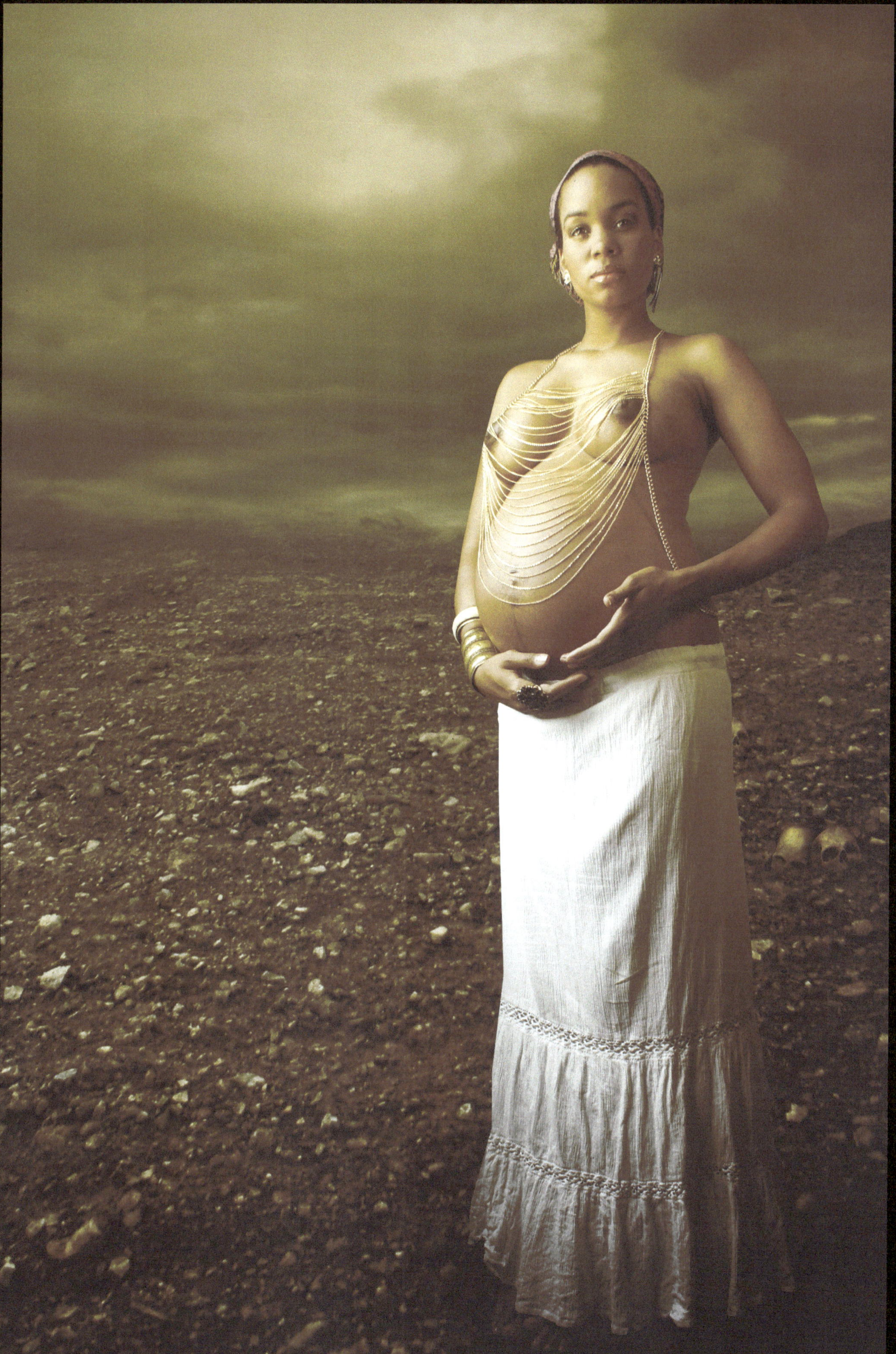

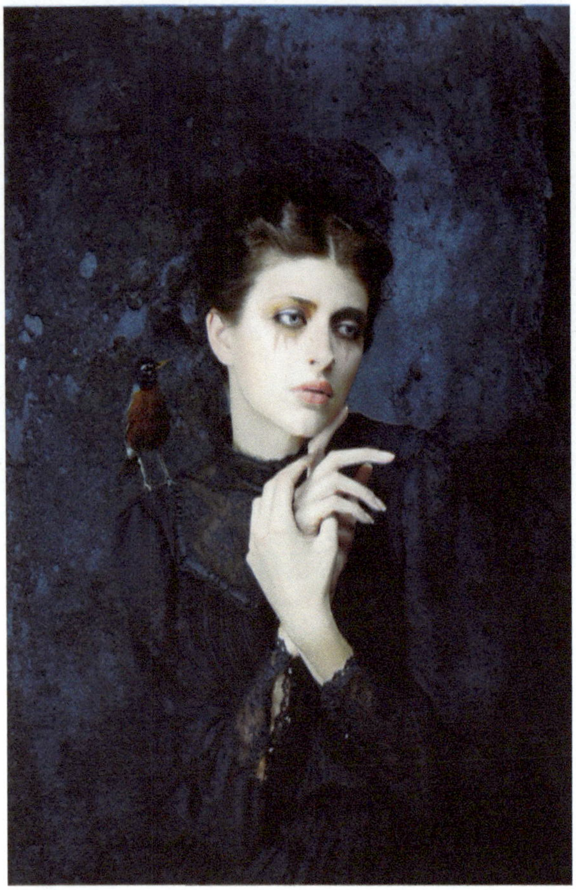

A Little Bird Told Me, digital media

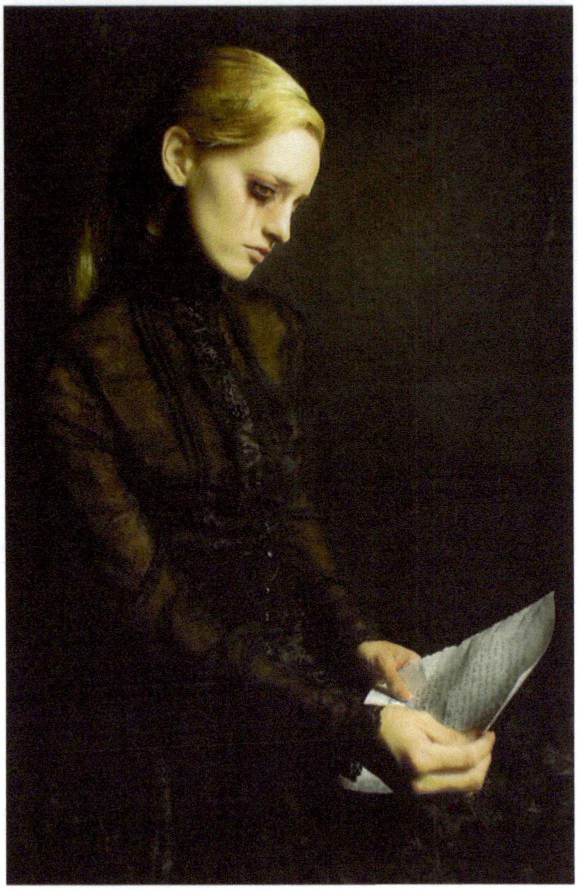

The Letter, digital media

Nocturne, digital media

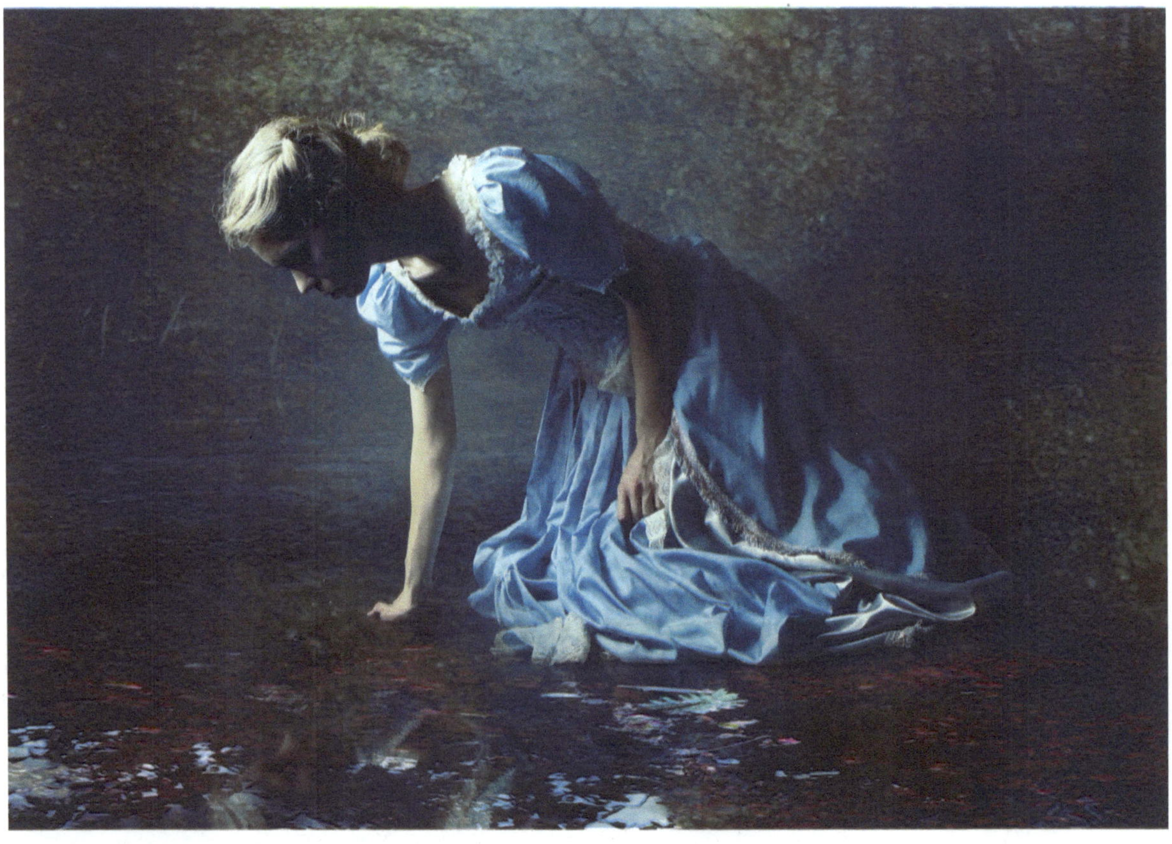

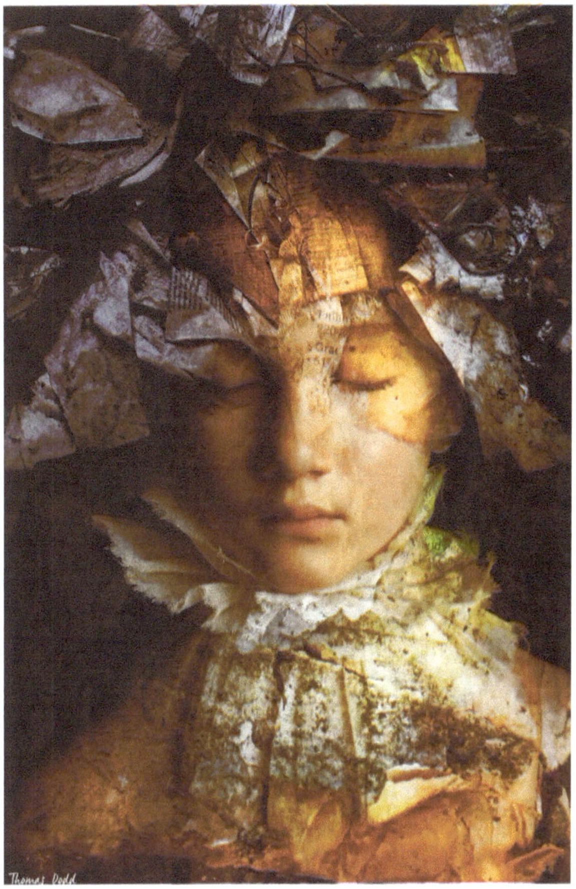

Dream into Memory, digital media

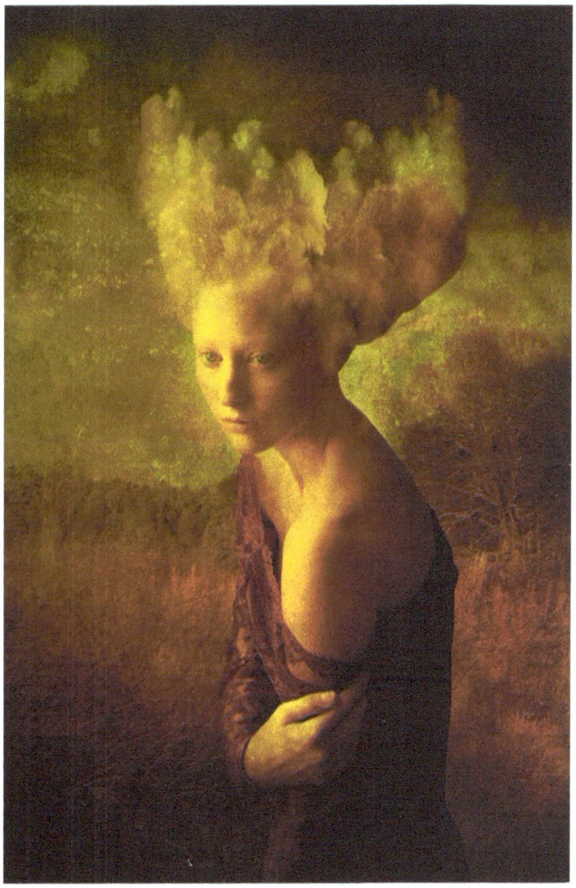

Head in Clouds, digital media

Force of Nature, digital media

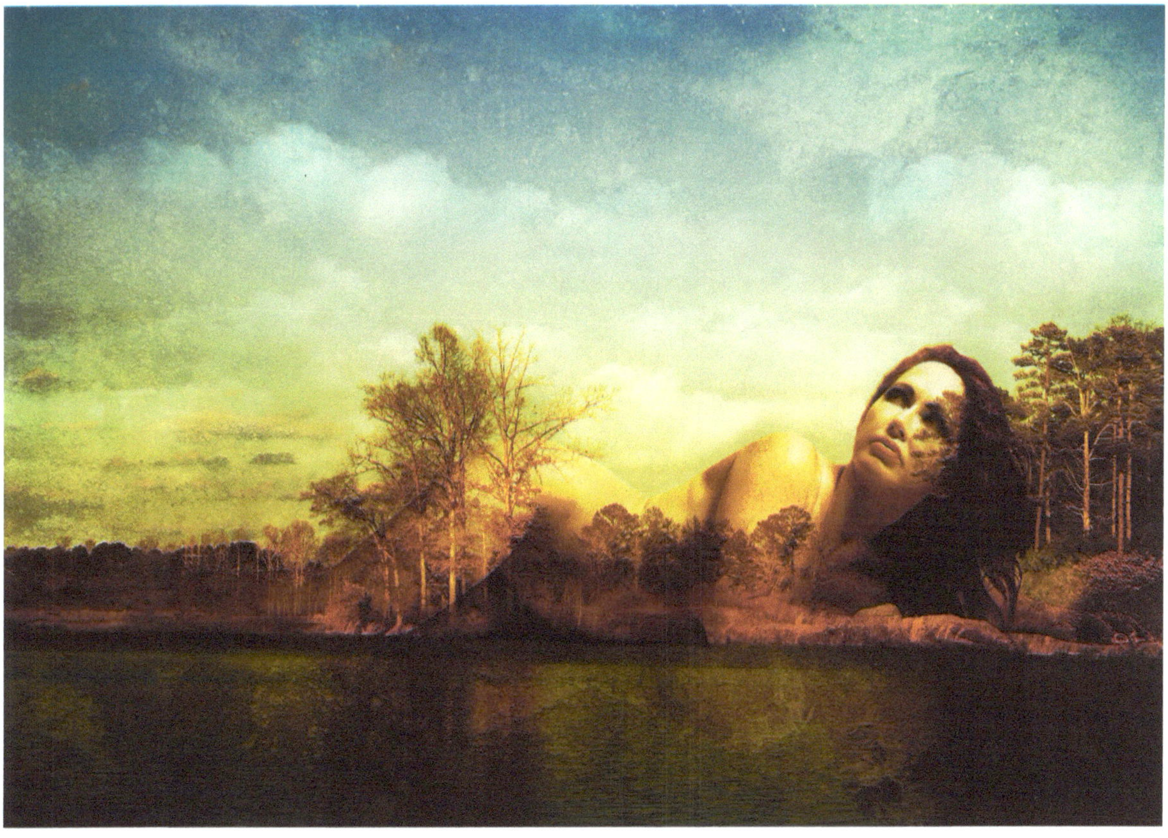

THOMAS DEMUTH

DIGITAL ART - GERMANY

www.artgalaxie.com

Thomas Demuth is a German digital artist. He was born in Hamburg in 1965. Getting a relatively late start on his career as a professional artist, he completed his education in 3D design in 2002.

Rather than referring to himself as a digital artist, he prefers the term "digital alchemist," seeing the computer as the oven where he places his ingredients, the software as the fire below the oven, and his art as the gold that appears like magic when the process is over.

Thomas is highly skilled in the use of 3D rendering software. He is known for producing top-quality photo-abstract images based on polygon mesh structures, a style that he has named "Polygonismus." Working with a mathematical mind, he is always trying to reduce his art to its most basic parts, using polygons sparingly.

This approach leads to intense complexity in his work and some level of abstraction as well. While other artists aim for higher resolution, he is focusing on the beginnings of the polygon, exploring their early stages in a greater depth than anyone ever has before.

Thomas draws influence from history, religion, and anthropology. The message that he is trying to express via his work is one that is highly relevant in the modern world, one that ought to be frightening for anyone who becomes conscious of the monstrous consumption that has become a party of everyday life.

Ecce Homo Fooltime, digital media

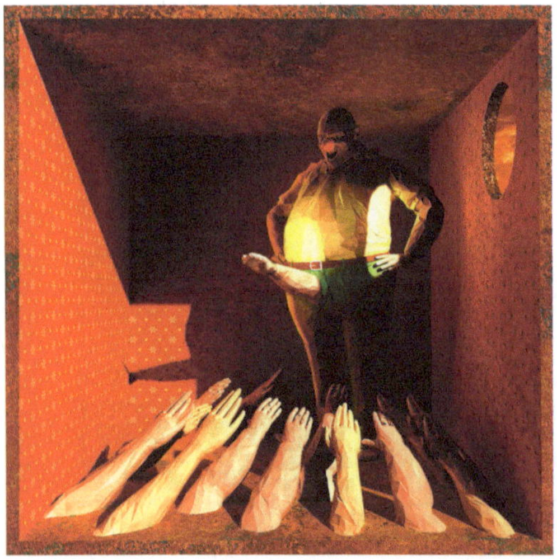

Triumph of Death, digital media

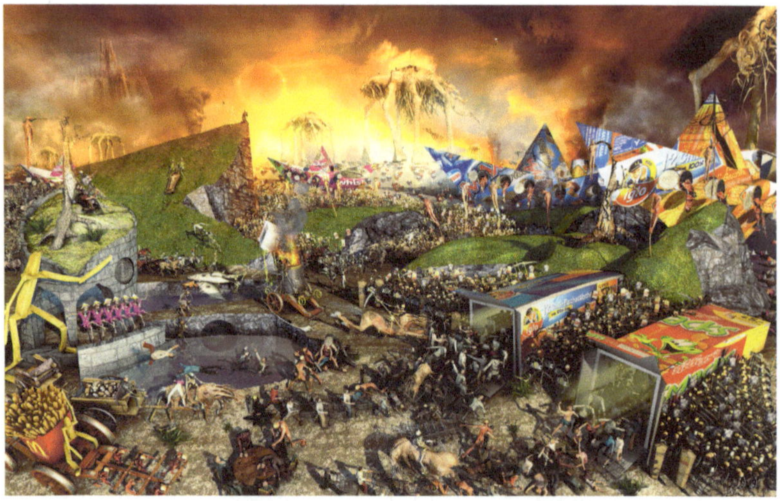

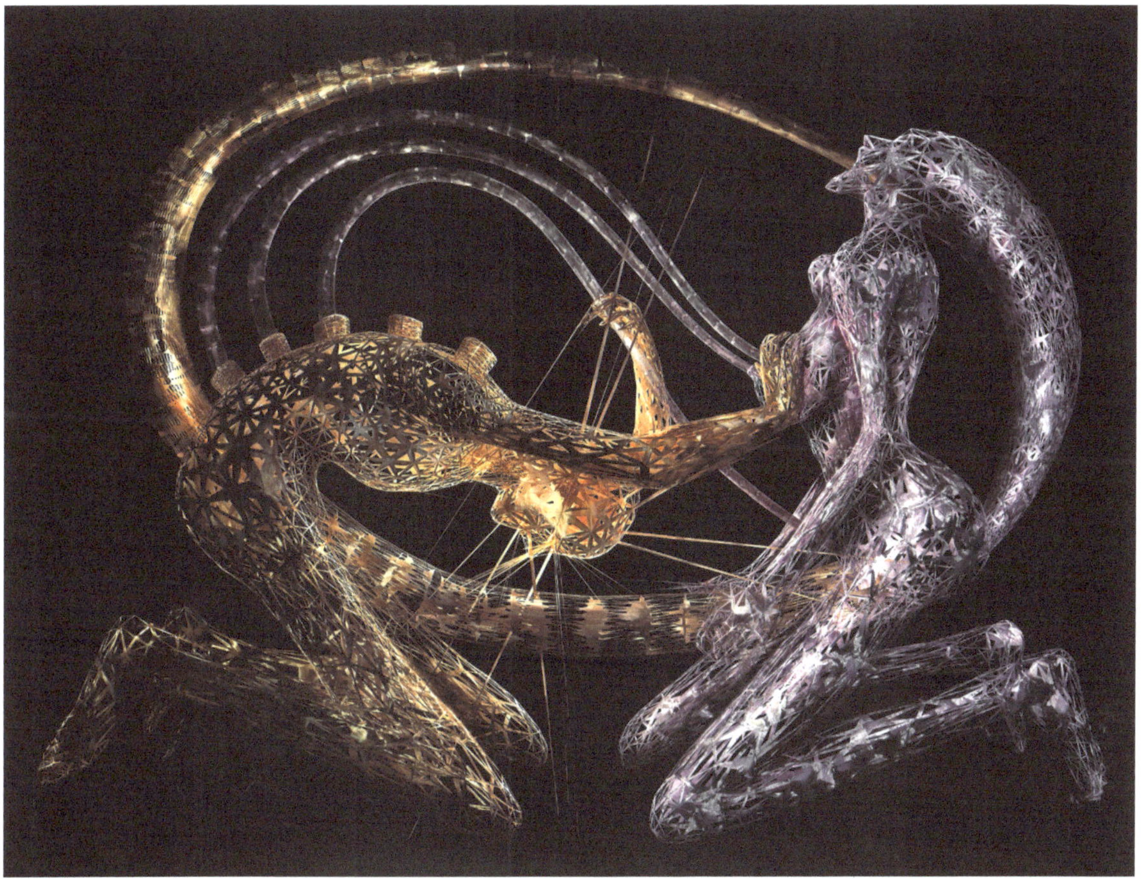

Polyeroticon Erotopolygonal, digital media

Consumata Prima Materia (Consumed Raw Material), digital media

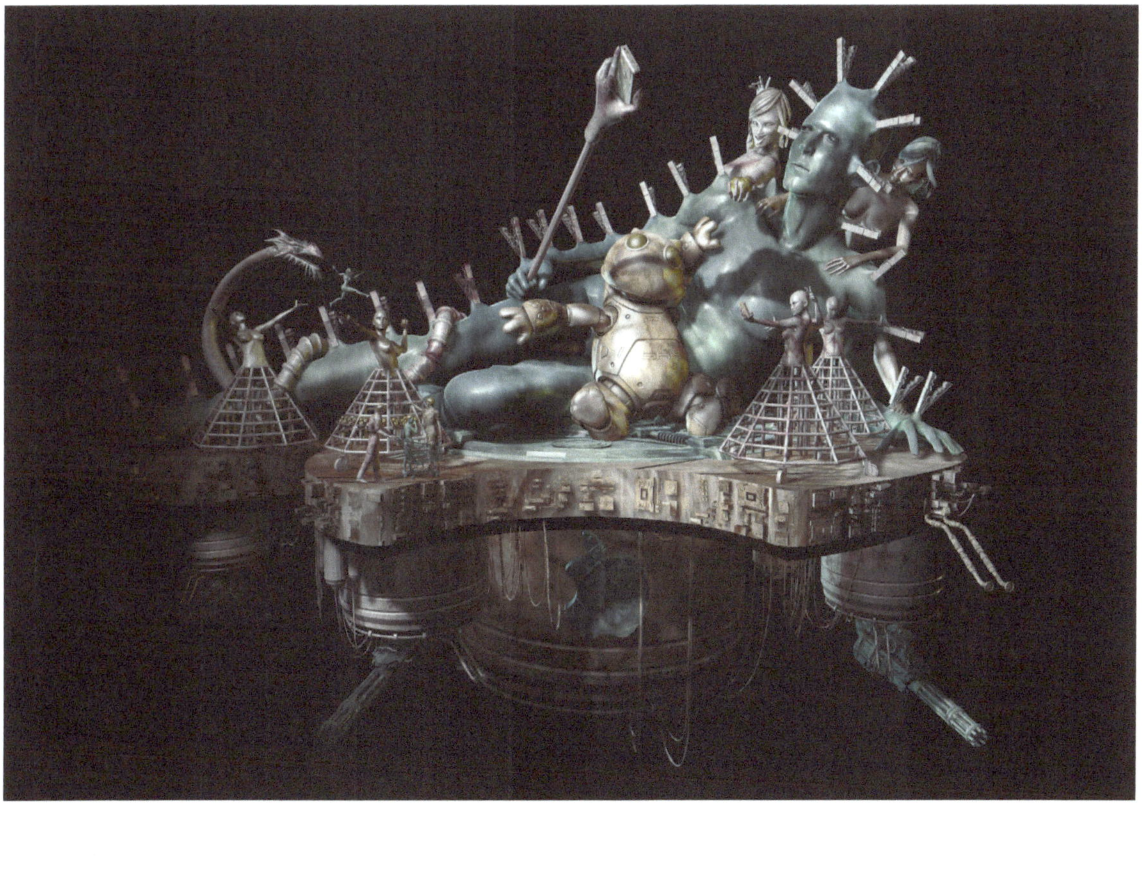

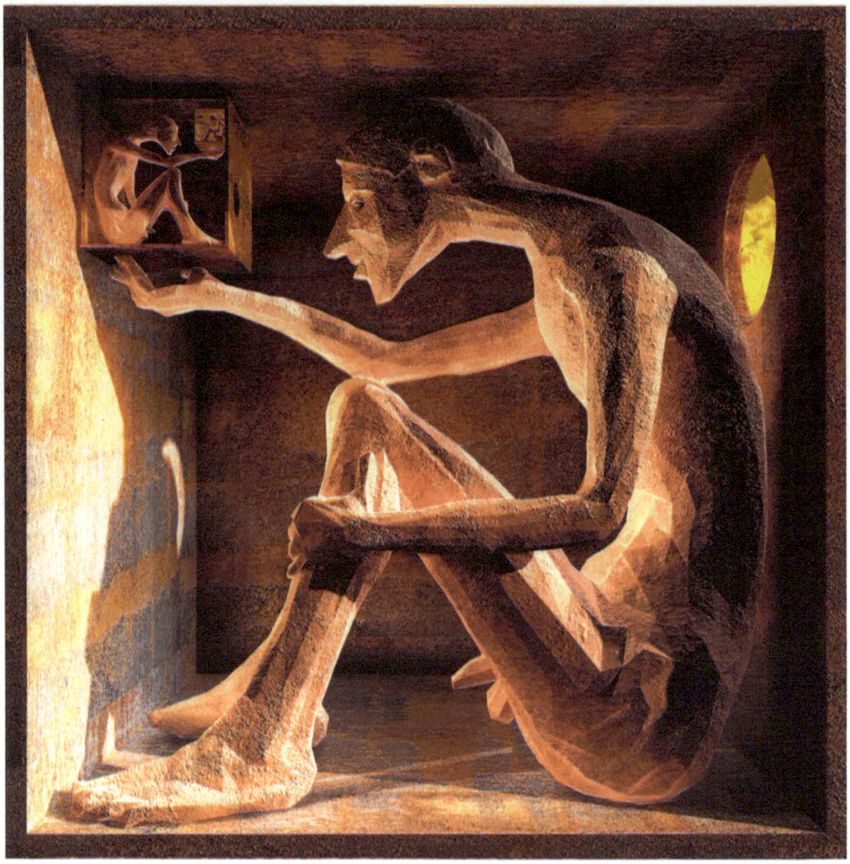

Ecce Homo, digital media

Ecce Homo Exodus, digital media

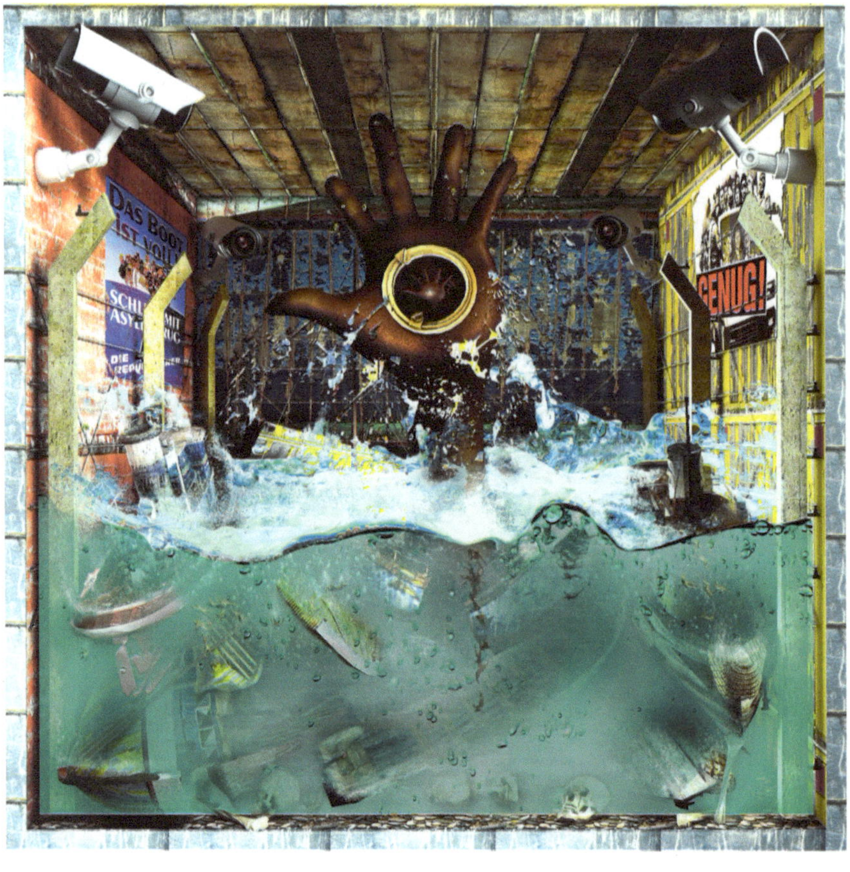

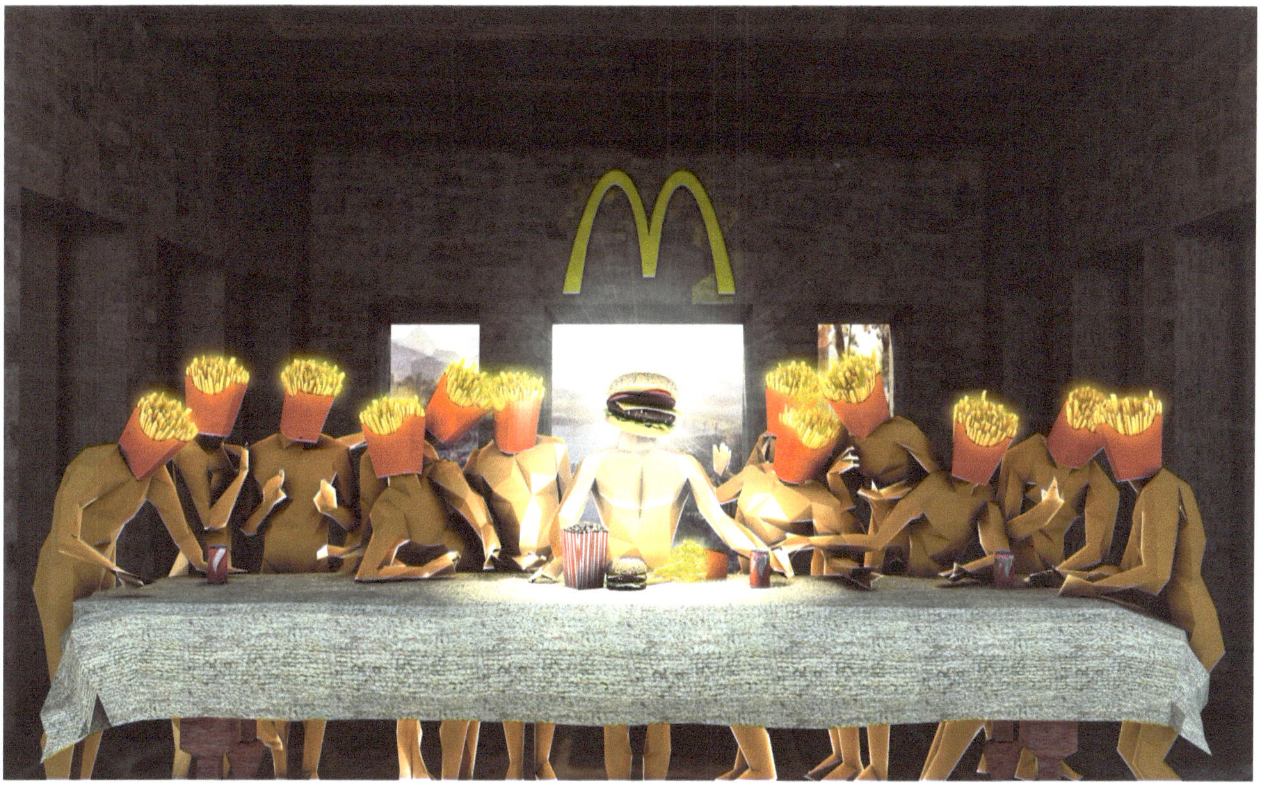

The Supper, digital media

Guernica, digital media

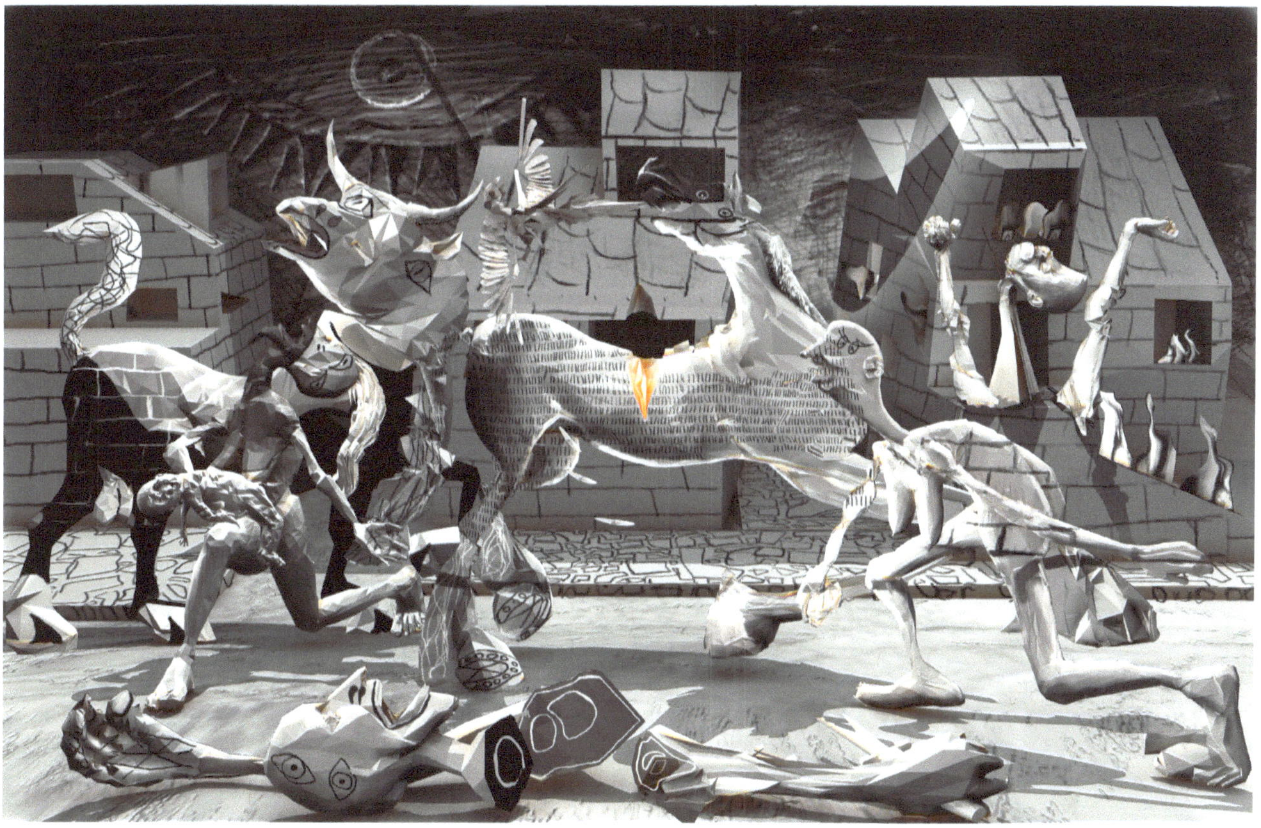

Milton Keynes UK
Ingram Content Group UK Ltd.
UKHW052010030823
426242UK00003B/27